*The* SWAN *of the* WELL *by* TITIA BRONGERSMA

*The* SWAN *of the* WELL
*by* TITIA BRONGERSMA

Eric Miller

McGill-Queen's University Press
Montreal & Kingston • London • Chicago

© McGill-Queen's University Press 2020

ISBN 978-0-2280-0338-0 (cloth)
ISBN 978-0-2280-0489-9 (ePDF)

Legal deposit fourth quarter 2020
Bibliothèque nationale du Québec

Printed in Canada on acid-free paper that is 100% ancient forest free (100% post-consumer recycled), processed chlorine free

This book has been published with the help of a grant from the Canadian Federation for the Humanities and Social Sciences, through the Awards to Scholarly Publications Program, using funds provided by the Social Sciences and Humanities Research Council of Canada. Funding was also received from the University of Victoria.

We acknowledge the support of the Canada Council for the Arts.

Nous remercions le Conseil des arts du Canada de son soutien.

*Library and Archives Canada Cataloguing in Publication*

Title: The Swan of the well by Titia Brongersma / Eric Miller.
Names: Miller, Eric, 1961– author, translator. | Container of (work): Brongersma, Titia, 1650–1700. Bron-swaan. | Container of (expression): Brongersma, Titia, 1650–1700. Bron-swaan. English.
Description: Poem in Dutch with English translation on facing pages. | Includes bibliographical references and index.
Identifiers: Canadiana (print) 20200288873 | Canadiana (ebook) 20200289039 | ISBN 9780228003380 (cloth) | ISBN 9780228004899 (ePDF)
Subjects: LCSH: Brongersma, Titia, 1650–1700. Bron-swaan.
Classification: LCC PT5611.B76 B76 2020 | DDC 839.311/3–dc23

Set in 10.5/13 Dutch Mediaeval and 10.5/13 Singel
Book design & typesetting by Garet Markvoort, zijn digital

*for* ELLY DULL-SIMON

# CONTENTS

Acknowledgments
ix

Introduction
xi

Illustrations
liii

## *The* SWAN *of the* WELL
1

Index of First Lines (English)
527

Index of First Lines (Dutch)
533

# ACKNOWLEDGMENTS

I would like very warmly to thank Mark Abley, my editor at McGill-Queen's University Press. E.J.G. Reker and W.A. Braakman at Special Collections at the University of Groningen assisted me greatly in April 2015, when I first began this project, and again in January 2020. Monique Dull has offered encouragement and insight throughout. Richard Ratzlaff lined up two astute external readers. Lia van Gemert contributed profoundly. Absent her expertise and generosity, the book would be a lesser thing. Freya Sierhuis also notably enriched the project. I am grateful to Elly Dull-Simon for hosting my visit, in the summer of 2014, to Drenthe in the Netherlands, where the idea of translating Titia Brongersma first occurred to me. The English Department at the University of Victoria has supported my research. My children, Ben and Wimmy, relished exploring the *hunebed* at Borger as much as Brongersma did some centuries before them.

Eric Miller
January 2020
Victoria, BC

# INTRODUCTION

*Brongersma to Her Reader*

Opening Titia Brongersma's 259-page volume of verse *De bron-swaan – The Swan of the Well* – published in Groningen, Friesland, in 1686, we come across at once the poet's address "To the Reader." She advises us to look at the back of her book for a list of errata. She confides she hopes "a second impression will achieve a superior degree of polish." An amended edition never followed. Its absence is one mystery enveloping this artist. Nobody knows when she was born, or when she died. And, although scholars such as Martine van Elk have illuminated the circle of women who published in the seventeenth-century Netherlands, still Brongersma's attainments remain underlit. She wrote from remote Frisia. Saluted by local enthusiasts as Sappho reborn, she expressed in more than thirty poems, which were conscious of their sexually dissident strain, an impassioned attachment to a woman – her friend Elisabeth Joly. She initiated archaeological investigation of the Drentish cromlechs – called *hunebedden*, "Hun's tombs," because some (not Brongersma) assigned the origin of these megalithic monuments erroneously to fifth-century Attila's horde.

Even apart from the poet's intellectual and erotic exceptionality, *The Swan of the Well* stands on its own merits as an outstanding specimen of late-Renaissance poetry. Its audience should rightly comprise more than specialists in women's, Netherlandic, or early modern studies. In committing myself to translating – to restoring and promoting – Brongersma's work, I honour her skill and bravery as well as her love of life, of literature, of antiquity.

*Sources*

Visiting Dokkum, a town not far from Leeuwarden, in Friesland, the Netherlands, in 1873, the French tourist Henri Havard tasted a spring rising in a meadow. "This water," he reported, "is the best in the country, and on being analysed during the last epidemic of cholera it was found to be of the purest kind. To its use is attributed the small number of victims to the different epidemics which have raged in Dokkum at various times, and the ancient chroniclers aver that it had the reputation of curing fevers, preventing hydrophobia, and restoring health to the infirm." He went on to record a "common legend" that credited the pool's existence to a saint's wonder-working. The holy man Boniface, "riding near the spot, and his horse becoming thirsty ... stretched forth his hand, and the animal struck the ground with its hoof, and immediately water sprang forth."[1] Havard nowhere mentions the poet Titia Brongersma. Yet her birthplace is assumed to be this same Dokkum – a settlement itself attested as far back as 240.

Since she published her verse while still reckoned young, Brongersma must have been born around 1650. The eventual author of *The Swan of the Well*, with its plentiful fountain imagery, probably grew up in a village long known for its wholesome – even consecrated – waters. Happily, the tale of St Boniface's horse chimes with a Hellenic and heathen antecedent, that of Pegasus. In a word, Dokkum can boast its own Christianized Hippocrene, or "Horse's Well." The Roman poet Ovid figured among Brongersma's favourite authors. In Ovid's *Metamorphoses*, Minerva reports the existence of a spring, newly pierced on Helicon's side by the stamping of a prodigious winged steed. Her interlocutor, Urania, muse of astronomy, concurs with the goddess: *est Pegasus huius origo / fontis*, "Pegasus is the source's origin."[2]

Boniface, by origin a Wessex monk, began converting the godless Frisians in 716. After he had ministered to Hesse, Thuringia, and Bavaria, rebellious pagans martyred him at Dokkum. The sixteenth-century commentator Cornelius Kempius – who Latinizes his and Brongersma's hometown into *civitas Doccumana* – notes that an abbey in his day still enclosed Boniface's well. Pilgrims hoped to imbibe a cure from it. Henri Havard's nineteenth-century account would justify their belief scientifically. But, preceding Titia Brongersma's birth by several decades, the Reformation had suspended the veneration of both Boniface and his well. When the nearby Catholic city of Groningen fell to Prince Maurits in the famous siege or "reduction" of 1594, the neighbourhood turned Protestant overnight. In Dokkum, the parish church became Dutch Reformed; and Brongersma's only overt allusion to St Boniface ornaments her Protestant "Eulogy over the body of J. de Bruyn, preacher at Dokkum." The university founded in Groningen in 1614 adopted a Calvinist tone. Ulrik Huber, a son of Dokkum and a contemporary of Brongersma, professed Calvinist theology at Groningen in 1686, the year of *The Swan of the Well*'s launch. In debates at nearby Franeker, in his capacity of juridical theologian, he argued that human reason cannot alone establish communion with the Holy Spirit and that we must rely, therefore, each of us, on its *internum testimonium*: a private revelation that becomes deeper the more we inwardly – individually – prepare for it.[3] Brongersma's love for Elisabeth Joly may have compelled her to realize in a different yet analogous mode the disparity of the outer world and its so-called common sense from the soul's imperatives. Her poetry resulted.

Aquifers flowing from elsewhere than from St Boniface's faith fill the well where Brongersma's Swan presides. Yet childhood recollections of his story may have inclined her to a love of sources literal and allusive, secular and divine. She tends to prefer a neoclassical to a Christian spring; and, when she modulates her language of fonts and fountains into a Christian key, she prefers to draw precedents from Scripture rather than from the lives of the saints.[4]

## The Freedom of Frisia

The epithet locals have long attached to Friesland puns defiantly: *Vrij Friesland*. To be "free" describes a condition of liberty. Just as easily, however, it acknowledges deprivation. Like the past of her Frisian homeland, the life of Titia Brongersma bears the impress of this ambiguous duality. Patriarchal authorities necessarily articulate the poet's birthright. Despite a place on the fenny verge of Denmark and Germany, Friesland enters written history early. Brongersma won, as an artist, the support of classical scholars at the academies of Groningen and Franeker. And it is the Roman historian Tacitus who enucleates, it may be, the essence of the Frisian myth or predicament, as it may have both encouraged and limited her. In his *Annals* (13, 54), he narrates the adventures of two Frisian princes. He Romanizes their names as Verritus and Malorix. They star in an anecdote coloured equally by humour and bloody-mindedness.

Tacitus describes how these footloose Frisians, assuming the vacancy of the banks of the Rhine, settle their dependents there. Local Romans regard them as squatters. Verritus and Malorix respond by taking their case all the way to Rome. They view the theatre of Pompey, but cannot grasp the concept of drama. Shown the senate, they perceive the mass of *patres conscripti* variegated by a number of men not in togas, but in outlandish costumes. Their guide tells them, his perplexed guests, how these foreigners have distinguished themselves by their devotion to the interests of Rome. Tacitus continues: "Insisting no mortal could surpass Germans in either arms or loyalty, the Frisians swept forward and took seats among the senators. The ardour of this impulse, the purity of this ambition, instantly won them esteem. Nero made both chieftains citizens on the spot. Then he ordered them to evacuate the vicinity of the Rhine."[5]

This story could epitomize the fortunes of Friesland as such, up to Brongersma's time. The Frisians affect a strategic bumpkinishness, and show tenacity. As for the centre whose sophistication they covet and hope to emulate, it is rich in every way. But it rewards servility, labouring (in Tacitus's tale) beneath the very Nero whom Brongersma's own verses will reproach, more than a millennium later, for matricide. Upstart in a way, the University of Groningen, founded in 1614, presumes to impart the humanist tradition, according to Rector Ubbo Emmius's grand *Edictum perpetuum* or "Eternal Promulgation," from within a polity so independent – a member only of the Hanseatic League – it endured the vicissitudes of centuries as a virtual city-state.[6] Paris, Oxford, and Cambridge had preceded by almost a half millennium the foundation of this school. Reflecting on his homeland, Rector Emmius wrote, "In truth Frisia is free, habituated to doing things its own way. It will not take orders from foreigners or tolerate subordination. For the sake of liberty, a Frisian willingly faces death."[7] Brongersma's four funny and confident pastoral poems in the Frisian language – a rarity in the period – manifest the audacity of her wry allegiance to native voices. Not long deceased, Gysbert Japiks (1603–1666) had pioneered the publication of literature in this language.

A boast traditional in Brongersma's milieu – "Every Frisian is a noble" – has some merit. Friesland never bowed its shoulders beneath the yoke of feudalism under which regions to the south of it stooped. The bishop of Utrecht's forces failed to subjugate the Frisians at the Battle of Ane in 1227. The Hollanders were defeated at the Battle of Warns in 1345. No overlord controlled Frisia during the Middle Ages. It was only in 1579 that the Treaty of Utrecht assimilated Friesland to the Dutch Republic or Seven United Provinces. Riven by civil war, the region did fall in 1524, its rebelliousness imperfectly subdued by the Holy Roman Emperor Charles V of the Burgundian Habsburgs. Brongersma herself writes in ignorance of the verdict historians will pass on the United Provinces of her later epoch. They tend to concur in the discouraging verdict that the Golden Age of the Netherlands had already ended in 1648, before she ever took up a pen.[8] But Bernhard von Galen, the bishop of Münster, had besieged Groningen unsuccessfully in August of the *rampjaar* or *annus horribilis* of 1672. Brongersma must then have been a girl. Her direct reference to this bloody incursion is limited to an epigram that only addresses the invasion in terms of the botanical emblems of the hostile parties, Louis XIV's France and Charles II's Britain, as well as Bernhard's Münster.

### *The Woman of the Well*

When Carel Pieman brought out Brongersma's book from his press "between the markets" in the university city of Groningen in 1686, a parade of Frisian scholars, preachers, and poets – all male – joined to praise her in their prefatory verses to *The Swan of the Well*. Several times they emphasize her relative youth. Though her age at the time cannot be ascertained, the poet's name can tell us other things. The surname Brongersma is indigenously Frisian. The "-sma" ending indicates that, in the past, those who held the name got that identity from the neighbourhood in Frisia where they then dwelled. The poet punned habitually on *bron*, the first syllable of her surname. According to Van Dale's *Groot woordenboek hedendaags Nederlands*, *bron* means *vanzelf uit de grond opwellend water* – "water that wells spontaneously out of the ground." Brongersma's Swan – her "Well-Swan" – occupies and animates just such a gratuitous spring. Dokkum, famous as the site of St Boniface's miraculous fountain, bore in Brongersma a daughter whose surname equipped her with a further motive to favour the topic of spring-waters.

As for "Titia," it seems a piece of neo-Latinity. Either it abbreviates "Laetitia" (a female name signifying "merriment") or, possibly, signifies on its own the idea of strength. A Frisian antecedent, roughly homophonous with "Titia," "Tjeda," may have preceded the general adoption in Friesland of the more polished or aspirational proper name. The *gens Titia* of ancient Rome was a patrician clan. Although Brongersma's family did not apparently hold any aristocratic rank, her vocation and her themes refined her sufficiently in the eyes of acquaintances. She praised the local gentry, and she exercised the artist's right to confer the nobility of her laurel wherever she saw fit. Thus the regional surname "Brongersma" and the Romanized "Titia" providentially unite to convey the poet's up-welling patriotism together with her ambition to combine humanist urbanity with the avowal of female experience.

## Ludolph Smids

Titia Brongersma's most effective champion held the post of doctor of medicine at the University of Groningen. Ludolph Smids also wrote belletristic prose and poetry. In 1685, he published his eighty-page *Gallerye of te proef van dichtoefeningen, met noodige verklaaringen verrykt* (*Gallery, or experiment in poetical exercises, enriched with annotations*) with Carel Pieman in Groningen. Smids dedicated this work, a verbal "gallery" of legendary women, each treated separately in rhyming couplets, not to Brongersma but to a notable female poet of the time, Katharina Lescailje. She lived from 1649 to 1711. Her reputation, unlike Brongersma's, enjoyed posthumous revival fairly early, in 1731, with the issuing of a careful edition of her verse. Lescailje supplied a dedicatory poem for Smids's enterprise, dated 1 April 1683. In his book, her tribute received pride of place, coming first among Smids's poetic laudators. Titia Brongersma, however, authored the *second* set of complimentary verses prefacing his book. The same verses appeared a year later in her own volume, *The Swan of the Well*. Smids shared a publisher, Pieman, with Brongersma; and some of the eminences offering praise in his *Gallery*, J.A. Rappardus and Johan Jacob Monter, belong to the roster that, in 1686 – soon after the *Gallery*'s appearance – extolled Brongersma's own collection. Lescailje, the woman to whom Smids dedicates his whole *Gallery*, grew up not in the hinterland of Groningen but in Amsterdam. Unlike Brongersma, she lived in the epicentre of literary activity. After 1679, she ran her late father's printing and publishing enterprise.

Smids's *Gallery* sketches notorious and illustrious women from history, canvassing both the Graeco-Roman and Judaeo-Christian traditions. A small etching adorns his frontispiece. With outspread wings, four birds frame a cameo.

The oval inner space of the cameo depicts a further bird. This prominent individual surmounts a stratum of dense cloud. A flock, evidently belonging to the same species, flutters below the grim weather, striving, it would seem, to lift themselves past its level. A bat and an owl keep them doubtful company. The Greek motto bending across the top of this vignette exhorts, "Wing your way above the cloud." The flock aspires from a condition of benightedness toward serene skies, enlightenment. The bird that has already got to the heights does not abandon its fellows. Given his topic and his dedicatee – Katharina Lescailje – Smids must assume an audience comprised of women as much as of men. His book's epigraph, culled from the historian Sallust, manifests the generous will to encourage everyone's voice: "*Omnes homines, qui sese student praestare caeteris animantibus, summa ope niti decet ne vitam silentio transigunt veluti pecora; quae Natura prona, atque ventri oboedientia, finxit*" – "All human beings who would distinguish themselves from the remainder of animate creation should strive with their utmost powers not to pass through this life in silence like herd animals, whom Nature has made to stoop and obey only the insistence of their bellies."[9]

## *Katharina Lescailje*

If Smids deserves to be called Brongersma's foremost masculine vindicator, Katharina Lescailje may, of all her female contemporaries, inspire her most as an instance of successful literary practice and articulate sexual solidarity. The dramatist and poet Lescailje developed and maintained a network of intellectual women. *The Swan of the Well* includes the acknowledgement of a tribute from Lescailje. Brongersma composes a sonnet in which she compares the Amsterdam writer to a rose, and associates her with Apollo. Martine van Elk has recently brought attention to an exchange of verse in 1672 and 1673 between Katharina Lescailje and the writer Cornelia van der Veer (1639–1704).[10] Although van der Veer and Lescailje's correspondence did not see print until more than half a century had elapsed, the ten friendship poems traded between Lescailje and van der Veer so strongly resemble Brongersma in imagery, diction, and topic that I believe Brongersma may well have seen them in manuscript form. If Brongersma did not actually read them, their existence still proves that a common rhetorical reservoir fed the minds and filled the inkwells of talented women of the period.

Indulging a practice thoroughly familiar from *The Swan of the Well*, Lescailje puns on van der Veer's name. *Veer* means "feather," and suggests therefore both an authorial pen and a high-flying vatic pinion. A pair of Lescailje's pieces regrets van der Veer's departure on a journey (to Briel), and celebrates her safe return. Just so, Brongersma will deplore her dear friend Elisabeth Joly's absences abroad, and rejoice in her reappearance. As for van der Veer, she displays jealousy kindred in tone to that of Brongersma's Joly poems when Lescailje overlooks van der Veer's birthday, and when she prefers to spend New Year's Eve with the poet Sara de Canjoncle. Like Brongersma, Lescailje and van der Veer refer to Momus the god of mockery, imagine the laurel as the token of writerly election, divinize local water bodies, allude to Polyphemus's awkward adoration of the nymph Galatea, recur to Dido's tragic love of Aeneas, and use the figure of the source (implicitly female) to image both secular and holy inspiration. Van der Veer's phrasing notably anticipates and may directly influence Brongersma's, especially in "*Aan de konstige en soetvloeijende dichteresse Catharina Lescailje*," "To the artful and sweet-flowing Poetess Catherina Lescailje," quoted by van Elk:

Godts helybron heeft soo smakelyk een voght,
Dat, die haar proeft, laat d'Hipocreen verschalen.

Van Elk translates the couplet thus:

God's holy fount has such delicious liquid
That whosoever tastes her, will let Hippocrene go stale.[11]

Elsewhere, Lescailje envisages van der Veer's namesake quill bathing in the waters of eternal life. At such moments, Brongersma's Swan appears to swim not far off.

Katharina Lescailje lived and wrote in awareness of female precursors and contemporaries in Dutch literature. They were numerous. They include Anna Roemers Visscher (1584–1651), Catharina Questiers (1631–1669), and Anna Maria van Schurman (1607–1678). Brongersma's acquaintance with Lescailje, a most distinguished writer of her own sex, richly complements her engagement with the male intellectual and impresario Ludolph Smids.

### *Brongersma's Circle*

Brongersma's *Swan of the Well* is a big book, just as its emblematic bird is big. Including the *eer-gedichten* – prefatory, laudatory verses by various hands – it comprises 259 pages and 259 poems. Fifteen of these poems commend Brongersma's enterprise, indicating the intensely sociable character of the work. Men contributed the complimentary pieces, save the sixteenth and last. Brongersma herself composed this expression of gratitude to a literary adviser, the learned Odilia S. Scherff, who assisted the poet with the book's section of explicitly Christian poems. The roster of male intellectuals honouring the poet's art includes Nicolaus Blancard, rector magnificus of the College at Franeker; Johannes Mensinga, rector magnificus of Groningen University; Andreas ten

Have, a preacher at Pekela; Ludolph Smids, the Groningen doctor of medicine, poet, antiquarian, playwright, and polymath; Samuel Mun(c)kerus, a writer; Mattheus Gargon, a preacher and poet; Adriaan Tijmens, a poet of Leeuwarden; Jan Adolf Rappardus, an intellectual; Johan Jacob Monter, a littérateur located in Assen; and Joannis Fedensma, a painter reputedly fond, like Brongersma, of Ovidian motifs. Brongersma's masculine acquaintanceship also encompassed the artist E.J. de Wolff, engraver of her frontispiece; the printers J. Purmerënt and H. Vlaak; and the publisher Carel Pieman. The range of female associates testified by the contents of *The Swan of the Well* is as extensive.

Before the procession of masculine *eer-gedichten* even begins, Brongersma prepares the reader for the upcoming prominence of this fact by inserting an eloquent "Dedication to the extraordinary and illustrious women of Groningen." For long stretches, in fact, as this prose dedication suggests, *The Swan of the Well* approximates the genre practised by her patron Ludolph Smids: the poetic gallery of unusual women. Perhaps the remotest ancestor of this literary kind appears in Homer, when (at the suggestion of Persephone) Odysseus reviews the shades of Tyro, Antiope, Alkmene, and the rest, in Hades. A more proximate influence on both Smids and Brongersma was Johan van Beverwijck (1594–1647). Van Beverwijck's 1643 exercise in panegyric *Uutneymentheyt des vrouwelicken geslachts* or *Excellence of the Female Sex* argues for "the superiority of a woman's brain and intelligence over a man's."[12]

Brongersma's apostrophe of the living ladies of Groningen shows her faith that she can both identify and affirm who among her peers deserves the status of "illustrious" or "extraordinary." Her sentiment of solidarity with her sex expresses itself in the collective noun *jufferdom* or "womankind." By her power, often (even exhaustively) celebrated, of draping laurels round the temples of her friends and betters, Brongersma emphasizes an artist's elective faculty of exalting whomever she chooses. Other women or female entities she treats belong to history and legend: Zenobia, Tomyris, Ceyx. At least one addressee, Elisabeth Joly, appears (often under the courtly pseudonym of Elise) as the object of sentimental – sometimes erotic – love. Dutch scholars such as Lia van Gemert have plausibly classified Brongersma – called Sappho reborn by contemporaries – as lesbian.[13]

### The Life and Songs of the Swan

Not only a common publisher, Carel Pieman, but also engravings of birds connect Ludolph Smids's *Gallery* with Brongersma's *Swan*. E.J. de Wolff's frontispiece for Brongersma's *De bron-swaan* depicts her bird standing on stout legs in a pool's shallows. Water has collected under a tree-tufted, cloven rock, out of which its source pours. Wings raised and fanned, de Wolff's swan challenges us. These birds can inflict bruises, even shatter human bones. Yet defence may engage the bird less here than inspiration. Or this swan – adopting the pose of a regenerated phoenix – may protect her patronesses. Six women drink at the well whose overflow brims the pond. They linger round an aedicule featuring an arch excised from the living rock. Despite their affectation of contemporary Netherlandic costume, de Wolff's female figures could comprise a majority of the nine muses. De Wolff correctly implies in his engraving that Brongersma's muses slake their thirst not so often on Helicon as in her own landscape. The scene includes a windmill and a tiered spire, a weathercock atop it. Yet her concept of musedom flows at last from Hesiod, from his Hippocrene – the "horse's well" that irrigates the Greek visionary's Boeotian peak.

Throughout her book, Brongersma deploys the titular Swan of the Well, that large and brilliant bird, as totem and proxy. The poet assumes her splendid creature can sing. The preferred verb is "warble." In Brongersma's fantasia, that avian music is never (or almost never) the adieu of legend, the famous swansong. But could there be a poeticism more exhausted than the swan? A jaded reader may fetch a sigh. Was this commonplace not exhausted already in 1686, when Pieman brought out and de Wolff illustrated Brongersma? At first glance, the poet does not seem even to bestir herself to innovate. What is her bird, after all, but the standard tuneful specimen? The male notables of Groningen flock to second Brongersma's image in their fifteen prefatory verses, comparing her to the swan of Dirce, Pindar; to the Venusian swan, Horace; and to the swan of the Rhine, the great Joost van den Vondel. Erinna, Alcman, Vergil, and Anacreon benefited in their time from this stale comparison. Anyone who frequents the resorts of swans will know the real thing sings quaintly, if at all. Norman Douglas, in his *Birds and Beasts of the Greek Anthology*, makes us certain that the ancients themselves, who circulated the commonplace of a melodious swan, often differed over the talents of the actual bird. "What," he asks, "of those allusions to the song of the swan, which is described sometimes as loud (by Antipater of Thessalonica), sometimes as soft (by Antipater of Sidon), and always as beautiful? For the music of this bird is here treated not as a poetic fable, but as a bald fact."[14] The exasperated Douglas hypothesizes a drastic "change in literary taste."[15] The spectacle of pretty plumage might have encouraged the tactfully deaf attribution of a lovely voice to match. So Shakespeare sometimes makes a noble physique the heritable concomitant of aristocratic birth. Douglas quotes a rustic in Lucian as incredulous as any modern listener: "we do see a swan now and again in the marshes; and a harsh feeble croak their note is; crows or jackdaws are sirens to it."[16] A curious reader may rightly ask, "What *kind* of swan is depicted in the frontispiece of Brongersma's book?"

E.J. de Wolff offers us the image of a species faintly ambiguous. The artist deviates from responsible ornithology. An observer of symbolist predilections might allocate the bird to hybridity: a mongrel half-swan, half-phoenix. It participates in the iconography of both. But the dark bulb at the base of its upper mandible almost certainly identifies the bird as what the modern Dutch call a *knobbelzwaan*, literally a "knob-swan." The name emphasizes a black protuberance that swells above the nostrils of the bird's orange beak. De Wolff's *Bronswaan* has opened her bill. Presumably she makes a noise. Neoclassical decorum would ordain some utterance infused with euphony.

Linnaean nomenclature, developed after Brongersma's time, calls this bird *Cygnus olor*. English speakers know it as a "mute swan." They engage in a case of over-correction from the habit of imputing music to the bird, because this species (in the phrasing of the Audubon Society's *Master Guide to Birding*) can produce "snorts, grunts and hisses," and is therefore not silent.[17] Since the nineteenth century, mute swans such as de Wolff's have been introduced all over the globe. If, with your inner eye, you project an ornamental lake, you probably envisage mute swans drifting across it. These waterfowl make their most agreeable sound flying. Their wing feathers excite a sweet whistling. The *Master Guide* transcribes the noise thus produced as *vaou, vaou*. The human ear can detect it as far as half a mile off.

### A Frisian Bird

Brongersma, however, was Frisian. Her Swan carries connotations peculiar to Friesland. The poet's work demonstrates the uncommon career of commonplaces, as indigenous impulses adapt them. Does the seventeenth-century landscape of Groningen and Drenthe peculiarly influence the halo of associations attaching to swans?[18] In that district, before the development of dykes, floods often inundated settlements. Villagers resorted to the raising of artificial mounds – *terpen* – to which the population might retreat when the waters rose.[19] Anthony Bailey tells us these *refugia* from floodwaters "were built between 300 BC and ... AD 1100." He adds "there are some 180 *terp* villages and towns in Friesland now."[20] Excavations in the interiors of *terpen* have turned up numerous flutes, some contrived from the bones of mute swans. In volume three of *Vogels in Friesland*, G. Elzinga offers a photograph of pipes with up to six holes drilled in (variously) the radius and the ulna of this species.[21] The dead – not dying – swan thus literally offered the opportunity of "swansong": a truly mortal musicality. Here is a variant of the pastoral owing little to Mediterranean precedent. Did Brongersma learn of the existence of such instruments? Were they still manufactured? She interested herself in antiquities, especially the megalithic *hunebed* of Borger, a monument she explored with Jan Laurens Lenting (or Lentinck) in 1685. Whether the transformation of a swan's wing-bones into flutes was a practice known to her or not, Brongersma must certainly have been aware of other dimensions of the swan's significance in her sphere.

Swanneries and swan wardens subjected mute swans in Friesland to close management from the Middle Ages onward. The matter of swan-right preoccupied legislators. The conspicuous birds offered brash embodiments of status. Swan-yards confined a minority of the birds for fattening and the spit. Others became regulated objects of the hunt. In 1343, the swannery in Waterland and West Friesland acquired fully 3,653 swans, presumably from similar enterprises elsewhere. Custodians marked birds on the beak or foot to prove ownership. The Fries Museum in Leeuwarden displays a proprietorial metal *zwanering* incised with the year 1647, made to encircle the throat of a bird. Swans obviously abounded in Brongersma's Friesland. They signified things foreign to ancient Greek and Roman writers. An artist of her ability, however, could merge Mediterranean tropes with Frisian idiosyncrasies.

As Friesland is to the southern heart of humanist Europe, so is Brongersma to the masculine milieu of late seventeenth-century literature – and even, arguably, to the very female authors who furnish her nearest parallels. Both the Amsterdam printer Katharina Lescailje and the court wit Aphra Behn (ca 1640–1689) enjoyed metropolitan advantages Brongersma lacked.[22] On all these grounds, the poet's apparently commonplace Swan must be deemed a *rara avis*. De Wolff was shrewd to introduce into his frontispiece formal reminiscences of the prodigious phoenix. Swanneries in Friesland kept punctilious *zwanenboeken*, "swan-books."[23] Did Brongersma intend to derive part of her title's impact from the precedent of this archetypically Frisian genre?

Despite the references to her Swan's enchanting warble, the poet also repeatedly characterizes the bird's voice – and her own – as "hoarse" and "throaty." These epithets emerge early in *The Swan of the Well*. In her preliminary "Dedication to the extraordinary and illustrious women of Groningen," she conveys a wish to her audience: "So may you always attend to [the book's] throaty music, proclaiming (as it does, throughout the world) your worthiest and most deserved glory." Brongersma's exhortation has – it is true – a fortuitous sister in the rhetoric of her contemporary Margaret Cavendish's address "To all noble, and worthy ladies" at the outset of her 1653 *Poems, and Fancies*.[24] But Brongersma specifies the *huskiness* of her voice. The Dutch phrase is *schorre gesangen*. She may confess (regret or boast) a personal quality – the real character and timbre of her own speech, or singing. And she may evoke another classical tradition, a small body of lore more empirically accruing around the figure of the swan. The epigrammatists of the *Greek Anthology* sometimes extolled the bird's fantastical musicality. Roman poets, however, found a different glamour in a more naturalistic audition of swans' calls. Take the anonymous *Pervigilium Veneris*, celebrating the springtime night watch of the love goddess – possibly a composition of the third century. This piece informs us *iam loquaces ore rauco stagna cygni perstrepunt*, "now the garrulous swans bugle with a hoarse voice across the ponds." Andreas Rivinus's edition of this poem observes that Vergil provides a model here: *dant sonitum rauci per stagna loquacia cygni*, "The hoarse swans raise a noise in the garrulous sloughs." Brongersma's adjective *schorre* functions much like *raucus*. Both adjectives communicate ideas of hoarseness, harshness, roughness, hollowness.[25] Let the epithet offer an acoustical token of inveterate Frisian disdain of suaveness – as well as of Brongersma's unbroken will to speak, which may have masculinized any sounds that she dared to make in the wondering, uneasy ears of her Dutch audience.

### The Swan as Character and Reader

The conceit of the Swan unifies Brongersma's book. It debuts in the fifth poem of Brongersma's collection, which fuses elements of riddle, epigram, and *ekphrasis*. The "aegis" is Minerva's shield (sometimes breastplate). The addition of the gorgon's petrifying head rendered this item of armour offensive as well as defensive. From the decapitated Medusa leapt the winged horse Pegasus:

> Riddles for Anna de Haas, the door to whose cellar is decorated with
> Medusa and Methuselah, with an owl and a swan
>
> What is that Owl doing, respectable familiar of Minerva,
> Just at the threshold of the wine-god's vault? –
> The bird dissipates the soporific
> Fume of grapes so revelry, less stuporous,
> Should better serve his Lady's ends.
>
> But why is a Swan here, with the heads
> Of the eldest of men and of the gorgon Medusa? –
> Wisdom cherishes those grown silver-haired and wise,
> While Minerva with her aegis defends this house.

Here the Swan floats at the threshold of symposiac pleasure amid emblems of decent comportment and sage restraint.

Brongersma uses the Swan to invigorate the venerable genre of the invitation, practised in antiquity by the likes of Catullus.[26] The bird's pond offers a setting in which to manifest the playful energies of intellectual friendship. Possibly the house in which Brongersma lived was called the Swan of the Well.

> To Miss S. T[er] H[orst], an invitation to come visit the Swan of the Well
>
> Darling Swan, don't leave my Swan paddling
> All alone. Come and splash with her in the well
> Even if it causes you a little bit

> Of trouble. She does despise solitary
> Swims, so spread your wings and float on them
> In flight to relieve her singularity
> Obliging me, too – your lonely Titia.

The invitee, sharing the speaker's avian form, presumably also shares her literary bent.

Describing the vagaries of the Swan's habitat, Brongersma supports the meteorological record of the years when the creature took flight. She thus assists conjecture about when she composed some verses. The Great Frost of 1683 and 1684 froze the Thames for two months. Off the coast of the Netherlands the salty North Sea itself congealed to a distance of some kilometres from shore. In Brongersma, the severity of the freeze circumscribes social pleasures. It does not suspend or destroy the Swan's sturdy profession of friendship.

> Too cold to print
>
> Now it doesn't snow as light as the petals
> Of winter roses, and the well's water
> Has frozen solid. My darling Swan
> Would rather hunker down, soft crown stuck
> Beneath her moulting wing. She waits to know
> If she will ever pluck a May's *mignonne*
> Blossom beside a Ram who spins and kicks
> In the sprouting meadow, delighted
> As he is by song. But meanwhile steady
> Friendship persists, flourishing all year
> Like the elm and vine of fable.
> They twine tightly, still more tightly
> As the tendrils spiral, and tree and berry
> Exchange their traits, woven as one.
> Let winter frown, they grow green regardless,
> And prosper in spite of all that envies them.

Cold as frost, envy opposes the poet's friendship, as (elsewhere) it opposes her poetry.

Even absent the vexatious topic of her close friend Elisabeth Joly, Brongersma will mingle (like Dickinson and Kafka, in this one respect) contrary accents of diffidence and ambition. The Swan not only issues invitations; she also receives them. Possibly Katharina Lescailje invited Brongersma to visit her in the cultural capital, Amsterdam, where Lescailje's family ran a bookshop and a printing press.

On an invitation to swim in the River IJ

Should I dare where so many eagles glide
To wallow, trying the patience of the IJ?
Ply these web-feet game for any waters
In such lucid, subtle, polished eddies?
Forgive my brag. My heart has never yet
Gone under. Sound policy has secured me
The general privilege of paddling. No
Aquatic monster could withstand my courage,
Or flare of sudden fire abash my coming.
A bulky daemon's grimace wouldn't baulk me.
But the toxic snake of a taunting critic
Craving endless rounds of senseless quarrels
Makes me linger, think, swim, and slide
Under the kinder banks of the Grunoos, adrift
On the current of a richer meditation.

And what *was* "the current of [that] richer meditation"? Brongersma's Swan is a well-read bird. I have already avowed my belief that the poet consulted manuscript verses by Katharina Lescailje and Cornelia van der Veer. She also composes and translates French lyrics, and offers her own Frisian eclogues. Praising Elisabeth Joly, Brongersma mentions that her friend has mastered three languages: at least so much is true of the poet herself.

Brongersma's book indicates acquaintance with both of Homer's epics, with Hesiod's *Theogony*, with Herodotus, with Plato, with Theocritus, with the Vergil of *Eclogues* and *Aeneid*, and with the Ovid of both *Heroides* and *Metamorphoses*. Some linguistic echoes suggest Brongersma specifically read Jonas Cabeljau's version of *Heroides*, which came out in 1657. The Swan memorializes Pierre de Ronsard (1524–1585). Brongersma may have read or seen Molière's *Mariage forcé*. She knew Honoré d'Urfé's *L'Astrée* (issued in five volumes between 1609 and 1627). The poet repeatedly borrowed a copy of Giovanni Battista Guarini's *Il pastor fido* (1590). She celebrates the long-lived playwright Joost van den Vondel (1587–1679). She paints a word-picture from Pieter Hooft's play *Granida* (1605). Possibly at the instance – or through the imitations – of her friend Ludolph Smids, she shows broad acquaintance with Giovanni Boccaccio. Brongersma often chooses airs from contemporary French opera, especially works by Philippe Quinault (1635–1688) and Jean-Baptiste Lully (1632–1687), including *Atys*, *Proserpine*, and *Le triomphe de l'amour*. These airs, detached from their dramatic settings, may have entered into her sphere via the periodical *Le nouveau Mercure galant*. Brongersma mentions two notable visual artists – Pietro Testa (ca 1611–1650) and Nicolaes de Helt Stockade (1614–1699). The latter is famous for his depiction of Ovidian motifs. Brongersma's Swan likes to echo the Song of Songs and the Psalms. The life, death, and resurrection of Christ engage her, sometimes passionately. However provincial her surroundings, Brongersma was by any standard a cultivated woman.

*Beginning and Ending*

Apart from the image of the bird, does a scrutable principle govern the overall organization of Brongersma's *Swan of the Well*? Like Lescailje and Smids, the author demonstrates a Baroque consciousness of literary kinds. Her book's title aspires to exhaustiveness: "rhymes in several genres ... including panegyrics, spiritual meditations, songs, descriptive pieces, birthday poems, eulogies, epithalamia, translations, complimentary verses, poems to accompany gifts, and riddles." Brongersma often, though inconsistently, introduces clear divisions into her book, announcing with the name of a genre the beginning and end of a particular series of pieces reducible under the advertised category. The reader therefore encounters individual poems of an announced kind ("sonnet," for example) as well as more comprehensive rubrics (epithalamia, spiritual verse, ekphrastic poems, birthday poems, elegies, and *omgeefsels* – verses intended to go along with presents).

One method of interpreting a volume of poetry is to examine the first and last items in it, its imaginative alpha and omega. Classical scholars sometimes call the piece inaugurating a book the *program poem*.[27] We may decide, less esoterically, to call the piece that concludes it the *envoi*. Brongersma starts with what she herself denominates a sonnet: "The triumphant lily-shrubbery of Groningen, rife with buds and blossoms."

> Dewed with pearl-like drops, your base supports
> An arch a Caesar would admire. The flower
> Brightly flaunts its garlands – rings
> Of spreading sprigs, ascending buds. Queen,
> Leafy splendour comprising variants,
> Neither Asian nard nor Attic thyme
> Infringes on your fame, for you combine
> The best of both and each, like a wing,
> Contributes to waft you off to glory.
> No one can stunt you and keep you down.
> Your crest transcends all staleness.
> Towering, you preserve your lily-blessing against
> The biting snake, the stinging scorpion. Neither

Can lodge in Groningen's contented garden.
You cast them out. You win the battle.

This short though sumptuous piece (a true – fourteen-line – sonnet in Dutch) articulates Brongersma's distinctive ambition. She may play on her own given name. Titus commissioned the most famous of Roman triumphal arches. This emperor, who vanquished Jerusalem in 70 CE, bore a name suggestive of "Titia." He had the monument raised in the city centre, the forum. The historian Mortimer Wheeler, discussing triumphal arches, perceives in them the perfect embodiment of Rome's arrogance. These "monstrous toys" embody ideally "the combined majesty and ostentation" of the belligerent empire.[28] Brongersma's reader must pass under her revisionist archway to cross the threshold of her book. Just as in this first, isolated sonnet, the poet will balance Graeco-Roman antiquity against Frisian modernity throughout *The Swan of the Well*. Groningen – a university town – will remain the hub of her intellectual world, appearing (in fact) less often as Rome than as Athens.

A lone opening flanked by columns and panels pierces a triumphal arch. An attic storey carved with a dedication tops the gate. The enormous structure extravagantly recalls a deed of conquest. Brongersma modifies the concept for her own ends. The prominence she grants to flowers reflects well-known aspects of seventeenth-century Netherlandic culture. This horticultural emphasis persists obviously into the present day. Brongersma knows too that flowers come associated with women, and with women's arts. The triumphal arch thus admits an added measure of female implication. If the original Roman gate crassly imagines victory as eternized penetration across a *limen*, then Brongersma alters this idea decidedly. Garden flowers embody cooperation between nature and art. In the northern hemisphere, efflorescence is a seasonal matter. Yet perennials can endure. Blossoming shrubbery partakes of both stability and transience, unlike insensible Roman stone raised to brave devouring time. The sonnet insists, moreover, that Groningen's perfumes surpass any known to the ancient empire that contrived triumphal arches: a Frisian-inflected instance of Renaissance "outdoing." Not Asia Minor or Greece could ever produce so sophisticated a bouquet.

Unlike masonry, flowers spontaneously grow. Plants decay and recuperate; marble or granite passively weathers away. In Brongersma, fame – a poet's dearest wish – flits in the volatile and sensuous guise of an aroma. Less overweening than Roman precedent, the arch that Brongersma praises still avows a win. Groningen's lily-shrubbery supposedly deters dangerous pests. Neither poisonous snake nor scorpion can transgress the arch's lovely prohibition. A Christian whiff of Eden – paradise regained – freshens the end of Brongersma's sonnet. Whereas lapidary Rome declared in the lucid testimony of its incised attic storey the fixed identities of victor and vanquished, Brongersma's last line testifies that – by coming into existence at all – her book has defied the odds, as the antithesis of what would prevent its coming into being. In the universe of *The Swan of the Well*, scorpions and serpents stand for the envious.

What about the conclusion? Brongersma may seem to sound a charmingly trivial note. After all, the *envoi* of her book belongs to a minor genre, the riddle:

> I vary like the winds to which
> I can attach at will and when
> Boreas planes on frigid wings
> He stiffens me in brittle shards
> So I lengthen into pendent crystal
> Bearing my daughter on my lips.
> Apollo bathes me in his balmy
> Breath that softens me, loosens
> Me up again, reborn
> In the very act of vanishing.

The answer to the enigma posed by the speaker's identity would appear to be "water." We have receded from Brongersma's Swan to the elementary medium in which the Swan swims – the substance of her pool.

Like the flowers of Groningen's triumphal arch, water submits to a cycle. Flowers bud, blossom, wither, are succeeded by fruit, and (like wild swans) return. In the northern hemisphere, water passes through a parallel series of states. Brongersma's riddle instances vapour, ice, and liquid. The poet often adduces Ovid, and metamorphosis enchants her. As a woman, she changes the tradition every time she touches it. Her valedictory icicle melts and, in keeping with the bias that inventively adapts commonplaces to female experience, its daughter is the liquid water drop. Sunny Apollo, one of Brongersma's presiding gods (not always unchallenged), recurs as the enabler of transformation and, implicitly, of poetry.[29] If E.J. de Wolff's frontispiece Swan adopts the stance of the un-killable phoenix, here a humbler assertion of death, rebirth, and matri-lineage finds expression. Brongersma, heir to Greece and Rome, female friend of Groningen's male intellectuals, both asserts and annuls her speaker's existence. She materializes and she vanishes in a thoroughly aqueous way, a shape-shifter's way. The book "vanishes" as we cease to read it. Physically it remains. It lingers, too, in memory. Brongersma's Dutch disappears in my translation, only to re-condense – such is my hope – in plausible Canadian English.

## *Elisabeth Joly*

Brongersma addresses thirty-two poems of *The Swan of the Well* to Elisabeth Joly, to the figure of Elise (sometimes assimilated directly to Elisabeth Joly), or to members of the Joly family. That gifted family includes (in the order of their appearance, in verse dedicated to them) Maria, Magdalena, Judith, Catharina, Philip, and Jacobus. Brongersma celebrates each one of them for proficiency in an art. Maria Joly stitches silk embroidery into linen; Magdalena makes an ingenious cap with an attached veil; Judith paints watercolours; Catharina manufactures artificial flowers; Philip paints pictures, to which he subjoins mottoes; and Jacobus manufactures deluxe books. The poet credits Elisabeth with epistolary eloquence, with a flair for embroidery, with painterly talent, with polyglot fluency, and with outrageous physical allure vaguely specified. The person of the beloved, however, remains un-particularized, except for her jet-black eyes. The Laura of Petrarch's *Rime Sparse* has eyes described in the same way.[30] The topic of Joly influences many poems that omit direct mention of her. Even Alcyone, daughter of Aeolus, lamenting on the coastline for her beloved Ceyx (and destined to be transformed, with him, into a kingfisher), becomes, in her place, a type of Brongersma's regret at Joly's departure by sea.

Lia van Gemert has identified several outstanding features of the verse exclusively dedicated to Elise or to Elisabeth. She observes "the theme of transvestism." Most strikingly, Brongersma's speaker adopts the persona of Cléonte in relation to Elise.[31] Van Gemert rightly observes the masculinity of this courtly name. Intriguingly, one (female) Cléonte has a role in Aphra Behn's *The Dutch Lover* of 1673 – coincidence, it would seem, rather than influence.[32] Van Gemert calls Brongersma's erotic mode "Petrarchan." This is a just general epithet, provided that strong modulations of love-elegy, deriving from Brongersma's engagement with Ovid, are allowed to supplement the tendency. Van Gemert guesses what may have happened between the poet and her friend:

> Putting the implications of the material together, the story behind this poetry might be as follows. Titia Brongersma had an intimate and emotional relationship with Elisabeth Joly. Their mutual happy feelings changed when Brongersma went too far in her physical demands; because her honour was at stake, Joly could no longer see her, although she regretted this. Brongersma knows Joly is out of reach for ever and has to satisfy herself with admiration at a distance. Meanwhile she knows she will never love somebody else the way she loved Elise. She does not seem to know how to judge her own feelings: are they chaste or is she a morally corrupt person?[33]

Van Gemert's hypothesis illuminates especially the pertinence of an idea of "honour." Meanwhile, the example and art of Aphra Behn, Brongersma's contemporary in England, heir to the same broad European tradition as the Frisian writer, may provide tools to refine the pursuit of a specifically rhetorical appreciation of *The Swan of the Well*.

Van Gemert's remarks on "transvestism" hint that Brongersma, when she depicts the figure of Elise or Elisabeth, evolves ways of embodying and expanding a sentiment of sexual flux. The method offers the poet artistic opportunities close to the kind Aphra Behn explores in "To the Fair Clarinda, Who Made Love to Me, Imagined More than Woman":

Fair lovely maid, or if that title be
Too weak, too feminine for nobler thee,
Permit a name that more approaches truth:
And let me call thee, lovely charming youth ...

Thou beauteous wonder of a different kind,
Soft Cloris with the dear Alexis joined;
When ere the manly part of thee, would plead
Thou tempts us with the image of the maid,
While we the noblest passions do extend
The love to Hermes, Aphrodite the friend.[34]

Behn and Brongersma realize the degree to which the practice of poetic gallantry – its manhood, its womanhood – is an artifice: a matter of address.

A Clarinda or an Elise permits a poet to animate on the beloved's behalf two age-old, complementary, and artificial systems of rhetorical expectation. Hence Elise now equals Achilles, now languishes like a maiden.[35] For Behn, the problem of "honour" and same-sex desire, which van Gemert imagines colouring Joly's responses to Brongersma, at once intrudes. Behn sidesteps it with a flourish:

In pity to our sex sure thou wert sent,
That we might love, and yet be innocent:
For sure no crime with thee we can commit;
Or if we should – thy form excuses it.

Behn's last line – "The love to Hermes, Aphrodite the friend" – distinguishes the god from (yet still fuses him to) the goddess. The result of their conjunction, the famous hermaphrodite, tarries therefore in the *process* of generation.[36] Behn's act of apostrophe, alternately constituting a male and a female object, fluctuates so elusively that it exempts the speaker from a lapse into the vice or sin that, van Gemert argues, Joly and Brongersma thought might sully a platonic affection. "To the Fair Clarinda" sets in play a poetic "wonder of a different kind": a perpetual motion machine vibrant with ambiguous *courtoisie*. Its grammatical fulcrum may be the caesura made by the last line's comma. But the true crux is the word "friend." Publishing her poem in 1688, two years after Brongersma's *Swan*, Behn recruits the reader as witness to friendship, to love, even to (imaginary or visionary) copulation – factors once personified by the Greeks in the figure of Philotes.

Prior to Joly's introduction, within just the first few pages of *The Swan of the Well*, the reader encounters Lady Isabella Catharina Maria, Baroness van Heerema; a female van Glinstra, possibly Eritia van Glinstra; one Anna de Haas; a certain Susanna Wilmson; and the celebrated queen of Palmyra, Zenobia. Then comes the intimate friend Elisabeth Joly. An invocation of the great goddess, Nature, follows Joly's entrée. The impartial-seeming adjacency of aristocrats and commoners and figures of legendary resonance is characteristic. Ludolph Smids's *Gallery* distributes its women by the logic of taxonomy. Brongersma's gathering coheres more by association.

Whatever the order in which Brongersma *wrote* her poems, a new reader construes them according to *The Swan of the Well*'s existing arrangement. Therefore Elisabeth Joly's first appearance deserves special notice. Droll circumstantiality protracts the title of this occasional piece: "On Miss E[lisabeth] J[oly]'s inaccessibility so long as the water's surface alternately froze and thawed, and people could get about by neither boat nor skate blade." Brongersma begins by asking her friend for advice. Perhaps Joly rejoins with the witty conceit that inspires this epistolary poem. Its theme is none other than obstacles to correspondence. If Joly is destined to be a muse like Laura or Beatrice, her debut in *The Swan of the Well* may also affirm her role as articulate to the point of some co-authorship. The reader instantly surmises that any exchange between Brongersma and Joly suffers impediment from the start. The solution – the sighs of the separated may, with the goodwill of the breeze, mingle at a halfway point to which neither party can get in person – evokes, even while it modifies, an ancient commonplace: the union of lovers' breath. Plato's epigram is one forerunner, perhaps:

> As I kissed Agathon,
> My soul was on my tongue.
> Poor thing, she came hoping
> To go across to him.[37]

Poet or beloved evidently seized on the opaque aura of semi-permanence that breath takes on, when expelled in cold weather. These visible puffs might embody sufficient durability to survive and coalesce with those originating far off in the lungs and mouth of a friend:

> If the sky would relent a little then
> We could line up and send off thousands of sighs
> Compounded of the steam we exhale. Sped
> On their course, oh may mine meet yours midway.

The reader of Petrarch need only examine the first stanza of the first poem of his *Rime Sparse* to find the invocation of sighs (*sospiri*): but the physical conditions that Brongersma describes (icy waterways, cold mist) belong to Friesland.

The poet has placed her Petrarchan *jeu d'esprit* and its sister piece, "To Elise, on the fresh clemency of the weather," so as to imply, at the outset of *The Swan of the Well*, the beloved's similarity to Zenobia, Syrian queen, on the one hand, and to the Frisian goddess Natura, on the other. The exalted poetic neighbours between whom Brongersma embeds the image of her friend function to amplify Joly's significance. Elisabeth is regal and divine, exotic and autochthonous. Brongersma infuses her vision of the Palmyrene monarch Zenobia, who flourished in the third century, with both martial and intellectual heroism, strengths reinforced by her fidelity to an assassinated husband, Odenathus.[38] The exalted tenor of the piece may derive a warrant from the treatise "On the Sublime," long attributed to Zenobia's courtier, Longinus, whom the poet favourably mentions. Brongersma's subsequent poem on the *hunebed* – a megalithic monument at Borger, not far from Assen, now reckoned to be five thousand years old – forms a contrast with the world of Zenobia. Palmyra was an exquisite city. The *hunebed* at Borger consists of enormous, rugged, undressed stones. Brongersma dismisses any theory of Mediterranean influence on the *hunebed*. With some sly humour (it would seem), she even brags that this Frisian prodigy surpasses all the remains of Hellas and of Rome. She alludes to Thebes of the Seven Gates only to depreciate that storied polis. The poet insists that the tremendous *hunebed* served as a temple to the goddess Nature, or Natura – and, more importantly, can be a temple to Nature *again*.

To be a *woman* who praises Zenobia is to innovate on the tradition valued at the University of Groningen by men such as Ludolph Smids. To praise Nature with a woman's song is to honour the might of a *numen* universally revered, but here assigned an accessible oracle. Between Zenobia and Nature stands Elisabeth Joly. Situated thus she assumes lineaments like a figure from Thomas Gray's "Elegy Written in a Country Churchyard" (1751), denied by the bounds of circumstance the crown that might have befitted her. Yet she is endued – despite personal obscurity – with the Frisian birthright of womanhood natural and divine.

A pair of poems of Ovidian inspiration, "The Despairing Canens" and "Canens reproaches Circe," features a female speaker, gifted with the capacity of song in an Orphic degree, who wastes away to tears and mist under the oppression of the sorceress Circe. Circe had transformed Canens's male beloved Picus into a woodpecker (Linnaeus has ensured that the family of woodpeckers remains the *Picidae*). Recklessly true to his love, Picus had spurned the overtures of the daughter of the sun. Ovid's *Metamorphoses* compares the dying Canens to a swan. The ordering of *The Swan of the Well*'s verse here characteristically modulates canonical, Old Master-worthy topics into a more intimate register of experience.³⁹ Canens's magically thwarted love refracts the poet's frustration. "Too cold to print," however, asserts the survival of friendship through the harshest of winters, using the ancient marital commonplace of the elm and the grapevine, substantiating by implication, at least, van Gemert's general argument that Brongersma conceives of herself as married, after a fashion, to Elisabeth Joly.⁴⁰ Ovid recounts how Vertumnus, Italian god of seasons, adopts the counter-sexual guise of a crone to court Pomona, goddess of fruit. To seduce the object of his obsession, he points to the elm and the grapevine, extolling the advantages of their mutual assistance. Pomona consents; the deities wed.⁴¹

A portrait features in the inventive "On the adored truss of yellow auriculas that I have set above the picture of Elisa in my study." Auriculas are a cultivated form of primrose native to Europe. Brongersma emphasizes the traditional femininity of flowers by heightening the beautiful masculinity of the speaker's beloved:

> You comprise, Auricula, an entire
> Gem-like garden in your many-blossomed
> Self, pent flaunting in a ribbon your yellow
> Like the bride of a potentate.

Celebrating the power of art and nature joined in a plant that gardeners favour, the poem proceeds to an *ekphrasis* of the beloved's portrait. In it, Elise wears an embroidered blouse. The reader has already learned of Joly's skill in needlework. The auriculas will wilt; the speaker promises constantly to refresh them, in the manner of a wreath; and she perceives how her verse itself weaves a verbal crown that will never wither. Wonderfully, then, Brongersma celebrates four domains of human artistry: the gardener's, the painter's, the embroiderer's, and the poet's:

> Already the petals wilt so I will weave
> Them in spite of time's damage into
> A crown for Elise, destined in these lines,
> At least, to crown her for as long as she lives.

"For Elise" joins those verses that complain of the physical distance between the beloved's dwelling place and the poet's. They are "damned to correspondence." The speaker wishes she were Icarus – an unpromising case, until it is surmised that this Icarus would plummet into Elise's arms: a heavenly plunge, sealed with a kiss. The speaker expresses the casual desire of becoming a swan, since she cannot assume Icarus's wings. Possibly this poem, in its aggrieved modesty, documents the *original* adoption of the bird to the poet's cause. Does it mark the very occasion when the governing motif of Brongersma's book stirred under the poet's hand? If so, the eloquent creature hatches from the desire of arranging to talk with Elisabeth as much as out of any tradition, whether Ovidian or Frisian.

Four poems to Elise declare their occasional nature. "On Elise's departure for France," "On Elise's dangerous going into France," "On Elise's unexpected taking sick and suffering," and "On Miss E[lisabeth] J[oly]'s bold curiosity" form a discrete series. To go to France is to aggravate already dismal circumstances of mutual impediment:

> You look unmoved. Isn't it enough the River
> Ee separates us since infernal Scylla
> Waits there, and Charybdis barks with gaping
> Lips? Even if she doesn't devour everything
> Still she deals wounds. You know very well
> What cliff faces of violence clap together
> Between us.

Here Brongersma confuses and thus conflates the traits of Scylla and Charybdis, monsters that threatened Ulysses. She may distantly echo Petrarch, who also evokes these Homeric obstacles (*Canzoniere* 189). Forces in local society as well as geography obstruct the poet, her poetry, and her friendship with Joly. The "cliff faces" crashing together evoke Homer's Roving Rocks.[42] Brongersma closes her plaint with a recollection of the first poem in *The Swan of the Well* to mention her best friend – "On Miss E[lisabeth] J[oly]'s inaccessibility," with its imagery of deputized breath. She enriches the motif, further, by use of Brongersma's favourite vocal epithet, "hoarse":

> Send a sigh on the wings of the wind.
> My sobs will toss and gust to meet it halfway
> And bring their hoarse greetings, every day.

"On Elise's dangerous going into France" adopts a different strategy. If the poem on Elise's departure reproaches the absconding beloved for widening the distance between them, then this piece insinuates moral risk. The speaker calls Elise "naïve." Furies lurk in Brittany. Scylla and Charybdis have emigrated to France from their former stations on the River Ee. Elise is a Proserpina tempted by a flower, liable to rape by the lord of the underworld. The beloved hurls herself wilfully into thorny bushes; wilfully, she treads the brink of an abyss. The helpless speaker concedes Elise has already made up her mind to leave.

"On Elise's unexpected taking sick and suffering" depicts Joly ailing, now back in Friesland. The speaker apologizes for responding huffily to a missed visit on Elise's part. She did not know fever had laid her friend low. The poet goes to call on her. Peeking into the sickroom, she glimpses Elise stretched out on her canopied bed. Death himself materializes, shaking a mortal dart. The shocked speaker verges now on petrifaction, like Niobe; now on deliquescence, like Egeria. The teary nymph Egeria became a well, a case of liquefaction blending decorously with Brongersma's perennial theme of spring-waters.[43] The poet would become an Orpheus to Elise, her Eurydice – testimony at once to love and to the "transvestism" van Gemert identifies in *The Swan of the Well*.[44] But "On Miss E[lisabeth] J[oly]'s bold curiosity" assures the reader of the beloved's recrudescent strength. She strides into the midst of a moving column of cavalry, earning the honourific "Amazon." Joly surpasses her male peer Achilles. Equalling him in warrior-hood, she exceeds him in intellectual attainment. A measure of the martial tone that inflects the picture of Zenobia invades these verses. The poet, however, cautions Joly against the "murder and bloodthirst" that breed "in the tingling fifes of the muster."

"A Zephyr for you, my most beloved and honourable Elise" takes up and modifies the topic of "How to keep up communications whether it freezes or it thaws." Petrarchan sighs and sobs gust through *The Swan of the Well*: but this capriccio abstracts the nature and effects of a loving exhalation into a balmy Aeolian god. The Socrates of Plato's *Phaedrus* chooses a breeze to exemplify the ideal reciprocity of (as it happens) same-sex relations: "the beloved is amazed at the good will of the lover ... And as he continues to feel this and approaches and embraces him ... then does the fountain of that stream, which Zeus when he was in love with Ganymede called desire, overflow upon the lover, and some enters into his soul, and some when he is filled flows out again, and as a breeze or an echo leaps from the smooth rocks and rebounds to them again, so does the stream of beauty ... return again to the beautiful one."[45] In Brongersma's vision, even Tempe – a valley already ideal – intuits its incompletion and its yearning, once the delicious ethereality of the western wind arouses it.

A brief tribute to Elisabeth's hitherto unpraised relative, Jacobus Joly, follows. He binds opulent books. The poet compares the clasps of his artisanal editions to the turtledoves that draw Venus's car. This erotic language may obliquely describe Brongersma's own book – not *The Swan of the Well* as such, but the collection of love poems to Elisabeth Joly dispersed within the broader volume. The idea that a slim volume of amorous verse abides under the wings of the more miscellaneous *Swan* gains credibility because Brongersma repeats and varies the same imagery in widely separated poems. The next relevant verses, entitled simply "Cléonte to Elise," liken the sad speaker to "a turtledove that moans and sits / On her dejected perch, a windmill's cable." The same genus of bird that adorns Jacobus's special editions here delivers a lover's complaint. After deploying an indigenous Frisian image (the windmill), the speaker, like a swain in Vergil, engages in sad colloquy with Echo, who lives – very conventionally –

among resonating rocks. The fusion of homely Netherlandic detail (a windmill's cable) with a classical crag and nymph epitomizes Brongersma's method.

"To Elise en route from Palts-Tweebrugge" finds Joly returning from a duchy of the Holy Roman Empire. Daybreak and the glowing beloved approach in unison. The poem comes astonishingly close in tone and topic to Katherine Philips's "Orinda to Lucasia." Philips's poem likewise imagines the likeness of the female friend and the sun:

> Thou, my Lucasia, art far more to me,
> Than he to all the under-world can be;
> From thee I've heat and light,
> Thy absence makes my night.[46]

Horses pull Elise's vehicle, not turtledoves. The beloved has been the toast of wayside taverns. The speaker abases herself. She compares herself to the Oceanid Klytie, whom the sun-god jilted. The allusion insinuates Elise's fickleness. Hyperion loved Klytie, but soon transferred his attention elsewhere. Forlorn she twisted her face after his daily passage, transformed by this hopeless adoration into the guise of a heliotrope.[47] In Brongersma's verses, Elise flickers between the roles of female Aurora and male Hyperion. The explanation for Joly's chronic inconstancy may lie in her capacity to love either a woman (namely, Brongersma) or a man (the undoubted preference of her society, possibly seconded by her own desire). The speaker concludes her encomium of Elise with a confession of dependency. She plays reflective moon to Elise's solar radiance. The return of Elise from Palts-Tweebrugge precipitates joy – and triggers insecurity.

"Thyrsis full of longing" features a speaker besotted with Elise. His pastoral name derives ultimately from the first of Theocritus's *Idylls*. This Frisian Thyrsis climbs dunes to gain a prospect of the sea. He longs for Elise; he would be her beacon; he would like her to come back astride a dolphin's back. She is his Palinurus. This reference to a helmsman in Vergil's *Aeneid* bears a burden of ambiguity. Sleepily tumbling from the ship he was steering, Palinurus swam to shore only to have ruffians, discovering him at the tideline, peremptorily slay him. Of course Thyrsis would behave otherwise if Elise were to emerge from the surf. Yet even when the beloved rests safely nearby, she presents a problem. "To the sleeping Elise" relishes optimum proximity: "Her cruelty sleeps in her who is my truest part." The poem mounts a plea for the maintenance of universal silence, in order to protract the poet's voyeuristic pleasure in the passive spectacle of a slumbering friend. "To Elise, on our latest farewell" discovers in the nearness of the weeping beloved an object of rich delectation. Tears beautify Elise, who murmurs "Never forget." The speaker, in Brongersma's paradoxical valediction, promises she will obey the command. But to fulfill it, she will at the same time continually commemorate (and thus refresh) her attachment. A farewell that never ends is difficult to distinguish from an ongoing conversation. Van Gemert may base her argument for the decisive alienation of the friends Brongersma and Joly on this particular poem.

"On a picture of Elisa: Cléonte to Elise" rehearses the series of mythological parallels by which Brongersma has constituted the figure of the beloved. After a *blazon* vaguely inventorying Elise's allure, the beloved is likened, successively, to Mars; to Diana (haughty goddess of the wild, of lust for dreamy Endymion, of the bloody chase); to an Amazon (militant womanhood); and, at last, to Helen (the personification of female appeal). Elise flashes and shimmers amid the interstices of masculine and feminine codes. Some male entities are aggressive (Mars); others compliant (Endymion). An Amazon goes to war. Helen bears the blame for ten years' armed struggle. The painting itself must most resemble Helen, as the object of the viewer's arbitrary projections. "On a picture of Elisa" ends with the admission of relief. The desire to praise is an appetite that has demanded to be satiated. The speaker, aroused by visual art, gives words to her desire and achieves significant form. Its shapeliness "calms" the speaker – almost like the physical release that she craves, and Elise will not grant.

The "story" of Brongersma and Joly continues with "To the chaste Diana, Miss Elisabeth Joly who, with her nymphs, goes hunting near IJlst in pursuit of the deer." Did Joly really pursue the chase? This Diana is a "cold and continent nymph"; the arrows she carries are the glances of her "inestimable eyes." The neglected speaker depreciates herself as the goddess's most negligible quarry. The speaker, like a deer, has been "run to earth." Diana hardly notices this predicament. Brongersma thus invents yet another scene of masochistic abjection. The speaker solicits her own persecution. "Thyrsis to Elise," written, unusually, in French, follows the harsh picture of Joly as fierce yet neglectful Diana. The poet names Zephyr; the agreeable odour of the western wind recurs. The good smell emanates directly from the beloved, who resembles a "peerless rose." This conventional compliment heralds the brief and sensuous "On a bouquet the young Flora bestowed (Miss Heringa van Eysinga presented the flowers to Philis, namely Miss Elizabeth Joly)." The unembarrassed blossoms of this poem crave "to open, / Quickly, and blow, and die: / Die upon your bosom." But the ecstatic wish is entrusted to the innocent intermediary Miss van Eysinga.

Brongersma dedicates the whole ekphrastic section of *The Swan of the Well* to Elisabeth Joly, "the brilliant and virtuous." The Swan herself here performs a panegyric of Joly the painter, apologizing, as is her wont, for her incapacity to praise the beloved as well as she deserves. Once again, the Swan is "hoarse." "On a painting of Elisabeth Joly, a woman as virtuous as artistic" takes its place in the gallery of other described artworks. Here Joly's mental attainments receive emphasis, not the charm or power her person may exercise. "Virtue and knowledge" are Joly's chief qualities. In this last description of Joly, she is both a Minerva – a chaste intellectual warrior – and an independent Daphne, in inalienable possession of her own laurel.

One more poem remains, an enthusiastic *genethliacon* or birthday poem in Brongersma's section devoted to this genre: "On the birthday of that most richly virtuous and ingenious young woman Miss Elisabeth Joly." The poet associates her beloved's August birthday with the period in the middle of that month (13 or 14 August) during which Athens celebrated the Panathenaea in honour of its patron goddess. Brongersma emphasizes the female exclusivity of that festival: "Women performed the rite." In the course of the poem, she shifts ground from the temple of Minerva, decorated by her acolytes, to a Frisian celebration. We learn that Joly knows three languages. Here, as *The Swan of the Well* begins to conclude, where Brongersma's elegies cluster, the poet observes the anniversary of the day on which Joly began to live. The poet says she would gladly grant the beloved a superadded, a second life. Failing to furnish that superhuman gift, she pledges instead to render permanent poetic service.

Scrutinizing the body of Joly poems, we discover recurrent topics. Breath stands for the intimacy of mutual affection. Lovers' breath can blend entirely: a pleasure the poet cannot otherwise consummate. We grieve on a beach; we witness wretched acts of supplication; we endure bitter weather. We fret about the beloved's faithlessness – possibly with the opposite sex – and admire the poet's contrasting constancy. Biographical readings easily mislead. Literature furnishes its own content, even as it furnishes form. Consider the fabrications of Elizabethan sonneteers, or of the Roman love-elegists who influenced Brongersma. The poet certainly studied Ovid's epistolary *Heroides* with care. Therefore the story of the friendship between Brongersma and Joly remains largely – happily – the story of writing. As for its mood of pining and repining, the verse tends to find its occasions when Joly is unavailable. Epistolary exchange palliates the calamity of a total severance. The relationship appears to consist of ruptures as much as of unions, whether they take the form of geographical displacement (Brittany, Palts-Tweebrugge) or the poet's suspicion of Joly's wandering eye. If all Brongersma's feats of inventive appreciation do not wholly absolve a difficult friend, the book evolves lovable structures in which to lodge the poet's fascination. Here is the gift that the Swan of Dokkum has passed to us, her posterity.

*Archaeology*

When I visited Borger, in Drenthe, in 2014, I rode a black bicycle beneath shade trees, the airy majority poplars, passing long farm fields, and once seeing stalking across the ground that fairy-tale bird the stork. Although this was Titia

Brongersma's country, I saw no swans. The dominant waterfowl was the exotic Canada goose. But from the meadows sang in antiphony with its kind a small finch called a *geelgors* or yellowhammer, with that tonal largesse of songbirds which confers natural citizenship on any audience. Bogs in Drenthe have preserved millennia-old corpses and wheels – even a wooden temple the size of a garden shed with hornlike projections at each corner, making paganism appear (in the Drents Museum at Assen) as homely as the practice of hanging of nest-boxes throughout a suburban yard. In Borger, a tranquil town, stands the *hunebed* where, on Pentecost, 1685 (the seventh Sunday after Easter), with her friend Jan Laurens Lenting (or Lentinck), Brongersma made what may have been the first archaeological reconnaissance of this megalithic monument.[48] The *hunebed* is contemporary with Stonehenge. Experts have bestowed on the civilization of its builders the name of Funnel Beaker Culture. It flourished between 3350 and 2700 BCE. At eighty feet (or 24.4 metres), and composed of forty-five immense boulders, the Borger monument is the longest of its kind. Jan Albert Bakker notes that the vicinity of Borger derived its name, as early as 1648, from the "cluster of *hunebeds*" distinguishing it.[49] Superstition in those days held that witchy "White Women" haunted the vicinity. According to Alfred Sadler, Boniface – the saint who opened Dokkum's holy well – ordered the destruction of the *hunebedden*, those foul shrines of idolatry. Florentius Schoonhovius (1594–1648) even accused the ancient inhabitants of the region of forcing strangers to creep through the gaps between the great stones while enduring the murderous enthusiasm of a dung-pelting mob. After this maltreatment, ritual slaughter supposedly awaited the wretches.[50]

The trilithons of Salisbury plain loom taller than *hunebedden*. But a *hunebed* has what Stonehenge lacks: a roof. Nine stones furnish the ceiling at Borger. A row or gallery of close-set side stones and capstones contributes to make a chamber nine feet (2.7 metres) broad. The *hunebed*'s amiable appearance – it has the look of a lazy, shambling animal halted to rest or to bask – precociously embodies the Dutch virtue of *gezelligheid* or "coziness," though an aura of preternatural force still blazes from it. The monument inspires pleasantly mingled awe and fondness. The Funnel Beaker people who erected the *hunebed* gathered glacially deposited granite erratics for their project. What did Brongersma make of this spectacle?

In 1579, a Dutch predecessor, recording or succumbing to Catholic *daemonomania*, bestowed the ugly name of *Duvels Cut* or *Daemonis Cunnus*, "Devil's Cunt," on the monument. Brongersma's reappraisal, extolling the goddess *Natura* or Nature, redeems the *hunebed* as an honourable testimony to the eldest of female divinities. As late as 1660, the artist Johan Picardt portrayed a *hunebed* assembled not by diabolical forces, but by giants.[51] Sadler reports a legend that these giants bowled the stones into place from a mile's distance.[52] Brongersma dismissed this fantasy. Her frank curiosity also drove her to dig beneath the trilithons. She unearthed urns so fragile they crumbled once retrieved into the light. Here is what she wrote about the experience:

> Praise of the *hunebed*, or the prodigious heaped pile of boulders at Borger, in Drenthe
>
> I stand like one to stone turned staring
> At the stacked rocks, boast of heroic Huns
> Apparently, who willed the building of a
> Monument to secure a footing on glory's
> Sheer gradient. No. This mass congeals a dream of
> Resentful giants upreared, vying with godhood
> Though they say Mulciber's thunderbolt split
> It, flaring, into fragments. Could it be a pyramid
> Dragged into place? Or a grave? For this gross,
> Craggy cumulation encloses in
> Its substrate carcasses, ancient sacrifice.
> No. More likely it is Natura's marble
> Temple where she desires that her divinity be
> Honoured. She would hear at the verge of her ninefold
> Threshold nothing beyond a song of praise.
> Let Thebes boast of walls tall enough to scrape
> The sky, this rocky monster will outlast her,
> No force though great can crack it all to bits.
> Come nymphs, and come you rustics of Drenthe,
> Make splendid with your praise this mineral palace
> That would be piled with flowers. Render to Nature
> What is elementally hers, and her tribute.
> I offer in a hoarse and throaty voice a song
> Of praise to extol this marvel of a cave and
> Prepare the oaken crown to deck the immense
> Castle of boulders.

Brongersma uses a poetic form made famous by her namesake Sappho: the *priamel*.[53] A priamel dramatizes a series of choices. The writer rejects all of them in favour of the last. Vainglorious Huns did not stack the *hunebed* of Borger.[54] Nor did rebellious giants. Although Brongersma found funerary jars inside the monument, she does not consider them evidence that the *hunebed* functions as a mausoleum. Instead, Brongersma restores the *hunebed* to the goddess Natura. The instrument of that restoration is her poem itself. Within hearing of the university city of Groningen, with its faculty infatuated (as she, too, often is) by the Greek and Roman classics, she makes the *hunebed* a resonator for a divinity of her own sex. Nature has the advantage of equal indigeneity and universality. She is Frisian, she is worldwide.

Renaissance writers often resort to an idea of "outdoing." Brongersma vaunts that her *hunebed* leaves the literary precedent of Thebes in the dust. Tongue in cheek, Brongersma may temper her Frisian pride with irony. Why should the poet refer to Thebes of the Seven Gates? Legend says a male mage, Amphion, raised the blocks of that city's walls merely by making music. Brongersma thus implies that, together, her modern power of incantation and the goddess's ancient *hunebed* eclipse the canonical achievements of a son of Zeus. *Natura*, in Brongersma's understanding of the case, may signify a neo-platonic as well as a Drentish entity. Her *numen* could resemble the one described by that compelling singer, Lady Philosophy, in Boethius's *Consolation* – *Natura potens* ruling the universe by law and love.[55]

The following poem by Brongersma's champion, the physician Ludolph Smids, appears in the first volume of an anonymous book issued in 1843, entitled *Drenthe in vlugtige en losse omtrekken geschetst door drie Podagristen*, or *Drenthe in quick, loose sketches by three sufferers from gout*.[56] Smids adopts the perspective of an archaeological specimen that, in a display of sensibility, rebukes the modern excavator for intruding on a private grave:

On the Swabian urn dug up in pieces beneath the so-called *hunebed* at Borger, to Titia Brongersma

I rested on a bosom before I was buried
Surpassing the whiteness of milk, of lilies.
This hard earthen urn was kissed by lips,
Lips whose affection none can praise enough.
Wet with hot tears, O Titia, I witnessed
A youthful woman of the north stuffing my belly
With mortal remains for she sat on the paving
Of stones before the funeral altar, and sifted
The ashes of her darling out of burnt raiment.
She choked in her woe, her sorrow: in embracing
That grey urn she looked as if she would die.
You climbing into the unguarded structure, curious,
Dug me up, learnedly parsed my fragments,
A cruel sagacity, for I have not seen day
Since the Saxon died, the Dane and wild
Swabian. O lady, what would you do now
With these potsherds? Lay them down again, cover
The relics and remains and close me up again
As what I was and I am, a faithful lover.

Smids in all likelihood calls the urn "Swabian" under the influence of the Roman Tacitus, who (in *Germania*) named the Suebi the region's dominant people. Brongersma conjures the goddess Natura anew with her song. Smids decides, however, to eroticize an urn burial, imagining a lovely woman mourning someone dear to her. Who has died the poet leaves unclear, but the lady who laments is youthful. In her rejoinder, Brongersma modifies Smids's image of bereaved, voluptuous femininity, explaining her reasons to the artifact:

> Reply to the charming verses the most learned Mr Ludolph Smids sent me, on the topic of the shattered urn
>
> You consider it alarming, unrestful
> That people exhumed you who once far more
> Cheerfully saw the surface of the earth.
> It is as good as kisses from many lips
> That your earthen worth is now extolled.
> I felt for you, salt tears thickly coursing,
> Soaking through your opening to the bottom
> Where remains lay packed in you, while I kneeled
> In front of you, the crumbly stuff sifting
> From the burst seal burial long sanctified.
> I looked at you, oppressed, and immersed myself
> In ancient woe. There you appeared: lifeless,
> Condemned to death in the grimy grave of such
> An uncanny monument, all broken potsherds
> (A sight to distress my eyes) crushed under
> Hard stones. I moved you into sunlight's warmth
> And walked bravely with your relics, away.
> I dispose your epochal, occult mortality
> Before the gaze of all, with a lover's care.

Brongersma transforms the grief of long-dead strangers, by the ministry of her intellectual love, into the austere and kindly sentiment of curiosity – curation as caring. She does omit to say how hard it was to preserve the remains she uncovered. Today Dutch archaeological law, as though inspired by Brongersma's experience, abides by the dictum *opgraven is vernietigen*, "to dig up is to destroy."[57]

### Heroines

Brongersma read Ovid deeply. Her work often alludes to his *Metamorphoses*. She depicts the plight of the lovers Ceyx and Alcyone, eventually reunited as a pair of those strong and beautiful birds, kingfishers; the transmogrification of Daphne, for whose afterlife as the poetic laurel she shows ingenious sympathy; Picus's adoption of a woodpecker's form under the wand of Circe, and the dissolution of his beloved Canens into mist and tears; and the renunciation of Cipus, who refused, in defiance of an oracular pronouncement, to become monarch of Rome: he settled for being the squire of a suburban estate. Brongersma also alludes to Ovid's *Heroides*, in which the titular women compose epistles to defaulting men. But the heroines she chooses to celebrate derive just as often from the compilations of Giovanni Boccaccio (who died in 1375) and her friend Smids's *Gallery*. Not passive chastity, but strenuous sovereignty over the disposition of one's body interests Brongersma. "Hippo" is here a female name; the poet's ultimate source may be Boccaccio. The story goes that Hippo's body eventually washed up on the shores of Ionian Erythrae. People there revered her tomb.

> Greek Hippo springs courageously into the salt barrens of the sea to escape pirates, willing to die rather than live in shame and slavery
>
> Woman, who will trumpet your deed? Say what
> Triton, disentangling Siren snared
> In fishing net, more bravely dove down into
> The deepest nether brine? Hippo, how firm
> Your heart, though barren ocean tossed you
> Heaving inhuman waves all salt. Despair
> Solicited you: integrity outweighed
> Mere life. What is treasure? Pirate gangs
> Like it – like to rape: a woman's booty.
> Groan instead, suffocate and thrash.
> An Attic shore-grave closes up your corpse
> In its barren lap. Your disaster draws
> Tears from my eyes. May I nurse the thought
> Of you here on the coast, and lament
> Your death? Philosophy and Poetry
> Drone and pound like the surf, as in your time,
> With just the note the Athenian sang. Who is
> Fit to make Hippo's reputation deathless?

Brongersma's rhetorical question could imply that she believes herself as "fit" for the task as any prior contender.

Relying on ancient sources, Ludolph Smids enrolled in his 1685 *Gallery* Zenobia, queen of Palmyra. Brongersma depicted the same topic.[58] It is worth comparing their disparate portrayals of this figure. First Smids:

> This is Zenobia, queen of the Palmyrenes.
> Doffing a silver helmet she would disclose
> Her sex had not her breast betrayed that
> Already, behind her waving banner's curve.
> Roaming the scrub she tests her mettle on
> Lions and tigers, piercing through their thick
> Flanks. The man she loved could not best her
> Even in his prime, when she was still princess.
> Now she is dead Odenathus's lovely widow.
> What wonder she leads proud campaigns
> To trouble fat Egypt and rich Asia?[59]

Brongersma conceives of Zenobia outside of a governing conceit such as Smids's tour of a gallery of women. Her circumstantial title may reflect the intent of describing an imaginary painting:

> Zenobia, widow of the prefect Odenathus, the most modest and audacious woman in the world, defeats the Persians and fights a lion while mounted on her horse.

> See Zenobia the queen like Achilles come again
> Riding over there, leading another charge
> While fighting off a lion and the Persian
> Both, her lance smeared boldly with hostile
> Blood, spattering droplets over Caesar's marble
> Throne. Her victory boasts its splendid spoils
> And becomes her more than a crown of pearl.
> She has got gold to beat the loot of Croesus
> And performed feats to equal Alexander's.
> Pyrrhus's spirit is hers. He never made a mistake,
> By Scipio vested in virtue's robes. Her great
> Mind was a gift Marcellus came to value.
> Trajan would approve her divine virtue.
> Rome acclaimed her like a goddess, her image
> Fixed in costly designs. Odenathus,
> See your surpassing woman now, glory
> Of her sex, inestimable treasure, tomb
> Raised to sublime Longinus's intellectual
> Apex, to dearest Cassius's, where Pompey
> Already had sown laurel for you, sir, and her.
> The beacon burns with coupled heat and light.

Zenobia – whom I discussed before, in connection with Elisabeth Joly – married the Roman prefect of Palmyra, in the province of Syria. After her husband's assassination (for which she was not responsible), Zenobia ignored Rome's interests. Emperor Aurelian attacked and vanquished her, and took her to Rome in chains. There she may have married the senator Marcellus Petrus Nutenus. Ruling only until 117, Trajan long preceded Zenobia, but he was the first Roman emperor to deify women associates. Brongersma may imply Trajan would have apotheosized Zenobia, had he enjoyed the opportunity. Brongersma's poem depicts the queen of Palmyra beset by natural and political foes, by a beast of prey and a horde of enemies. Marshalling the names of Achilles, Alexander, Pyrrhus, and Scipio, the poet endorses epic violence. By comparison, Smids's poem emphasizes Zenobia's female form ("her breast") as well as her prowess as a hunter and general. It does not contrast her abilities with any other individual man than her late husband. Unlike Brongersma, Smids ignores the Syrian queen's encouragement of culture.

Brongersma remembers with a dramatic monologue another queen – the Scythian Tomyris, who ruled the Massagetae. Herodotus (480–425 BCE) says she won the most violent battle in all history:

> After Cyrus the Persian had subdued the east, including the king of Babylon, he used deception to kill the son of Tomyris, the Scythian queen, and a third of her army. Vanquishing the invader, she had the man decapitated, and sank his head into a bag of blood with the idea he could at last satisfy his lust for that drink.

The queen speaks

Cyrus, was it not enough to lay waste the east
And topple Babylon with your steel? Insatiable
Guest must you rage, invading all remaining
To me – talents, thoughts, mental strength? You
Ambushed my son. I did not weep. I plotted
My revenge on you, who won only by a ruse
That triumph. My hand thrust the killing spear,
And you, with all your might, I reduced to nothing
Insofar as human beings can. I had
Your envious head severed from your torso
And plunged it in a pouch of blood up to the ears
So you could glut your thirst, finally full.
Bloodhound, dog of loathing, you didn't tire
Of murder's gore. Now drink until you puke.
Don't forget to sound the horn insisting "Mission

Accomplished" – by me, Tomyris, laurels
Wrested from you, to wreath womankind.

Cyrus seized and killed Spargapises, Tomyris's son. Her heir, made drunk, could not fight back. The queen swore she would give her Persian enemy more blood than even he could stomach. In 529 BCE, her army defeated his. Tomyris fulfilled her vow, sinking the head of her child's killer into a leather sack brim with gore.[60] In this angry queen, Brongersma may have found an image to unite two of her favourite themes. Her Swan more serenely incarnates the first of these motifs: the strength of female love and ambition. Her indelible Frisian allegiance may support the second: an insistence on integrity and on liberty.

## *Diction and Orthography*

I reproduce in this facing-page translation the orthography of the 1686 edition of Brongersma's poetry – the only edition. She composed the majority of her work in Dutch, but she included four pastorals in West Frisian. Some asperity may sour their droll air, inasmuch as they gauge the fates of female personnel: bawdry, drudgery, matrimony, and the marks of class division (a lady, for example, rejoins with standard Dutch to a Frisian-speaking farmwife). Van Elk notes that women publishing in the Netherlands in Brongersma's period usually stopped publishing as soon as they got married.[61] The gifted Katharina Lescailje remained unwed, and so persisted in her public career.[62] Whether Brongersma married after 1686 is unknown.

The language of most of Brongersma's verses is comparable to that of Ludolph Smids. To a modern reader of Dutch, the manner has become archaic. But it remains as comprehensible as (in the English tradition) John Milton's. Still, there is a difference between Brongersma and Smids to be stressed. Carel Pieman brought out Smids's *Gallery* in 1685, and *De bron-swaan* in 1686. In the former case, the compositor shows more consistency and accuracy. Whoever set Brongersma's type more often, I discovered, represented words as they might be *pronounced* rather than as they should be *spelled*. In translating, therefore, I sometimes had to say individual phrases over and over again, before attempting to locate their probable analogies in seventeenth- and eighteenth-century Dutch dictionaries. Either Brongersma or the compositor, or both, had a good ear and markedly improvisational spelling. Proper names (to choose one example) presented a formidable, but enjoyable puzzle.

Brongersma supplies a list of errata, but the compositor contributes not a few of which Brongersma takes no account. Typeset errors tend to be simple and I have corrected them. Here are examples of such corrections: *steme geschal* becomes *stemgeschal*; *Druken, Drukken*; and *greep's, greep s'*. Lia van Gemert clarified for me the sense of some particularly perplexing passages.

## The Translation

No complete translation of Titia Brongersma exists, apart from this one. Nevertheless a handful of individual poems have inspired artful renditions. *Women's Writing from the Low Countries 1200–1875: A Bilingual Anthology* features three poems wittily translated by Myra Heerspink Scholz.[63] Brongersma always follows the protocols of rhyme and metre. Wanting to reflect that formal disposition without obliging myself to quaintness, I forsook rhyme – but retained the discipline of metre. Most of my lines submit as best they can to the dictates of trimeter, tetrameter, and pentameter. A notable minority of Brongersma's poems prescribe the air – usually from contemporary French opera – to which they should be sung. The poet's compositor often badly garbled the tags or titles from these source airs. I did my best to discover Brongersma's musical intentions. In this regard, Nederlandse Liederenbank was an especially valuable resource (liederenbank.nl). Elsewhere, Brongersma affixes French mottoes to her poems. These were easy to translate. So were the rare verses the poet herself composed in French. To identify figures whom Brongersma mentions, biografischportaal.nl often gave good hints.

## Notes

1. Henry Havard, *Picturesque Holland*, 62–3.
2. See *Metamorphoses*, v. 254–63.
3. See Aza Goudriaan, "Ulrik Huber (1636–1694) and John Calvin."
4. Her book does, however, offer testimony to friendship with probable Catholics, such as Anna Margareta Broersema, who evidently honoured the Dominican order with an artful banner.
5. My translation. I rely on the Latin text of Tacitus, *Annals XIII–XVI*.
6. Groningen remained a member of the Hanseatic League from 1282 to 1669. A good Latin school preceded the foundation of the university in this city. The autonomy of Groningen ended in 1499, when Duke Albert of Saxony incorporated Groningen and Ommelanden into a Burgundian province.
7. See von Martels, "Ubbo Emmius, the Eternal Edict and the Academy of Groningen," 416, n54. The original, drawn from Emmius's treatise *De Frisia et Frisiorum Re Publica*, which I translate, reads, "Re vera libera Phrisia est, suis utens moribus: exteris nec parere sustinet, neque dominari cupit. Haud invitus Phriso pro libertate mortem oppetit."
8. Israel, in his *Dutch Primacy in World Trade, 1585–1740*, claims that the Golden Age begins around 1590.
9. My translation.
10. See van Elk's splendid essay "True Fire, Noble Flame."
11. Ibid., 166, n21.
12. See van Gemert's "The Power of the Weaker Vessels," 39.

13 Van Gemert asserts Brongersma "presents us with the problem of lesbianism," in her pioneering "Hiding Behind Words?," 33.
14 Douglas, *Birds and Beasts of the Greek Anthology*, 108.
15 Ibid., 109.
16 Ibid., 110. Douglas attributes his version of Lucian to E.W. Fowler and F.G. Fowler (*The King's English*). Living in the second century, favoured toward the end of his life by Emperor Commodus, Lucian composed satirical dialogues.
17 Farrand, *The Audubon Society Master Guide to Birding*, 142.
18 The Netherlands of Brongersma's period made a departmental distinction between "provinces" and "landscapes." Until 1795, Drenthe was a landscape overseen by a *drost* or bailiff.
19 The word *terp* is etymologically close to the English "thorp," an archaic word designating a village.
20 See Bailey's *The Low Countries*.
21 See Elzinga's brief essay "Biwurke fûgelbonken út de fryske terpen," which comprises pages 945 to 959 of van der Ploeg, et al., *Vogels in Friesland*, vol. 3. The photograph of swan-bone flutes appears on page 954.
22 The English Aphra Behn, fictionist, playwright, and poet, displayed, like Brongersma, a fascination with the place of women in life and literature. She also eagerly panegyrized the representatives of the state. Her laureate-like Tory partisanship is similar to Brongersma's support of the House of Orange.
23 In present-day Leeuwarden, Tresoar – the Frysk Histoarysk en Letterkundich Sintrum – possesses swan-books from 1574, 1635, 1638, and 1647. See the article "Recht van zwanenjacht in Friesland" on sneuperdokkum.blogspot.ca, the blog of the Historische Vereniging Noordoost-Friesland te Dokkum. This entry was posted in 2008, and I last consulted it on 27 May 2018.
24 See Cavendish's *Poems, and Fancies*.
25 See *Anonymi, sed Antiquae tamen Poetae elegans et floridum Carmen de Vere communiter Pervigilium Veneris*. I quote line 83 of Rivinus's edition. He remarks that the phrasing derives from Vergil's *Aeneid*, book 11, line 458.
26 I refer to Catullus 13, *Cenabis bene*.
27 Bruss interprets an epigram thus in his "A Program Poem of Alcaeus of Messene." Similarly, Lafleur explains in his "*Amicitia* and the Unity of Juvenal's First Book" that the Roman writer's opening poem is "intentionally programmatic, designed by Juvenal to foreshadow themes, characters, situations that will be more attentively explored later on" (158).
28 See Wheeler's *Roman Art and Architecture*, 158.
29 The sun in Brongersma on occasion jilts his paramours such as Klytie, a nymph who devolves into a heliotrope.
30 See Sonnet 151.
31 Van Gemert, "Hiding Behind Words?," 38.
32 In Molière's *Bourgeois gentilhomme* (1670), Cléonte is a young lover of Lucile who disguises himself as a Turk. In at least one seventeenth-century Italian drama, Cléonte is a female character.
33 Van Gemert, "Hiding Behind Words?," 41.

34 See Behn, *Oroonoko and Other Writings*, 262. In the period, "to make love" can mean mere gallantry – sweet talk.
35 In fact, the career of Achilles includes episodes of cross-dressing. His mother, Thetis, attempting to exempt him from service in the Trojan War, hid the hero in female costume among the girls at the court of Lycomedes, king of Scyros. Odysseus detected the fraud by setting weapons in front of the young women; Achilles's interest in these appeared too keen. Such a story courts sexual confusion, only to repudiate it. "Clarinda" suggests "Clorinda," the name of a woman warrior who figures in Tasso's *Gerusalemme liberata*.
36 Ovid relates the story of Hermaphroditus in the fourth book of his *Metamorphoses* (306–88). The ardent nymph Salmacis fuses herself with the progeny of Hermes and Aphrodite: *neutrumque et utrumque videntur*, "neither man nor woman – and both – they seem" (379). Ovid's narrator, Alcithoë, imparts a negative emphasis to the union: she says that it undermines virility and permanently pollutes Salmacis's lake. But this bias reflects her opposition to the worship of the androgynous Bacchus. That god eventually transformed her into a bat.
37 Translated by Sinclair, *Selections from the Greek Anthology*, 27. Manifesting a different sort of love, Dido's sister Anna wants to receive the queen of Carthage's last breath: *extremus si quis super halitus errat,/ore legam*, "If any last exhalation strays from your mouth I will take it in" (*Aeneid* 4.683–4). Ludolph Smids refers to Plato's epigrams in his 1685 *Gallerye* (77), although Brongersma may never herself have read the one I reproduce.
38 As will be seen, Smids also depicted Zenobia, in his *Gallerye* of 1685.
39 From the time of Theocritus, Circe – with Medea – becomes the type of a maleficent enchantress. The commonplace is altered when a woman decides to invoke Circe's power. Seventeenth-century etchings and paintings by artists such as Antonio Tempesta and Luca Giordano portray the transformation of Picus and Canens's distress.
40 Van Gemert, "Hiding Behind Words?" 38.
41 See Ovid, *Metamorphoses* 14.642–771.
42 See Homer, *The Odyssey* 12.61–72.
43 Numa's widow Egeria appears in the fifteenth book of Ovid's *Metamorphoses*.
44 Veyn's *Roman Erotic Elegy* lays out the features of this literary kind.
45 See Plato, *Six Great Dialogues*, 117. There is no evidence that Brongersma read this particular dialogue. I draw the connection.
46 Katherine Philips, known as the "matchless Orinda," lived from 1632 to 1664. An unauthorized collection of her poems appeared in the year of her death, and a proper edition in 1667. I rely on Paul Hammond, ed., *Restoration Literature: An Anthology* (Oxford, UK: Oxford University Press, 2009), 236–7.
47 See Ovid, *Metamorphoses* 4.206–70.
48 "Megalithic" is a technical term not in circulation until 1839.
49 See Bakker's *Megalithic Research in the Netherlands, 1547–1911*, 31.
50 See Sadler's "The Hunebeds, or Cromlechs of Holland."
51 Bakker reports that the etymology of *hunebed* is, precisely, "giant's bed" or "giant's tomb" (*Megalithic Research in the Netherlands*, 28).
52 Sadler, "The Hunebeds," 57.
53 See Sappho, "Fragment 16" as rendered by Anne Carson in *If Not, Winter*, 26–9.

54 Attila's Huns penetrated into Europe far enough that they briefly had influence of a kind in the Frisian sphere.
55 See Boethius, Book 3.2 of *The Consolation of Philosophy*, 236–9.
56 The "sufferers" were the Dutch regionalists A.L. Lesturgeon (1815–1878), D.H. van der Scheer (1791–1859), and H. Boom (1810–1885).
57 Lukas Koops, author of *Het geheim van het grootste hunebed*, uses this admonitory aphorism as a chapter title.
58 Fanatics opposed to any testimonies of paganism, such as the Temple of Bel, have recently blown ancient Palmyra to bits. They beheaded the Syrian city's elderly chief curator, the scholar Khaled al-Asaad.
59 Zenobia appears as no. 41 in Smids's work of his 1685 *Gallerye* (31).
60 For an account of these events, see Herodotus's *Histories* 1.205–15.
61 Van Elk raises the question in *Early Modern Women's Writing* (260). Women whose poetry might advance a husband's career sometimes continued to publish.
62 See van Elk, "True Fire, Noble Flame," 162.
63 This excellent anthology, the chief editor of which is Lia van Gemert, appeared with Amsterdam University Press in 2010. The relevant poems may be found between pages 320 and 329.

## Bibliography

*Anonymi, sed Antiquae tamen Poetae elegans et floridum Carmen de Vere communiter Pervigilium Veneris*. Edited by A. Rivinus. Leipzig, Germany: Apud Joannem Presstum, 1644.

Bakker, J.A. "De opgraving in het Grote Hunebed te Borger door Titia Brongersma op 11 juni 1685." *Nieuwe Drentse Volksalmanak* (1984): 3–16.

– *Megalithic Research in the Netherlands, 1547–1911: From "Giant's Beds" and "Pillars of Hercules" to Accurate Investigations*. Leiden, the Netherlands: Sidestone Press, 2010.

Bailey, Anthony. *The Low Countries: A History*. Boston, MA: New Word City, 2018.

Behn, Aphra. *Oroonoko and Other Writings*. Edited by Paul Salzman. Oxford, UK: Oxford University Press, 2009.

Blank, Paula. "Comparing Sappho to Philaeris: John Donne's 'Homopoetics.'" *PMLA* 110, no. 3 (1995): 358–68.

Boethius. *The Consolation of Philosophy*. Translated by H.F. Stewart, E.K. Rand, and S.J. Tester. Cambridge, MA: Harvard University Press, 1990.

Bruss, Jon Steffen. "A Program Poem of Alcaeus of Messene: Epigram 16 G-P (= A.P. 7.429)." *Classical Journal* 98, no. 2 (2002/3): 161–80.

Catullus. *Catullus: The Poems*, 2nd ed. Edited by Kenneth Quinn. London: St Martin's Press, 1988.

Cavendish, Margaret. *Poems, and Fancies*. Menston, UK: Scolar Press, 1972. (Orig. pub. 1653.)

Collinson, W.E. "The Frisian Poems in Titia Brongersma's 'Bronswaan.'" *Modern Language Review* 19, no. 1 (1924): 84–94.

de Jeu, Annelies. *"'t Spoor der dichteressen": Netwerken en publicatiemogelijkheden van schrijvende vrouwen in de Republiek (1600–1750)*. Hilversum, the Netherlands: Verloren, 2000.

Douglas, Norman. *Birds and Beasts of the Greek Anthology*. New York: Jonathan Cape, 1929.

Farrand, John, Jr, ed. *Audubon Society Master Guide to Birding*, vol. 1. New York: Knopf, 1987.

Feitsema, Tony. "Onbekinde midfryske skriuwers (XIII)." *Us Wurk* 17 (1968): 25–43.

Goudriaan, Aza. "Ulrik Huber (1636–1694) and John Calvin: The Franeker Debate on Human Reason and the Bible (1686–1687)." *Church History and Religious Culture* 91, nos. 1/2 (2011): 165–78.

Havard, Henry. *Picturesque Holland: A Journey in the Province of Friesland, Groningen, Drenthe, Overyssel, Guelders and Limbourg*. London: R. Bentley & Son, 1873.

Herodotus. *The Histories*. Translated by Aubrey de Sélincourt. Harmondsworth, UK: Penguin, 1986.

Homer. *The Odyssey*, vols. 1 and 2. Translated by A.T. Murray. London: William Heinemann, 1966.

Israel, Jonathan I. *Dutch Primacy in World Trade, 1585–1740*. Oxford, UK: Clarendon, 2002.

Jensen, Lotte. "Centrum van vriendinnenkring, Titia Brongersma." In *Met en zonder lauwerkrans. Schrijvende vrouwen uit de vroegmoderne tijd 1550–1850. Van Anna Bijns tot Elise van Calcar*, edited by R. Schenkeveld-van der Dussen. Amsterdam: Amsterdam University Press, 1997.

Lafleur, Richard A. "*Amicitia* and the Unity of Juvenal's First Book." *Illinois Classical Studies* 4 (1979): 158–77.

Lesturgeon, A.L., D.H. van der Scheer, and H. Boom. *Drenthe in vlugtige en losse omtrekken geschetst, door drie podagristen*. Coevorden, the Netherlands: D.H. van der Scheer, 1843.

Lynch, Hannah. *Toledo: The Story of an Old Spanish Capital*. London: J.M. Dent, 1910.

Meijer Drees, Marijke, "Het roemrugt'bre jufferdom van Groningen: Over *De bronswaan, of mengeldigten* van Titia Brongersma." In *Klinkend boeket: Studies over renaissance-sonnetten, voor Marijke Spies*, edited by H. Duits, A.J. Gelderblom, and M.B. Smits-Veldt, 151–7. Hilversum, the Netherlands: Verloren, 1994.

Ovid. *Metamorphoses*, vols. 1 and 2. Translated by Frank Justus Miller. London: William Heinemann, 1984.

Pipkin, Amanda C. *Rape in the Republic, 1608–1725: Formulating Dutch Identity*. Leiden, the Netherlands: Brill, 2013.

Plato. *Six Great Dialogues*. Translated by Benjamin Jowett. Mineola, NY: Dover, 2014.

Ralegh, Walter. *Selected Writings*. Edited by Gerald Hammond. Manchester, UK: Carcanet, 1984.

Sadler, Alfred. "The Hunebeds, or Cromlechs of Holland." *Journal of the British Archaeological Association* 26, no. 1 (1870): 53–8.

Sappho. *If Not, Winter*. Translated by Anne Carson. New York: Knopf, 2002.

Schenkenveld, van der Dussen. *Met en zonder lauwerkrans: schrijvende vrowen uit de vroegmoderne tijd 1550–1855: van Anna Bijns tot Elise van Calcar*. Amsterdam: Amsterdam University Press, 1997.

Sinclair, Andrew. *Selections from the Greek Anthology*. Bristol, UK: Weidenfeld and Nicolson, 1967.
Smids, Ludolph. *Gallerye of te proef van dichtoefeningen, met noodige verklaaringen verrykt*. Groningen, the Netherlands: Carel Pieman, 1685.
– *Schatkamer der Nederlandsse Oudheden*. Amsterdam: Pieter de Coup, 1711.
Tacitus. *Annals XIII–XVI*. Translated by J. Jackson. London: William Heinemann, 1981.
van der Aa, Abraham Jacob. *Nieuw biographisch: Anthologisch en critisch woordenboek van Nederlandsche dichters*. Amsterdam: De Grebber, 1844.
van der Ploeg, D.T.E., et al., eds. *Vogels in Friesland*, vol. 3. Leeuwarden, the Netherlands: De Tille, 1979.
van Elk, Martine. *Early Modern Women's Writing: Domesticity, Privacy, and the Public Sphere in England and the Dutch Republic*. London: Palgrave MacMillan, 2017.
– "True Fire, Noble Flame: Friendship Poetry by Katharina Lescailje, Cornelia van der Veer, and Katharina Philips." *Early Modern Women* 7 (fall 2012): 157–89.
van Gemert, Lia. "Hiding Behind Words? Lesbianism in 17th-Century Dutch Poetry." *Thamyris: Mythmaking from Past to Present* 2, no. 1 (spring 1995): 11–44.
– "The Power of the Weaker Vessels: Simon Schama and Johan van Beverwijck on Women." In *Women of the Golden Age: An International Debate on Seventeenth-Century Women in Holland, Italy and England*, edited by Els Kloek, Nicole Teeuwen, and Marijke Huisman, 39–50. Hilversum, the Netherlands: Verloren, 1994.
van Gemert, Lia, ed. *Women's Writing from the Low Countries, 1200–1875: A Bilingual Anthology*. Amsterdam: Amsterdam University Press, 2010.
Veyn, Paul. *Roman Erotic Elegy: Love, Poetry and the West*. Translated by David Pellauer. Chicago, IL: University of Chicago, 1988.
Virgil, *Virgil*, vols. 1 and 2. Translated by H. Rushton Fairclough. London: William Heinemann, 1986.
von Martels, Zweder. "Ubbo Emmius, the Eternal Edict and the Academy of Groningen." In *Christian Humanism: Essays in Honour of Arjo Vanderjagt*, edited by Alasdair MacDonald, Zweder von Martels, and Jan Veenstra, 399–418. Leiden, the Netherlands: Brill, 2009.
Wheeler, Mortimer. *Roman Art and Architecture*. London: Thames and Hudson, 1964.

Title page (*opposite*) and frontispiece (*overleaf*) of *De Bron-Swaan* (1686).
Images courtesy of the University Library Groningen, with special thanks for
the assistance of Evert Jan Reker

# De BRON-SWAAN,
## Of MENGELDIGTEN
### VAN
# TITIA BRONGERSMA
Bestaande in Lof-Gedigten, Geestelijke stoffen, Gesangen, Af-beeldingen, Verjaar-Gedichten, Lijk-klachten, Bruylofts-Sangen, Vertalingen, Byvallen, Omgeefsels, en Raatselen.

Tot GRONINGEN,

Gedrukt, By CAREL PIEMAN, Boekdrukker tussen beyde Markten; Anno 1686.

Mejuffr. Bronsbaas volgens
hare eigeverklaring, zie het woord
aan den Leeser, was haar eerste werk,
waarvoor hij verschooning vraagt,
het welk haar echter schijnt te
hebben aangemoedigd, en heeft later
dos wegts een proef aan gees=
=telyke gezangen en gedichten,
Hemelsche Orgeltoonen geti=
=teld, van haar candt gewe
gemaakt. Zie hierover A. v. d.
bl: cath:d Nederl: letterk:; 3 dln bl:359
by Lamb:t Bidloo in zyn Pan Poetic
en by het Aanhangsel op Witsen Gey
vers Verdicta 1844 1:ste deel.

V: Dam van Noordeloos
Rotterdam.

GRONINGER BRON-SWAAN
Van Titia Brongersma

# LA SEIGNEURIE DE GRONINGUE subdivisée

## LA SEIGNEURIE DE GRONINGUE
subdivisée en toutes ses Iuridictions
Dressée sur les Memoires les plus Nouveaux
Par le S.r Sanson Geographe ordinaire du Roy
A PARIS
Chez H. Iaillot, joignant les grands Augustins, aux deux Globes
Avec Privilege du Roy pour vingt Ans
1692

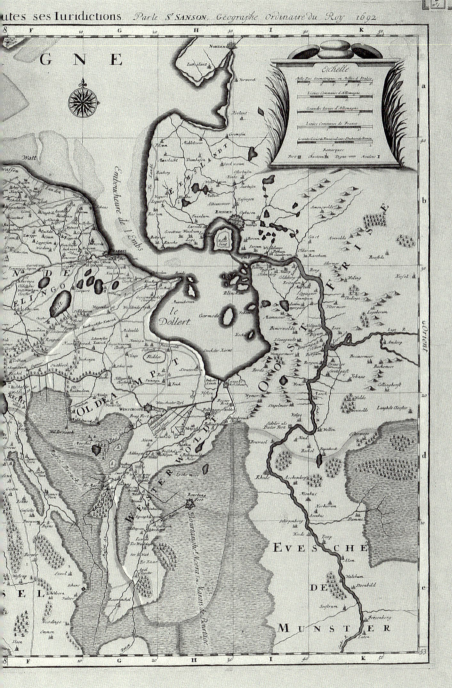

(*previous page*) Map of Groningen and environs (1692). Dokkum, Groningen, and Borger are clearly marked; (*above*) Etching of Titia Brongersma seated near the *hunebed* at Borger in 1685, taken from Ludolph Smids's 1711 *Schatkamer der Nederlandsse Oudheden*. Images courtesy of the University Library Groningen, with special thanks for the assistance of Evert Jan Reker.

The *hunebed* at Borger in 2014. Photograph by Monique Dull.

*The* SWAN *of the* WELL *by* TITIA BRONGERSMA

Groninger Bron-Swan
Van Titia Brongersma

✦ ✦ ✦ ✦ ✦ ✦ ✦ ✦ ✦

*The* SWAN *of the* WELL *of* GRONINGEN
*By* TITIA BRONGERSMA
✦ ✦ ✦ ✦ ✦ ✦ ✦ ✦ ✦ ✦ ✦

# De Bron-Swaan,

## Of Mengeldigten

## van

## Titia Brongersma

◆ ◆ ◆ ◆ ◆ ◆ ◆ ◆ ◆ ◆ ◆ ◆ ◆ ◆ ◆

Bestaande in Lof-Gedigten, Geestelijke stoffen, Gesangen, Af-beeldingen, Verjaar-Gedichten, Lijk-klachten, Bruylofts-Sangen, Vertalingen, Byvallen, Omgeefsels, en Raatselen.

Tot Groningen,
Gedrukt, By Carel Pieman, Boekdrukker
tussen beyde Markten; Anno 1686

# The SWAN of the WELL

## or RHYMES IN SEVERAL GENRES

### BY

## TITIA BRONGERSMA,

including panegyrics, spiritual meditations,

songs, descriptive pieces, birthday poems, eulogies,

epithalamia, translations, complimentary verses,

poems to accompany gifts,

and riddles

Published in GRONINGEN
between the markets by CAREL PIEMAN,
in the year 1686

Aan den Leeser

Versoeke de goetheyt te willen hebben, dit mijn eerste werk voor lief te nemen schoon het op de hoogste leest niet geschooyt is, dog even wel tot vermaak van de goede Gonst-genoten is aangeregt, en de Druk of Letter-fauten die (door te grooten hast, of andersins) hier en daar sijn in geslopen, sullen gelieven te soeken aghter in het Boeck, al waar se sijn aan getekent, op dat men het gene daar door gerabraakt: wederom kan herstellen en beter verstaan. hope dat het met de twede Druk beter gepolijst en vermeedert voor U.E. Oogen sal verschijnen, verschoon dan dese misgrepen, en neem geduldt in de miswoorden op te soeken.

Blijve V.E. Verpligte Dieneresse,
T.B.

To the Reader

Muster the goodness to take up my first work indulgently, though its appearance falls short of ideal. My objective is consistently the connoisseur's delight. Correction of flaws in the edition or defects in the imprint that managed, out of haste or the like, to creep into the text, should be looked for in the back of the book. They are enrolled there to minimize confusion, to amend and guide understanding. With luck a second impression will achieve a superior degree of polish, and be generally improved for the reader. Excuse therefore the oversights, and please take the time to consult the list of errata.

I remain your most obliged servant, T.B.

Op Draght
Aan het voortreffelijke, en Roem-rugtb're JUFFERDOM, van
GRONINGEN.

Kome U.E. Waardigheden op-dragen uyt een goede genegentheyt dese mijne *Bron Swaan, of Mengeldigten*, niet om haar waarde, nog om hoe datse behoren te wesen, maar om hoe danig dat se sijn, hoe wel U.E. Heusheyt groot genoeg is de mis-grepen voor by te sien, soo heb ik nogtans altijt schroom-agtigh geweest dese *mengelingen* in het Ligt te brengen, door dien altoos de bitse nijdigers met Adder-tongen steken, niet alleen op sulke mindere saken als de mijne, maar selfs op de onberispelijkste, soo dat de alder door Lughigste verstanden selfs sulkx onder worpen sijn, wil my dan geerne mede onder werpen dat te verdragen soo ik U.E. maar mag behagen, en de Soylisten, en Momisten nog toewensen (uyt een goet hert) dat se het beter mogen maken, en de zege voor my weg slepen, maar

Dedication to the extraordinary and illustrious
women of Groningen

With ardent affection I come dedicating to you, high
excellencies, this my *Swan of the Well*, my rhymes
in several genres, not on account of their merit or
their quality but for what they are – even if your
discretion must indulge the persistence of some
unexpunged errata. I always have been shy about
bringing this miscellany into the light. Incessantly
the snappish enviers sting with their adder tongues
not only lesser enterprises such as mine, but also the
least blameworthy endeavours. Therefore seeing that
every talent, even, has to endure the assault of the
extravagantly empty-headed, I would gladly undergo
the same treatment myself. Out of a full heart, too,
I wish those lonely repiners and votaries of Momus
would show me they can do better – and wrest my
victory away from me.

maar men seyt tot een spreek woordt, dat de beste Stuyr-luyden altijt op het Landt staan, of die het minste weeten, het meeste te seggen hebben, 't is dan gemakkelijker te berispen, als te verbeteren, dogh sal de gift Swangere Nijt haar Swadder laten uyt braken, en my wapenen met het schildt van gedult, en genoeg laten sijn mijn Gonstelingen haar begeerte te voldoen, en U Mee Jufferen versoeken: met haar te willen aanvaarden dese *Bron-Swaan* (:schoon met geen Fenix pluymen verciert:) die U.E. nogtans sal laten hooren haar schorre gesangen, en bereyt is U.E. aller Roemens waarde waardigheden Loffelijk de werelt voor te dragen, waar toe de pligt, en U.E. verdiensten haar verbinden, en my doen seggen.
*Dat ik ben Hoog Ed. ge-Eerde, en Roemens waardige Jufferen mee Jufferen U.E. genegene en Geringsten Dienares.*

TITIA BRONGERSMA
**NICO-**

But there is an old saying pertinent to the case: "The best helmsmen never venture out to sea." Oh, another maxim occurs to me: "Those who know least have most to say." It is thus easier to insult than to surpass. Yet let the prodigiously fertile Envy bring forth her brood, that horde of muttering critics, still I will raise my shield of patience and a sufficiency of what I desired will be fulfilled and I will look to you, best incarnation of womanhood. In your name please accept this *Swan of the Well* (simple though it may be, no panache of phoenix-plumes garnishing it). So may you always attend to its throaty music, proclaiming (as it does, throughout the world) your worthiest and most deserved glory. Duty and the remembrance of your assistance compel the bird, and all my acts recount those good offices. I remain your most willing and most humble of servants, women most worthy of fame among women.

TITIA BRONGERSMA
NICO-

*Eer-Gedichten.*

## NICOLAI BLANCARDI, LEIDENSIS,

Epigramma extemporale,
In Poemata virtute & ingenio ornatissimae virginis
*Titiae Brongersma.*

Quod tuba Virgilii, lyra Flacci, altusque cothurnus
    Annaei, et Latiis sal Juvenalis erat;
Id Belgis sua cum *Brongersia* plectra tetendit,
    Ingenio certans omnibus, arte prior
O Frisiis nova Musa tuis, o Carmine posthac,
    Te quoque cum superes, non habitura parem.
Cedite Germani, Gallique, Italique, Britanni,
    Crede mihi, nullum majus in orbe decus.

*Scriptum in arce Siardaea, M DC LXXXVI*
*Kalendis Iunii.*

❖ ❖ ❖

Dus vertaald.

Roemt, Romen, op't gedreun van Marôs Helden-Sangen;
Op Flacci soete Lijr; op Sen'cae treur'ge prangen;
Op d'aerd'ge prikkl'en van den snêgen Juvenael,
Op Nasos Liefdes-Rijm, of and'rer Sangers prael,
Ons Nederlant kam meed'op Sangeressen roemen:
Kan onder Romens roem haar *Titia Brongers* noemen:

                                                            Ons

Poems in Honour of Titia Brongersma

An extempore epigram on the goodness and ingenuity of the most distinguished Miss Titia Brongersma's verses, written in the citadel of Sjaarda on the first of June, 1686*

By Nicolaus Blancard, from Leiden

What the trumpet of Vergil, the lyre of Horace,
The buskin of Seneca and the stinging salt
Of Juvenal did for the people of Latium:
The same the lute of Titia Brongersma
Will do for us Belgians. Her truth and talent
Equal theirs – her craft surpasses them.
Muse without precedent among the Frisians,
Since in time to come you will continue
To prevail, fated to be nonpareil:
Germans, Gauls, Italians, Britons – they
Yield. No greater glory lights the earth.

❖ ❖ ❖

Dutch version [of Blancard's epigram]
By H.E.M.†

Boast, Rome, Vergil's epic trumpet's blare.
Boast Horace's sweet lyre, Seneca's dire plots.
Boast the base sting of acid Juvenal.
Boast Ovid's love-rhymes, or another singer's
Skill: our Netherlands acclaims a poetess,
Matching Titia Brongersma's fame

---

* Blancard composed this epigram in Latin. "Sjaarda" is an alternate name for Groningen. Nicolaus Blancard held the post of Rector Magnificus in 1685 at the College of Franeker. Brongersma's occasional poem for the centenary of that institution appears later in *The Swan of the Well*. Married to Maria Eversdijk, Blancard was born in 1624 and died in 1703. Like Brongersma, he displays his grasp of genre by associating canonical authors with particular literary kinds. His emphasis is explicitly patriotic.

† The mysterious initials "H.E.M." may reflect a compositor's error. Since Johannes Mensinga's own contribution immediately succeeds Blancard's epigram, "H.E." may reflect the printer's misconstruction of "J." The author turns Blancard's Latin verse into Dutch.

Ons' Frieslant praalt op haar met meerder eer en recht'
En haar een groene krans van Lauwer-blaeden vlecht:
Sy derft kloekmoediglyk met haere Titia pronken,
En tegen Hoge-Duits', en geest'ge Franssen lonken,
En Italiaesch vernunft, en Engelsch' aerdigheit;
Jae stelt selfs boven die haer Titias waerdigheit.
                                                H.E.M.

✦ ✦ ✦

In Poemata cura ac ingenio elaborate à Lectissima ac Ornatissima
Virgine TITIA BRONGERSMA.

Laudamus veterum monumenta perennia Vatum,
    Quousque modos Atthis, cultaque Roma dedit.
Ingeniis nihil his illustrius Orbis habebat,
    Et quot erant vates, credidit esse Deos.
His titulis Hellas, his aemula Roma superbit,
    Atque aliis Phoebus vix bene notus erat
In partem laudum successit Belgica Tempe,
    Et vagus huc venit ex Helicone chorus,
Pieridum, Phoebique chorus; seque Ipse videndum,
    Praesentemque dedit vatibus ipse suis.
Iamque pares Belgae Graijs Latiisque Camenis,
    Invidiam & lauros iam meruere mei.
Invidiam & lauros, dignissima praemia vatum,
    Et quod scriptores nomen in astra ferat.
Quaeque mares olim capiebant praemia soli,

                                                Hac

With Rome's, for Friesland praises her on convincing
Grounds, and winds her a green laurel crown.
Let Friesland vaunt her singer with all verve.
Lofty German, vivacious French, lucid
Italian, candid English? Titia conquers.

♦ ♦ ♦

On the sophistication of the well-wrought poems by
the learned and distinguished Miss Titia Brongersma
By Johannes Mensinga*

We praise perennial monuments of ancient
Bards and the Attic measures Rome, the refined,
Learned to practise. Then the globe harboured
No minds brighter than those poets', and they
Were judged to equal gods. With titles like that,
Hellas and her successor Rome vaunted
Poets – Phoebus hardly received more honour.
Now a Belgian Tempe assumes in turn
The right of this degree of praise. From Helicon
Wanders the Pierian chorus to assist the spirits
It has chosen. Our Camenae earn now
The envy and the bays that Greece and Rome
In their time won – surest signs a writer's
Name will be lofted to the stars. If ever
A woman deserved a wreath, she wins that dowry

*Johannes Mensinga, born in 1635, held the post of Rector Magnificus of Groningen University in 1682 to 1683, again in 1683 to 1684, and finally in 1691 to 1692. He died in 1698. Horace boasted (*Odes* 3.30) that he, first of the Romans (*princeps*), naturalized Greek measures to Latin verse. Mensinga tells a story of how culture inherits culture, not only by his open avowals but also by his alternation of Greek and Roman terms ("Pierian" is sheerly Greek, whereas the name "Camenae" designated the indigenous Italian muses).

[4]

Hac etiam in Belgis faemina dote placet.
Titia testis erit Brongersia, Frisia virgo,
    Et Patriae & sexus Titia grande decus.
Illa lyra numeros, calamo canit illa, tubaque,
    Quos numeros vellet Lesbia virgo suos.
Hisque modis vivax capiet per secula nomen,
    Et laudem à serâ posteritate feret.
Atque aliquis dicet; vates hoc carmine fecit
    Invidiam populis, invidiamque Viris.

JOH. MENSINGA

♦♦♦

Aan de vond, Deugt, en konstrijke Dichteresse, Juffer TITIA BRONGERSMA, Op Haar BRON-SWAAN. OF MENGELDIGTEN.

Als ik u Bronswaan sag, ging my mijn Geest ontspringen,
De defticheidt desselfs deed my dit Vers afdringen,
    Mijn Zang-Heldin hielt aan en kon niet stille zijn
    Sy was verheugt voor 't licht van sulk een zonneschijn.
Sy deed 't beswangert breyn seer gratichlijk ontsluyten,
Om dit tot uwer Eer, tot waarde lof te uyten,
    Die uwe Bronswaan leest, die moet verwondert staan,
    Vw gulde Versen recht in vreugd' het herte slaan.
Geestrijke Iongkvrouw 'k zeg, gy zijt een bloem der bloemen,

Een

Now, here – among us Belgians. Frisian Titia
Brongersma will secure the splendours
Of her land and sex. She masters lyre,
Pastoral flute, trumpet and the poet
Of Lesbos could only desire her craft.
Such skill will keep her work alive for ages
And sustain her praise down to remotest
Epochs when another pen must avow
Brongersma the envy of peoples and of men.

◆ ◆ ◆

To the ingenious, virtuous, polished poet Miss Titia
Brongersma, on her *Swan of the Well*
By Andreas ten Have, preacher at Pekela\*

Once I'd seen *The Swan of the Well*, my spirit
Surged. Your distinguished book inspired these
Verses. My muse, unable to be silent,
Encouraged me. Your sunshine warmed her
Invention. She unsealed her pregnant mind, happy
To express your worth in praise sincerely.
Whoever reads *The Swan of the Well* must be
Astonished. Your golden lines make the heart
Rejoice. Ingenious woman, flower
Of flowers, ornament of the age to bring

\* Brongersma also includes in her book a piece in praise of ten Have and his restoration of the Reformed Dutch church at Pekela. Here the preacher himself reflects aspects of her poetry. He alludes to her generic variety by listing the diverse arts she celebrates, as practised by her circle of acquaintances ("charcoal, chalk – needle"). Aptly for a clergyman, ten Have shifts from the performance of neoclassical and secular touches to close his poem with a sentiment proper to a sermon: a reminder of eternity. The topic of envy often recurs in the verse of Brongersma's supporters. It is a conventional *topos* to accompany the celebration of literary achievement, or the recognition of genuine pettiness from some quarters of the poet's society.

Een Cieraadt van ons tijdt daar Doccum op mach roemen
    Als u geboorte plaats, ja Groningen met een,
    Der konst bemind'ren tong, bralt uw lof in't gemeen.
Schoon bitze nijdicheydt mocht komen op te dond'ren
Weest niet verzaagt, laat u sulks doch geen zins afsondre
    Van u voornomen werk, gaat voort in spijt van haar,
    De vuil afgonsticheydt is maar een g'ring gevaar.
Roem van ons tijdt gy kondt ten rechten gaan uitdagen
Natuire met Pinceel, die uw werk ooit an zagen
    Konstrijke Titia gemaakt met kool, of krijt,
    Of ook door Naaldewerk, stonden verbaast, verblijdt.
Doch Iuffer Brongersma vermitz seer haast verdwijnen
Der menschen goede gunsten konsten, wilt dan mijnen
    Voor't aardtsch het Hemelsche, vliegt boven't sterren Hof
Met uwe schandre Geest, daar men staag bromt Godts Lof.
    Mijn Lot, Is Godt
    ANDREAS TEN HAVE.
    Predikant ter Pekel A.

♦ ♦ ♦

Op de selfde

Moet ik dan dichten? en hoort gy na geen' verschoonen?
Daar 'k my soo droef vertoone,
't Hooft stuttend', met mijn hand;
Daar gy de Lier siet opgehangen an de wand?

                                        Daar

Fame to Dokkum since you were born there,
And to Groningen as well. The tongues
Of art-lovers extol you abroad. Let Rancour
Snarl – don't despair. Don't let it distract you
From your outstanding work advancing
In spite of Spite. Vile Envy's just a petty
Peril. Glory of our days, you challenge
Nature with your brush. With transport, gifted
Titia, and surprise, people looked on what
You'd wrought with charcoal, chalk – needle, even.
But, dear Brongersma, knowing people's love
Like all art perishes too soon, savour
My affection and the arts before you must
Exchange earthly life for heavenly,
Your brilliant mind piloting you above the stars
To where God's constant praise resounds.

God keeps me on the straight and narrow.
ANDREAS ten Have.
Preacher at Pekela.

◆ ◆ ◆

On the same
By Ludolph Smids\*

Must I compose verse? No exemption?
Do you see me now head in hand, the lyre
Hung up on the wall? The laurel there,

\* Brongersma's most prominent patron, Ludolph Smids, published his collected poetry in 1694. Among other works, including a drama that Brongersma praises, he compiled an alphabetical *Schatkamer der Nederlandsse Oudheden*, or *Curio-Cabinet of Dutch Antiquities*. He celebrated Brongersma for her archaeological and poetic reconnaissance of the *hunebed* at Borger. Here Smids assumes the reliability of his honouree's literary judgement. His image of pooling tears is a ludicrous instance of tasteless hyperbole, whereas Brongersma often resorts to more defensible or decorous exaggerations. The teasing intonation (detectable even when Smids, in another poem to Brongersma, impersonates a buried urn unearthed by her) transmits affection, respect, and perhaps some condescension.

Daar gy de Lauwer, van uw heusheyd my geschonken,
     Verdort siet, en beklonken?
          Daar u den Inkt, en Pen,
Genoegh anwijsen, met hunn' schimmel, wat ik ben.

Sal ik van 't singen van uwe blanke Bronswaan singen?
     Ah! ah! de Tranen springen
       (Anschouw ik maar de Son)
Ten ogen uiten: en 't Nat stroomt zamen tot een Bron.

't Is wel. Ik heb genoeg. Gy sult niet meêr begeren,
     O Swaan! 'k sal u vereeren
     Met geen' onnosel Dicht,
(Wiens flauwe luyster voor uw' schoone pluimen swicht)

Maar met mijn Tranen neen met vloeyen de kristallen.
Ah! laat u daarin vallen.
     Swem, Swaantjen, in die Bron,
Tot TITIA, seg: dit is 't al, het geen hy kon!

LUDOLPH SMIDS, M.D.

♦ ♦ ♦

OP DESELFDE.

Klinkdigt.

Soo staat u Bron-Swaan dan in het gareel geslagen,
Geestrijke Brongersma, der Sang-Godinnen eer,

                                         Ter

Withered now – was that once pressed on me?
There ink and pen prove in dried-up
Neglect what sort of writer I am. I sing?
Sing of the shining *Swan of the Well*? The tears
Jump to my eyes, as when they confront the sun.
My eyes are streaming, like her spring. Just as
Well. Don't ask for more, Swan. I shouldn't
Glorify you oafishly. Tasteless
Prattle brittles, set beside such smooth
And glamorous plumage. My tears pour out
In crystal floods, in which, my dearest Swan,
You may paddle, until Titia cries "Stop! That's
Impractical – utterly fantastical."

♦ ♦ ♦

On the same
By Samuel Munkerus*

Sonnet

*The Swan of the Well* wears a bridle finely
Tooled, to brilliant Brongersma's credit,
The goddess of song whom that bird met

* Samuel Mun(c)kerus appears in the historical record between 1686 and 1698. The Swan of Dirce (or Thebes) is Pindar; that of Venusium, Horace. Mun(c)kerus runs through several of Brongersma's topics in succession, by way of compliment (Arachne the weaver; Polyhymnia, muse of sacred song; the bestowing of Daphne's prestigious laurel; and the poet's disposition to write occasional verse, with the aim of eternizing ephemeral celebrations). "Grunoos" is an alternate name for Groningen.

Ter goeder uyren steek' hy af van Grunoos veer
Om uwe schranderheyd het Heel-al door te dragen
Geen and're Swaantjes wenst de Kuysheyd voor haar wagen:
Want geen haar Feest-toon houdt soo net na haar begeer,
Als 't welke singende beswangert met uw leer
Durst dat van Dirce en Venusium uytdagen.
Dus tart g'ook met u Naalt Aragnes kunstight' haar,*
En Polyhymnia in maat met keel of snaar,
Ik twijg' uw Tekenkonst, en rare wasse vrugten.
  Die vogelen en Mensch bedriegen door haar schijn,
Dat hand en tand uyt lust daar aan geslagen zijn,
  O Kunst'naars dese maagd elk voor sijn kroon doet dugten.

SAMUEL MUNCKERUS

*andersteyken-doek, of Gaas.

♦ ♦ ♦

De selfde weder aan de selfde.

Men noemt U Titia, als Febus Priesterinnen,
Nog Brongersma, dat is de eer der Hengste-bron
Nooyt eygender men u, Mejoffrouw, noemen kon,
Het nood-lot spitzde wis op soo een naam uw sinnen.
Dies stoft nu Groningen op uw belaurwde haren,
Als Lesbos op Sapphò, als Theben op Korinn?
Haar Letterhelden zijn verrijkt door een Mannin',
Die maagd een wonder schoon papiere kint kan baren.

♦ ♦ ♦

Men-

At Grunoos's ford at a propitious moment
To lift up wit in flight across the globe.
No other swan could usurp your virtue, since
None celebrates the fête precisely right
But she who out-sings (pregnant with your learning)
The Swan of Dirce, and the Venusian swan.
The fineness of the web you weave beats
Arachne's. Your finger on the string
Excels Polyhymnia's. What rare
Ripe fruits are those you portray. Bird
And man alike blink, dazzled by this
Brilliance than which no light burns
Brighter. Who has the skill in proper
Dread to weave for this woman her garland?

♦ ♦ ♦

From the same hand, for the same woman*
[by Samuel Mun(c)kerus]

Let Titia be your name when you are Apollo's priestess.
Brongersma is best when you visit the muses' well,
For *bron*, in our tongue, means "source." Neither name
Entirely embodies you, young woman:
Necessity demands our wits combine your proper
With your surname to comprise your essence.
May we draw a parallel and say
Groningen is to your belaureled locks
As Lesbos to Sappho's, Thebes to Corinna's?
A woman enriches the roster of literary heroes
And brings forth prodigious paper children.

♦ ♦ ♦

* *Mannin* is the word for "woman" that Mun(c)kerus chooses for use in his second-last line. This sounding language has a Biblical cadence, and brings with it a hint of scriptural pomp; at the same time, it emphasizes, perhaps, Brongersma's unusual place as both the mother of poems and the equal of male writers. Mun(c)kerus playfully explores the fortuitous doubleness of Brongersma's name: its Graeco-Roman and indigenous Frisian halves.

Op deselfde

Zwijgt grijse logen-eeuw, verdigtzel heeft nu uyt
Geen droevig Zwanen-treur nog doodt-bereit geluit
Voorspelt wanneer het dier den laatsten snik zal geven:
Dees eerst-geboren Zwaan, die hier in 't bron-nat speelt.
Bekoort elk door haar zang; maar schoon sy zò zoet kweelt,
Zò zal haar toon nogtans haar doen onsterflijk leven.

M. GARGON

♦ ♦ ♦

Op deselfde. Klink-digt.

Verdigte God heên vliedt, vliedt negen zang-godinnen,
Weg dubbel spitse berg, daar 't hengste-hoeve nat
Uyt den gereten steen zoet ruischelende spat,
Dat zinnen-roerend sap, dat roert voortaan geen zinnen.

Hier springt een ware Bron, hier kan men droppen winnen,
Die d'alderwufste Geest van sin-stram maken rat.
Hier klinkt een hooge toon, hier is een mengel-schat,
Van jeder een bemint, vvijl's andren doet beminnen.
Zo mengelt Titia een geestig mengel-stof,
En krijgt door Mengel-konst een onvermeng'bre lof,

                                                                                     Daar

For the same woman
By M[attheus] Gargon*

Silence, leaden listless age! Listen.
That's no dreary swansong expressed
In the pangs of death when the bird
Sobs her melancholy last.
This new-born Swan sailing in the well
Enchanting every listener with song
Warbles so sweetly she will never die.

◆ ◆ ◆

For the same woman†
By M[attheus] Gargon

Phantasmagoric god, flee –
Nine muses flee. Away with Parnassus
Of the double summit where
By the pasture, gushing from
Broken rock, a spring burst out
Murmuring, offering a drink that led
To ecstasy, that leads to ecstasy
No more, from this day forward. Here bubbles
A true well. Here you can quaff a cup the
Illuminated spirit fills with the fluent
Wisdom of its phrases. The note
Exalted rings out, treasure varied
So what speaks to you specially
Endears you to it: others
Will love other things. So Titia
Mixes a felicitous blend
Acquiring by mixed art unmixed
Praise. The ninefold sisters ought

* Mattheus Gargon was preacher and rector at Vlissingen after 1707. He published a book called *Walchersche Arkadia* in 1715. Bucolics predominate in that work. He also painted. He seizes on Brongersma's innovative representation of the swan, and proves his readerly sagacity when he isolates and echoes her faith in rebirth.

† Gargon catches Brongersma's ambivalence about the Graeco-Roman pantheon and myth-system. Dante has a similar attitude when he both evokes and would silence a Roman predecessor (*Inferno*, Canto 25, line 94): *Taccia Lucano*, "Let Lucan be silent."

Daar zelfs het negental nooit met heeft mogen prijken:
Want 't zangheldinnen rot bezat niets in 't gemeen,
Indien men waarheid by verdigtzels mag gelijken.
Of 't is volmaakter nog in Brongersma alleen.

M. GARGON

♦ ♦ ♦

Op de Groninger BRON-ZWAAN, Van den zoetvloeyende
Digteresse Juffr. TITIA BRONGERSMA,

O Brontje! dat weI eer zyn oorspronk heeft genomen,
Van Pegaas Hoeve slagh, op 't toppig Helicon;
Gy die omringelt zyt met puyk van Lauwer-boomen?
     Waar in dat hem verMaakt de blyde Morgen Zon:
Als hy de weer-glans kaatst, met vreugd aan alle kanten,
Maakt dat elk droppel schynt, als held're Diamanten.

Dan speelt dit spiegel-nat met dankbaarlyke swieren,
     En geeft een weeder-min, van 't geene zy bezit:
Terstont stremt 't Nat tot enkt, de Lauwer tot papieren,
     De Eed'le Dichtkunst pronkt, en treft het hoogste wit
Daar sulk een Brontje vloeid, so dierbaar uitgelesen
Bedenkt! Wat moet dan niet, dit Swaantje waardig wesen.
Daar swemt dat Beestje heen op peerle moere baaren,
     En kweelt zielrekkende so liefelyk en soet:
Dat sy de Ryn Swaan soekt en d' Y Nimph t'evenaere

En

No longer to preen. They supply
Nothing worthy. For poetry
And truth, please read Brongersma.

❖ ❖ ❖

On *The Swan of the Well* of Groningen by the fluent
poet Miss Titia Brongersma
By A[driaan] Tymens*

Little well deriving from the hoof-stamp
Of Pegasus on Helicon's pinnacle,
You who rule crowned with the splendour
Of laurel-leaves, reveling in morning's glad
Sunlight, brilliant weather streaming pleasure:
In every quarter dew is cloudless diamond.
The mirror-like well-water's swirl-inscribed.
What does it reflect? The wetness dries into ink,
The leaves of the laurel have resolved into paper.
The noble art of poetry attains
Its topmost height. From the spring come cries
Intelligible, charming, only
Think what the darling Swan doesn't merit.
The sleek creature glides borne on pearl-like
Pool – a voice to touch the soul so dulcet
Rivals the Swan of the Rhine, the IJ's Nymph
    too, and

* A.J. van der Aa says Adriaan Tijmens, a minor Frisian versifier, lived in Leeuwarden. This connoisseur especially liked dramatic poetry. Ludolph Smids, acknowledging Tijmens's regionalism, called him a "phoenix flaring in native plumes." The virtue of Tijmens's poem consists in the way it assimilates Brongersma's Swan now to literature, now to the process of producing literature. All the while, it still grants to the bird a kind of autonomous existence. Ted Hughes's *Crow* furnishes a parallel figure – different in other respects, to be sure. Tijmens alludes to Joost van den Vondel with the epithet "Swan of the Rhine." The Nymph of the IJ is probably Katharina Lescailje.

En door een hemelval verrukt het têer gemoet
Tot lust, en yver, om die Zangers na te streeven:
Men siet hier Sappho, neen, den Mantuaan herleeven.

Zy spreit heur vlerkjes uit, en laat elk 't singen hooren,
  Zy strooyt haar sachte pluim als goude letters neer
Op't glad papier, en streelt dus t'effens ziel en ooren:
  Zo wint hier Brongersma de Lauwerkrans van eer,
Ia, streeft voorby elk een om meerder roem te haalen.
  En dooft met haare stem, 't geluit der Nachtegaalen.

In Leeuwarden den 13 Octob. 1686 A. TYMENS

◆ ◆ ◆

Op de Bron-Swaan Van de Ed: in kunst, wetenschap en deugt uytmuntende Juffr. TITIA BRONGERSMA

Wie durft, vermaarde Sang-Heldin,
  Maar met een swakke vêer,
Gaan treeden Pallas Tempel in,
  Dit hangend' U ter eer?
Hoe durft hy, die noyt dichten kon,
Toch naad'ren tot uw' Swaan-Bron?
Maar, Sangeres, uw' waardigheyt,
  En hoogh begaafde Geest,

              Die

Rapt by a ravishing bolt from heaven, the bird,
Brim with longing and passion, yearns to equal
Sappho and even the Mantuan, who rise again.
She spreads her wings and opens wide her beak.
She shuffles soft plumage. Golden words
Entrusted to happy paper, she can stream
Into ears and souls. So Brongersma earns
Supreme laurels, drowns the nightingale's lament.

♦ ♦ ♦

On *The Swan of the Well* by Miss Titia Brongersma,
the skillful, the learned, the virtuous
By J[an] A[dolf] Rappardus*

Who dares, famous heroine of song,
Equipped with a weak quill only,
Enter the temple of Athena intending
To do you honour? How could a man
Who cannot write verse dare to
Take up your Swan? But, singer, your
Gifted spirit and goodness encourage
Him. Your modesty's forgiving.

* Jan Adolf Rappardus (or Johan Adolph Rappardus) enrolled as a student at Groningen in 1675. He married Hermanna Pickards. His daughter Catharina was born in 1688. Rappardus perceives – and amplifies – the generosity latent in Brongersma's courteous, complex refusal to mimic the conventional (masculine) poetic pose of asserting a master's vatic assurance.

Die brengt hem tot vermeetelheyt,
    Uw' heuscheyt dekt hem meest;
Ghy Nimphjes, komt het slecht te pas?
Begiet hem met een waater-plas.

Uw' Bron is als het Hoeve-nat
    Van Helicons valley,
Schoon had men dan een gulp gehadt,
    Als men dien Maagden-Rey
Maar sien mag, en het soet gekweel
Mag hooren uyt uw Swaantjes keel.

Verschoon dan, soet Dichterin,
    De drift van sijn gemoet,
Een goede wil, zyn krachten min,
    Een heusche siel voldoet,
Want wie kon doch, met eenig blijk,
U, Vriesche Sappho, zyn gelijk?

J.A. RAPPARDUS

♦ ♦ ♦

Op de

You nymphs, if I falter, splash me
With plenty of chastening well-water.
How much your pool resembles Helicon's
A sip and the sight of your muses proves
With the warbling that cascades from
The throat of your little Swan, sweetly.
Pardon then, dear poet, inadequate
Talent that would from strong delight
Attain a decent end. For who at a stroke
Becomes, O Frisian Sappho, your peer?

♦ ♦ ♦

Op de Titel-Print Van de Groninger Bron-Swaan, uit-gegeven,
door de Digtkunstige Juffr. TITIA BRONGERSMA

Een Maagd, Apollo toegewijd,
    Schenkt ons (al grimt de bitse Nijd)
Een geestig Boek, vol Mengel-dichten,
    Van soete stijl, beschaafd en net?
    'T is recht een lieflijk oorbanket,
'T strekt tot vermaak, en om te stichten.

De Teeken-geest, verbeeld ook hier
    Een ruwe Rotsteen op papier,
Ten Toppunt bogtigh opgesteegen,
    Waar uyt dan mild een Aader vloeyd,
    Die tot een Bron of Beekje groeyd,
Dat ruyschend' nêerwaards komt gezeegen.

    Een blanke Swaan! Verlustigd' 't oogh,
    Die spreid haar wieken naar om hoogh,
En dobberd' soetjes op de baaren,
    Haar Hals gekruld, bekoorlyk kweeld?
    Waar door sy hert en zinnen streeld,
Aanminniger dan duisend snaaren.

                                                              Den

On the frontispiece of *The Swan of the Well*
of Groningen, by Miss Titia Brongersma
By Johan Jacob Monter*

A woman vowed to Apollo, young,
Gave us (though snappish Envy gnashes)
A vivid book of various verses
Stylish, sophisticated, beautiful.
In this life, it's right to prepare
A pleasing feast for the ear, to amuse,
To mark occasions festively.
The hand that etched the frontispiece
Drew a rough boulder rearing
Up, from which a gentle vein
Of water flows until it swells
Into a stream, rustling downward,
Filling a consecrated pool.
A white Swan spreads her wings
While her webfeet paddle. Neck
Bent, she calls charmingly
Bringing to song her heart and mind
More alluring than a thousand
Chords struck from an orchestra.

* A friend of Ludolph Smids, Monter lived in Assen. Brongersma celebrates this place not far from Leeuwarden. A.J. van der Aa notes that Monter contributed to a 1685 collection of Groningen poetry. Monter echoes phrases from Brongersma's verse while practising one of her favourite modes, *ekphrasis* (a verbal rendition of a visual work of art).

Den oever van dit helden Kil,
Bezoomd door Jufferschap, die stil
Met 't hol der handen water scheppen?
Dan zy uyt 't hagelwitte Vat
Elkàar toebrengen 't Edel Nat,
Welk Bronvocht zy begeerich leppen.

Groninga toond zigh in 't verschiet,
Als opgetoogen, mits zy siet
Die suivre BronSwaan! wiens gesangen,
Zo ryk, en deftigh toegeregt,
Aan haare kroon, een Paarle hegt,
Die daar sal glansryk' eewigh hangen.

Hoogdraavend draafd haar Heldentoon
En Treur-gezangh, hoe soet en schoon
Kan uyt het oogh noch traanen dringen.
Haar Feest-Dight minlyk toegesteld!
Van wien Haar Lof-en Jaar galm meld,
Dies BRONSWAAN! gaat onsterflyk zingen.

O Puyk van Grunoos Maagdeschaar!
Ruk Lauwer-telgen by elkàar?
Maar neen! hou u slegts staagh verbonden
Haar geest te roemen, 't geefd meer glans,
Dan een geplukten Lauwer-krans,
Waar mê zy is genoegh omwonden.

JOH:JACOB MONTER

♦ ♦ ♦

Aan

The seductive cool of the banks a band
Of women circles, silently
Scooping water in hollow palms.
They offer from those gleaming cups
The noble drink, lap spring-water.
Groningen promises to be
Buoyant in spirit when she reads
The purest *Swan of the Well*,
Songs so opulent, magisterial,
Thoughtful, like a pearl to her crown
Fastened that will glimmer there
Attached forever. Headlong rush
The Swan's heroic numbers, tragic
Register so sweet and clear what eye
Could refrain from tears? Her festal
Songs felicitously contrived,
Panegyric, anniversary
Resounding. This *Swan of the Well* will
Immortally echo on. Glory
Of Grunoos's womankind! Do these
Women twist Daphne's descendants
To crown one another? No.
They unite to extol your mind.
It gives off more light than a spray
Of leaves plucked from a tree. But me?
I am happy to bind her a garland.

◆ ◆ ◆

Aan De vond-en trand-rijke Digteresse Juff. TITIA BRONGERSMA
Op de Tijtel-plaat van haar Groninger BRON-SWAN, of
MENGEL-DIGTEN.

Waarom zit hier Apoll, en 't Negental,
Niet op de boord, van desen water-val?
En waar om hoort men hier geen stemgeschal
    Gehuwt aan Snaren?
Is 't ruischend nat, dat uyt dees steen-reep vliet,
'Tzin roerend zap van den Parnassus niet,
Dat men Apol, noch geen der Musen ziet,
    Op d'oever waren?

Dees Juffer-schaar, die d'ene d'andre trekt,
Vangt dan vergeefs het water dat hier lekt,
Indien dat niet de logge Geest verwekt,
    Tot rijm en dichten.
Licht maakt daarom de lang-gehalsde Zwaan
Op't roey-tuich van haar veren zulk een Baan:

                                      Licht

Verses in honour of the inventive and stylistically
rich poet Miss Titia Brongersma, reflecting on the
frontispiece of *The Swan of the Well*\*
By M[attheus] Gargon

Why doesn't Apollo preside with his nine
By the side of this cascade? And why do we
Not hear the sound of lyre-strings in harmony?
Isn't that stony conduit channelling Parnassus?
Is there really no sign of the god and his muses?

This troupe of women, each encouraging the rest,
For nothing gathers the water lapping here
If the taste doesn't waken the spirits to metre.
Lightly the long-necked swan wings her way there.

\* By refusing in his *ekphrasis* to identify the women at Brongersma's well with Parnassian muses, Gargon may indicate how the poet chooses to honour a plurality of female acquaintances in the course of her book.

[No pagination]

Licht wil sy na de bron van Pegaas gaan,
    Om daar te zwichten.
Neen, neen, ik dwaal, neen, 'k heb het recht gevat,
Geen hengste-bron uit dese klippen spat,
Maar Titia, verschaft dit Geestich nat,
    Dat elk wil drinken.
De witte Swaan verheft haar ook om hoog
Om aan Apol te zeggen, dat zy zooch
Uit dese bron, veel smakelijker tooch,
    Als hy kan schinken.

                          M. GARGON

♦ ♦ ♦

Aan de Waterscheppende Juffers in de Tijtel-prent van de Bron-zwaan Of Mengel-dichten van de Geest-rijke Poëtersse
**TITIA BRONGERSMA**

Staakt ijverschaar, staakt desen strijd,
  Het water van dees Beek kan uwe dorst niet stillen;
Want hoe gy drinkt met meerder vlijt,
  Hoe gy zult uit dien bron meer droppen drinken willen.

                        Mors mihi vita
                        M.G.

♦ ♦ ♦

                                Ter

She should go and yield to Pegasus's spring!
No, no – I am simply raving. This is not
The horse's well that spurts from these rocks
But Titia's, the inspiring source everyone
Wants to taste. Her dazzling Swan transports her
High to tell Apollo she decants a liquor
That quenches thirst better than his brew.

◆ ◆ ◆

On the young women who draw water in the frontispiece of *The Swan of the Well* by the most fanciful poet Titia Brongersma\*
By M. G[argon]: "Death to me is life"

Stop, people! Stop competing for this resource.
A stream such as that cannot quench your thirst.
Whoever drinks here will with increased fervour
Crave to drink more from the well, and still more.

◆ ◆ ◆

---

\* Gargon's emphasis on the frontispiece derives in all likelihood from his vocation as a painter. He playfully imagines the women depicted in that picture as vying to get a drink. Why did he choose to append the Latin motto "Death to me is life"? He may be playing with the idea of the *fons perennis*. The deathless fountain of literature slakes the unquenchably recurrent thirst of mortal imagination. Or "Death to me is life" may be Gargon's personal motto, here a seal of approval.

Ter eeren van het schrander en weergaloos Werck, van de
verstandige Juffer MeJuffr. TITIA BRONGERSMA.

Uyt uwe groote Geest en wonderbare wercken,
Mejuffer Middagklaar kan ick daeruyt bemerkken,
De waarheyt van 't verhaal 't geen Nasoos Phenix veer:
In sijn herscheppings boeck, hoogdravend' stelt ter neer.
Hy beelt Deucalion ons voor met steens te planten,
Doch uyt geen lompe key maar 't puyk der diamanten,
Soo reken ick Iuffrouw u af-komst, want u Geest,
'k Behoef geen meer bewijs, bevestigt alder meest.
Mijn stellingh, want ik sie rees voor hun glory swigten,
D'uytnemenst uwer sex wiens deftige Gedichten
Gy verder overtreft dan aen den Hemel-trans
De Son de sterren doet door gadelose glans,
Selfs Sapho staat bedeest, ja valt uyt spijt aen 't wenen,
Nu Titia verrijst, nu is Sy uyt geschenen.

           J.H. FEDENSMA
           Schilder.

◆ ◆ ◆

               Aan

In honour of the ingenious, peerless work of the
brilliant Miss Titia Brongersma
By J[oannis] F[edensma]*

Your poems show so much intellect, dear woman,
I see as clear as the noon hour the truth
Of Ovid's story of the phoenix in his book
Of transformations thrillingly set down,
And Deucalion planting stones, not
Crudities: superb diamond. The fable,
Poet, is a portent of your future. Your talent
Makes me advance this claim, and add to your
Glory, outstanding genius of your sex. Your verse
Excels its rivals as at the gate of heaven
The singular glister of the sun dims the stars'
Feeble twinkle. Even Sappho stands
Abashed, concedes defeat now Titia looms
Up – now brilliant Sappho, herself, is outshone.

❖ ❖ ❖

* Joannis Fedensma, a painter who moved in the circle of Ludolph Smids, draws imagery and phrasing from Brongersma's poems. He notes her fondness for Ovidian motifs. When he decides to cast her as Deucalion, he reflects Brongersma's own habitual literary equivocation between male and female spheres. Spared by Jupiter from drowning in a universal flood, Deucalion and Pyrrha (who had retreated to safety onto the slopes of Parnassus) repopulated the earth by throwing stones behind their shoulders – *ossa magnae parentis*, the bones of their great mother, as the oracle of Themis elliptically described them (*Metamorphoses* 1.383). As soon as they hit the ground, Pyrrha's missiles became women, Deucalion's men. The image of the stony earth as *progenetrix* recurs in Brongersma's poem on the *hunebed*. Brongersma's defiance of norms imposed on women may affect Fedensma's choice to have her work bring forth men: Deucalion only produced, or reproduced, his own sex. The generative power attributed to rocks conceivably recalls the mineral magnificence of the *hunebed*.

Aan de Ed. Deugtrijke seer Geëerde, en in kennis uytmuntende
Juffer MeJuffer OUDILIA S. SCHERFF haar Ed. opdragende de
LofGedichten, en Geestelijke stoffen in't besonder.

'K Had lang mijn schacht gedoopt om't blank papier te smetten,
Soo my 't ontsag daar van niet hadde doen beletten
Om V alwaardigheyt te off'ren mijn Gedigt,
Waar door ik door de reên ten hoogsten ben verplicht
Wijl dat van al wat leeft voor het verstant moet wijken
Soo met een Pallas dan voor Iuno d'Eerkroon strijken,
Want waar de luyster van de Son der kennis straaldt
(:Die al de flikk'ring van de wereld overhaaldt:)
Daar Triomfeert dat Licht, soo heerlijk opgeresen,
Het geen men uyt V oog kan sonder scheem'ring lesen.
Soo ooyt Groninga vvaar bekroont met vvetenschap
Door Iufferdom, soo treedt gy me op d' eerste trap,
En sleept de Lauw'ren weg. O! schand're Amazone
Vergun dat ik mijn Swaan door uwe Naam mag kronen,
En dat haar Bronne boordt door u mag zijn geëert
Het geen al over lang van herten is begeert,
Waar voor het Swaantje dan haar stem sal laten horen
(Hoewel wat schor) dog, Is tot uwen dienst geboren,
Het spreyt' er wiekjes, en fingt reets met sagt geluyt
De groote wond'ren van V Ed'le gaven uyt.

❖ ❖ ❖

De Gro-

Dedication to the eminently virtuous, honourable, and learned Miss Odilia S. Scherff of, especially, my poems of praise and my verse on spiritual themes*

My dipped pen abstained a while, from staining paper.
Awe restrained my hand from daring to compose
Verse for you, so worthy. I'm obliged.
Every reader must respect your mind,
An Athena seizing the prize, prevailing over
Juno, because where the sun of knowledge
Glows (brightening the universe it convinces),
Light rejoices in a triumph, uprisen
Gloriously. The clearness of your eye
Dispels, forbids obscurity. If ever
Groningen won laurels by thinking
Women's efforts, allow me now to mount
The victor's podium, to crown my Swan
In your name, please. May you honour my
Well-side, with your presence. That place is not
Desired by all. Therefore the little Swan
Cries out, hoarsely, for she was hatched to serve
You. She flaps her wings, begins to proclaim
The miracle of your innate nobility.

◆ ◆ ◆

* Brongersma's contemporaries would understand Juno as the goddess of decent wifedom, Athena as goddess of the armed and independent mind. Odilia Scherff did eventually marry Winandus Fredell. They had a child in 1705. Titia Brongersma herself writes this tribute. As in her book's dedication to the women of Groningen, she attaches the idea of "hoarseness" or "throatiness" to her Swan. The attribution becomes as insistent as a Homeric epithet.

# DE BRON-SWAAN

*The* SWAN *of the* WELL*

* The 1686 edition does not in fact have a title page to distinguish the sequence of prefatory, dedicatory poems from the body of Brongersma's own work. But the book's pagination only begins with her sonnet "The triumphant lily-shrubbery of Groningen, rife with buds and blossoms."

[1]

DE GRONINGER Triompherende LELY-STRUYK
Verciert met Bloem en knoppen. Sonnet.

Hoe staat die tronk bedauwd met pereldroppen
Verheven op de Keyserlijke trans,
Hoe brald die blanke bloem met hare krans
Omkringeld van haar aangegroeyde knoppen.
Haa Koningin, en puik-loof aller spruyten,
    Geen Nardus, noch Himet bereykt u naam,
    U grootheyt drijft op vlerken van de faam:
Want niemant kan U in een engte sluyten,
U kruyn schiet door bedampte swerken heen.
O! vaste hoek-pylaar hoe ongemeen
Bewaard gy voor het gift uw Lely-dalen,
    Soo dat geen bitse Slang, noch Scorpioen,
    Kan in't bevredigt hof van Gruno Woen
Maar drijftse voorr, en komt de zeeg behalen.

◆ ◆ ◆

Aan

The triumphant lily-shrubbery of Groningen, rife with buds and blossoms*

Sonnet

Dewed with pearl-like drops, your base supports
An arch a Caesar would admire. The flower
Brightly flaunts its garlands – rings
Of spreading sprigs, ascending buds. Queen,
Leafy splendour comprising variants,
Neither Asian nard nor Attic thyme
Infringes on your fame, for you combine
The best of both and each, like a wing,
Contributes to waft you off to glory.
No one can stunt you and keep you down.
Your crest transcends all staleness.
Towering, you preserve your lily-blessing against
The biting snake, the stinging scorpion. Neither
Can lodge in Groningen's contented garden.
You cast them out. You win the battle.

◆ ◆ ◆

* This sonnet sets the tone for the entire collection. As the poet ushers us into her book, she offers conquest as a case not of imperial annexation, but rather of exclusion. Nard is spikenard, or the amber-coloured aromatic oil derived from that plant. Thyme honey is found throughout Greece, but the most famous originates near Mount Hymettus, in Attica.

[2]

Aan de Hoogh-Edel, Welgeboren Juffer, Mejuffer
ISABELLA CATHARINA MARIA, Baronesse van Heerema,
toen haar Ed: Song onder 't speelen.

Wie hoor ik daar soo Hemels onder t' spelen
     Gelijk een Engel quelen,
Is 't een der Musen die haar gorgel slaat
En onder Phaebus lier sig hooren laat?
Neen, neen 't is Isabel een pronk der aarde,
     't Is Catharijn die waarde
Die Suyv're die een Sappho hier verbeeld
Wijl zy door hand, en stem elk d'oren streelt.
't Is Herema die van Apol beschonken
     In Lauwren staat te pronken,
En die door hem werdt op Parnas geleyd:
Waar dat voor haar al lang is plaats bereyd.

◆ ◆ ◆

Aan de Hoog-Edele Vrouw Mevrou E.V.G.

O! Friesche Hof-pomoon, en suster van de Musen,
Hoe opend gy de wel van haar geleerde slusen
Op Blessums Helicon, waar het gehoefde paard
Door 't klatsen van sijn voet U wond'ren openbaard:
En doet U konsts-rivier met Aganippaes dropen
Van 't tweegespitst Parnas de wereldt overlopen,

                                        Soo

On the noble, high-born young
woman, Lady Isabella Catharina Maria,
Baroness van Heerema*

What can I hear in this mundane place?
It delights me like an angel's warbling.
Does one of the Muses perform aloud,
Flanking Phoebus? No, it's Isabel,
Ornament of this earth, it's Catharina
Meritorious and pure, who plays the role
Of Sappho, finding admission to every
Ear with her fingers' skill, her vocal beauty.
It's Heerema who, inspired, rewarded
By Apollo, guided by him, finds the spot
On Parnassus reserved for her advent.

❖ ❖ ❖

To the truly noble Mrs E[ritia] V[an] G[linstra]†

Garden-haunting Pomona, Frisian sister
Of the Muses whose elegant well brims
On Blessum's Helicon where, as he paused,
The horse struck open your wondrous spring,
Aganippe's waters also feeding
Your streaming art – two sources sliding
From double-crested Parnassus to us:

---

* Baroness van Heerema, born around 1656, married Titus van Essum in 1699 at Bodum, Groningen. She died in 1725. Like many seventeenth-century poets, Brongersma makes her first address to a member of the nobility. Already she displays her penchant for ringing changes on a person's plurality of given names. Petrarch's play with Laura's name is the canonical instance. The Baroness earns Brongersma's attention for her artistry: the object of the poet's praise is the woman's vocal gifts and artful playing of a stringed instrument. The eccentricities of Brongersma's compositor (often evident in the rendition of people's names) has been brought into the best possible conformity, here as elsewhere, with usages established by present-day Dutch historians (exemplified, for instance, in the entries available at biografischportaal.nl).

† Eritia van Glinstra lived from 1655 to 1714. She had married Hector van Glinstra, and was buried in Dronrijp, three kilometres from Blessum. Blessum lies near Leeuwarden. Ovid associates the spring of Aganippe at the base of Helicon with Hippocrene – the source higher up the slopes, legendarily evoked by the hoof-blow of Pegasus. The Muses were sometimes called the Aganippides. Brongersma celebrates a fellow writer, and thus allocates van Glinstra a poetic spring to match the well in which her own Swan swims. An alternative though unlikelier female candidate for Brongersma's dedication

[3]

Soo dat, waar maar de faam haar loftrompetten slaat,
Sy ons her rugt'bre roem van Glinstra horen laat.
Van Glinstra glinsterend' gelijk de hemel sterren
In welkers redenglans het Ore moet verwerren
Ja met een woordbesluyt ik dat dit treflijk beeld
Veel eer van Goden, dan van Menschen is geteeld.

♦ ♦ ♦

Aan Juffrouw ANNA de HAAS. Die genood waar pekelharing
te eeten dog: niet komende wierd haar Ed: eene gesonden,
die dus spreekt.

Dewijl gy niet en koomt om my de nek te breken
Ter plaatse waar men u op mijn waardy gaat noôn:
Soo koom ik selver hier, om my op u te wreken
Op dat gy seggen moogt de Haring spant de kroon,
Want als gy scheurd, en rijt, mijn vlees met grage tanden
Als dan bewoon ik eerst den versen Oceaan:
Wiens baren my doen up de Frieschen oever stranden
Daar my het Britse, meyr door 't golven heeft doen gaan.

♦ ♦ ♦

Aen de selve Die op haar kelder deur geschilderd hadde het hooft
van Medusa, en van Methusalem, met een Vyl, en een Swaan.

Vrage.
Wat doet den Uyl, de Eer-staf van Minerve
Juist aan den ingank van de Wijngodts zaal

antwoord

Wherever Fame puts the trumpet to her lips
It proclaims the far-reaching renown of Glinstra,
Glinstra glistening like the celestial stars
With such a glitter of glamorous language
The ear would resist, and cannot. The greater
Share of glory the gods nurture, not men.

♦ ♦ ♦

To Miss Anna de Haas whom I invited to a dish of
pickled herring. Since she couldn't make the date,
I sent her one – who made this speech:*

You missed the moment to rend sweet, briny
Flesh from my bones, at the place, from the plate
Appointed. Now I've come to make it right,
As in the fable "The Herring Takes the Prize,"
Beating out the flounder, setting her snout
Permanently out of joint. When you tear me
With gratified teeth remember that I lived
In the refreshing tide. It pushed me into
Shallows and onto the Frisian beach, the British
Impelling me there more than the ocean current.

♦ ♦ ♦

Riddles for Anna de Haas, the door to whose cellar
is decorated with Medusa and Methuselah, with
an owl and a swan†

What is that Owl doing, respectable familiar of
    Minerva,
Just at the threshold of the wine-god's vault? –

is Eelkje van Glinstra-Bouricius, a poet. Eritia seems a more credible recipient by virtue of her connection to Blessum. Brongersma puns on the name "Glinstra," using in Dutch a verb that evokes glimmering and glistening – an effect partially reproducible in translation. Pomona, a Roman divinity, presided over fruit trees.

* As a Dutch folktale begins, all the salt-water fish decide to hold a race. The flounder takes the lead, the herring trailing it closely. A herring's eyes, situated on the sides of its head, prevent it from seeing directly in front. Vision impaired, the fish surmises it has triumphed, shouting, "I won the prize!" But the flounder, a flatfish, actually reached the finish line first. The proof is that it bashed its snout hard against the terminal marker. The impact resulted in a physical peculiarity characteristic of all flounders as they appear today. Like the herring, the flounder suffers from distorted seeing. Its eyes appear to sit atop the fish's head: hence the supposed liability to collision. The tale offers an aetiology for the flounder's crooked nose. Brongersma's voluble herring explains why its multitudinous comrades might be caught along the Frisian coast. The English fishing fleet has harried them there. Of Brongersma's Anna de Haas nothing is ascertainable.

† Brongersma combines riddle with *ekphrasis*. The severed head of petrific Medusa was fixed to Minerva's aegis, the goddess of wisdom's shield or breastplate, thus rendering that defensive piece an

Antwoord,
Om dat die geur de dofheyt doet versterven
Mits wakkerheyt hem dient tot zegepraal.

Vrage:
Maar daar's een Swaan, en 't hooft van't ouwste der ouwden
Met het Medusen Hooft'ant: dat wert getoont
Om dat de Wijsheyt wert voor grijs gehouden,
En Ook, om dat daar selfs een Pallas woond.

◆ ◆ ◆

Aan de Ed. Juffer SUSANNA W. Die een korvie met bloemen
gesonden wierd van Karitate.

Wel hoe Susann: wat stuyrd u Karitate?
Sijn 't bloemen; dat is vreemd kent zy u niet?
Die bloem tot bloemen send doet nergens bate;
Want in u selfs, gy selfs een bloemtie siet.

◆ ◆ ◆

DE MUSCH versoeckt de Nagtegal te Singen.
       J.J.J. A.D.B.

O Philomel, beween niet meer u ongeluck
K'weel liever op de kruyn van Penus kroost u sangen
Fluyt soete tilpertien, ey gargle tiuk tiuk tiuk
Gy doet me naar u stem en Veld deun seer verlangen.
Slaa kleyne Orgel krop, slaa met u Tongsken aan
Gy sijt de strikken van Vorst Thereus al ontsprongen

                                              En

The bird dissipates the soporific
Fume of grapes so revelry, less stuporous,
Should better serve his Lady's ends.

But why is a Swan here, with the heads
Of the eldest of men and the gorgon Medusa? –
Wisdom cherishes those grown silver-haired and wise,
While Minerva with her aegis defends this house.

◆ ◆ ◆

For the noble Miss Susanna W[ilmson] to whom
gratitude has sent a basket of flowers*

Well, Susanna, what does gratitude send you now?
Flowers? That's odd. Doesn't she know you better?
Flowers on flowers add nothing to the sum
Since you yourself are the consummate blossom.

◆ ◆ ◆

The sparrow attempts to sing like the nightingale†
J.J.J. A[ngenis] D[e] B[lasco]

Philomela, give up grieving old
Misfortune. Sing instead the wreath
Of Peneus's daughter. Whistle mellowly.
Gurgle *took-took*. Your voice's rustic
Music intimately stirs me. Little
Organist, sound every chord. And touch,
Little tongue, every note you can.
Don't you see you've escaped Prince
Tereus's bonds, and adopting new themes

offensive weapon. Bacchus moderates the austerity of wisdom, as in Plato's *Symposium*; in Genesis, Methusaleh lived fully 969 years. The Greek Minerva offers one image of philosophical depth; the venerable descendant of Adam another.

* Susanna Wilmson married Jacob Groothuys, an infantry lieutenant. Regimental records attest that the ceremony happened on 12 January 1684. In her epigram, Brongersma uses two words for "love": *karitas* and *minne*. The first expresses itself in good works; the second in courtly service. The association of women with flowers, implicit in the program poem's triumphant shrubbery, becomes specific in this poem.

† In the third line of these verses, Brongersma's compositor offers the obscure name "Penus." The poet, however, probably urges the nightingale to address the tale of Daphne, daughter of the river god Peneus (her epithet in Ovid is *Peneia*). The virtuosic nightingale is properly a laureate: and – a telling fact, in Brongersma's vision of the world – by dint of talent she has overcome (or *should* overcome) the past. By situating a bird of legendary resonance in a peaceful, modern Frisian garden, Brongersma prepares the reader for her fluency in the rendition of antique topics, such as Zenobia's reign. The onomatopoeic representation of Philomela's music is Brongersma's own. Pales is a female divinity – goddess-guardian of pastureland.

[5]

En met een nieuwer toon, en taallit aan gedaan:
Schoon sijne moetwil u die hadde uyt gewrongen
Gy moogt nu vry met vreed in dese Rosegaard
Wel singen tuyt, tuyt, tuyt. En vrolijk tierelieren
Wijl gy van Pales, en haar Nimfen werd bewaard
Die u O! lieve dier met Liesig mos Beswieren,
En toyen 't Nestien op, dat voor u werd bereyd
Wanneer ge af geslaaft door Galmstrijd 'toog komt luyken
U slaap koets is van Pluym op takkies neer gespreyd
Ver wulleft met de blaan van groene hage struyken,
Sie daar, ey Beesie sie, hoe yder is verlust
Op u behaaglijkheyd, en nog sit gy gescholen
In een gekloofden holm, denk hoe g'het hert ontrust
Nu gy u meer voor my, als and'ren hout verholen,
Ik tierp op u gebeen mijn wil'tsang rustig uyt
Waarom misgond gy my dan u gewiek't geluyd';

♦♦♦

Zenobia Weduwe van de Keyser Obdenatus overwint de
Persianen: en tegen een Leeuw strijt te Paarde sittende,
die de Kuyste, en moedigste Vrou van de werelt was.

Sie daar Zenobia de Koningin
De Paarden alseen twede Achil berijden,
En ginder weer een Veltslag voeren in
Om tegen Persiaan, en Leeuw te strijden,
Haar dapp're speer bemorst van Vijants bloet
Druipt vlietend' af op Caesars Marm're troonen

Daar

Renew your art? It's a long time since
He dominated you. In this rose garden
Expatiate in safety. Keep chanting
*Towt-towt, tiralira*: Pales protects you.
The nymphs defend you and, dear creature,
Upholster with whorls of moss the nest-cup
Shaped for you, after echoing antiphony
Has tired you out. Let down and malleable twigs
Pillow your tented bed draped in folds
Of green. Look, darling beast. We're all pleased
By the delight you provoke from the fork of
Holly oak. Think how you ease the heart.
Linger with me longer, before you visit
Other woods. I chirp my natural note
For you. Why grudge me your melody?

◆ ◆ ◆

Zenobia, widow of the prefect Odenathus, the most modest and audacious woman in the world, defeats the Persians and fights a lion while mounted on her horse.*

See Zenobia the queen like Achilles come again
Riding over there, leading another charge
While fighting off a lion and the Persian
Both, her lance smeared boldly with hostile
Blood, spattering droplets over Caesar's marble
Throne. Her victory boasts its splendid spoils

* Brongersma may engage in *ekphrasis*, with a particular painting or engraving in view. Zenobia married the Roman prefect of Palmyra, Lucius Septimus Odenathus, in 258. They waged war on the Sassanid Persians. Assassins murdered both her husband and her son. Emperor Aurelian ultimately vanquished Zenobia at Antioch. Taken in chains to Rome, she may have married the senator Marcellus Petrus Nutenus. Brongersma assumes this second marriage, and Marcellus's respect for his wife. Cassius Longinus, a member of Zenobia's court, wrongly credited with the composition of the influential tract "On the Sublime," lived from 213 to 273. The onset of a natural foe (the lion) and a political foe (the Persians) creates some Longinian "sublime" effect. Brongersma may consider Pompey (or Gnaeus Pompeius Magnus, 106–148 BCE) a proper antecedent for Zenobia, because she relies on authorities who claim this general first absorbed Palmyra into the Roman territory of Syria.

[6]

Daar het triumph haar Zegepralen doet
En meer bepronkt dan duysent Perrel Cronen.
Zy staat verrijkt met Kresus goude staf.
En aangedaan met Alexanders daden.
Met Pijrhus geest die nooyt mis oordeel gaf
Door Scipio gegort in deugts gewaden.
Marcel heeft haar scharp sinnigheyt geleert.
Trayanus met Rechtvaardigheyt beschonken.
Waar door se wert al seen Godin ge Eert
Tot Romen, daar haar Beelt is uyt geklonken
In kostele porfijr, haa! Obdenat
Sie nu die Kuysch, en groote Roem der Vrowen
Wel eer voor u een onwaardeerlijk Schatt
Haar Tombe op Cassius de wolkberg bouwen

Daar waar Pompeë de Lauwer heeft geplant
Voor u en haar; waar nog sijn houtmijt brant.

◆ ◆ ◆

Op 't af sijn van J.E.J. Toen het froor, en Doyde; soo dat men onder, nog over, kon

Wat raat Iolij nu 't Water leyt beschorst
Nu men door Sneeuw de Cristalijne stroomen
Ver dikt siet, en geen Brief kan Overkomen:
Wijl dat het met een ijs-vloer is bekorst,
Tis Borëas genoeg nu by mag braden
Sijn kil Befrosen Borst, hy wermer gloet.
Van Orithia, die nog overladen
Van min, hem door haar Minlijkheden voet.

Aeh

And becomes her more than a crown of pearl.
She has got gold to beat the loot of Croesus
And performed feats to equal Alexander's.
Pyrrhus's spirit is hers. He never made a mistake,
By Scipio vested in virtue's robes. Her great
Mind was a gift Marcellus came to value.
Trajan would approve her divine virtue.
Rome acclaimed her like a goddess, her image
Fixed in costly designs. Odenathus,
See your surpassing woman now, glory
Of her sex, inestimable treasure, tomb
Raised to sublime Longinus's intellectual
Apex, to dearest Cassius', where Pompey
Already had sown laurel for you, sir, and her.
The beacon burns with coupled heat and light.

◆ ◆ ◆

On Miss E[lisabeth] J[oly]'s inaccessibility so long as the water's surface alternately froze and thawed, and people could get about by neither boat nor skate blade*

What do you advise now the river stops
Suspended, and through thick ice we
Only glimpse the fluent stream, and can
Exchange no letters since a floor of ice
Like magic has congealed, and it is so
Cold Boreas would warm his shuddering breast
With Orithyia's ardent glow, thawing the god
By applying her love – her loveliness? The thought

* The god of the north wind, Boreas, seized Orithyia, daughter of Erechtheus the king of Athens and the Naiad Praxithea. Brongersma's poem – the first in *Swan of the Well* addressed to Elisabeth Joly – assumes Orithyia's reciprocation of the divinity's feelings. Socrates himself refers to the myth of Boreas and Orithyia in the course of Plato's *Phaedrus*, a dialogue in defence of erotic feeling. Sighs are a commonplace Petrarchan love symptom. Brongersma and Joly may innovate in perceiving, and exploring lyrically, the visible pseudo-solidity of vaporous breath in cold weather, fancifully dispatched in the manner of aerial *billets-doux*.

[7]

Aeh! dat heeft my al veel te lang verdrooten
Geloof me soo ik kon ik brak het Glas,
Of glee op schaatsen langs de gladde plas
(Tot u:) die my so over hout af gesloten,
Of dat den Hemel wou wat milder sijn
Om duysent suggies, die we alle beyde
Uyt wasemen, te regten op een lijn:
En op de koers van u, en my, aan leyde.

Op dat se onder weeg in het ontmoeten
Malkaar, van wegen ons, dan mogten groeten

♦ ♦ ♦

Aen ELISENE. Toen het weer Ontdooyde.

Het is dan eens gelukt groot-Vorst van Aguilon
   T'ont grendelen u Bron,
Die gy tot spijt van my soo hert hebt doen verstijven
Dat men daar op wel kan met stale pennen drijven
O wreedaart, hat ge dan geen deernis daar ge saagt
   Mijn bange borst belaagt
En daar gy wist hoe seer dat Eliseen begeerde
Dat ik haar met een brief, (soo lang gewilt) vereerde
Dog niemant klaagt ligt aan een anders leet, of smert
   Al raak het schoon aan 't hert.
Nu 't is genoeg, ik sie het water soeties dertlen
Dat weer op nieuw de soom van 't hoenvelt koomt bespertlen
Dat my doet hopen (wijl ik vrees voor geen gevaar)
   Dat nu de Baan is klaar

            G. a

Has oppressed me, too long. Believe me
I would smash the glass if I could, or glide
On skates over the slippery surface, or
If the sky would relent a little then
We could line up and send off thousands of sighs
Compounded of the steam we exhale. Sped
On their course, let mine meet yours midway.

◆ ◆ ◆

To Elise, on the fresh clemency of the weather*

Grand Duke Aquilo mellows, unlocks your source
Which once was so irksomely inflexible
People could scribble on it with skate blades.
But gusty bully, show me pity. You lay soft siege
To my shy breast, and you know how strongly
Elise has wanted a letter from me, so long longed for.
But a stranger's misery is difficult to feel.
Yet it's enough for me to witness water playing
    sweetly
That surges up from the moorhens' fenland
And fills me with hope (since I have no fear)
That the way is clearing. Go then, my letter, go.

\* These lines may record the end of the Great Frost of 1683 to 1684. The long suspense of a hard winter, congealing even ink, followed by the resumption of fluency, stands in interesting relation with the next poem. There Brongersma records her encounter with the *hunebed* at Borger. The huge monument stands derelict and mute at first, because it is misunderstood. Ignorance has hitherto prevented the goddess Natura's temple from resuming its ancient, abiding function. The poet's song releases the shrine from silence's *frozen* enchantment – analogously as spring melts ink for epistolary use.

[8]

Gaa dan mijn letters gaa, gaa: maar wilt ondertussen
Soo g'in haar handen valt, voor my die driemaal Kussen
Seg dat ik wens, in plaats van U. by haar te sijn
        Of dat se waar by mijn:
Daar, waar wel inkt bevriest, maar nimmer mijn gedagten
En dat ik haar altoos met groot verlang sal wagten.

♦ ♦ ♦

Loff Op 't HUNNE-BED, of de Ongemeene, opgestapelde Steen
hoop Tot BORGER. IN DRENTHE

'K Staa, verbaast dees Steen Mijt aan te schouwen,
'T schijnt dat wel eer, het dappre Hunnenschap:
Daar heeft gewilt een Denk-plaats op te bouwen
Om soo te streven op de Eere Trap.
Neen 't is't gestapel daar een drom van Reusen
Door wraak gehitst, het Godendom bestreet,
Dog die men sag tot morsel selfs verkneusen
Door 't Blixsem vier van Mulciber gesmeet.
Of 't sijn alleen getorste Pieramijden,
Of Tomben, want dit grove berg gewas
Besluyt in haar gewelfsel, van voor rijden
Nog tot een blijk, geheylgde offer-ass.
Neen 't is veel eer Naturaas Merbre Tempel
Waar in sy wil dat men haar Godheyt eert
En aan de voet haars neegentalge Drempel
Niet anders dan een Lofgesang begeert

                                  Laat

Find your way into her hands: pass on three kisses
And say I wish I were in your place, with her –
Or she with me. My ink may have frozen:
   my thoughts
Remained warm as ever, and I still expect her
With a longing never suspended or diminished.

♦ ♦ ♦

Praise of the *hunebed*, or the prodigious heaped pile
of boulders at Borger, in Drenthe\*

I stand like one to stone turned staring
At the stacked rocks, boast of heroic Huns
Apparently, who willed the building of a
Monument to secure a footing on glory's
Sheer gradient. No. This mass congeals a dream of
Resentful giants upreared, vying with godhood
Though they say Mulciber's thunderbolt split
It, flaring, into fragments. Could it be a pyramid
Dragged into place? Or a grave? For this gross,
Craggy cumulation encloses in
Its substrate carcasses, ancient sacrifice.
No. More likely it is Natura's marble
Temple where she desires that her divinity be
Honoured. She would hear at the verge of
   her ninefold
Threshold nothing beyond a song of praise.

\* On 11 June 1685, Pentecost (the seventh Sunday after Easter), with her Borger friend and host Jan Laurens Lenting (or Lentinck), Brongersma conducted what may have been the first archaeological excavation of a *hunebed*. This megalithic monument, now designated D27, is the longest of its kind in the Netherlands. Reporting that Germany preserved the Pillars of Hercules, Tacitus may offer a garbled account of *hunebedden*. *Hun* does not designate an ethnic group, as Brongersma supposes: it is an archaic word for "giant." (The megalith was thus called a "giant's tomb.")

## [9]

Laat Theben vry nog poggen op er, Muyren
Die schier in't hoog bereykten 't wolk gespan
Dit Rots gevaart, sal langer konen d'uyren:
Geen kragt hoe groot haar Force quetsen kan,
Coom Nimphies, en gy Drentsche Herderreyen
Bepronk met Loof, dit Borger Steen-Paleys
Wilt top en kruyn met Bloemen overspreyen,
Schenk aan Natuir daar van haar deel, en eys,
Ik nuyr dan met verheescht: en schorre toonen
('tSy wat het wil:) tot roem dees wondre Grott
Een Lof-liet, en berey de Eyken kroonen:
Waar mee 'k bepruyk, het groote Keye-slott.

◆ ◆ ◆

Let Thebes boast of walls tall enough to scrape
The sky, this rocky monster will outlast her,
No force though great can crack it all to bits.
Come nymphs, and come you rustics of Drenthe,
Make splendid with your praise this mineral palace
That would be piled with flowers. Render to Nature
What is elementally hers, and her tribute.
I offer in a hoarse and throaty voice a song
Of praise to extol this marvel of a cave and
Prepare the oaken crown to deck the immense
Castle of boulders.

♦ ♦ ♦

DE SWABISCHE LIJKBUS, by brokken, tot Borger, onder de
Huinebedden, uit de grond gehaald, aan TITIA BRONGERSMA

    'K heb op een boesem, eer men my begroef, gerust,
Die melk, ja lelien in witheid ging te boven;
    Die treurig aarden vat is van een mond gekust,
Een mond, wiens vriendlijkheid men nooit genoeg kon loven.
    'K sag my, O TITIA, van heete traanen nat,
Terwijl een Noordsche maagd mijn buik vol beend'ren propte,
    Daar sy, voor 't lijkaltaar, op Keiselsteenen sat,
En 's minnaars aaschen, uit verbrande kled'ren klopte.
    Sy scheen te stikken in haar droefheid, in haar rouw,
En, in 't omhelsen van de grauwe bus, te sterven,
    Die gy, geklommen in het onbesuist gebouw,
Nieuwgierig opgraaft, en beklaaglijk stoot an scherven,
    (Foei, wreede wijsheid!) daar ik nimmer daglicht sag,
Daar ik, sorgeloos, stond onder deese steenen,
    Sint hier de Sax, en Deen, en woeste Swabe lag.
O Maagd, waar wildge nu met deese scherven heene?
    Leg neder, overdek de beenderen, en de fles,
En strek me wederom een trouwe minnares!

♦ ♦ ♦

On the Swabian urn dug up in pieces beneath the
so-called *hunebed* at Borger, to Titia Brongersma*†

I rested on a bosom before I was buried
Surpassing the whiteness of milk, of lilies.
This hard earthen urn was kissed by lips,
Lips whose affection none can praise enough.
Wet with hot tears, O Titia, I witnessed
A youthful woman of the north stuffing my belly
With mortal remains for she sat on the paving
Of stones before the funeral altar, and sifted
The ashes of her darling out of burnt raiment.
She choked in her woe, her sorrow: in embracing
That grey urn she looked as if she would die.
You climbing into the unguarded structure, curious,
Dug me up, learnedly parsed my fragments,
A cruel sagacity, for I have not seen day
Since the Saxon died, the Dane and wild
Swabian. O lady, what would you do now
With these potsherds? Lay them down again, cover
The relics and remains and close me up again
As what I was and I am, a faithful lover.

♦ ♦ ♦

* A poem by Ludolph Smids appears in the first volume of an 1843 travel book, *Drenthe in vlugtige en losse omtrekken geschetst door drie Podagristen*, or *Drenthe in quick, loose sketches by three sufferers from gout* (152). It was printed by D.H. van der Scheer, in Koevorden. Van der Scheer was one of the authors. The other two were A.L. Lesturgeon and H. Boom. Quoted in 1843, Smids says Brongersma found a number of pots, red and blue in colour, some with two and some with four handles.

† Ludolph Smids calls the urn "Swabian" under the influence of Tacitus, in all likelihood. In his Germania, the Roman historian identified that land's most widely prevalent tribe as the Suebi. Smids eroticizes his scene of antique grief, expressing the sentiment of sacrilege or violation that would inhibit archaeological reconnaissance.

Replijk op het aartig Vers van de Hoog-geleerde HEER
LUDOLPH SMIDS: my toe-gesonden Aan de gebroken LYK-BUS.

GY sijt dan als het schijnt verstoort, en ongerust,
Om dat men u (die eer veel mond'ren gingt te boven)
Ontgraven heeft, gy wert soo wel als doen gekust
Van veele, die daar door u aart, en waarde Looven
'k Had deernis met u, wijl nog 't soute trane nat
Drong door u hals tot aan de gront van 't ingepropte
Geraamt' ter wijl ik voor u op mijn knyen sat
En 't keyeg stof van u gewyde Deeg'len klopte.

'k Sag

Reply to the charming verses the most learned
Mr Ludolph Smids sent me, on the topic of the
shattered urn.*

You consider it alarming, unrestful
That people exhumed you who once far more
Cheerfully saw the surface of the earth.
It is as good as kisses from many lips
That your earthen worth is now extolled.
I felt for you, salt tears thickly coursing,
Soaking through your opening to the bottom
Where remains lay packed in you, while I kneeled
In front of you, the crumbly stuff sifting
From the burst seal burial long sanctified.

* Brongersma deflects the erotic
pathos of Smids's poem.

[10]

'k Sag u verdrukt, en mee gedompelt in de Rouw
Daar gy als levenloos, in't duystre Graf most sterven
Schoon 't onderwelfsel van soo'n treffelijk gebouw
Besloot het overschot van u verbroken scherven,
Daar waar het, dat ik u met droeve Oogen sag
Hoe gy getorst, geknelt laagt onder herde stenen
En in het Sonne ligt met eygen hande lag
Dies stap ik moedig met u overblijfsels heene.
En stel de beendren, en u lang bedolven vles
Voor yders Oog, en strek u voor een Minnares.

♦ ♦ ♦

EERGEDICHT, Op het inhalen van Sijn Vorstelijcke
Doorlughtigheydt d'HEER PRINS HENRICK CASIMYR, by
der gratie Godts, Vorst van Nassauw, &c. Met Sijn Doorlughtige,
Hoogh-gebooren GEMALINNE AEMILIA. By der gratie Godts
PRINCESSE VAN ANHALT, &c.

Myn Sangh-Nimph wil dat ik (wijl yder sigh vermaakt
In't aansien van de nieu opgaande Somer-Lighten)
Mijn schorre fedel slaa, die nauwelijkx kan righten,
De gront-geluyden, waar soo hoogh een luyster blaakt.

Dog

I looked at you, oppressed, and immersed myself
In ancient woe. There you appeared: lifeless,
Condemned to death in the grimy grave of such
An uncanny monument, all broken potsherds
(A sight to distress my eyes) crushed under
Hard stones. I moved you into sunlight's warmth
And walked bravely with your relics, away.
I dispose your epochal, occult mortality
Before the gaze of all, with a lover's care.

◆ ◆ ◆

Poem in honour of the reception of his princely
Illustriousness, the Lord Prince Hendrik Casimir by
the grace of God sovereign of Nassau etc., with his
distinguished noble Consort, Amalia by the grace of
God Princess of Anhalt etc.*

The sight of fireworks tinting summer skies
Thrills the crowd and me. The nymph inspiring
My music would evolve a theme blazing
That brightly, on her humble fiddle strings.
My talent's faint, but duty compels me
To make some music for an occasion

* Hendrik Casimir II, stadholder of Friesland and Groningen, who lived from 1664 to 1696, married Henriette Amalia of Anhalt-Dessau in 1683. He became the first hereditary stadholder of Friesland. Brongersma can write laureate-style verse – like John Dryden, her contemporary – when she addresses civic themes. In this period Aphra Behn, too, composed artful verse propaganda for a ruling dynasty, the Stuarts. Brongersma's similarity to such British writers derives not from any direct influence, but from participation in a common historical and rhetorical milieu. "Stadholder" literally means "lieutenant," but the office is supreme in its jurisdiction. At this time, the Netherlands had two stadholders – one of Holland, the other of Friesland.

[11]

Dog sal, schoon my de magt ontbreekt, mijn pligt nog tonen,
In 't nuyen sonder maat, (dewijl m'het hoeve-nat
Nooyt heeft besprengt dat uyt der Musen spring-rots-spat)
Voor 't Heylig paar, wiens Lof verdient veel Lauwer-kronen.
Welkoom dan Casimir welkoom Aemilia,
Welkoom doorlugte Twee in U bemuirde wallen
Daar g'op de Eer Troon sult als Goude Sonnen brallen
Schoon U de Nijt volgt met verwoede schreden na.
't Aal-Oude Helden-schap van U Roem-rughbre Oud'ren
ô Vorst! straalt met een glans op 't blanke Harrenas
Van het Nassauvvsche puik, waar in men eertijts las,
De Dappre Daân, die ghy, nu torst op Uwe schoudren.
Leef langh met U Forstin, als Vader in het Rijck.
Droog af het klamme voght der biggelende tranen!
Soo lang door vrees gevoet van Uwe Onderdanen,
En zijt een Numa in dit vrye Republijck.
Weest als een Hercules, die in de vlam der Stieren,
Sijn strijdbre hand-knods velt, en zegen so het Lant:
Dat in het gloende vier van Neeringloosheyt brant,
Op dat men U Berook, en stook, met Vreughdevieren.
En Gy ô Anhalts Pronk, die al seen blijde Dagh!
In 't krieken van U Lent tot Troost zijt op geresen:
Wilt ons een Moeder, en U Prins een Pallas wesen:
Die door een wijse-raat aanvaart het Groot Gelagh.

Soo

Without a peer, even when I have not drunk
My fill of water from the well of Pegasus.
The blessed couple merits every wreath.
Welcome therefore Casimir, welcome
Amalia, welcome illustrious couple
To your sturdy ramparts. There enthroned
You will shine like the sun in spite of Envy
Who stalks after you, already. The heroic
Venerable fellowship of your everywhere
Renowned forebears, Ruler, beams glittering
On the bright armour of Nassau's glory
Engraved on which are scenes of history,
Brave deeds depicted that now are buckled
On your shoulders. Live long with your consort
As Father of the State. Dry the tears prompted
By love for your subjects, and be the Numa
Of this free republic, Hercules to rope
With strong hands the reckless bull and quash
Corruption in the marketplace, in trade.
You will turn that wildfire to a glow of joy.
And you, Anhalt's splendour, dawning blithe
In the birdsong of a new day, be our mother
And to your prince a Pallas wise in counsel,
Sage suggestion gaining great prestige.

Soo sal den Hemel Vooght u schoont' en Deught bekroonen,
ô Rijx Princes, En Wy, wijl 't swangere Metaal,
Sigh van'er last ontgort, uyt roepen altemaal
Leef langh, leef langh, ghy moet in onse Vesten woonen,
De Groote Moogentheyt, en Trotse Borgery
Verselt met Mavors-Stoet verheffen hunne Lancen,
Het vrolijk' Nimphe-dom bereyt U Eere-kransen;
En offert al de Maght aan Uwe heerschappy.
Het Klock-geklangh, en 't schel geluyt der Velt-Schalmeyen,
Kornetten, en Klaroen, slaan galmen in de Lught,
Wijl 't vliegent Solfer-werck vermaaklijk neemt de vlught,
Waar 't sigh met swermen weet, dan hier, dan daar te spreyen,
Dus siet men Hendrick, (en Aemilia, altans)
Verwellekoomen, die in Grunos weerbre Ermen,
Door 't Prinslijck Tucht-Swaart sal d'Onnoselheyt beschermen,
Daar Hy de Leyt-star is, en een bewalde Schans.
Daar hem met hant-geklap: de Scharrend' Ondersaten
Toe wenschen; dat door Hem (dien Braven Lauwer-helt)
De Vry bevryde-Staat, magh warden staagh herstelt,
En soo een Heerscher blijft, in 't Lant, der Lantsche-Staaten;

◆ ◆ ◆

Gesangh

Heaven's guardian cleanse you, crown you
Princess, while the guns' labouring metal
Births best wishes with a bang! And dwell
A long time in our fortress. Mars's attendants
Launching missiles guarantee our might
While all the nymphs weave splendid wreaths
Bespeaking dominion, and bells and shawms,
Cornets and horns reverberate beneath
The flying rockets sumptuously clustering,
Scattering – pledges of hospitality to
Hendrik and Amalia, always, in Groningen
Where the princely sword of law will defend
Innocence, for he is the star from which
We take our bearings, and he is our redoubt.
Permit the laugh, allow applause commending
This hearty champion worthy of his laurel
By whom our free and liberal state may stay
Restored, he sojourn here united always
With our pride, our United Netherlands.

◆ ◆ ◆

[13]

Gesangh der Groninger Maaghde-Rey.

Toon, Nymphes des Eaux.

Hoe Heerlijk bralt dien Puik-Son in het westen,
Hoe Lieflijk beflikkerts' het Princelijke hert,
Dat door haar Glans vermeestert wert,
    En waar op hy gaat vesten
Sijn gans vermogen, want dien Morgen Roos,
Die hy uit duisent aangenamen geuren koos,
    Die komt hier dan nog ten lesten,
Bestormen door 't minlijk gesigt:
Dien Helt, voor wien selfs Mavors swigt.
Plukt Mirthe-blaan, en groene Lauwerieren,
Bestrengel dit paar met Ydalisch cieraat,
Wijl Cipria geboogen staat
    Om haar voort op te cieren,
Ah! roeptse ah! mijn schoonheyt is nu niet,
Een andre Venus heeft dees Mars in haar gebiet
    Koom laat ons haar Feest-dag vieren
Wijl Anhalt, Nassauw is soo waart,
En Peleus, met sijn Thetis paart.

❖❖❖

Welkoom-groet aan WILHELM GEORG FRISO, By der Gratie Godts Prins van Nassauw, &c.

WElkoom gewenste Prins welkoom Wilhelm Georg,
Weest Friso wellekoom in Grunoos grijse muuren

                                                      Diens

Song of the young women of Groningen

Air: "*Nymphes des eaux*"*

As gorgeously burns your glorious sun
In the West, so brightly sparkles, too,
Your princely heart that in the sun's radiance
Finds its pattern when he celebrates
To the fullest of his powers because his
Rose of the morning, chosen from thousands
Of vessels of good scent, approaches to
Quench the fires of him who, stormed by that
Exquisite face, remains a hero before whom
Even Mars stops boasting. With Cyprian
Myrtle, Idalian laurels twine this pair.
All cry "My beauty is no more," for another
Venus has this Mars in her possession.
Come let us adore her feast day: Anhalt
By Nassau is cherished. Peleus has Thetis.

◆ ◆ ◆

Felicitations to Wilhelm Georg Friso, by the grace of God Prince of Nassau etc.†

Welcome longed-for Prince, welcome Wilhelm
Georg, be welcome Friso, welcome within
Groningen's grey walls whose sturdy locks

* "*Nymphes des eaux*" is a melody that may derive from Philippe Quinault and Jean-Baptiste Lully's opera *Atys* of 1676. Louis XIV adored this *tragédie en musique*. In the opera, the goddess Cybele transforms a mortal who scorns her love into a god and a pine tree. The island of Cyprus is endeared to Venus, and the town of Idalium is sacred to the goddess. Brongersma's own poem – retaining a mythological ambience, but subordinating tragedy – is the first of many in *The Swan of the Well* to draw on the melodies of Versailles for a template.

† Wilhelm Georg Friso, born in 1685, died the next year. Brongersma often uses the Biblical image of the flourishing cedar tree. A source for her allusion is Psalm 92:12: "The righteous shall flourish like the palm tree: he shall grow like a cedar in Lebanon."

[14]

Diens sterke grend'len zijn voor V een vaste Borg:
Wiens roem [al grimt de nijt] veel eeuwen sal verduuren.
Welkoom Nassauwse Spruyt, en eerst geboorne soon
Van Casimir, en van Aemilia: die waarde:
Dat puyk-heeld waarlijk wart te voeren staf, en kroon,
Wijl d'Eernaam van haar. Lof vervuld de ganse aarde.
Leef lang O! jonge Spruyt, was op tot heyl, en luk
Gelijk een Ceder-boom geplant in Sions dalen:
Groey, bloey in vreed, en al d'onheylen van ons ruk,
Op dat elk een mag in uw schaduw adem halen,
Plant hijr d'Olijve tak, en schenk haar vettigheyt.
O! kleyne Koester-Vorst: wijl u de Lauwerieren
Door V Al-ouwt geslagt voor lange sijn bereyt
Waar V de Fama mee begint te overswieren;
Den Hemel gun [die reets van uwe moet getuygt]
Dat gy de schreden volgt van V Doorlugte Oudren,
(En brave dapperheên, uyt volle teepels suygt,)
Die V het heldenkleed doen gaspen aan de schoudren,
Op dat g'als Jason wint de Deugt: dat gulden vagt,
En 't giftig Drakenest verdelgt door Dolk, en Degen,
Dat gy tot heul van 't Lant tot Wijsheyt wert gebracht,
Om soo de ware Kerk te hoên door 's Hoogsten zegen,
Wert een Ulisses (als Vvader) in beleyt,
Een Hercules in magt, en een Achil in 't strijden,
En stel V Groote Naam tot een onsterflijkheyt
Om Grunoos volkren, en der Friesen te bevrijden.

❖❖❖

Op het

Ensure for you a mighty fortress's renown
That (baulking grumbling Envy) will last long
Ages. Welcome, branch of Nassau and firstborn
Son of Casimir and of Amalia, the dear.
Glory tarries for your crown and guiding staff.
In her splendid name the whole world extols you.
Live long youthful scion, grow in health and
Like a cedar planted in Zion's dales
Prevail, flourish, mature in Peace, avert
All disaster from us so each and every
Person may draw under your shadow easy
Breath and plant her olive branch, dispense
Her fatness. *Mignon*, cute Prince, closely
Snuggled, your dynasty prepares you laurels
And Fame begins to whirl your name about.
Heaven says – precociously you show –
You follow in the footsteps of exalted elders
Sucking gallantry and valour from brimming
Nipples, clasping the vestments of a hero
To your shoulders, in future virtue a Jason
Assuming the Golden Fleece, stabbing dead
The toxic dragon – help to your land until
Wisdom governs and the true Church receives
The highest benediction. Be like your father –
Ulysses in policy, Hercules in strength,
Achilles in the field and keep your name
Imperishable, in protecting the liberty
Of Groningen and the Frisian people.

◆ ◆ ◆

[15]

Op het Panegyris of openbaar VREUGDEN-EEUW, Van de
vermaarde Academie tot Franeker, die den 29. Julij 1685.
Is ingewyt, en nu naa verloop van een Eeuw, op den
24. Septemb. 1685. gedachtenis wort gehouden. Als mede

Aan de Hoog en Doorgeleerde Heer, mijn Heer NICOLAUS
BLANCARDUS, Historischrijver des Graaflijkheydts van
Zeeland, &c. Ouste Professor in d'Unieerde Provincien eerste
R. Magnificus van de tweede Eeuw.

Laat vry de snege Frank, en 't deftig Spangien pralen,
De schrandre Britt, als ook den dapp'ren Itaaljaan.
Laat Duytsland met'er glans de wereld overstralen,
 En Holland flonk'ren als een nieuw ontwolkte Maan.
Laat dese pronken met geleerden in haar Rijken
 Op gulde Zetel pragt; 't beroemde Friesen-land
Hoeft met haar Hogeschool voor geen van dien te wijken,
 Want haar befaamt gerugt bromt uyt aan alle kant.
Hoe heerlijk heeft gebloeyd dien sitstoel aller wijsen,
 Waar Gods geleertheyt op de eerste Eertrans sat;
Waar Themis mild'lijk deed haar koesteringen spijsen:
 Terwijl de Heelkonst schonk sijn kostelijke schatt.
Wat oppermeesters sijn aan d'eerste tijd verscheenen?
 Wat ligten blonken doen Vorst Ludwigh stalen kling

              De

On the festal assembly, or public centennial
celebration, of the illustrious Academy at Franeker,
first inaugurated on 29 July 1585 and officially
commemorated on 24 September 1685 – dedicated
to the eminent and deeply learned Mr Nicolaus
Blancardus, historian of the Landgravate of Zeeland
etc., senior professor in the United Provinces and
first rector magnificus of Groningen's second century
in existence.*

Let French *esprit*, Spanish solemnity
Freely discourse – British sense, Italian
Gallantry, too. Let Germany brilliantly
Illuminate the world, Holland glisten
As a brightened moon escaping cloud.
Let them boast scholars expert in their fields,
Each on a gilded chair. Friesland renowned
Need not, given her College, acquiesce
To any contender. Her faculty evokes
Rumours of glory over the gossiping globe.
How this seat of learning has prospered where
Theology occupies the highest step,
Where Themis temperate, gentle, nurses her
Darlings, while medicine administers her
Priceless treasure. Tell what inspiring figures
Have flourished in our first century, after

* Blancard authored the epigram with which *The Swan of the Well*'s series of commendatory verses begins; his contribution echoes this poem, with its survey of national types. Themis, a consort of Zeus, personifies justice and (appropriately for Brongersma's occasion) summons assemblies. Since the poet marks the university's centennial, she looks back as far as 1585. Willem Lodewijk, stadholder of Friesland, managed to penetrate Spanish-held Breda in a peat barge, and to overwhelm the occupier's garrison. Victory in Groningen eventually followed. Peace with Spain was concluded by the Treaty of Münster, in 1648. Arrian, governor, friend of Hadrian, philosopher and historian, lived from 86 to 145 CE; he is most famous for his *Anabasis*, or *Journey Upcountry*. Theodore Beza, a church reformer, defended John Calvin.

[16]

De vrye Fries bevrijd'? wat Sonnen sijn verdweenen,
    Wiens ondergang als doen bragt veel verandering.
Daar nu dien Blancard komt dien lof cruyn op te streven
    Met arends wieken, nu de twede Eeuw begind,
Die door sijn yver doet Demosthenes herleeven,
    En waar het mensdom weer een Cicero in vind.
Daar van tuygd Arriaan, die Alexanders daden
    Ten top punt voerd; die gy, O grote Redenaar,
Door uw besneden schagt griefd in vergode bladen,
    En brengt d' onsterflijkheyt sijns naams in 't openbaar.
Wat Griek heeft ooyt geleeft, of wonder der Latijnen,
    Die gy niet hebt doorsnuft, en in het ligt gebragt?
Wat luyster hebt gy niet als een Apol doen schijnen
    Op Casimir, die als een Caesar werd geagt.
Gy wijt dan heylig in voor 't oog der Tabbert scharen
    Het vrolijk Eeuw-gety, waar dat de Lauwer-kroon
Als overwinnende bepruykt uw silvre hairen,
    (Heer Nicolaes) wijl gy beklimt de Eere-Throon.
Daar g'op het konst-slot, en 't cieraad der moed'ge Friesen
    Als Hoge-leeraar mee voor lang sijt ingehuld.
Daar g'op het kleyn Atheen elk 't grootste doet verkiesen,
    Wijl 't met een overvloed van kennis is vervuld.
Daar g' door uw lof-reen, en vertoog schaft honigraten,
    En 't luysterende rot een lekker oor-bankett;
Daar g'schenkt een mond-kost aan de greetge Letter vraten,
    Die gy hebt aan de diss van uw Parnas geset.
Waar de Catones, en de Bezaas 't all belonken,
    Waar Balden swieren, en Galenen besig zijn.
Waar Aristotelen staan in 'er rang geklonken,
    Wijl yder van hun smaakt der Goden Nectar-Wijn.

                                          Daar

Prince Lodewijk's steel freed the liberal Frisian?
What sun has sunk, whose setting altered all?
For Blancardus comes striving after that crown
Winged like an eagle as our second era starts
Who in zeal revives Demosthenes,
In whom we find another Cicero.
His resolve equals his Arrian's, who chronicled
Alexander's feats most excellently
Whom you, great editor, wielding shrewd pen
Inscribing divine pages, sent amended
Into the public sphere, to last forever.
What the Greek and what the Roman read
You too have read, all of it, and shared with us.
For Casimir you have like an Apollo
Polished splendours to more splendid lustre
Respecting that great author, like a Caesar.
Go then glorious in the eyes of the gowned,
The genial current of the age. You are best
And the laurel wreath sits well on your silver
Hair, most honourable Nicolaus, as you settle
Into the chair of merit. Abide long
In the castle of art – jewel of staunch
Frisians, our beloved professor.
In our little Athens all defer to the greatest
Overflowing with knowledge, panegyrics
Dripping like honeycomb, banqueting the ear.
On eager plates you offer food for the table
Of your Parnassus where Catos and
Bezas sparkle, where Baldwin glows and
Galen is busy and Aristotle will not budge
From his assured height and they sip the nectar
Of the gods on high, in bliss. There sage

[17]

Daar wijse Senecaas slaan met haar Engle tongen
    De vreugde-galmen uyt, wijl van het negen tal
Het blijde feest-lied wert door choor-maat op gesongen;
    Waar onder ik mijn lier op 't soetste stellen sal.
Die schoon geen Hemel-trant doet uyt haar tonen vloeyen,
    Maar pligtswijs voor uw kweeld, met wensing dat voortaan
't Roem rugtbre Boek paleys met uw in heyl mag groeyen,
    En op het metselwerk van Sions Bouw-heer staan.

◆ ◆ ◆

Aan de Hoog-geachte Juffer CLARA GERLACIUS.

Vergeef me dat ik V naa waarde niet kan roemen,
Alleen sal ik mijn gonst, u gonstig bieden aan,
En U O! Klara (: die men waarlijk klaar mag noemen)
Doen aan het sterren-hof by d'and're ligten staan.
V needrigheyt doet my een stoute daadt aanvaarden
Om V te nooden op de soom van dese Bron,
Waar 't Rots gevaart voor lang een klaare stroomâar baarde
Die noyt haar vlietend nat so waardigh schenken kon
Als nu, wyl 't Nimphedom gelyk de Son komt brallen
Op d'oever van de beek waar in het Swaantje singt
(Schoon het niet naar behoor V streeldt met beemel vallen)
Maar die V door haar stem nogh tot de wolken dringht.
En die een Lof-liedt sal (so lang haar tyt mag duyren)
Vytgalmen, en altoos van Vwe gaven nuyren.

◆ ◆ ◆

Aan

Senecas sing angelically echoing
Joy, the ninefold sisters choiring, among whom
I set my lyre in the sweetest place.
No adequate tones issue from its strings,
But possessed by love and duty still it
Vibrates with the wish that from now on
The palace of letters should augment the strength
Of its fame under your guidance, and I
Remain at hand while Zion's briskly building.

✦ ✦ ✦

To the highly esteemed Lady, Clara Gerlacius*

I could not possibly express your worth.
Allow me then the privilege of reverence.
Clara, how right that to address you always
Is to invoke the "clear," the "bright," the "famous."
You multiply lights in heaven, join the stars.
Your decency makes you countenance
The boldness of an invitation to my well's
Rim, where the rocks give birth to clear waters
Never before offering swift refreshment
So worthily as now, because an instance
Of nymphdom bright and clear as sunlight visits
The banks of the pool where this little Swan would
Falter, fail and fall short but that the theme
Of you transports her song to the very zenith.
Until she dies it will blare your talent's fame.

✦ ✦ ✦

\* Clara Gerlacius, daughter of Groningen's mayor Tjaard (or Tjaerd) Gerlacius, was born in 1658 and died in 1694. Adam Camerarius painted her with the mayor's other children in 1665. Brongersma's tribute manifests the poet's delight in punning on people's names.

[18]

Aan de seer ge-eerde Juffer OEDILIA SCHERFF.

Verwaardig my dat ik V eer-naam roem
O! braave Scherff, en dat ik V mag cieren
Met myn Gedigt, in plaats van Lauwerieren:
Of Myrthe groen, of Veen Pallas noem,
Want V verstandt toondt dat ghy zyt gebooren
Vyt Iovis breyn, dien grooten Blixem Voogdt.
Die niet alleen het meeste ront beoogdt
Maar die door V syn wond'ren brengt te vooren,
Soo sal ik dan (wyl ghy syn dochter zyt
O! schand're Geest, V gaaven eeuwig looven
En voeren die op wieken heen naar booven
Waar noyt het minst' van Uwe Deugt verslyt
Maar daar ghy aan het sterren dak sult praalen,
Gelyk een Son: die t' al kan overhaalen.

♦ ♦ ♦

Tamyris Koningin van Scythen, naa dat Cyrus Koning van Persen, gans Orienten, en den groot magtigen Konink van Babel had te onder gebragt, en haar eenige Soon: met de darde part van haar heyr had bedriegelijk verslagen, overwon Cyrus, het hem't hooft af kappen, doodt zijnde, sette dat in een bloedt-bat: om eens sat te drinken.

De Koninginne spreekt.

Waart't Cyrus niet genoeg dat gy gans Orienten
En Babel had verwoest? door 't staal? onsaad'bre gast,

Moest

To the admirable Odilia Scherff*

Forgive me for magnifying your name,
Gallant Scherff, and glorifying you
With a poem in lieu of laurels or green
Myrtle or – apter yet – the status of Pallas,
Since your mind attests your birth from Jove's
Own brain – great guardian of lightning who not
Only watches over the globe, but also
In you brought forth of himself a marvel. Therefore
Brilliant spirit, celestial daughter, I'll praise
You endlessly, and bear you up on wings
Where attrition will never wear away
Your virtue. You'll glitter in the starry vault
Like a sun to inspire everyone.

◆ ◆ ◆

After Cyrus the Persian had subdued the east,
including the king of Babylon, he used deception to
kill the son of Tomyris, the Scythian queen, and a
third of her army. Vanquishing the invader, she had
the man decapitated, and sank his head into a bag
of blood with the idea he could at last satisfy his lust
for that drink.†

The queen speaks

Cyrus, was it not enough to lay waste the east
And topple Babylon with your steel? Insatiable

* Odilia Scherff eventually married Winandus Fredell; a child was born to this couple in 1705. In the last and sixteenth of her book's prefatory verse dedications, Brongersma herself probably composed the praise of this woman's talents – again with a comparison to the intellectual goddess Minerva (otherwise known as Pallas Athena).

† Brongersma's long title functions like a history painting's. Herodotus relates that Cyrus captured Spargapises, the son of Tomyris, queen of the Massagetae, while that man lay stupefied with wine. Unless the tyrant released her son and withdrew to the limits of her territory, she promised to give Cyrus more blood to drink than even he could stomach. Tomyris found Cyrus's corpse, and fulfilled her threat by pushing the dead man's head into a skin brim with human blood. Herodotus says Tomyris sealed her oath by the chief divinity of the Massagetae, the sun. The preceding poem, to Odilia Scherff, an acquaintance of Brongersma's, features the same luminary, and perhaps gives a glimpse of how Brongersma went about ordering these particular poems. Ludolph Smids's poetic *Gallery* of famous women includes Tomyris.

[19]

Moest gy nog Woeden in mijn Ov'rige talenten
Naa gy mijn eenig Soon hadt al te snood verrast,
Doch weende daarom niet, maar stelde my te wreken
Aan U, die niet als door bedrog de zege won.
Ik heb U selver met mijn speren door doen steeken
En U met al U magt vernietigt, soo ik kon.
Ik heb U' t grimmig hooft van 't lichaam af doen klinken
Dat in een bloedt-bat staat tot aan de Ooren toe,
Op dat gy eens u dorst versaadt, en sat moogt drinken
Want gy dog nimmer waart van 't mensche moorden moê,
Daar bloethondt, daar suyp U rot brakens toe dan dronken,
Basuyn nu uyt wie dat U t'onder heeft gebragt,
Tamyris is't die met U Lauw'ren sig sal pronken:
En kronen met haar daadt het vrowelijk geslagt.

◆ ◆ ◆

De Grieksche HIPPO springt gemoedigt in de baren: om de Roovers te ontkomen, liever willende met eerc sterven, als in schande, en slaafs te leeven.

WIe sal O! Griekse maagt, V daadt trompetten?
Wat Triton sag ooyt moediger Siereen
'T gevaar ontsnappen van haar schakers netten,
Schoon hy beoogt het hol der diepste Zeen.
Wat moet O! Hippo heeft V hert doen stijven?

Ah!

Guest must you rage, invading all remaining
To me – talents, thoughts, mental strength? You
Ambushed my son. I did not weep. I plotted
My revenge on you, who won only by a ruse
That triumph. My hand thrust the killing spear,
And you, with all your might, I reduced to nothing
Insofar as human beings can. I had
Your envious head severed from your torso
And plunged it in a pouch of blood up to the ears
So you could glut your thirst, finally full.
Bloodhound, dog of loathing, you didn't tire
Of murder's gore. Now drink until you puke.
Don't forget to sound the horn insisting "Mission
Accomplished" – by me, Tomyris, laurels
Wrested from you, to wreath womankind.

◆ ◆ ◆

Greek Hippo springs courageously into the salt
barrens of the sea to escape pirates, willing to die
rather than live in shame and slavery*

Woman, who will trumpet your deed? Say what
Triton, disentangling Siren snared
In fishing net, more bravely dove down into
The deepest nether brine? Hippo, how firm
Your heart, though barren ocean tossed you

---

\* Giovanni Boccaccio in his *Famous Women* says Hippo was a Greek who saved herself from rape by pirates by casting herself into the ocean. Her body washed up on the shores of Ionian Erythrae; people there revered her tomb. Brongersma's allusion elsewhere to figures such as Tancred suggests her familiarity with Boccaccio's writings – possibly through Ludolph Smids's. Boccaccio died in 1375.

## [20]

Ah! vreesde gy 't gewelt der baren niet?
Hoe dorst ge, op die wreede baren drijven?
Maar't waar dat V de wanhoop daar toe riet,
V kuysheyt waar V waardiger als 't leeven;
Dat dagte gy, dog't is ook 't grootste schat,
En 't deftigste juweel, maar gy moest sneeven
Elendige, en stikken in het nat.
Waar van d'Attische strandt noch kan getuygen.
En bergt u Lichaam in haar dorre schoot.
Sy koomt de tranen: om u ramp te suygen
Van d'Oevers af, en treurt mee om u doot,
De Philosoofsche, en Poëtische klangen
Die dreunen noch door 't hooren van de faam
Op tonen van Atheensche maat gesangen
't Geen maakt V een omstervelijke naam.

◆◆◆

Aan de konst-lievende Juffer Me-juffer JOHANNA FOLCKERS

Het schijnt dat gy Minerv' haar goude draân,
En't weef-tuyg, met de konst-riem hebt ontdragen,
Wijl dat ik haar verstoordt sie heene gaan
Naar't Negen-tal: om die haar noodt te klagen.
Neen, neen ik mis, sy vraagt het Susterschap
(Die het Parnas met reyen gaat vercieren)

Om

Heaving inhuman waves all salt. Despair
Solicited you: integrity outweighed
Mere life. What is treasure? Pirate gangs
Like it – like to rape: a woman's booty.
Groan instead, suffocate and thrash.
An Attic shore-grave closes up your corpse
In its barren lap. Your disaster draws
Tears from my eyes. May I nurse the thought
Of you here on the coast, and lament
Your death? Philosophy and Poetry
Drone and pound like the surf, as in your time,
With just the note the Athenian sang. Who is
Fit to make Hippo's reputation deathless?

♦ ♦ ♦

To the art-loving Miss Johanna Folckers\*

Minerva snatches your golden yarn, your weaving
Loom with its cunning strap, in a huff going
Off to the Muses, to complain about her plight.
No. I have it wrong. She asks that sisterhood
(Who dignify Parnassus with their chorus)

---

\* Minerva jealously excelled not just in intellectual power, but also in the art of weaving – as Ovid's story of her challenger Arachne makes famous. Arachne's tapestry superbly depicted the devious loves of the gods. Once struck by the enraged goddess, Minerva's rival hanged herself. The goddess saved Arachne, however, by suspending her at her loom – as a productive spider. Brongersma entertains briefly a conventional idea of the volatile and petty goddess: then grants her Minerva magnanimity.

[21]

Om U te stellen op de boven-trap:
Daar Sy U wil bepruyken met Lauwrieren.

♦♦♦

Op het geestig borduyren van Juffer ELISABETH JOLY.

Arachne heeft het Lof van V geweven,
En naar de konst in haar tapeet gedreven,
Hoe gy altans als een Apelles maaldt,
Wanneer g'een Lent' doet planten door V naaldt
Op 't zijdeveldt, en hoe V vinger greepen
Met goudtdraadt om festoen, en kringels sleepen,
Soo dat de Konst-Godin sig acht gehoondt,
Doch tegens dank V met haar Lauwren kroont.

♦♦♦

Op het aardig dansen, singen, en speelen, van de H.Ed.G. Juffer ANGENIS De BESCO.

SONNET.

Staa Cypria! U sool begint te kraken,
Gy danst niet op de maat, seyt Momus, maar
De Besco doet de zaal door 't swieren blaken:
En sweeft op het een blik der schimmen waar.
Gy Callioop houw op van 't heesche galmen,

't Is

To place you on the highest step, where they
Will set the woven laurel on deserving brows.

❖ ❖ ❖

On Miss Elisabeth Joly's ingenious embroidery\*

Arachne has woven a visual hymn to you –
Tapestry after the example you set, an Apelles
In graphic skill when you sow a springtime
On the silken meadow, knotting yellow thread
In circlets and festoons so the very goddess
Of this art, itching to scoff, can only rule
You merit the crown that (look) she twists for you.

❖ ❖ ❖

On the most noble, honourable Miss Angenis de Basco's enchanting dancing, singing and playing†

Sonnet

"Stand aside, Cyprian goddess: in dance
You are no peer," mocks Momus, "of Miss de Basco
Who blazes through the hall floating, whirling
On the eye, with the grace of a vision. Hold
Your peace, Calliope, don't shrill in song

\* Elisabeth Joly, Brongersma's most frequent poetic addressee, here receives the mingled tribute of the victimized Arachne and the reluctantly generous Minerva. Apelles (Alexander the Great's favourite painter) was reckoned by the ancients to be the supreme artist in his medium. The floral motif recalls *The Swan of the Well*'s program poem.

† A son of Night, Momus is, from the time of Hesiod forward, the god of satire. The *allemande* originated, as the name suggests, in Germany. To perform this processional dance, couples formed a line, extended their paired hands forward, and paraded back and forth with stately steps. Brongersma alternates between dismissing and embracing the Greek and Roman pantheon.

[22]

't Is Sy die U in't singen overwint,
En ciert haar tuyt met U gewonnen palmen,
Waar meê Sy ook haar blonden lokken bint.
Terpsichora gy moogt U vingers nijpen,
En't blanke Elp met angst, en vrese grijpen,
Wijl dat een Nimf', of eer een aarts Godin
U steld ten toon, die 't luyst'rend oor komt streelen
Wanneer se gaat een Alamande speelen,
En voerdt daar door tot lof haar prijskroon in.

♦ ♦ ♦

Op het aardig kante naayen van Doek, van Juffer MARIA JOLY.

GY zijt gewis de konst school door getreden,
Wijl gy van doek een bloem-perk hebt gewrogt.
En weet daar of door' t puntig staal te smeeden
Het swierend' Loofwerk, waar wert in gebrogt
't Graveersel van de vond uyt V gebooren,
Doch sal daar voor goet-aardige Mary
V op mijn Lier de Loftoon laten hooren:
En kransen V met mijne Poëzy.

♦ ♦ ♦

Op het

For Miss de Basco sounds far sweeter, decking
Herself with the palm she won from you,
In her blonde hair disposing it. Terpsichore,
White with fear, must want to pinch her fingers
Who touches the ivories, since a nymph or, rather,
Earthly goddess shows exactly how to play
The *allemande* – so exquisite to listeners
She takes in this department, too, the crown."

♦ ♦ ♦

On Miss Maria Joly's delightful lace stitching
of a picture*

Who would doubt your education in art,
Planting a flowerbed in a linen cloth
With a thread and steel needle swooping
In lines as fine as those of an engraving?
Such is your skill for which, interesting
Mary – good Mary – my lyre resounds its praise
Crowning you thus with a garland of words.

♦ ♦ ♦

\* Brongersma begins a series of
complimentary epigrams, dedicated
(it would seem) to members of
Elisabeth Joly's family.

[23]

Op de konstig kappe, en nette-strikken van
Juffer MAGDALENA JOLY.

Gy weeft, en knoopt van zy, en nette-garen
Veel strikjes t'saam, en breydelt tot cieraat
De wuffe golvjes van U bruyne hairen,
Daar 't uytgespan op hersen-standers staat:
Waar uyt een bron van gaven komt gevlooten,
Die niet alleen de nieuwe vondt omvat
Die Pallas volle kruyk heeft uyt gegooten,
Maar die U oversproeyt, en drenkt in 't nat,
So dat gy niet alleen weet wel te stricken
Maar door U geest, een ijder doet verquikken.

◆ ◆ ◆

Op de snege geest, van Juff. J.J. CARBON.

SWijg Hermes, en Rethorica houw stil,
Of duyk vry onder 't schaauw van velt gordijnen:
Hier leyt V roem, en achting in geschil,
Nu dat Carbon haar reden-glans laat schijnen,
Gelijk een Son, die in de dageraat
Haar stralen schiet, om d'afgerolde droppen
Te lekken van het kruyt, en Lely knoppen:
Waar op haar ruchtbre naam gesneden staat.
Want Sy behoeft de Taal-godt niet te wijken
Nog Cypris selfs, waar van se d'Eer komt strijken.

◆ ◆ ◆

Aan

On the ingenious cap and veil contrived by
Miss Magdalena Joly*

You have woven and tied together a headpiece
Of many threads connected, quaint caparison
For the crisp little curls of your brown hair
Distinguishing the thatchwork of that deep mind
Out of which your talent springs that not alone
Devises this chic invention issuing from
Pallas Athena's full jug: since your every thought
Gushes, refreshes. Just the art of hat-making? Over-
Flowing genius, you invent floods of pleasures.

◆ ◆ ◆

On Miss J.J. Carbon's nimble mind†

Quiet down, Hermes. Rhetoric, be silent
Or creep behind the curtains Natura weaves.
Carbon has won the debate, and is the greater
Controversialist, contrarian, orator –
A sun that at break of day shoots her rays
To lick the rolling dewdrops from leaves
And buds of lilies. Her reputation is secure
And she should cede neither to the god
Of smooth talk nor to the Cyprian goddess,
From whom she snatches our acclamations.

◆ ◆ ◆

\* This poem fuses into a single argument two images favoured by Brongersma throughout her book: the art of weaving and the element of water. The former belongs traditionally to the female sphere, as a chore and an avocation: the latter, to the physiography of Friesland and the habitat of swans.

† Possibly a compositor's error renders the surname of a relative of Mattheus Gargon, one of Brongersma's supporters, as "Carbon."

THE SWAN OF THE WELL ◆ 95

[24]

Aan de sneege en seer Ge-Eerde Juffer JOHANNA CATHIUS.

'K Heb lang gewenst haa! Cathius te pronken
Met V gewijde naam op het papier,
Omwonden met een telg van Lauwerier
Die V voor lang van Phoebus is geschonken,
Waar V de Sang-rey sal doen onder brallen:
Wijl gy, sijn Nigt, (uyt Pallas breyn geteeldt,)
De Eer verdient, die selfs V selfs vereelt.
Door minlijkheeden, en noch boven allen
Sult zijn bekranst, dees last is my gegeven,
Neemt dan niet qualijk dat ik V bekroon
Met mijn gedigt; het is der wijsen loon
Te werden opgeciert, en soo verheeven.

♦ ♦ ♦

Aan de konst-lievende Juffer J.V.B.

WAarom verschuylt U Sonne-Schijn
In 't hol van Pontus baaren;
Schuyf op het schaam geverft gordijn,
Laat vrees haar kroost bewaaren.
Vertoon met Febus u paruyk,
Die schijnt van goudt te blinken:
Met hem U glansig oog ontluyk,
En laat de moet niet sinken,

            Want

To the witty and greatly esteemed
Miss Johanna Cathius*

I want to boast about you, Cathius,
Putting your lucky name on paper
Wound together with some laurel
Bestowed a while ago by Phoebus
Whose choir, too, will brag of you
Since you – his niece – burst out
From Pallas's brow, and earned
Your glory before he came around,
And entirely without him. Your grace
Above all wins the prize. The pleasure
Is mine – patience with the poem
Crowning you. Consider it the right
Of the highly gifted to receive gifts.

❖❖❖

To the art-loving Miss J.V.B.

Why hide your light in the depths of the sea?
Push aside Humility's painted curtain.
Leave obsessive Fear to monitor her spawn.
Show with Phoebus your face. With him
Blossom and sparkle. Courage! Your own

---

\* Brongersma adapts Greek myth for her own purposes. Zeus swallowed Metis after a prophecy foretold she would bear a son greater than him. Hephaestus wielding an axe relieved Zeus's subsequent physical agony by splitting open his forehead. Athena sprang out: an intellectual birth. Here the poet imagines an acquaintance emerging from Athena's brow, a conceit that dilutes the paternal legacy – as does the de-emphasis on Apollo.

[25]

Want selfs U Geest die dringt U aan,
Daarom doorsnuft de boeken,
Soo sal ik meet e beurte staan,
En U met Rijm besoeken.

♦ ♦ ♦

Aan de seedige Hoog ge-eerde Juffr. BARBERA SYGERS.

'K Souw wel wensen V te noden
Op het Rijm-banket der Goden,
En op Pegaas lekkerny,
Maar dewijl gy door de wolken
Soekt het heyldigt aller tolken
Vyt een Hemels Poezy:
Sal ik V daar mee niet moeyen.
Maar hoop dat gy soo moogt groeyen,
Als een Ceder aan de Soom
Van een Beek, en dat een zegen
V ten vollen sy verkregen,
En bestort een vreede stroom
Vyt gegoten van hier boven,
Dat gy reden hebt te loven
Hem, die naa sijn raats besluyt,
V daar toe heeft uyt gekosen:
Wijl ghy pronkt in Sarons Rosen,
En steekt boven and'ren uyt.

♦ ♦ ♦

Op het

Soul drives you to put your nose in every book.
I want a part of that: and write these words
Knowing you are a reader – and will read them, too.

◆ ◆ ◆

To the virtuous and highly respected
Miss Barbera Sygers*

I would like, a lot, to invite you
To the rhyme-feast of the gods,
To sample Pegasean sweets:
But given that, from your eminence
In the clouds, you parse already
Every interpreter, chapter and verse,
Should I be so rash? Let me at least
Wish you may flourish as a cedar
On the banks of a river and win
The fullest triumph, peace streaming
Like that river only because you choose
To praise God, in accordance with His
Wisdom. Flaunt therefore the Rose
Of Sharon that outshines all the others.

◆ ◆ ◆

* Annelies de Jeu says Barbera Sygers lived from around 1660 to 1690. The Song of Solomon declares "I am the rose of Sharon, and the lily of the valleys" (2:1). Some identify this plant as a hibiscus, others as a variety of tulip. The Old Testament generally associates cedar trees with moist locales.

[26]

Op het geestig boetseeren, in Was, van Juffer JUDITH JOLY.

DOe dan Pomoon het masker van de Oogen
Op dat se siet wie haar de roem ontrekt:
't Is Judith die door wonderlijk vermogen.
De fruythoorn heeft voor elkx gesigt ontdekt,
En toondt een kriek, een pruym, een peer, citroenen
Dog ijder aan sijn rank, en d'holle vrugt
Gemengelt onder een aan Loof festoenen,
Waar op de fama slaat haar lof-gerugt,
En wil dat ijder haar ter eer sal vlegten
Een Tuyltjen, om dat op haar kruyn te hegten.

♦ ♦ ♦

Op het geestigh bloeme maken van Iuffer CATHARINA JOLY.

Ik sie de bloem-Godes ter schuyl gekropen,
En bloost nu sy V korfjes siet gevuldt
Met Lely, en gemaakte Rose knopen,
Waar mee gy hebt V hairlok opgehuldt,
Natuir staat stom, en schaam-roodt, wijl de bladen
Geformt zijn als Laurier, soo ongemeen
Dat Febus selfs verbaast, wie kan versaden
Het oog in dees V konst, daar niet alleen
Sig menschen; maar haar Goden in verwond'ren
Die tot V Eer dit komen uyt te dond'ren:

En roe-

On Miss Judith Joly's skilled clay and wax models

Unfasten the blindfold from Pomona's eyes
So she can see the glory ebbing from her:
Cornucopian Judith depicts the horn
Of plenty – cherry, plum, pear, and lemon
Curvy, each with its proper leaf attaching
Mixed with others in festoons so charming, Fame
Ripens quickly, spreads the suggestion, "Now
Let us gather flowers, weave the bouquet
Into the garland Judith merits and will wear."

❖ ❖ ❖

On the inventive flower-making of Catharina Joly

I see the goddess of flowers bend and blush
Spying little baskets you filled to the top
With lilies and with artificial rosebuds
With which you have secured locks of hair.
Nature is dumbstruck, flustered red at leaves
Formed perfectly after the precedent of
Apolline laurels, so well, in fact, Phoebus
Blinks astonished. Mortals glut their eyes
On these, your works of art, but gods also

[27]

En roepen t'saam haa! Katharijn gy zijt
Een Flora, en een wonder van ons tijt.

♦ ♦ ♦

**LOF GESANG**

Assen Lusthof, Pronck Valeye
    Daar de Drentsche Bos' Godt pan
Met sijn Canna gaat ter Reye
    By de braafste Nimfies, van
Haar gehugt, langs digte boomen
    Daar het vlietend' Beekie rilt
En sijn dertelende stromen
    Over 't hanged' Tackie tilt.
Daar de Schaapjes aan de Heyde
    Overgroeyt met Loof, en kruyt
Knabblen't geurigs't uyt de weyde,
    Waar soo menig Balsum Spruit
Laage water valtjes decken
    Daar de klim de Eycke kust
Om't gedagt ten Top te trecken
    En te strelen in die Lust.
Daar men bettjes spreyt van bloemen
    Om met Psiches Rust, in schaauw
Van't geboomt, die Plaats te roemen,
En't bedruypen van den Daauw
Daar de Harders Rose kransen
    Vlegten, elk sijn Hoederin,

Waar

Come to gawp and thunder their approbation
Crying "Catharine! Flora! Marvel of our time."

◆ ◆ ◆

A song of praise*

Pleasure garden of Assen, glorious valley
Where sylvan Drenthe's Pan to the summons
Of his reed pipe dances rounds with nymphs
Petite and debonair, abiding by thick-trunked
Trees where the river's glimmer gushes
Lapping sweeping overhanging branches,
Where lambs on heath all dense with grasses
And with herbs crop aromatic leafage
So many soothing simples sprouting, riffles
Creasing standing water, where oaks kiss
Air, dilate their crests' dimension, and long
Boughs loosely stream in rangy
Space, and people strewing beds of petals
Rest like Psyche and Amor in the shade,
Dew dropping, herdsmen winding rosy
Wreaths each keeping watch and sighing in

* This energetic loco-descriptive poem mixes observation with the desire to outdo canonical landscapes. Pindus designates a mountain range in northwest Greece. Enipeus is a river. Homer calls its waters the most beautiful of any on earth. Oreads are nymphs of the high places. Assen is a small city south of Groningen, originally constructed around a nunnery, close to Borger and to the *hunebed* that Brongersma elsewhere commemorates. Her supporter Johan Jacob Monter lived there.

[28]

Waar sy onder groene Transen
    Sugten klagen van de min.
Daar men Orfeus Lier hoor klincken
    Op de maat van Hemel sang
In wiens vreugt sig souw verdrincken
    Selfs Leernesse water-Slang,
Pisa souw haar wout verlaaten
    Met de kuise Iageres
Oreas haar Bergen haaten
    En het steyl gekruynt Cipres.
Pindus 't struiklig velt vergeeten,
    Iason liet het Gulde Vlies,
Enipeus souw sijn geseeten
    Stil, by 't Popelige bies
Om met d'Asser Heyligheden
    Op de Loff kar van het Lant
Zegepralende te treeden,
    Wijl het is der Goden Plant.

◆◆◆

Het lof van Assen

Roemt dan Achaïa nog op 't Trotse bos Stymfaal!
Ik roem veel meerder van de Asser hooge Eyken
Geen Tempe (schoon s'haar lof doet steyg'ren in Tessaal)
Of Lyceosche Berg, noch Pergus kan bereyken
Dit Lust prieel: maar in Astreé haar adem schept
En uyt die Bron-aar met de Drentsche Themis lept.

                                               Daar

Green arcades such sad amours, and Orphean
Strings vibrate and illustrate Uranian
Love, felicity in which Lake Lerna's
Dire hydra might drown, Pelops give
Up all his rage, the Oread of stark
Hauteur scorn mountain altitudes
With cypress adorned askew, Jason forget
The Golden Fleece and Pindus resign the shrubby
Plain and Enipeus renounce his lovely seat
Beside the lowly rushes to climb aboard
The cart of praise with Assen's blessed, to prance
Proclaiming triumph, for here we find God's
Personal plantation.

❖ ❖ ❖

The praise of Assen

Boast, Achaea, Stymphalia's proud wood.
I praise more ardently Assen's lofty oaks.
No Tempe, the wonder of Thessaly,
Or Lycaean peak, or Sicilian Pergus can surpass
This bower of bliss: Astraea breathes easy
Wading spring-fed waters with Drenthe's
Themis. There they relax, where sumptuous

[29]

Daar 't dertle, en 't weelderig loof sig breydelt top in top,
En daar men Philomeel de kruynen siet bespringen
Wanneer de soete Lent doet gorgelen haar krop
En op de topjes laat haar eygen veltdeun singen,
Daar 't Lommerige Wout de Nimfjes strekt tot dak
En kranst haar hoofden meer als Dafnes Lauwertak.

Laat Sperchius vry met de populiere kroon
Sig pronken, die de soom van sijne vliet doet groeyen,
Laat Pan de pijnboom mee verheffen tot sijn Troon
En Syrings Rietpijp op sijn ackers maar doen loeyen,
Het schelle Keeltje van den Asser Nagtegaal
En 't Bloemrijk dal, verpogt, en dooft het Altemaal.

♦ ♦ ♦

Aan de wijs-giergige Juffer EUPHEMIA MECHTELDT
SCHYR-BEECK.

EUPHEMIA 'Vaart, V geest, en Goet gerugt
O! wijs-begeer'ge Maagt slaan galmen in de lugt,
En dringen midden door de t' saam getrokken swerken
Wijl V de fama draagt op uytgespannen vlerken,
Want waar de Leersugt heerst, daar bloeyt de weten schap.
En streeft tot boven aan de steyle Hoef-vliets trap.
Waar Phaebus liersang wert ten wolken op gedreven
Wiens Hemel-vallen doen de starveling herleeven,

En

Foliage fuses trees by their tops. Philomela
Darts from bough to bough when vernal sweetness
Fills her mouth with gurgling song and from
The branch-ends she whistles rustic music
Where the nymph is roofed in forest shade
Rewarding her more richly, far, than Daphne's
Famous laurel. Let Sperchius* vaunt his poplar
Crown rooted on the banks of his fine flood.
Let Pan the pine tree elevate to a throne
And Syrinx's reed squeal of her loamy domain.
The clear throat of Assen's nightingale and
The vale heavy with flowers must prevail:
One out-sings, the other out-scents all rivals.

◆ ◆ ◆

To the ever-curious Miss Euphemia
Mechteldt Schyr-Beek

Euphemia, may your quick wits and obvious
Goodness find an echo far and wide
Storming heaven from below. For Fame
Extends wings and ascends since where
The hunger for learning is urgent there

* Sperchius is a river – and a river god – of Thessaly. It originates on the heights of Pindus.

[30]

En rucken uyt de borst een hert vol greetigheyt
Ten aan sien tot de Konst, en yder maakt bereydt:
Om door de kennis tot volkomentheyt te raken.
Klim dan, Mechtildes, wilt die klare beek genaken,
Slorp heyl'ge dropen uyt die Christaline Bron,
En suyg de stroom-aar leeg van Grunoos Helicon,
Leert daar met Pegaâs op Parnas V vlugge pennen
Opregten, en V voor de thiende Musa kennen.

✦✦✦

An de Amstelsche Puky Bloem Jr. KATHARINA LESCAILJE op het versoek, my enige van haar Ed. Versen te senden.

SONNET.

Gewyde Roos, Godinne aller Bloemen,
Die op de soom van Amstels Y-Bron bloeydt,
En weeldrig op Apolloos sang berg groeydt,
V sullen al de spruyten heylig noemen.
V malse blatjes vol bevalligheyt
Verquikken 't blakend' Hert, en sijn gereegen
Aan 't snoer van Artzeny, en Cypris Zegen,
Wijl haar de prijs door V wier toe geleydt.
Wanneer 's op Ida souw het Vonnis halen,
En gy O! Perel-bloem der Zuyder dalen
Vergun dat ik my in V geuren queek,
Ruk maar een knop (schoon 's is van 't minste blosen)
Ter zijden af, (haa puyk van Gijsbregts roosen:)
Die ik te pronk dan op mijn boesem steek.

✦✦✦

Aan

Blooms erudition and it reaches
Higher, after heights where the horse's
Well is flowing and, to the strings of Phoebus,
Song rises, likewise. The leavings, even,
Lapsing down, revive the starving and make
The pent heart beat almost free of the breast
Breaking in its ardour for art, inspiring
All to reach completeness, passion inquiring.
Climb then, Mechteld: disturb the clear stream:
Gulp blessèd mouthfuls from the glassy spring,
Suck dry the streamlet of Groningen's
Helicon. With Parnassian Pegasus
Study, wings lifted: you're the tenth Muse.

♦ ♦ ♦

To the marvelous flower of the Amstel, Miss Katharina Lescailje, on her sending a few noble verses to me*

Sacred rose, goddess of flowers,
That blooms on Amstel's banks, by the
Wellspring of IJ, and blows on
Mountain slopes of Apolline song,
Holy ought all your shoots to be called.
Your petals and leaflets full of charm
Quicken the blazing heart, and strung
In the Healer's garden they wreathe
The Cyprian's triumphs. On Ida she
Wears you when she would win
The contest. Pearl of flowers of southern
Vales, wrench a silken bud, even the least
Of them. Gem of Gijsbrecht's spoils, Glamour
Herself fastens you to my breast.

♦ ♦ ♦

* Katharina Lescailje lived from 1649 to 1711. The posthumous publication of Lescailje's two books of poetry and one of drama translated from French was intended to counter the financial loss to her family when the privilege of printing plays was taken from them in 1731. Brongersma may incidentally allude to dramatist Joost van den Vondel's 1638 *Gysbreght van Aemstel*. Vondel's play is set during the siege of Amsterdam in 1304. A speech from that drama may have influenced Brongersma's sonnet: "Ah, hedge-rose, a breath from your red mouth – a little light from your soul – my rose, my dawn hour. Stir my faint spirit as a wind caresses the garden." Vondel was a friend of the Lescailje family. The Cyprian goddess is Venus; the Healer, Apollo. The Amstel and the IJ are the celebrated rivers of Amsterdam.

[31]

Aan Juffr. S.T.H. Haar nodende by mijn Swaantje aan de Bron te koomen.

Ey Swaantje laat mijn Swaan niet sonder Swaantje roeyen,
Maar wilt u haastelyk by haar in't brontje speyen,
Het wagt V daar met smert, want 't swemt niet graag alleen,
Sprey uyt V wiekjes, en drijf op u Pluymtjes heen,
Gy sult haar sekerlijk in't eensaam sijn verligten:
En my, V TITIA daar door te seer verpligten.

◆ ◆ ◆

Replijk op het aardig en sinrijk Vers, van de Hoog-geleerde
Heer LUD. SMIDS
Med: Doctor tot Groningen doen ter tijt

WAt liefde draagt gy tot de Nijt
Koont gy de afgunst selfs om ermen?
Kan Ys een hete, borst ververmen,
Wat liefde draagt gy tot de Nijdt
En haar te strelen sijn verblijdt
Gy siet de gladd, en grof vergifte kringel slangen
Met bossen in'er hair, soo vuyl en dik beslijmt,
En nog koont gy haar aan die etter schouders hangen
  Om kussen die bemorste wangen:
  Waar aan gy avregts sijt gelijmt
My dunkt nu dat gy hebt de blintheyt in U oogen
  Ey, vaag de Vliesen af,

            Waar

To Miss S. T[er] H[orst], an invitation to come visit
the Swan of the Well\*

Darling Swan, don't leave my Swan paddling
All alone. Come and splash with her in the well
Even if it causes you a little bit
Of trouble. She does despise solitary
Swims, so spread your wings and float on them
In flight to relieve her singularity
Obliging me, too – your lonely Titia.

♦ ♦ ♦

Reply to the perceptive, beguiling verses of the most
learned Mr Ludolph Smids†

What kind of love can conciliate spite?
Can you actually embrace Envy, in person?
Can ice thaw, really, to a warm heart? What kind
Of love could soothe, caress ill will? You, sir,
Ride the shoulders of the sneaky, slippery,
Crass and toxic serpent tangled, foul and
Thick with muck, and kiss, sir, its caked cheeks
Though it defiles you, despite your valour. You can't
See properly. Your judgement wears blinders.

\* The invitation poem is a genre of long standing. Catullus and Horace practised it. Here "Swan of the Well" may be the name of Brongersma's house as well as a stand-in for the poet herself and for literary conversation – a home and a source of inspiration at one and the same time.

† Ludolph Smids's poem in honour of *The Swan of the Well* humorously pleads Smids's poetic exhaustion and ineptitude. Brongersma's verses may partake of similar facetiousness. The commonplace of literary envy (*livor* in Ovid and other Roman poets) comes up often in *The Swan of the Well*. To embrace envy is paradoxical because no manoeuvre can placate it. Brongersma rejects Smids's apparent premise. She praises, however, the artfulness with which the intention has been expressed.

[32]

Waar is U verstant gevlogen
'K vrees gy hebt U selfs bedrogen
Want gy delft U eygen Graf,
Het schijnt gy stelt U vreugt in U verdriet te maken,
Gy quetst U met U eygen naaldt,
En selfs een wond vol afschriks haaldt,
Ik moet U grote dwaasheyt laken,
Dus wert ge dan tot loon voor gout, met loot betaalt.

✦✦✦

De Wanhopende Canens

HElaas is Picus dan niet meer te vinden
Heeft Circe hem verandert in een Spegt,
Wel aan ik sal dan weer om mijn Beminde
Doen Blijken dat ik ben voor hem opregt.
Heeft sijne trouw: haar ontrou soo geschonden
Dat hy de straf onnosel dragen moet,
Soo heeft hy dan aan my sijn trouw gevonden
Die om hem stort een brakke trane vloedt
Aan dese Tiber, die het vogt sal mengen
In sijne vliedt, ah! Picus, Canens smelt:
Sy voelt haar af gemat door 't nat te plengen
En in een Mist-wolk om V min gestalt.

Ah! wat is schoonheyt, Iuegt, en wel te singen
Niet als een rook, in haar veranderingen.

✦✦✦

Aan-spraak.

Gy hebt dan snoode tover-boel
Mijn Picus soeken te verleyden,

En

You've fooled yourself. You as good as dig
Your grave. Your goodness increases your distress.
You prick yourself with your own needle,
And give yourself a disgusting wound. I would
Love to laugh at your absurdity and so
Give you in exchange for your perfect gold, lead.

◆ ◆ ◆

The Despairing Canens*

Picus, oh, has vanished: Circe has changed him
Into a woodpecker. Should I prove my love,
Prove I am his sincerely? Can I trust his
Loyalty? Her wantonness disfigured it, or
Transfigured it. Must my innocent endure
The punishment? Though I cannot find him
I embody in human shape his faithfulness yet,
Which, on his behalf, drips and pours salt tears
By godly Tiber, who mixes in his flood
My essence – for Picus! Dearest, your Canens
Melts now and mists away shedding herself,
Turned into fluid, into fog, out of love for you.
Grace, youth, a singing voice – what are they? –
Her metamorphosis leaves only pale air.

◆ ◆ ◆

Canens reproaches Circe†

You filthy cauldron of magic, have you
Injured Picus and parted him from me

* Ovid tells the story of Picus and Canens in the fourteenth book of his *Metamorphoses*. Picus, son of Saturn, king of Latium, loved the nymph Canens, whose song possessed almost Orphic power: *rara quidem facie, sed rarior arte canendi*, "Rare in looks, that's true – yet rarer still her talent for singing" (14.337). But the enchantress Circe lusted after Picus. She got him alone by enticing him to chase a phantom boar. He refused Circe, so she converted him into a woodpecker. Ornithologists still call the woodpecker family the *Picidae*. As for Canens, Circe let her waste away, lamenting, into thin air. Ovid compares this death to a swan's. Thus Brongersma's animal familiar or alter-ego obliquely adorns the bleak story: *Verba sono tenui moerens fundebat: ut olim / Carmina iam moriens canit exequialia cygnus*, "She was pouring out her words in her grief in a soft voice – as a swan, while dying, is said to sing its own eulogy" (429-30). Brongersma usually sees Circe as malevolent.

† Canens's name means "the singing woman." Though her song has the power to move inanimate things, still this nymph is stifled by the magical daughter of Helios. Many of Brongersma's poems feature male powers oppressing female personnel: the figure of Circe alters that emphasis. As for the woodpecker, Romans considered it a bird sacred to Mars. It fed Romulus and Remus. Augurs paid the behaviour of woodpeckers special attention. Brongersma refers later in her collection, in a poem to the Baroness van Heerema, to Canens.

[33]

En droevig van my af doen scheyden
    Waar om ik my vol pijnen voel.
Mijn soet gesang wel eer gepresen
    Dat herde rotsen murwen kon.
    Waar 't bos sig door bewogen von,
En vloeden stilde hoe hooch geresen,
    Doch daar ik mijn geminde Lief
Her hert op 't meeste mee kon strelen,
(Het geen hem dogt de ziel te ontstelen)
    Dat waer, als ik mijn stem verhief,
Die sie ik my door U benomen
    O! moorderesse van mijn vreugt,
Daar hy vast pikt in holle bomen:
    Wijl ik verdruyp door ongeneugt.
Kan dan sijn vlugt, en mijne tranen
    U wraak niet blussen, Circe? Neen,
Schoon dat de lucht haar water-kranen
    Ontsluyt, of dat ik eeuwig ween.

♦ ♦ ♦

Droom, van Eliseen.

Wat wil dit wesen van V twee gespleten tong
Als pijlen, die me door de boven lip been drong
Doen ik uyt blijtschap V een welkom kus quam geven,
O! droom, die droom doet my in angst, en vrese leven
Ik heb't orakel van Apol daar om gevraagt,
Die my op 't droevigst' in dat droef geval beklaagt;

En

Filling me to the brim with pain? My sweet
Song so praised before could make the hard
Stone tender, animate the woods and calm
Floods however high they rose. The music
Infused itself into my beloved like light.
Who could conceive of stealing the soul?
But as I raised my voice you took even my
Music, murderess of my joy. He drums
Hollow trunks of trees everlastingly
While I droop in anguish. His flight, my tears –
Don't they quench your cruelty, Circe?
Must the firmament break open
All its fountains, or I sob for all eternity?

♦ ♦ ♦

Dream of Elise\*

What does it mean – your tongue split in two
While arrows pierced my upper lip just when
From sheer happiness, I wanted to kiss
You? Dream: you have filled my life with dread.
I consulted Apollo's oracle about it
Who pitied me in my plight, predicting the worst,

\* The dream related here (probably in connection with Elisabeth Joly) invites intepretation. A forked tongue belongs in fact, and by tradition, to a snake. As *The Swan of the Well*'s program poem already testifies, snakes do not play positive roles in Brongersma's imaginary world. The arrows that pierce the speaker's upper lip must remain ambiguous. Eros shoots arrows. Lips are used for speaking and kissing. Why the upper lip? Men grow moustaches there. Is Elise's affection diverted from Brongersma's speaker to a male rival? Or the arrows could represent unkind words issuing from Elise's forked tongue, and lodging painfully in a tender place. Lia van Gemert has argued credibly that this poem commemorates a major crisis in the relationship between Brongersma and her friend Elisabeth Joly.

[34]

En voorspeldt dat gy my eerlange sult bedriegen
Hoe trouw ik ben, en dat V trouheyt sal vervliegen,
Het geen den Hemel hoed, die 't avregts keren wil
Op dat daar tussen ons ontstaa geen hert geschil,
Maar dat ik op V Eedt, en schrift 't geloof mag bouwen
Gelijk gy op mijn woordt V vast'lijk moogt vertrouwen.

◆ ◆ ◆

Te koudt om te Drukken.

Het sneewt nu niet als winter-rosen,
Waar door het Bron-nat leit befrosen,
    Mijn Swaantje durfter nu niet uyt,
    Het steekt sijn hooftje weer in't ruyt,
En 't wacht of 't noch eens mocht gelukken
De bloemtjes in de May te plukken.
Daar 't met de Ram in't Lente-groen
Door Sang lust d'eerste swier wil doen.
    Of vaste vrintschap, die altijt
        Bloeyt, en klevende is,

Gelijk het klim den olm met vaste taken bindt
En door en weder door haar taye ranken strengelt,
Daar sig het eene met hyet ander siet door mengelt
En als gevlogten in haar eygenschappen vindt.
Die schoon de winter grimt, nog groendt in tegenstrijden
En klimt, en bloeyt, en wast in spijt van die 't benijden.

◆ ◆ ◆

                              Aan

Foretelling you would betray me soon.
I will remain true, but you flee fidelity.
Heaven protect those who do not stray.
Yet no bitter quarrel has divided us.
Therefore I found on your vow and letters
My trust, as you may rely on my word.

◆ ◆ ◆

Too cold to print*

Now it doesn't snow as light as the petals
Of winter roses, and the well's water
Has frozen solid. My darling Swan
Would rather hunker down, soft skull stuck
Beneath her moulting wing. She waits to know
If she will ever pluck a May's *mignonne*
Blossom beside a Ram who spins and kicks
In the sprouting meadow, delighted
As he is by song. But meanwhile steady
Friendship persists, flourishing all year
Like the elm and vine of fable.
They twine tightly, still more tightly
As the tendrils spiral, and tree and berry
Exchange their traits, woven as one.
Let winter frown, they grow green regardless,
And prosper in spite of all that envies them.

◆ ◆ ◆

* For Ovid and other authors of antiquity, the elm wrapped round with a vine stands for marriage. Book fourteen of *Metamorphoses* supplies the canonical instance. Vertumnus, Italian god of seasons, would beguile Pomona, the mistress of orchards, with the observation that the grape and the tree benefit each other whenever the latter becomes the support of the former. Brongersma follows later European writers in expanding the ambit of the image's significations to encompass friendship. The weather of the poem probably corresponds to the intense Great Frost of 1683 to 1684. The poem may regret an interval or occasion of cool sentiment between Elisabeth Joly and Brongersma.

[35]

Aan de Konst-lievende Juffer KLARA BARTHOLS.

HIer send' ik de Trouwe-herder
(Die u hoort in eygendom)
My geleent eens wederom.
Doch bedank uw, en wil verder
Dat ge my hier in verschoont
Wijl ik heb te lang dees bladen
Uw onthouden tot mijn schade
Moogelijk zijt gy gehoont,
Want U goetheyt heeft voor desen
My ge-eert door U person,
'k Ben soo lange niet gewoon
Uw te missen, wat mach't wesen
Seg doch Klare klaarheyt van
Uw verblijf, zijn dit de Reden
Daar ge laast beloft' van dede
'k Weet niet watter marren kan
Of heb ik de mermre Trappen
Van uw steylen Helicon.
(Waar ge slorpt een Nectar Bron)
Al te stout op komen stappen
'k Bid vergeef me die misdaat,
'k Sal mijn hakend' hertje spenen
Van uw leck're Hipocrenen,

Nu

To the art-loving Miss Klara Barthols*

I send *The Faithful Shepherd*. It's
Yours. Over and over I borrowed
The book, and dare to thank you though
I kept it much too long, as you know –
I'm embarrassed. Maybe you're
Ironic to indulge me with a visit.
I couldn't get used to not seeing you.
Klara, you're all "Clarity," bright,
Candid, radiant, open, sane –
Happy. I don't believe the stream
Will tell on me, if I've presumed
In a daydream to clamber up
The marble steps to your Helicon,
Where you sip nectar from the source.
Forgive me my misdeed, Klara –
I'll unlatch my little heart
And wean it from your delicious
Hippocrene. Though my doting

---

\* Annelies de Jeu says Klara Barthols lived from 1669 until after 1684. According to Henk Duits, Brongersma refers to Giovanni Battista Guarini's *Il pastor fido* (*The Faithful Shepherd*), published in 1590. This comedy set in Arcadia became especially popular in the Netherlands after 1650; the poet may refer to a Dutch version of the work. Pastoral inflections occur in many of Brongersma's poems – even her poem about the *hunebed* at Borger. The speaker's pledge of fidelity suits the tendency of her reading material. She uses the frank language of breastfeeding in connection with her customary image of the inspirational source.

[36]

Nu het schijnt te zijn een quaat,
Maar sal evenwel noch blijven,
In gewoonte, voor als naa
Schoon uw gunst niet kan beklijven
Uw dienstwaarde .. TITIA.

♦ ♦ ♦

De Koninklijke Granida, en den herder Daiphilo.

'K Sag Daifilo het koele Bron-nat langen
Met slaafsche nedrigheyt aan sijn Princes
     Hy hoog hem voor die groote Lantvoogdes
Wie sijne Drink sta al heeft beleeft ontvangen:
Haar dorstig hertien sloeg wijl d' oogen drongen
     Dwars door het ster van sijn besaat gesicht
     Waar in sy vont soo grooten zede licht,
Meer als ze uytten kon met duysent tongen.
Dien blooden Herder voor haar neer gezegen
     Ah! sey hy 'k swijm, ah! help me Koningin,
     Ik waar ontzielt, en sturf om uwe min
Soo mijne staf, waar aan V Troon gereegen.
Waar nu ay! Mijn: dit riep hy als verslagen,
     Het geen Granide trof tot aan de ziel,
     Die moedeloos op sijne schouders viel,
Gy hebt my 't hert O Herder mee ontdragen.
Mits greep s' een snoer van Perlen van'er leden,
     Daar seyse Daifilo, dit is het pant
     Van mijne Trouw, mijn kuyse liefde brant
Tot V in deugt, schoon 'k wierd aangebeden

                                      Van

Vex you, I will stay true
Even if you revoke all favour
To belated Titia, your faithful servant.

❖ ❖ ❖

The royal Granida and the shepherd Daifilo*

I saw Daifilo with slavish submission by the cool
Well-water stoop before his mistress the great
Lady: avid she took his drinking cup,
Their gaze closing all the space that kept
Him from the light that shone from her face
Instinct with such fairness a thousand tongues
Would falter in the struggle to describe
That brightness. The candid herder close to her
Said, "I'm blacking out. Please help me, Queen,
My soul faints away, I die adoring.
The staff over which you hold entire sway,
I couldn't call it mine." He cried out like
A man conquered, striking Granida to
The heart, and in turn she fell on his shoulders.
"Shepherd, you pierce my soul. I love your pleas.
Here," she said, "Daifilo, take this string
Of pearls as a pledge my chaste desire burns

* Granida and Daifilo appear in Pieter Hooft's pastoral play *Granida* (1605). Betrothed by her father Cyrus of Persia to Prince Tissaphernes, Granida lost her way while hunting. She came across the shepherd Daifilo and his mistress Dorilea. Daifilo fetched water for the princess. Brongersma's poem recalls this act of generosity. Hooft's Granida excuses her tarrying with handsome Daifilo with these words: "I stop here to refresh myself from the midday heat, to slake my thirst from a cold cup: so may Ceres prosper your crop, and Pan defend your herds." Eventually, the pair flees to the woods to live a rustic life together. Tissaphernes magnanimously relinquishes his claim to the princess. Gerrit van Honthorst painted a scene from the drama in 1625. In his picture, the lovers rest in the forest. Tissaphernes and some soldiers approach to arrest the shepherd.

Van Cyrus naasaat niet souw op my winnen,
    Maar V O Roem van 't land, met V alleen
    Ben ik in 't hoeden van het vee te vreen,
En sal V boven al de Vorsten minnen.
Als gy de schaapjes drijft op klaver weyden,
    Dan sal Granied' de Haselare stok
    Als Scepter swaayen voor het witte vlok,
En die met V in Mirthe dalen leyden.
Dit Bossig wout, en Cristalijne watren
    Die aan de voet van dese Berg-fonteyn
    Haar oorspronk nemen in dit Rose pleyn,
Die sullen ons geval door wolken schatren.
Met sweegse, en den Herder viel ter aarde,
    Hy kuste heel verrukt die schoone hant,
    Die hem aan haar met vaste koorden bant,
En voor dees Twee een Aartschen Hemel baarde.
Voort wierd' daar ope de Heyl-basuyn geslagen
    Van Velt godinnen, en het Herderdom,
    Die dees bekroonde Bruyt, en Bruydegom
Met groote stacy deên ten Tempel dragen.

♦ ♦ ♦

Aan de snege Juffer **MARGARETA GRATEMA**. Toen sy me niet bond' op mijn Verjaar-dagh

Waarom mijn Nicht vergeetge my te binden,
Of is 't de pijn niet wart, aan mijn persoon
Een lint te spild'ren, of een Tak, of Croon,
Te schenken, of koont gy geen Bloemtjes vinden,

I

Virtuously for you. What Cyrus chooses
I do not want. You, glory of the pastures –
You alone I want. While tending flocks
I'll caress you, and love you above any
Prince as you guide white sheep to clover:
Granida herself will wield a hazel sceptre
Leading them with you into myrtle hollows,
Through branchy thickets, past glassy waters
Which from the lap of the mountain fountain out
Beginning to make their way across the rocky
Plain gurgling in delight at our dalliance,
In mirth diffusing a veil of modest mist."
Daifilo fell to the ground, and kissed in mad
Passion the perfect hand that linked him to
Her with unbreakable bonds, bringing down
To earth a heaven for the pair. The big bassoon
Sounded in salute to the meadow goddesses:
Country folk, ecstatic, led them to the temple.

◆ ◆ ◆

To the clever Miss Margareta Gratema, when she
omitted to bind me on my birthday*

Why did my niece forget to decorate me?
Wasn't it worth the trouble to tie a ribbon
Or a sprig to my person, or set on me a crown
As a gift? Or could you find no flowers?

---

\* Brongersma's poem could reflect a birthday ritual. Celebrants may have attached some meaningful trinket to the body of the person honoured.

[38]

Ik loof dat is de saak, maar soo gy wout
Mijn Jaardag vieren, om U drift te tonen,
Daar is wel stijkel-groen, om my te kroonen,
En ook wel klimmer loof: stil, dat is stout,
't Is waar gy weet men pronkt geen hooft met Cransen
Met sulkx, of 't moet een Prins, of Coning zijn,
Of een Poët, vermaart in daad, als schijn,
Die men verheft op Palm, of Lauwer Transen,
Want dit is in een graat, dog 'k ben te vreên
Soo gy m'U gunst maar slechts koomt op te dragen
Schoon door Een wens, ik wil niet anders vragen
't Is goet al wat, spruyt uyt genegentheên.

♦♦♦

Aan de Geestrijke Juffer CORNELIA BLANCKAARD.

Geen wonder dat men V als opgesloten siet,
En met een yversugt doorsnufflen geurge bladen,
Wijl V de wijsheyt dat voor lange heeft geraden,
Want waar die puyk son bralt daar gelt het maanligt niet.
Met regt hebt gy gekeurt dien Berg vol helle klanken,
Dien konstklip waar Apol het Top punt van Parnas
Gestigt heeft aan de soom van sijne Nectar plas:
Omstruykelt met het Loof van heyl'ge Lauwerranken.
Daar gy Cornelia (schoon gy de werelt haat,
En in V steenrots soekt het woeden te ontsluypen)
V in die Godendrank koont vol en drunken suypen:
Wijl g'V hoe ver gy zijt, op 't naaste vinden laat.
Lep dan het hoeve vogt, en toon een glans in 't duyster,

Stil

I believe that to be the case: yet you
Ought to observe my birthday, to show affection.
There is holly still to garland me, or ivy.
I'll stop, I'm presumptuous. True that
One does not adorn a head with a crown
Of such plants unless it belongs to a prince, king,
Or poet of great fame – so it seems – whom we
Revere with palm frond, or laurel. Since those
Cases are too grand and hyperbolic
I want you to show me your favour
By granting a single wish – and no more.
It all comes, after all, of affection.

◆ ◆ ◆

To the ingenious Miss Cornelia Blancard*

No wonder other people regard you as
A recluse. Retired your zeal culls the flowers
Of literature sweet of scent – your idea of wisdom.
Such a brilliant daystar reduces the rest
To moonshine. You choose the summit that
Resounds with joyful noise, the sheer drop
Of art where Apollo founded Parnassus
By the rim of his nectar well around which
Grow the scions of his holy laurel.
In contempt of the world in your rocky fastness
You strive to evade all the storms of passion.
You gulp your satisfaction in the drink
Of the gods, and cast your light into darkness. You

\* Cornelia Blancard may be a daughter of Brongersma's supporter Nicolaus Blancard.

[39]

Stil door V sijn al de Redelose Reen,
Dring met u breyne Tors door dikke dampen heen,
Op dat het mind're ligt, het meerd're niet ontluyster.
Doop daar u goude schacht in't blanke perel nat,
Dat uyt de Muir-reep komt met stralen af gevlooten,
En met een Hemel val van boven neer geschooten
Tot, daar het door de prang u moedig tegen spat,
Appel hoeft u Penceel, nog ik u kruyn te kransen,
Gy sijt O Pronk beelt van Driemaal drie Gesag,
Bepruykt door u Verdienst, en in de Nagt, een Dag,
En schuylt daar als bekroont in schaw van groene Transen.
Dien Blancken Phaebus, die sijn silverdradig hooft,
Voor u ontdekt, en toont tot u te zijn genegen:
Heeft u in't snoer van sijn Gezeegenden gereegen,
Wijl g'als een Pallas uyt sijn hersens zijt geklooft.
Dog ik beswijk, terwijl mijn pen haar laaste snikken
Uytboesemt, en versoek te werden vast geprent,
(Schoon my geen Helicon, nog Pegaas is bekent)
In u Gedagt, en wens my aan u hert te strikken.

◆◆◆

Mavors Wapen-vogel.

Ik hoor de oude haan van Mavors kraayen,
    Die in de dageraat hem hooren laat,
En 't hoender kot met pluymwerk koomt beswaayen,
    Daar hy verbreydt: het geen behelst de staat
Van 't groot belang' waar in geen uyllen herssen,
    Maar Marsias: de Regter is van als:
Schoon and're Saters op hun tanden knersen
    Om: seggen zy: sijn oordeel is maar vals,

Hoe-

Lift the rain of ignorance, with your mind's
Bright torch you pierce thick vapours, and prevent
The lesser from outshining the greater light.
Now wet the pearly page with a gold nib,
Every stroke shining where pen and paper
Merge, your ink falling like a beam of light
(Brave stain!), Apollo assisting at your
Stroke, and I at hand humbly to crown you.
Let the nine Muses offer you authoritative
Advice, adorned by deserving you who are
In the night a day; they shelter under your
Garland as beneath a colonnade. Blank
Paper gleams, blazes like Apollo
Who, exposing silver hairs in your honour,
Proves his favour, stringing you bead-like
On his necklace of the elect: for you
Burst from his heart like a Pallas. As for
Me I give up, my pen sighs its last
Word escaping from my bosom, delible,
Since neither Helicon nor Pegasus
Sponsor me wishing not to be blotted
From your thought – and writing, therefore,
As best I can, Cornelia, on your heart.

♦ ♦ ♦

Mars's heraldic bird\*

I hear the old cock of Mars cackle,
Daybreak his proclamation, and
He shakes his hackles strutting to
The henhouse, great-hearted, wise
To where real value lives, prevailing
As those fools ruled by Marsyas, once,
Do not. Remember how the pack
Of the satyrs ground their teeth muttering
"His authority is false," though when
Apollo flayed the hide from that braggart
Whom they despised, still they whined,

---

\* The cock is the emblem of right choosing here (in the image of his many hens). The weathercock offers by contrast an image of wrong choosing. Its essence is conformity to external forces. Marsyas the satyr, finding a flute that Minerva had rejected, mastered the instrument. He challenged Apollo to a contest. The muses judged Apollo superior. The remorseless god flayed the satyr. Why would Mars consort with Marsyas here? They share a first syllable and therefore a link. As Mars is a true power, so Marsyas may be a false one. Analogously, a living rooster far surpasses in initiative a weathercock – one example of which appears in E.J. de Wolff's frontispiece for *The Swan of the Well*. The cock and Marsyas resemble one another in having about them a crowd. Hens surround the cock; grovelling sycophants the satyr. That Marsyas appropriated Minerva's rejected flute may imply the spuriousness or secondariness of his musical ambition, by contrast with the cock's instinctive crowing and the god's triumphant lyre.

[40]

Hoewel s' om hem wel eer als wolven huylden,
    Wanneer Apol dien bul de huydt afreet,
En onder 't kreupel-bos van schaamte schuylden,
    Dog nu is't weer verkeert, maar wijl men weer
Dat sulke vogels met de winden waayen,
    Ist nut dat sig de weer-haan daar naa stelt.
Want dit gebroed weet sig met om te draayen,
    Waar't vonnis maar van wint-bol wert gevelt.

Dies seyt hy niemant weet op sulken toon te krijten
Als dese Haan, en kan wel tegen hondert bijten.

♦ ♦ ♦

Antwoordt aan Juffer A.E. COSTIUS.

Gy vraagt me of men op Parnas wel droog kan sitten
    En of de groote hitte
Van Febus stralend' ligt, de sterken ook versengt,
    Van die sig daar vermengt.
Men siet de Musen, om: beregt daar van te geven,
    Gemeenelijk haar neven
De Bron Aar plaatsen; om haar pluymen (wijl se spat)
    Te dopen in'er nat.
En wat den Hengst belangt, men leest nooyt dat sijn veren
    Door vogt, of brant verteren,
Maar wie! dat klavert op het hoog, (schoon ongeciert,)
    Wel wert Belauweriert.
Soo: heeft Apol my door sijn Clio eens doen weten,
    Die nessens hem geseten,
't Gordijn ontschuyt (en toont de Konst Berg in't verschiet)
    Wien elk haar hulpe biet

Om

The hyenas, and grovelling into
The bush hid themselves, scared?

But look – everything turns around.
Here's a rooster that capitulates to
Whatever breeze seems to be prevailing.
Weathercocks advantage us, don't they?
That brood knows so well to conform
Where Aeolus, the windbag, insists.
Consider how many, how very
Many, are just as craven, subject
To opinion – whose other name is fear.

❖ ❖ ❖

Answer to Miss A[nna] E[lisabeth] Costius*

You ask me, "Does Parnassus furnish
A safe resort? Do Phoebus's heat
And streaming rays burn even
The mighty who mix there?" Witness
The Muses giving opportunity
To those related to them, usually,
To soak their plumes at the well
While they splash. As for what
The winged stallion requires no one
Has alleged damage to
His feathers, either through fire
Or through damp. He grazes on
The peak without tack, naked,
Well worthy of his laurels.

Clio who sits beside Apollo
Acquainted me with the god
Lifting aside the veil, revealing
Reaches of art that rear higher.
She who implores Clio's aid
With an offering rising to

* Anna Elisabeth Costius lived from 1643 to 1719. Annelies de Jeu notes that only one poem of Costius's seems to have survived to the present day. She may have taught at a school.

[41]

Om, offer onderweeg, door onbeweegbre schimmen
    Belet quam in het klimmen.
Dog waar den Iver, en de Leersugt 't samen zijn
    Daar is geen moeyte, pijn,
Hoe Heuv'lig en Bestruykt, haar Toppen staan verheven,
    Men laat niet naar te streven,
Op dat gewijde Choor, waar men de Nectar suypt,
    Die van den Hemel druypt.
Daar is geen Noot, nog Doot, voor die met rijpe sinnen
    Een prijslijk werk beginnen,
Maar wie als Icarus verwaant bestrijt de Son,
    Of al seen Phaëton
De Goden tergt, die wert gestraft, bespot, gesmeten,
    Vermorselt en te reten.
Gy dan haa Costius, grijp Pegaas wieken aan
    Om opwaarts voort te gaan:
Waar V de Deugt verwagt, en met haar hant sal leyen
    In Geurge Mirthe-weyen:
Wijl g'hebt haar heylig Sog: door Hertelijke Min,
    Al lang gesoogen in.

Gy wilt uyt mijn vaatje tappen
't Nectar van de wetenschappen?
Jaa: ge wart dan wel vergult.
Maar, ge moest aan my eerst lenen
Volle Tonnen Hipocrenen:
Met u wijsheyt op gevult,
Seker, dan sout eerst gelijken
Prijs, en Roem, daar van te strijken.

♦ ♦ ♦

                                            Aan

The Muse, though hindered
By hard-hearted shades, comes
Ascending where there is neither
Toil nor pain but rough and brushy
Terrain exalted baulks the striver
Toward the precinct where nectar
From heaven dripping is drunk down.

No ordeal, no death imperils
The precious work begun, the mind
Mellow: but Icarus in conceit
Challenging Hyperion and
Phaethon pestering the gods – such that they
Smite, deride, dismember, requite
According to their deserts. Costius,
Hold tight to Pegasus's shoulders
Where the wings are rooted that
Vault you upward wherever
Your virtue would adventure. Under
Clio's guidance you will visit
Fragrant myrtle gardens. Since
The Muse has given you suck
Loving you, nursing you,
Would you taste my kilderkin
Of wisdom? You will glow like
Gold leaf, friend. Drink deep
Leaning on me, drink firkins
Full of Hippocrene, drawing
From the spigot equal praise
And fame.

◆ ◆ ◆

[42]

Aen de Tooverende Circe.

Gy doet my door U Const met Cippus schromen
Die mee gehoorent, niet dorst treden in
De hooge poorten, van 't Beroemde Roomen
Het Voester-huys, van Romulus Wolvin
Hoe sal ik dan! met Hoorens, geef me reden
Door Deuren in de Leeuw Stat konnen gaan;
'K stoot ligt de spitsen af in't binne treeden,
Of dekse met een Crans van klimmer blaan
Neen 't sal nog beter sijn daar uyt te blijven,
Men mogt me anders voor een Beest, ontlijven.

◆ ◆ ◆

A.J.M.J. Costius

De wijl gy Costius reets op de middel trap
Van 't hoge Klipgevaert der musen sijt gestegen
En aan de spring Rots bent geleyt door wetenschap
Waar uyt een ruyschend nat komt storteling gezegen
Die u gewiekte pluym bevogt heeft door sijn val
En die u schaft een Bron om sat daar uyt te drinken
Wiens risselende stroom, u meer bevloeyen sal
Wijl u de weetlust doet de sterren over blinken
Maar soo ge ijst, en vreest, te streven op die Trans
Of soo de weg testeyl schijnt om ten top te raken
Gort u met moet, treed' voort, men wint daar menig Crans
Die Phaebus schenkt aan die wie klavert met vermaken

Ik

To the wonder-working Circe*

Your art, Lady, placing these horns on my head
Puts me in distraught Cipus's predicament
Who dared not pass through the lofty gates
Of famous Rome, foster home of Romulus's
She-wolf. With these horns, what reason could
Induce me to enter the leonine city,
Unless I hid the tips beneath a laurel
Crown? Better to stay outside the limits
Lest I be slain, mistaken for a beast.

❖ ❖ ❖

To my gentle lady J[udith] J. Costius†

Pausing at the midpoint, Costius,
Of the Muses' mountainside,
You taste the stream that chuckles as
It blesses, starting from the spring
The hoof once cleft in rock. To it
Wisdom led you. Now wet
Your plumage in the falling waters,
Drink the riffles' abundance, for
Your love of knowledge makes you
Glitter above the stars but
Chills and fear seize you, still,
In the struggle upward to
The summit. Proceed. Courage wins
Many crowns from Phoebus who
Bestows them on those who climb

* Cipus, a victorious general, grew horns on his head as he approached the outskirts of Rome (*Metamorphoses* 15.565–621). A soothsayer interpreted his horns as proof of the general's future kingship. A good Roman, Cipus renounced this destiny. Wreathing his horns in laurel, he avoided entering the city. Instead, he told the Senate about the prophecy. For his renunciation, Rome awarded Cipus an estate beyond the city limits. Brongersma departs from Ovid's precedent. She adds Circe, who inflicts transformations, elsewhere, on the loving couple Canens and Picus. Does Brongersma intend to introduce a suggestion of cuckoldry to the plight of Cipus? Rome features a Leonine wall, but it was raised long after Ovid's time (around 850).

† Judith is Anna Elisabeth Costius's sister. Their parents were Elisabeth and Cornelius Costius. Judith wrote a pamphlet entitled *Eulogy at the Funeral of the Blessed Maria Stuart* (1695). Both Anna Elisabeth and Judith composed poetry. Brongersma may place these verses here with playful intent; the Biblical Judith, Costius's probable namesake, appears in the next poem.

[43]

Ik sal dan: schoon mijn tree wat traag sijn, en te mat
Beklimmen 't struyklig spoor, en volgen u op't padt.

♦ ♦ ♦

De Woedende Leeuwin of de Lionsche Amasone, die haar
had verlooft aan een Edelman tot Lions: die haar veragtelijk
verliet, waar over gehoont, heeft Hem (: in Mans gewaat sijnde!)
aangeranst, soo als sy uyt de Comedie quam, en door steeken,
soo dat hy doot bleef liggen, voorgevallen tot Lions in de
Maant Januarij 1685.

Ik noem haar Lione.

Weg Dido, weg Lucretia
Weg Heydens rot, met al u spoken,
Lionaes offer is aan't rooken
Zy stapt de Fransche Judith naa:
En wint (: soo d'Eer daar is geleegen:)
De Lauwer kroon, door vuyst, en deegen.
Verrader roeptse als verwoet
Gy die vermaak neemt in de spelen
Van vreemdigheen op Treur Toneelen?
Coom nader, met een frisse moet.
Ik sal u leeren Maagden schennen,
En my niet meer te willen kennen,
Mits riegt se dwars den Schenner door

Die

Ingeniously joyous. Come
I'll climb with you, though my step
Will be slower than yours to follow
A path so difficult and obstructed.

❖ ❖ ❖

On the Amazon or enraged woman of Lyon engaged
to a nobleman of that city. Once abandoned and
mocked for being jilted, she disguised herself in
male clothing and ambushed her lover as he left the
theatre in January 1685, knifing him dead.*

I give her the name "Liona," or "Woman of Lyon"

Off with you, Dido – off with you, too,
Lucrece – off with all you heathen scum,
Parasitical ghosts. Let us instead
Burn incense for Liona, Judith of France
Honoured with a laurel crown in
The category of fist and dagger.
She yelled like mad, "Traitor, you're
Amused to go to the theatre, are you,
To watch strange spectacles on the tragic
Stage? Come closer if your courage
Is so cool. I'll teach you to shun a young
Lady's company." Farouche she runs
The absconder through, bereaving him

\* Possessed by Venus and Eros, infatuated with the Trojan prince Aeneas, the Carthaginian queen Dido slew herself with a sword. In the underworld, she snubbed the man for whom she had annihilated herself. Instead she sought out Sychaeus, her *amor pristinus* – the husband who had long predeceased her (Vergil's *Aeneid* 6.469–76). Lucrece killed herself rather than submit to rape by Tarquin. Judith seduced Holofernes, the general dispatched by the expansionist Nebuchadnezzar to take the seacoast town of Bethulia, which lay west of Babylon. He had gained control of the city's water supply. Bethulia was on the point of capitulation. Judith succeeded, however, in cutting off Holofernes's head. That success heartened her people's beleaguered forces.

THE SWAN OF THE WELL ♦ 135

[44]

Die zy de laatste snik siet geeven
Wijl hy berooft is van het leeven.
Daar seytse nog: dat hebt ge voor
De Trouw: soo trouloos my ontswooren
Gaa Rover daal in Plutoos Chooren.
Daar vlugt den dapp'ren Amasoon
En poogt soo 't onheyl te ontwringen
Terwijl haar 't hals-regt aan koomt dringen,
Dog dit is regt Bedriegers loon:
Geen Leeuw laat sig van Wolven terten
Een Vrouw trotseert vaak Manne herten.

♦ ♦ ♦

Op het Ver-Eert Trossje, geele Auriculen in de laate Herfst, die ik geplaatst heb boven de afbeeldinge van Elisa Hangende in mijn Schrijf-kaamertie

O Bloeyrijk Hof Iuweel Aurijkula
Die in u Spansel staat van Gout te prieken
Gelijk een Koninkx Bruyt, spijt Africa
Die ons met geuren tert, uw geur laat rieken
En in de sooren Herfst een Lente toont
Die op haar Bloos, Tapeet borduyr gewaden
Geschakelt heeft en soo haar hooft bekroont

Door

Of life with life-blood. "Slump there,
That's what you get for disavowing
Me. So go join Pluto's gang." She tries
To drag the cursed carcass off while
Menacing Justice lumbers after her, yet
His was the proper reward of jilting.
No lion indulges abusive wolves. A woman
Should not suffer a man's change of heart.

◆ ◆ ◆

On the adored truss of yellow auriculas that I have
set above the picture of Elisa in my study*

You comprise, Auricula, an entire
Gem-like garden in your many-blossomed
Self, pent flaunting in a ribbon your yellow
Like the bride of a potentate, and may
All the sweets of Africa infuse your perfume
Turning our sour autumn into a springtime
Who on her blouse has embroidered a border

---

* Auriculas are a variety of primrose, popular in the seventeenth century. Here Brongersma wittily switches the usual roles of art and nature in her verse. The flowers are real, the woman an image rather than a person.

[45]

Door veelderley geswier van Loof Cieraden
Gy sult dan wijl ge mee den Soomer hoont
En my uyt gonst uw Bloemtros is geschonken
(: Waar op ik stof in't prijsen van u schoont:)
In't Cabinet van mijn vertrek-plaats pronken
Daar 'k u nog schoon de blad'ren sijn verdort
Door tijts verloop, sal in de Lof-Crans vlegten
Van mijn Elisa: die gebeden wort
Soo lang se leeft u op haar Kruyn te hegten.

♦ ♦ ♦

Aan den stuyrsen Groot-Vorst van Aquilon, of wreede Winter,
toen het weer dooyde.

NU kan de Bron-Maagt eens haar asem weder haalen,
O! wreedaart, die ge hat in ketenen gesmeet
Van Christalijn, wijl gy op hagelwolken reet,
En deed' verstremmen selfs de grootste pekeldalen,
Waar Doris nog betruurt, haar kroost, door U verkragt,
Geen Eeuw geheugt ooyt van soo een Barbaarse magt,
Geen Galathé, nog Nimf van Cloris, dorst verschijnen,
Nog verfauwen: gy deed'al wat leven hadde quijnen,
Maar nu ist al gedaan U forse moer verweekt,
Nu Febus heerscher is, die U gewelt verbreekt.

Gaa

And crowned her head with multifarious
Leafy whorls, outdoing even high summer.
Though this truss was given from goodwill
Already the petals wilt so I will weave
Them in spite of time's damage into
A crown for Elise, destined in these lines,
At least, to crown her as long as she lives.

◆ ◆ ◆

To that big sulk, Grand Duke Aquilo, otherwise
known as Cruel Winter: at last the weather
has warmed\*

Now the woman of the well breathes free
Brute, you who pelted us with glassy
Pellets astride your hailstorm, freezing
The briniest resistant waters where
Doris mourns the children you violated.
No age recalls a power more barbarous,
No Galatea or nymph of Cloris's need
Question that, or faun. You made everything vital
Languish and pine. But now your rigid
Strength is slush, now Phoebus melts away

\* Aquilo is synonymous here with Boreas. He carried off Orithyia, daughter of King Erectheus of Athens. Her name means "mountain squall." Their daughter was the goddess of snow. Boreas assumed the form of a stallion. Hence Brongersma's allusion to Aquilo's horse.

[46]

Gaa by Orithia, gaa U by haar vernagten,
Die sal (mischien) u komst met meer verlang verwagten.
Want al te lang een Gast te spijsen
Maakt de vrientschap onbequaam,
Seker 't is niet om te prijsen,
Nog voor niemant aangenaam.

't Is dan best dat Elk haast keert
Naar sijn eygen vier, en heert.

♦ ♦ ♦

Aan de Hoog-waarde Deught, en Geestrijke Iuffer Me-Iuffer
IDA MARIA VEELKERS.

Gedoog O! puyk heeld van de geestelijke scharen
Dat ik mijn Digtveer in gesmolten perlen doop,
Of dat ik blat aan blad van geurge Lauw'ren knop
Om uw gewyde Cruyn daar mee te Eevenaren.
Wijl gy uw waarlijk voor een ijders oog doet kennen
Dat gy opregtelijk den rechten Ida zijt,
Geen Ida waar Enoôn versleet baar soetsten tijd
By Paris, maar wiens geest drijft voort op Arends pennen.
Dien Ida die door het beneveld's werk kan dringen
Met haar gewiekt vernuf, en toond met een dat zy
Daar in gezegend leefd', O! schandere Mary
Wat Lof-lied sal men van V deftigheden singen?

Want

Your clutch. Go to Orithyia, perhaps
She, the girl of the gale, may await
Your coming warmly. The guest who overstays
Converts a visit to a spiteful siege, tolerance
Shivers – dies. Sweep off on your mount
Therefore: storm away.

♦ ♦ ♦

To the gentlewoman as virtuous as pious
Miss Ida Maria Veelkers\*

Consummate model for all the righteous,
Would I could sink my quill in a solution
Of pearls, or plaited a fragrant laurel wreath
Pondered leaf by leaf, equaling the tribute
To the pattern of your worth. All eyes acclaim
You the justest of Idas, surpassing that
Ida where Oenone passed in sweet bowers her
Idyll with Paris, for on an eagle's pinions
Your spirit aspires: Ida, you soar past
The eloquence of that Phrygian woman's
Epistle, winged with the power of discernment
And dwell in blessedness, my brilliant Mary:
But what song of praise could convey

\* The Oread Oenone addresses a letter to Paris in the fifth poem of Ovid's *Heroides*, a book of heroic epistles addressed by women to their beloveds. Brongersma's language may echo the phrasing of Jonas Cabeljau's Ovid translation of 1657, *Letters of Complaint by Illustrious Ladies*. Cabeljau lived from 1632 to 1680. Brongersma takes the opportunity to distinguish between Christian piety and pagan sensuality. These spheres offer similarly rich opportunities for eloquence. The poet subordinates the rhetorical power of a lovesick nymph to that of a devout woman. The contrast was suggested, in all likelihood, by her addressee's name, "Ida." Miss Veelkers, by Brongersma's account, is a pious woman; whereas Ida in Ovid is the name of a mountain on whose slopes Oenone and Paris enjoyed carnal bliss. The poet's supposition that Miss Veelkers will recognize the pagan allusion says something about Miss Veelker's wit, tolerance, and learning.

[47]

Want gy haa! Veelkers kroost trotseerd be na de wereld
En straald gelijk de Sonn de dikke dampen door,
Gy baand naar Zions-top veel anderen het spoor:
Waar door uw Eer-naam bloeyd, en eeuwuwig blijft bepereld.
Maar schoon geen Hemelval uw luystrend' oor kan strelen
Van mijn ontvlerkt geluyd, dat minder is al niet,
Soo bid ik dat g'op Gonst, maar naar geen Rijmtrant siet
Die ligt V zedigheyt, en aandagt souw verveelen,
Dog waar de wijs-heyt met de reden sig gaat huwen
En waar beleeftheyt paard aan't Hemelsche verstand,
Daar Triompheerd de Deugt, die in V is gepland:
Soo hoef ik V dan om dees misdaad' nooyt te schuwen.

◆ ◆ ◆

Toe-Matie.

'K Dank U puyk van Sarons bloemen
Niet om dat ge my gaat roemen
Om het weynig dat men vind
In mijn geest, 't geen veel verblind.
Maar om dat ge my door reden,
De geheymen koomt ontleden
Van U soete Rijmery,
En gestigten Poësy,
Waar mee gy me koomt beswieren
Trots gevlochten Lauwerieren,
't Geen'k onwaardlich ben, doch sal
(Schoon me trof het ongeval
Van U gonst te moeten derven)

Noch

Your dignity that excels almost the entire world,
Daughter of the Veelkers, burning like the sun
Through clogging fogs, blazing a way
For others to find Zion's top, a feat for which
Your fame blossoms, precious as pearls, yet
I cannot caress your ear with divine language,
My flightless racket is less than nothing, depending
On your goodwill whatever metrical scheme
I choose, despite the boredom imposed on
Your exemplary judgement and virtue: for
Where courtesy and heavenly wit fuse
Goodness triumphs, so I need not even
Overcome this – my sorry insipidity.

♦ ♦ ♦

Abundance*

Gratitude to you, glory of Sharon's flowers.
Not that you go about spreading my renown
On the little basis of what my mind supplies
Which is not so very dazzling, rather
You persuade me of the mystery cohering
In your sweet rhymes and well-built verse
Which crown me sublimely in woven laurel
Of which I cannot be worthy yet I shall,
Even if the misfortune should occur
That you withdraw your favour, die

* The Song of Solomon declares
"I am the rose of Sharon, and the lily
of the valleys" (2:1). The addressee of
this poem is obscure.

[48]

Noch U Dienaresse sterven,
En geloof dat gy altijd
In mijn slecht geheugen zijt.

◆◆◆

Op't noden, in den Y-stroom te komen.
De Swaan spreekt.

SOuw ik daar soo veel Adelaren groeyen
Met mijn geswalp den Y stroom durven moeyen
En op dat klaar, en sagte golf Tapeet
Mijn treders setten, en die vloet beswemmen
Die al de vloeden door haar magt kan temmen
Vergeef me dat, dog 'k waar wel haast gereet
Soo my het hert voor lang niet waar ontsonken
(Schoon my het Sparen heeft sijn gonst geschonken
Om mee te plaatsen,) maar helaas; wat raat?
Geen waater monster souw mijn moet versetten
Nog barrening te komen my beletten
Soo ik niet vreesde voor een grooter quaat
Dat 's voor de gift-draak van de schimp Soilisten
Die geerne wil in strijt van tweestrijt twisten,
Daar hebt ge dan de reen waar om ik blijf:
Gedoken ondert lies van Grunoos wallen
Waar 'k ben bevrijt om in geen ramp te vallen,
En op de baaren van gerustheyt drijf.

◆◆◆

Aan Elisene.

Ag! moet ik dan so ver van V gescheyden blijven
    Daar men alleen door schrijven

V heus-

Your faithful servant and please believe you
Always remain in my memory however faulty.

♦ ♦ ♦

On an invitation to swim in the River IJ*

Should I dare where so many eagles glide
To wallow, trying the patience of the IJ?
Ply these web-feet game for any waters
In such lucid, subtle, polished eddies?
Forgive my brag. My heart has never yet
Gone under. Sound policy has secured me
The general privilege of paddling. No
Aquatic monster could withstand my courage,
Or flare of sudden fire abash my coming.
A bulky daemon's grimace wouldn't baulk me.
But the toxic snake of a taunting critic
Craving endless rounds of senseless quarrels
Makes me linger, think, swim, and slide
Under the kinder banks of the Grunoos, adrift
On the current of a richer meditation.

♦ ♦ ♦

For Elise

Must I remain so far from you,
Damned to correspondence, limited
To the civilities of letters? How

* The IJ runs through Amsterdam. Possibly Katharina Lescailje invited Brongersma to visit her in this capital of literature. But the uneasy poet, concerned about her reputation, would rather linger in Groningen. Brongersma sometimes likens male eminences to eagles, so this poem belongs to a subcategory of elaborate, possibly ironic expressions of diffidence at the menace of envy or ridicule.

[49]

   V heusheyt nad'ren kan,
Hoe dikwijls spreek ik daar met droeve klagten van.
En 't leckend' oog waar uyt de brakke droppels springen
   Een Ramp koomt op te dringen
   Aan mijn bedrukt gemoet,
Dat door de hoop van V te sien steeds wert gevoet.
Maar ach! Wanneer, wanneer: O wrede tussen wegen
   Koomt het V eens gelegen
   Dat ik mijn hert ontlast,
En het verlangen sus, dat lange hoe meerder wast
Tot V mijn Eliseen: ay! wouw Dedaal me gunnen
   Sijn wieken 'k souw dan kunnen
   Gemoedicht tot V gaan,
Of dat ik hadde maar de pluymen van een Swaan.
Ik souw de driften van den E stroom over plassen
   Om V te gaan verrassen,
   En al seen klis V leen
Aankleeven, maar helaas dees spooreloose reen
Verquikken my: als of ik waarlijk V omhelsde,
   En mont en lippen knelsde,
   Doch 't is maar enkel droom,
Vaar wel, en leef gerust tot dat ik by V koom.

      ♦ ♦ ♦

Op het Inkleeden van de H.E.G. Juffer ANNA MARG.
BROERSEMA. Die sich heeft gestalt onder de Banier en Ordre der
Dominicanes wiens patronesse is: S. Rosa.

Siet nu hoe Anna bralt in Bloem-festonnen,
En slorpt het leckre nat uyt Rose Bronnen

            Dus

Often have I complained about it,
Leaky eyes oozing brackish tears,
Misery crushing me, hope
Fed again – again suspended?
But when? When? Heartless stretch
The roads between you and a chance
To ease the heart, appease the longing
Insufferably swelling. Would, Elise,
Daedalus could grant me wings
To fly to you elated, or I
Became a swan. Above the Ee*
I'd soar and take you by surprise
And cleave to you, tight as a burr.
Baseless plans excite me
As if I embraced you, and mouth
Shut on mouth, that dream: dreamy
Solace till I come to you.

♦ ♦ ♦

On the phrases that the respectable gentlewoman
Anna Marg[areta] Broersema inscribed beneath
the banner and device of the Dominicans, whose
patroness is Saint Rosa†

See Anna revel in festoons of petals, and
Sip quintessence of rosy wells. A crown

\* The river mentioned here is the Dokkumer Ee.

† A servant in the Peruvian household of the infant Rosa saw the baby's face transformed into a flower of the same name. The eventual Saint Rosa became associated with the Dominicans from 1607. She mortified herself by sleeping on pottery shards and by whipping herself, hence the hints of voluntary pain in Brongersma's poem. In 1615, a Dutch pirate, Janis van Speilberg, looted Lima. Licensed as they thought by the iconoclastic Reformation, he and his brigands breaking into the Church of Santo Domingo with the intent of despoliation confronted the young woman ablaze with holy fire and holding up a monstrance. Terrified they fled, took ship, and abandoned their plans of thievery. Rosa died in 1617.

[50]

Dus net bekranst, schoon d'stijkel't voorhooft pijnt
    Nog even bly verschijnt.
Wel Margareet sult gy nu Rosies plucken
Uyt Saron: daar de Doorenties nog drucken
Hoe sagt, hoe mals haar blaties sijn: diens geur
    U lof bestrijkt op keur.
Gy toont: U Priesteres van dese tijen
En laat geciert U ordening in wyen
Met stacy, daar gy 't hullend kleet grijpt aan
    Om soo gepronkt te staan.
Voor uwe Mayesteyt in't hof der hoven
Om met de Cerafijns sijn naam te looven
Daar't wit gewaat: en't suyver hert moet sijn
    Als kost'le chirzolijn.
Dog Broersema ik wens dat gy u Dagen
Bevrijt moogt sien van droeve jammer plagen,
En Roosies plukt met Rosa naar u sin
    Die g'voert ten Hemel in.
Op dat (: hoewel U Peerel is gereegen
Aan't snoer van't hoog geheym:) de heylge segen
U Ziel bedruypen mag, daar d'Eeuwigheyt
    U kroning maakt bereyt.

◆◆◆

Op de ongemeene plaisierige Wandelplaats, de Cingel: buyten om de stadt Leeuwarden.

O Weeld'rig Yper wouwt begrandigt in V paden,
Met wat een herten lust heb ik V vaak betreen,
En in V Gallery veel uyren doen besteen
Om daar in't Boom-prieel mijn suffe geest t'ontladen.

                                           V kruy-

Of flowers may pain the brow with prickles
Yet provoke a state of bliss. Margreet, pluck
Sharon's growths. Those thorns ache, that leafage
Enriches, this odour you choose to praise on high.
You paint the priestess of the tides, consummate
The design in ecstasy, depicting the robe
Exquisite and majestic, for the court
Of courts in honour of His name together
With, whitely arrayed, the seraphim, heart
As precious crystal clean. I know, dear
Broersema, sadness and distress do not
Plague your days. You cull roses with Rosa.
At your will you can bring heaven near.
Your pearl is strung already on the string
Of imponderable mystery, and blessed
Benediction sprinkles you. Eternity
Prepares you, Anna, your crown.

❖ ❖ ❖

On the Singel, a singular and pleasing promenade on the periphery of Leeuwarden\*

Thick elm woods grown tall on every path,
With what a hungry heart I have wandered you
And in your galleries meditated hours
Embowered, unbending my mind. Your crowns

\* The East Frisian Count Enno acknowledged Emperor Ferdinand in 1657. His district became a fief of the Holy Roman Empire. Strictly speaking, Phrygia borders on Troy, but in this loco-descriptive poem Brongersma assimilates the locations in order to avow that Leeuwarden's beauties surpass those of the fabled city. Poplars would drip with amber if they were the metamorphosed sisters of Phaethon, in Ovid; whereas the anointing of fingers belongs to the ordination of Levitical priests in the Old Testament. Brongersma's praise of a great garden therefore synthesizes motifs from Greece, Rome, and Israel for the delectation of its female visitors.

## [51]

V kruynen die soo steyl tot aan de wolken schieten
Bekransen vaak mijn hooft, soo dat dees puyk-warand,
De Pallem-gaarden troftst van Keyser Ferdinand
Waar't Firesche Iufferdom haar vreugt komt door genieien.
Maar schoon dees wandel-baan, en effene boscagie
Dat Leeuwaards festen Croont, en Gragte boorden ciert,
Niet naa waardy van my mag warden belauwriert
Vergun dan dat ik V van eygen Telg pluymagien.
Berey een Lof-festoen, die ik ten toon mach rijgen
Aan 't Oude hoofsche spits: om uwe Cingel-Tuyn
Te stellen op haar Troon: end at ik uyt basuyn
V Roem: die grooter is, als 't opperhof der frijgen.
Wast dan als Ceders, en groey op tot Populieren,
Stort Amberdroopjes uyt, bedruyp V stigters hant
Die in soo juisten rey V Tronken heeft geplant,
En doet V Schoonheyt, met een Fenix vlerk beswieren.

❖ ❖ ❖

Aan de seer geagte Juffer S. WILMSONN, Onder de naam van Amaril.

EY! Amaril 'k versoek my niet te weyg'ren
Om klimmen op de eerste ondertrap
Van ons Parnas, daar U de wetenschap
Verwagt, en poogt U gonst te bien in 't steyg'ren.

Als is de top wat steyl, gy klaterd met gemak:
Want onder weeg, schuyld g'onder 't Lauwerdak.

❖ ❖ ❖

Op

Mingled in the clouds sheltered my head.
Splendid parkland, palmy garden planted
By Ferdinand, the emperor, here the women
Of Frisia come for pleasure. This system
Of trails and level wooded ground improve
Fortified Leeuwarden, adorn the canal bank:
Grant therefore that from your leafy plumage
I may prepare for descendants a festoon
Of praise, which I will fix to last in a high
Place of this old palatial terrain, setting
Your Singel on her throne, and trumpeting
Your fame brighter than the Phrygian
Citadel's. Like a cedar flourish. Stretch
As a poplar lofty. Ooze amber drops.
Anoint the fingers of your founder, who
Set your trunks in sightly rows and like
A phoenix with wings lifted, renew. Renew.

◆ ◆ ◆

To the respectable gentlewoman Miss S[usanna]
Wilmson, under the name of Amaryllis\*

Amaryllis, do not tempt or dare me
To climb the lowest foothills, even,
Of a mutual Parnassus: your knowledge
As well as kindness surpass my own
By so much. Your ease in ascent must
Subdue the famous steepness of the peak.

◆ ◆ ◆

---

\* Amaryllis is a pastoral name from Vergil's first eclogue. The hierarchy of genres governing poetic attainment was sometimes called the *rota Vergilii*, or the wheel of Vergil. An ambitious poet ought first to write bucolics, then georgics, and at last an epic, following the pattern of the Roman's career. The choice of courtly pseudonym for Miss Wilmson evokes the world of eclogue rather than of more ambitious genres. An amaryllis is also a plant producing large flowers: early in *The Swan of the Well*, Brongersma compares Miss Wilmson to a blossom.

[52]

Op een bonte gekruyste SPIN, Die eenige weken voor mijn vensterglas in haar net haar had verhouden, dog door een koude Noorde wind verjaagt, en haar uyt gespan gebrooken.

Aragne is verhuyst en haar Tapeet gebrooken
Door Borëas helaas! nu is mijn spintje voort,
Had ik de magt sy waar daar over al gewroken,
Maar vrees dat't arme dier in't woeden is vermoort.
Ey: Noortse beer wat deed' die kruysling V voor schade,
Sy ving maar vliegjes in haar nietig uytgespan,
Daar mee sy soberlijk haar holle buyk versade,
Minerv' hoeft haar nu niet te leggen in de ban,
En had om 't prijs lot met haar niet te horen weven:
Wijl s' Pallas door de vlugt van selfs de Eer komt geven.

♦♦♦

Aan de Hoog-geëerde Godtminnende Vrou Mevrouw S.S.G.A.

Ick weet wel dat ghy nimmer naamt behagen
Te slorpen van het Hipocrene-nat,
Want ghy hebt noyt die lasten willen dragen
Schoon het van selfs uyt Pegaas Bron-aar spat
Maar u gemoet dorst meerder naa die stroomen
Die Neboos drift doet uyt de Heyl-beek koomen;
waar Bethel en waar Hermons vette paden
Vol leckerny, de heemelingen voedt

Waar't

On a spider whose back bore the blazon of a bright
cross: she spun a web in my window weeks ago, but a
cold wind drove her away and destroyed her design

Arachne has lost a nest. For Boreas
Clawed that tapestry apart. Where has
The wee weaver fled? Could I, I would
Restore her to her corner, but fear
Furor squashed flat this feeble beast. Bear
Of bad weather, how might a puny bead,
Daubed with a cross, offend? Her modest loom
Engrossed inconsequential bugs. Her hollow
Belly's dome bulged with snacks seldom. Minerva,
Your ancient curse is voided. Arachne's rout
Leaves that goddess unrivalled in the world.

♦ ♦ ♦

To the estimable lover of God Madame S.S.G.A.*

I know well that you never take delight
In drinking from the spring of Hippocrene
Since you do not want to address the themes
Bubbling out from that fabulous fountain,
Preferring to it the waters that froth
From Mount Nebo's scree, and the holy
Brook in Bethel, and Hermon's aquifers

* Nebo offered the elevation from which Moses could look into the Promised Land. Hermon designates a cluster of mountains rising to the highest altitude in Syria. Bethel names a settlement on the legendary site of Jacob's dream of angels climbing to, and descending from, the gate of heaven. This poem may refract the one immediately preceding it. There the spider, though associated with Arachne, bore a Christian cross on its back. The image and action of mountaineering joins Parnassus with Zion. Brongersma substitutes scripturally sanctioned watercourses for her customary pagan wells. The identity of "S.S.G.A." is unknown.

Waar't Manna druypt, die d'honger kan versaden
wyl het daar vloeyt voor elk in overvloedt
Ik laat V dan beklimmen Sions drempel
Wyl ghy geen lust schept in der Musen Tempel
Dog eer ik sluyt, en eer ik u laat hooren
Myn laatste groet, so bid ik dat ge wilt
Aanvaarden dese gift uyt my gebooren
Waar door ge dan myn gans begeeren stilt,
En dat ik V mag door myn doffe klanken
Staag roemen, en V voor die Eer bedanken.

♦ ♦ ♦

Aan de Hoog-geëerde Vrouw Mevrouw W.V.B.G.B.

WIe streeldt soo soet mijn luysterende Ooren?
Wat nagtegaaltje doet haar keeltje horen,
Dat soo zielroerend' slaat al seen Siereen,
Is't Erato, of is't Melpoom? O! neen
't Is Philomeel die Wout-nimf die de bergen
Doet dreunen door haar stem, en die koomt tergen
Het Sang-rot waar dat Pegaas water plas
Af borteldt uyt de steen kloof van Parnas,
't Is zy die door 't betoverende singen
Kan door de herste klip, en Rotsen dringen
So dat de weder-galm kaatst door de lugt,
Voor wiens geruys dien blooden Echo vlugt,
De blanke Delta van Delius beluystert,
Is als verrukt, (schoon Nox haar glans beduystert)

En

Flush with dainties where manna drips that can
Satiate the hunger of every man and woman.
Then ascend Zion's side you who have
No taste for the Temple of the Muses yet
Before I come to the end of my salutation
Accept this specimen of my invention
Allowing me in metre constantly
To praise you and thank you for that honour.

◆ ◆ ◆

To the estimable Madame W.V.B.G.B.*

What streams so sweetly in my listening ears?
What thrush is that whose throat pulses with
Music that moves us like a Siren's voice?
Erato? Melpomene? No. It's
Philomela, the wood nymph who alters
The woods with her song and challenges
The stony fastness of Pegasus where
His hoof struck water gushing from the rock.
She enchants the hardest cliff, bewitches
Into reciprocity the roughest ground
Bouncing vibrations through the air,
Astride whose flight the naked Echo mounts.
Apollo's sister half-moon, half-mad muses

---

* The identity of the person to whom Brongersma dedicated this poem is unknown. Although she is the muse of tragedy, Horace addresses Melpomene as the inspiratrix of lyric verse. Erato presides over love poetry; her attributes are the roses and myrtles with which Brongersma's poem concludes. Philomela, the nightingale, here rejoices more than she grieves, yet the co-presence of Melpomene with Erato may darken the burden of her song.

[54]

En lacht haar toe, terwijl se hene gaat
De bootsschap brengen aan de Dageraat,
Die haar sal voeren op'er Rosse wagen
Ten Hemel, daar haar Lof-ster wert gedragen
Op wieken van de faam, waar Sy altans
Sal prijken met een Roose, of Mirthe-Crans.

♦ ♦ ♦

Aan de Geestrijke Vrouw, Me-vrouw M.C.F.

Men plukt nooyt druyven van een Distel boom
Nog vijgen van de stekelige Dorens,
Een Kreupelaar beklimt geen hogge Torens,
Nog schip drijft op van selfs in tegenstroom.
Soo dat van weetniets nooyt veel nuts kan komen,
Maar die verligt zijn, en het goet verstant
Beslijpen al seen ruwe Diamant,
Die konen door de tijt de wil betomen
Gelijk als gy die nimmer heeft verspilt,
Geen uyrtje om geen voordeel in te voeren,
Die leersaam zijt, en altijt heeft gewilt
't Sy wat het waar de konsten af te loeren,
't Geen is de spoor, en geessel tot de konst,
Waar door gy d' Lof-kroon wint, en ijders gonst.

♦ ♦ ♦

Aan de Juffrouw G.V.L.

U Deugt en aart, doet my aan U verbinden,
Hoewel ik niet kan offren tot een gift,

Als

As Night grows less definite, and laughs
When she goes off to bring a message to
Aurora with her rosy wagon conveying
Her to the height of heaven where the star
Of her glory soars on wings of fame forever
Garlanded by roses, or by myrtles.

♦ ♦ ♦

To the ingenious Madame M.C.F.*

Can you pluck grapes from thistles, figs
From thorns? Or can a sorely injured man
Climb a high gate, or a boat oppose a torrent
Deprived of means of propulsion? From
A know-nothing no knowledge can proceed.
But the enlightened and those of strong mind
Realize the promise of a diamond in
The rough. They bridle a will so well it is
As much as never to have squandered it.
Subdue every passing hour to its best
Use, and learn to entice from cover what
Could be, and must be, and will be learned.
Your strenuous track, the whip you ply,
Win both a crown of glory and wide goodwill.

♦ ♦ ♦

To Miss G.V.L.

Your virtue and personality oblige
Me to you so I give what I can, this
Gift of thanks, a makeshift display

---

* This counsel of intellectual discipline manifests Brongersma's devotion to the idea of the learned woman: a Frisian version of the *précieuse* or anticipation of the British bluestocking.

[55]

Als Dankbaarheyt, en dese letterdrift,
Die gy altoos van my oprecht sult vinden,
U goetheyt glanst tot yder als een son,
Waar mee gy veel begloort, en koont behagen,
Want nimmermeer m'u onbescheyden von,
Dies koom ik U dan om een saak te vragen
Dat is dit vers te nemen aan,
En steeds in uwe gonst te staan.

♦♦♦

Aan de seer geëeerde en goet-aardige
Juffer ANNA MARG. VALCKE.

WAarom verlaat ge soo de sterke wallen
Van Groningen, waar naa soo menig haakt!
Daar soo veel puyk van Lauwer-helden brallen,
En waar de Leeuw voor elkx beholding waakt.
Waar Themis school in mermer staat geklonken,
Waar dat Astree van dierbere Porfijr
Haar woning bouwt, en pragtig staat te pronken
By 't hoog Olymp, waarom verlaat gy't hijr,
En soekt V vreugt in't eensaam woudt te vinden,
Mint gy't geboomt' of't rillen van een beek.
Hier wandelt g'ook in schaduw van de Linden,
En 't stroomend' nat, schiet mee' door deese streek,
Of wilt g'een Telg, of Roos, of Lely plukken
Tot V vermaak, hier woont de Bloem-godin,

Die

Of the lettered zeal which will always serve
Sincerely in your cause. Your goodness
Like the sun glows for all, incandescing,
Assuring me you also incline to me.
I approach you then to ask a favour, namely
Please accept this verse and permit me
Constantly to bask in your benevolence.

◆ ◆ ◆

To the estimable and benevolent gentlewoman
Miss Anna Marg[areta] Valcke\*

Why do you forsake the ramparts of Groningen
When multitudes long to dwell within them with
So many great heroes of literature and the Lion
Keeping vigil? The school of Themis declaims
Its verse, Astraea raises a building all of
Precious porphyry – comely, flaunts herself
Before high Olympus. Why do you leave her
Divining some happiness in deserted woods
Doting on trees, on the trilling of a brook?
You can stray here in linden-shadow, too,
And waters gurgle shooting through this tract.
If you want to collect roses and lilies then
The goddess of flowers will entice you

\* Brongersma contrasts *rus* with *urbs*, country with city. Her friend prefers rural retirement, for which *Tyter* (the Dutch for Vergil's bucolic *Tityrus*) and amaranth (a never-withering flower) are metonyms. The poet concludes with a Catullus-like invitation. Astraea is goddess of justice. Across the Channel, John Dryden claimed, echoing Vergil himself in his *Astraea Redux* (1660), that this divinity returned to earth with the restoration of Charles II.

[56]

Die wel voor V een Krocus uyt sal rukken
Van haar paruyk om V te lokken in:
Dat Theben voor wiens hoog en ys're muyren,
Den Atlas schrikt, hoe krachtig in gewelt.
Waarom koont gy niet in haar vesten duyren,
Koom Anna, koom kies dan de stat voor 't Velt,
Koom Margareet, ey laat V tog bewegen,
Hier vloeyt Hymeth uyt Nectar Bronnen af,
Hier wert V Perel aan de Kroon geregen
Van Grunoos roem, hijr swaayt de vrede staf.
Kan al dees heerlijkheyt V niet bekoren,
Keer weder by den steedsen Amaranth,
By Tyter die voor veld gesang doet hooren
Sijn Fedel-snaar, kies dan de stat voor 't landt,
Soo sal ik V O! Valke komen noden
Op het Banket van mijn geringigheyt,
Schoon dat het is geen lekkerny der Goden,
Ik heb't nochtans ter eer van V bereydt.

◆ ◆ ◆

Aan de Eer en Deugdrijke Juffer A. GEMMENIG. Die versochte het Swaantje naa haar E[delen] te willen senden.

DAar koomt mijn Swaantje aan gevaren,
Haa! Gemmenig op U begeer,

'T kooft

Selecting a crocus from her headdress
As a token of her regard, and her power.
And how mighty that other power – lofty,
Steely walls of this Thebes before which
Titanic Atlas quails! Why not sojourn
Safe in these precincts? Choose the city
Over the wide world, Margaret. For here
Flow the honey of Hybla, nectar from the wells.
You yourself will flash as a pearl in the crown
Of Groningen's fame, where Peace waves
Her festive staff. Prefer such wonders
To fields of amaranth and Tyter croaking,
Sawing at a fiddle string. Remain in town
And I will invite you to a modest banquet.
We will not feast on the viands of the gods.
But bear in mind it will be made specially
For you and you only, my dear friend.

◆ ◆ ◆

To the honourable and virtuous Miss A. Gemmenig,
who requested that the little Swan be sent to her Ee*

Here comes my little Swan as per your request,
Gemmenig. She cleaves the chop with blithe

---

\* Sometimes the Swan is Brongersma's compilation of verse, sometimes Brongersma herself – or the spirit of her poetic gift and power, fusion of muse and writer and literature in its totality.

[57]

't Klooft met sijn borst de gladde baren,
En 't steekt nu af van Grunoos Veer
Om d'Esche waat'ren te bepeylen,
En 't Y, en 't Sparen te beseylen.
Doch of het door te grooten vlijt
Vermoeyt waar van het driftig roeyen,
Soo bid ik dat g'het gonstig zijt,
Want 't sal sig haast wel derwaarts spoeyen.
'Toont maar dat het U meer bemint
Als gy haar, die het slegs besint,
Om met de pluymtjes wat te speelen,
Of dat gy daar voor U plaisier
Het beesje graag wilt hooren quelen,
Siet soo gewillich is het Dier,
Doch soo g'het voor haar dienst wilt eenig eer betonen,
Soo sult g' (ik eyich geen meer) het met een kus belonen.

◆ ◆ ◆

Aan het kleyne, en Geestige Juffertjen ALEYDA FLUGGER.
Op het aardig Teekenen.

Wat Bloem festoenen staan op 't blanke Veldt,
Hoe naa heeft Testa daar ten toon gesteldt

Sijn

Breast leaving Groningen's waterways
To try Esch and IJ and to sail Haarlem's
Spaarne, yet if the bird despite her zeal
Should slow down being tired of all that
Sculling, let me plead in her behalf she's
Doing the best she can and, besides, she really
Has more love for you than you for her. Just
Caress her feathers, play a while with her
And have the patience to listen to her whistling.
She is devoted to your service. One kiss
Would consummate her bliss – she asks no more.

◆ ◆ ◆

To the enthusiastic and gamine Miss Aleyda Flugger,
on her charming drawings*

The field is bright with festoons of flowers –
Undoubtedly it's Pietro's work, Pietro Testa's.

---

* The precocious Aleyda Flugger was probably the daughter of Luderus Flugger, advocate of Groningen and the lands surrounding it (*Ommelanden*) after 1677. He may have died in 1694. Pietro Testa (1611 or 1612–1650), an Italian master of drypoint, influenced Dutch artists such as Hercules Segers and Rembrandt. Testa's work, usually mythological, can make even flocks of putti seem as natural as birds to the forest he populates with them.

[58]

Sijn konst in Schets op Schets door't deftig malen
Van Grif of Teken-pen: om prijs te halen,
Neen, neen ik mis 't is Fluggertjen dat Ligt,
(Dat wonder van haar tijdt) heeft dat gestigt.
Dat geestig kindt van Eenmaal Seven jaren,
Kan reets door Tekenkrijt veel vreemtheyt baren,
Haar naam, en daadt in Vlugge vlugtigheen,
Zijn wel geschooyt, en komen over een,
Soo dat Natuyr haar toont te zijn genegen,
Wijl's haar beschonken heeft met geest, en zegen.

◆◆◆

Aan Diana.

Als ik niet meer op aard' sal sijn
En aan het graf ben op-gedragen,
Soo denk gy nog wel eens aan mijn
Als gy de Linde-Boom gaat vragen
Wie dat haar schors de gunste deed,
En in 'er bast U namen sneed:
Die sal dan seggen ah! Diaan
Dat heeft U Philis selfs gedaan.

◆◆◆

Aan de Geestrijke Juffer SWAANTIE T.H.

Hoe koont gy met u Swane vlerken
Door boren lugt en dicke swerken?
De Swanen vliegen nimmer hoog
Maar blijven lag in yders Oog,

Doch

Yes, and all these sketches, too, done with
Graving tool and paintbrush. The man wants praise.
No. I'm wrong. It's little Flugger, luminary
Of our epoch, who has performed these feats,
Precocious spirit, only seven years old.
Your chalk can catch any curiosity.
Your name suits you, "Flugger," Flier,
Your name flies off on the backs of your
Winged artwork like a flock of doves
And everyone wants more of it and Nature,
Who blesses you, is happy to endorse your spirit.

♦ ♦ ♦

To Diana\*

When I on earth am no more,
Lying buried in my grave,
Please think of me when you pass
And ask the linden tree just how
It perpetuates the loving dead –
Ask why in its bark your name is cut.
The leafy thing itself, Diana, will sigh
"Phyllis – Phyllis in person did that deed."

♦ ♦ ♦

To the imaginative little Swan, Miss T[er] H[orst]†

How can you do it? You pass with your
Swan's wings through cloud, thin or thick.
But swans as a rule never fly high, stay low,
Remain in eyesight – yet the god of Delos

\* This epitaphic epigram is infused with motifs from Roman love-elegy. The lover imagines her own death. In life, she had incised her beloved's name in the trunks of trees. Her personal memorial impulse exhausts itself in hoping for the perpetuation of the knowledge not of her virtues, her talents, or her beauty – but, rather, of her love for Diana. Elise assumes the guise of Diana on occasion.

† The quasi-domesticated Mute Swans of Friesland may not have flown high, but (*pace* Brongersma) during migration wild swans certainly do. Feral species that might casually have visited Brongersma's neighbourhood in winter are the Bewick's and Whooper swan.

Dog Delius sterkt u met kragten
En voerdt u voort op konst'bre schagten
Tot boven op den Helicon
Waar gy beroerdt de Hengste bron
Door het beroemdt en vlugtig swemmen:
Daar gy het dierbaar vogt doet klemmen.
Aan 't sagte dons van u verstant
In wiens vermogen staat geplant
De Grootste gonst der Hemelingen
Die op Olymp u Lof-Liedt singen
En roepen 't saam koom aan Terhorst
Lest hier u leersaam-rijke borst.

◆ ◆ ◆

Op het Portrait van Juffer S.T.H. in gedachten,
en in 't afwesen gedaan.

Daar is het aardig beeldt
Gebooren uyt gedagten,
En uyt het breyn geteelt
Van mijn genegen kragten,
Waar ik Pigmalion
'K souwt 't leeven door 't aan-schouwen
In blasen, schoon ik kon
Niet als de Schets behouwen,
Denk hoe gy woondt in 't binnenst' van mijn Hert
Wijl gy soo naa van my getroffen wert.

◆ ◆ ◆

Aan

Strengthens you and leads you upward
On precious pinions to the top of Helicon
Where your fabulous swimming stirs
The old horse's well raising delectable
Waves. Your genius bright as your
Smooth plumage hears the praise of all
Olympus. They summon you thus,
"Come, Ter Horst. Read this verse
Commending that learned breast of yours."

♦ ♦ ♦

On the portrait of Miss S. T[er] H[orst] drawn from memory, in her absence

Here is the charming image deriving from
The mind alone impelled by its desire.
Were I Pygmalion, I would breathe life
Into what I can only look at. I grant
I just got down a sketch, but it proves how
Deeply inside, my friend, I always hold you.

♦ ♦ ♦

[60]

Aan de selfde.

Pallas heeft U uyt-gebroedt,
En Apollo op gevoedt,
Iuno heeft U pap geschonken
En g'hebt Lunaas sog gedronken,
Venus heeft U toe-gedekt,
Cupido weer op gewekt,
Hermes heeft U leeren praten,
Jupiter U lopen laaten,
Flora heeft U hooft vercierdt,
Fama U belauwerierdt,
En Euterp U leeren speelen
Op Cimbalen, Fluyt, en Feelen,
Dies sijt gy in alles rijk
En een Pandora gelijk.

♦ ♦ ♦

Cleonte aan Eliseen.

Gy segt ik ben een dief, en steel u rust,
Ah! dat ik soo veel kragt kon in u werken
Men souw me vinden in veel meerder lust
Als jemant nu kan aan mijn wesen merken,
Ik steel segt gy, gy steelt van my veel meer,
Ik steel maar rust, 't schijnt dat ge my koomt terten
'K heb van dat weynig maar alleen de eer,
Gy sijt een Dief en steeldt al menschen herten,
Geef weer aan mijn dat gy gestolen houwt
Ik sal de rust in 't rusten u weer geven,

't Is

To the same*

Pallas hatched, Apollo nursed you.
Juno spooned you pap from a pipkin,
You sucked at Luna's teat, Venus
Dressed you up, Cupid roused
And Hermes tutored, Jupiter
Bestowed his freedom on you,
Fame set laurel on your temples,
Euterpe taught you how to play
On cymbals, flute, and tambour: in
Your riches you resemble Pandora.

♦ ♦ ♦

Cléonte to Elise†

You say I am a thief and steal your rest.
I wish I had as much real power as that.
You would witness more joy in me by far.
I steal from you, you say. You steal from me
Much worse. So I steal your ease, an abstract
Conquest for which I gain mere illusory
Honour, whereas you take men's hearts. Return
What you have stolen from me and I'll give back

* An ambiguous analogy with Pandora serves to celebrate the addressee's abundance of favours.

† The male name "Cléonte" may have appealed to Brongersma, as belonging to a character in Molière's *Bourgeois gentilhomme* (1670). In her work, it appears usually to designate a male personage: but it retains the advantage of some contemporary ambiguity. Aphra Behn, for example, in her *Dutch Lover* (1673), offers a female character of the same name. This poem is the second in *The Swan of the Well* to feature the courtly lovers Cléonte and Elise.

[61]

'Tis seker als men op de reeden bouwt
Dat nooyt een Mens kan sonder hertjen leven.

♦ ♦ ♦

Aan Juffer S.T.H. onder de naam van Philis, die haar met een Mes in de hant sneed.

WAt sinnig staal geeft sulk een sneed:
In Phijlis handt, geen Deomeed
Sent hier het spits sijns Oorlogs speeren
Om Cijpris daar mee te beseeren:
Ik antwoord met een stille mondt
Haar eygen Mes heeft haar gewondt
Dog 'k sal soo sy wil Venus wesen
Haar als Dione weer genesen.

♦ ♦ ♦

Antwoort aan Philis die vreesde vergeten te warden van Cloris.

Vergeefsche sorg baart onrust in de geest
Waar om ist dog mijn Phijlis dat ge vreest,
Daar kan geen wimpel boven Phijlis swayen
Maar Phijlis sal het eelste puyksel maayen
Van Cloris gonst, schoon dat het Nimfedom
Van Gijsbreghts stadt my om en om
Beschansten met haar schoon't, neen wildt geloven
Dat u bevalligheyt het gaat te boven,
Wat baat my 't Goudt dat in de Mijnen rust,
Wat nut geeft fruyt als oog en monde niet lust,

Ik

Your lost ease. My case proves that old saying:
No one can live long without his sweet heart.

♦ ♦ ♦

To Miss S. T[er] H[orst], under the name of Phyllis*

What envious steel has cut such a gash in you?
Diomedes did not injure Phyllis's hand
With the harsh tip of his spear as when he
Wounded the Cyprian goddess. I must acknowledge
Rather her own knife has hurt her: but still I plead
Since she is a Venus, I'll as her Dione help
Her recover as fast as those who bleed only ichor.

♦ ♦ ♦

Answer to Phyllis who confessed herself fearful of being forgotten by Cloris

Worry does the mind no good. What can
You fear, Phyllis? As surely as a banner
Stirs in the breeze, Cloris's favour will
Always ennoble her Phyllis. Although
The pretty nymphdom of Gijsbreght's
City throngs around you no one would
Deny you, beauty, excel it. What good
Is gold that lies in the mine? What use the fruit
Neither eye nor mouth desires? I am like

* Dione (the female version of the name "Zeus") is sometimes represented as the mother of Venus. In the fifth book of the *Iliad*, Venus rescues her son Aeneas after Diomedes has wounded him with a thrown rock. Recognizing that he has encountered a deity not temperamentally suited to the battlefield, Diomedes hurls a spear at the goddess; it tears the skin of her divine wrist near the palm. She retreats, and is maternally soothed by Dione. Fierce Minerva meanwhile mocks the ornamental Venus, insisting that the injury must have originated from the pin of a brooch.

[62]

Ik ben gelijk een rots voor 't slaan der baren
Gy suldt het Cabinet mijns hert bewaren
Geen Y sche stroom Godes hoe rijk van glans
Draagt boven uwe Deugdt de Eere Krans
De vloden die aan Grunoos oever golven
Die houden my in u geheug, bedolven.

♦ ♦ ♦

Aan Althesibé

Althesibée uyt Jlio gesprooten
Sult gy Jtati nu geheel verstooten
Om dalia te plaatsen in U Hert?
O! Hemel gun dat ik in dese smert
Vergaa, of dat den Blixum neer komt storten
Om mijn verdriet daar over af te korten,
Of dat ik in U erm ontfang de Doot
Die gy my duysent maal t'omhelsen boot,
Neen'k leef en staa te vast op U verbonden:
Want wie een Eedt vernreekt, vervalt in sonden.

♦ ♦ ♦

Aan de Goet-aardige Dorimeen.

HOe sugt ge Dorimeen om dat u Tirsis laat
Die gy naar veel gebeen U gunsten hebt geschonken,
Of zijt ge droef om dat Silvander u versmaat,
En Damon die ge hebt betovert door U lonken,
Vertou niet altevast op Minnaars Eedt en wint,

Want

A rock for you, impervious to crashing
Waves. You are warden of my heart's hoard.
No River Ee, however sparkling-bright,
Goddess, can wash away your crown of glory.
The floods that kiss the banks of Groningen
Overwhelm me with thoughts of you.

◆ ◆ ◆

To Alphesibé\*

Alphesibé budding now and blooming
Do you uproot me from your heart,
And set Dahlia there where I was?
Heaven let me die of woe or
Lightning blast, abbreviate my pain
Or permit me, man, to die if
Only in your arms – yours, who once
Begged for thousands of embraces.
No, no! Suffer me to live that I may
Not sin, and may fulfill my vow
Staying faithful to it, and to you.

◆ ◆ ◆

To the good-natured Dorimée

Dorimée, you're sighing, aren't you?
You're heaving sighs now Thyrsis leaves you
To whom you gave your favour after many pleas.
Or are you distressed Silvander scorns you
And Damon, whom your eyes once bewitched?
Don't take seriously a lover's breathy vow.

\* Brongersma's compositor has
"Althesibé," but probably intends a
Gallicized version of Vergil's bucolic
name "Alphesiboeus."

Want't is het ligste stof dat men ter werelt vint.
De herders soeken slegs haar sinnen te vermaken
En schijnen seer verlieft, jaa sterven om U min,
Se stikken in verdriet, en dan in vlammen blaken,
Gelijk een Etnaas gloet, om U haar af Godin,
Een vleyers tong is sagt, maar s'heeft veel wederhaken,
Elendig acht ik die: die in die strikken raken,
Wanneer se als een Son U schoonheyt bidden aan,
En vresen dat ge d'een voor d'ander meer sult agten,
Dan menens dat ge zijt ten eenemaal voldaan,
Of dat se maken van U strafheyt groote klagten,
Neen, neen gedenkt dat vry versotte Dorimeen,
Sy lacchen als se zijn gescheyden, om die reen,
Laat Tirsis quijnen, laat Silvander tranen gieten
Laat Damon steenen, en bemin met onderscheyt,
Soo sult ge vaste Trou, in vastigheyt genieten,
Maar die te ligt gelooft, wert ligtelijk verleyt,
Men moet het huylen van de Crokodil ontvlugten,
Want dat vernist geween, doet menig deerlijk sugten.

♦ ♦ ♦

Aan de Hoog-Edel gebooren Juffer IDA ISABELLA RIPPERDA.

Waar vind' ik stof genoech en eer bewijsen,
O! Isabel, selfs Ida heeft geen groen,
Noch Rosen om aan V mijn plicht te doen,
Noch ik geen macht genoeg V deugt te prijsen.

V goe-

It's made of the flimsiest material to be found on earth.
Shepherds mostly look merely to refresh their senses
When they look lost utterly in love and ardent
Even to dying, choked by distress, scorched by
Its fire as though they swam in molten Aetna
Just for you – their goddess. Flattery's tongue
Is smooth, but indiscriminate, contradictory.
I'm your witness: they tie themselves in knots
When they praise your beauty like the sun
Hoping you will prefer one to the rest of them
And be satisfied, at last – or else complain
Endlessly of the punishment your pride metes out.
Dorimée, don't be besotted. They laugh when they leave
Going over their attempts to seduce you. Let
Thyrsis languish, then – let Silvander drench himself
In wet sadness – leave Damon his effort to astound.
Then you will command their fidelity, or attention.
Shun crocodile tears – glib varnish of fake
Pathos coaxing love from those who woo their doom.

◆ ◆ ◆

To the most nobly born Miss Ida Isabella Ripperda\*

Where can I find stuff equal to your quality
Isabel? Ida has not herself the green or rose
Proper to the task, nor I the power to paint

---

\* Brongersma may pun on "Ida" in the second line, equivocating (as in her poem for Ida Maria Veelkers) between her addressee's name and that of a Mediterranean mountain. Given the frequent bunglings of Brongersma's compositor, Ripperda could be a relative of the poet's supporter Jan Adolf Rappardus.

[64]

V goeden aart verbint my V te roemen,
En dwingt my dat ik op V gaven stof,
Want soo ik V naar V verdiende lof
Souw eeren 'k sou V Iuno moeten noemen,
Wijl staatigheyt V ciert en seer doet achten,
Vergeef me dan Hoog Adelijke Spruyt
Dees macht'loosheen, dog wil eer dat ik sluyt
My voeren in het minst' van V gedachten.

♦♦♦

Aan de Eerwaarde Konst-lievende Juffer ELISABETH CELOS.
Toen haar E. song.

Wat lief en soet geluydt slaat in mijn Ooren?
Wat Hemel-trant koomt my soo net te voren?
Ist een Siereen die voor Ulisses singt:
Neen't is Celos die met haar keeltje dringt
Tot door de dunne lucht, en bos, en velden,
Waar Faunen, Saters haar gesang vermelden,
Waar Filomeeltje duykt in 't Lauwer-groen,
Om luystren wat Elisabeth sal doen,
Waar selfs Apol verwondert haar moet loven,
Jupijn loert mee ten wolken uyt van boven,
Waar Juno 't hooft van schudt wijl dat se hoort
Die held're gorgel-toon die elk bekoort,
Doch Febus als verliest op haar gesangen,
Doet haar een kruyn Lok van sijn Dafne langen
Om haar te pronken, en te komen noodt
Op het Parnas, waar hy haar naam vergoodt.

♦♦♦

Plicht

Your merit. But your real goodness binds me to
The duty of your praise, compels me to make
Something indicative of your talents.
Honour to her in proportion to
Her worth! Let me call you Juno, you walk
With her dignity, deserve her stately
Kind of esteem. You noble branch of noble
Birth, excuse this exhibition of my weakness.
Let at least my effort lodge itself humbly
In the grand forbearance of your recollection.

◆ ◆ ◆

To the admirable and art-loving singer
Miss Elisabeth Celos*

Sweet noise delights my ears
Celestial as precise. A Siren
Such as serenaded Ulysses?
No. Celos. Her resonant throat
Loads with music the yielding breeze,
Forest and field where Fauns and
Satyrs define themselves by being
Within hearing of her who is all
Their talk, where small Philomela
Dives mute into her laurel bower
To study what Elisabeth can do,
Where Apollo himself dumbstruck
Speaks only to praise her, Jove
Staring from the cloud balcony
Above, Juno seduced by the song
No less than by the singer, infused
With that warbling, enchanting
And clear. Phoebus, rapt, approaches
Celos as she sings, and places on her hair
A crown got from Daphne saying, "Come
To Parnassus. I will deify your name."

◆ ◆ ◆

* Johanna Elisabeth Celos may have been born in Veendam, in 1665.

[65]

**PLICHT-OFFER** Opgedraagen aan de kunstlievende Liefhebbers, en Musicijns, Van DOCCUM.

Dus praalt Parnas met ongemeene luyster,
En lokt door haar vertoog een yders hert,
Sy maakt door 't ligt veel and're ligten duyster,
Dewijl zy meer dan yets verheven wert,
Want Phoebus selfs slaat Lier, en sagte Luyten,
Op een Vergode trant, wiens Hemel-klang,
De Kreyts van 't hoog der tronen schijnt te uyten,
Daar yder queelt een lieflijk Choor-gesang:
Iaa wie souw niet door sulke Orgel keelen,
Den ganschen Helicon, en Hipocreen,
De Grieksche magt haar wonderen ontsteelen,
En voeren het op Doccum-bergs Atheen:
Alwaar ik hoor soo meenich Gallem meng'len
Voor 't Altaar: daar Latonaas eenig Soon,
Het Maatgeluyt door sijn volmaakte Eng'len,
Belauweriert stelt op de Eere-Throon.
Hoe kan't dan minder zijn: dat ik (onwaardig
By sulk een Rey geacht) mijn schorre Feel,

Op V verdiensten slaa mits ik rechtvaardig
Vyt offer pligt V soete wonders queel.
Welaan volhard: en cier V Gorgel sluysen
Met Melody: op dat men roemen mag.
Hier swiert de wimpel van de Eelste Muysen
Die men ooyt op Parnas verschijnen sag.

♦ ♦ ♦

Op het

An occasional piece composed for the discerning
dilettanti and musicians of Dokkum*

Parnassus herself gives voice glittering
And in performance seduces
Everyone's heart and her light
Makes her rivals' dim, more proof
Of how meritorious her
Elevation. Phoebus strikes the lyre,
Sings and divinizes the listener
With a tone decorous to the highest throne
Where a lovely chorus warbles
In perfect concert yet still we ask
Who could sing accompaniment
Adequate to the power of that pipe organ?
Heliconian Hippocrene, the Greek
Maiden and all her wonders –
It's astounding here on the height
Of Dokkum's Athens. I hear
So many echoes mingling before
The altar where Latona's only
Son presides splendid on his dais
Laurelled, attended by impeccable
Angels. I am inferior to all this.
How should I detain the attention
Of such an assembly with my
Weak measure? What I sing
Honestly please accept as tribute
To your sweet marvelousness.
Keep performing, your own
Throats and melody best
Glorify, exemplify the reason
Of your praise. See how the standard
Of the muses flies from the peak of Parnassus.

♦♦♦

\* Dokkum is Brongersma's probable birthplace, a town less than twenty kilometres north-east of Leeuwarden.

[66]

Op het vertrek van Elisene Naar Vrankrijk.

VErlaat gy my Troulose Eliseen,
En siet gy niet hoe bitter dat ik ween
Om U Vertrek, hoe kan ik dat gedogen,
O hert van steen, en gy wert niet bewogen.
Ist niet genoeg dat ons den E-stroom scheyt,
Daar tussen bey de helsche Scyla leyt:
En daar Charibdis bast met open monden,
Schoon sy't niet al verswelg't soo geeft se wonden,
U is bekent wat klippen van gewelt
Vaak waren tussen ons belang gestelt.
Dan Draaken bits, en kort in een gedrongen
Diens nek ik heb met Herk'les knods verwrongen,
Waarom gy dik veel tranen hebt gestort
En my daar door tot klagen aan geport,
't Gedenkt my nog hoe gy met natte wangen
My als een klis bleeft aan de leden hangen,
Dan seyde gy 'k moet sterven soo gy gaat,
En Eliseen hier eenich blijven laat,
Maar ah! Cleonte sterft om't droevigh scheyen,
Sijn oogen doen niet dan U reys beschreyen.

Wat

On Elise's departure for France*

Faithless Elise, can you really leave?
Don't you hear how bitterly I'm wailing?
How can I take it, you stony heart?
You look unmoved. Isn't it enough the River
Ee separates us since infernal Scylla
Waits there, and Charybdis barks with gaping
Lips? Even if she doesn't devour everything
Still she deals wounds. You know very well
What cliff faces of violence clap together
Between us. I tied the neck of the snappish
Serpent in Herculean knots. It made
You weep hard, and made me protest. You
Clung to me wet-cheeked wrapping your body
To me tight as a burr crying, "Elise
Will die if you ever go away leaving
Her alone." But Cléonte dies instead,
Eyes blurred at your departure. What has

* As he laments, Cléonte characteristically mingles reference to local features (the River Ee) with classical personification and evident allegory. Brongersma possibly confuses the identities of Scylla and Charybdis, monsters escaped by Odysseus. Homer says Scylla has six heads, lives in a lair hollowed in a strait-side precipice, and sounds like a puppy; Charybdis the cyclonic monster three times a day alternates between exposing the sea bottom and spewing out a great volume of suppressed sea water. The "cliff faces of violence" may recall the Roving Rocks that Odysseus's ship managed to escape. Circe appears in her usual role as a malignant enchantress. Sobs that pass midair between parted friends revise a conceit in one of the first poems in *The Swan of the Well*: "On Miss E[lisabeth] J[oly]'s inaccessibility so long as the water's surface alternately froze and thawed, and people could get about by neither boat nor skate blade."

[67]

Wat loon verdient sijn lijden? wrede spreek,
Ontdankb're, ah! hoe is mijn hert soo week,
Ik smelt met Nestis in mijn eygen dropen,
En gy doet Lethes vloet te snelder lopen.
Baldadige vergeet doch nooyt den Eedt
Die gy my voor der Goden vierschaar deed.
Gy weet den hemel is het selfs beleden,
En 't staat in 't hert van U en my gesneden,
Doch sal nu dat de Blessche Bos-Godes
Gedompelt leyt in 't naare Lijk-Cypres,
U naamen kussen, en met groot verlangen
De tijdingh van U wederkomst ontfangen.
Gaa, gaa dan heen, en grens aand' Lely-strandt,
Voer U geluk met vreugt weer in ons lant.
Laat Circes Tover-konst U niet verblinden,
Stuyr my een sugt op wieken van de winden,
Mijn snikken gaan U stap op stap te moet,
En doen U alle daag een heuse groet.
Vaar wel dan met dees kus, mijn hert moet breeken,
Doch 't is genoech daar Traanen konnen spreeken.

♦ ♦ ♦

Op het vertrek van Eliseen naar Frankrijk, en de perijk'len onder weeg.

Gy gaat dan Eliseen Brittansche Leelien plukken
Vyt het Lovische-hof, misschien kon dat V drukken,

Want

His passion earned him? Tell me, ingrate. How
Could my heart be so weak? The lachrymose
Queen of the Dead melts in me, fills me
With tears. And you make Lethe's flood flow
All the faster. Wanton, do not forget
The oath that you before the gods solemnly
Swore. Heaven's witness is graven in
Our hearts. Yet now Blessum's sylvan goddess
Lies in her bitter bed, kissing your name
Hopeless and yearning. Just go – go and pass
The border of the lily-coast. May bliss
Pilot you cheerfully back into our
Country. Do not let Circe's sorcery
Blind you. Send a sigh on the wings of the wind.
My sobs will toss and gust to meet it halfway
And bring their hoarse greetings, every day.
Farewell, then, with this kiss (my heart must break).
Yet it suffices. The eloquence is all tears.

♦ ♦ ♦

On Elise's dangerous going into France*

Naïve lady, beset by pricking hazards,
Go right ahead. Pluck the lilies of Brittany
In Louis's court. Two fiery snakes

---

* In this poem, Scylla and Charybdis are accurately described. With her talk of Proserpina's rape by Pluto and her imagery of pricking, Brongersma's speaker appears concerned for Elise's chastity and safety. The regnant king of France is Louis XIV.

## [68]

Want al te stout bestaan veroorsaakt ongelukken
    Gy kent de prijke niet.
Den Ingank wert bewaart van twee paar vierge Draken,
Die door haar mont, en neus, een ganse Hel uytbraken,
Wiens sterke Solfer-vlam het sterre-dak doet blaken,
    Daarom wel voor V siet.
Megare, Tisiphon, met sulke rasernyen
Daar moet gy Eliseen: in 't eerste tegen stryen,
V Heldenmoet en kan V daar van niet bevryen
    Of g'most een Iason zijn.
Noch vint gy Scyla die de Sicyljaanse plassen
Doet spatten in de Lucht door 't yselijke bassen,
En waar Caribdis doet de Zeên ten Hemel wassen,
    O tweede Proserpijn!
Wagt u en wilt de Bloem der Goden niet genaken,
Wat middel Eliseen soo Pluto u quam schaken,
Cleonte kon de hoon van dat gewelt niet wraken,
    Sijn machten zijn te swak.
't Is beter dan dat gy dit opset af wilt breeken,
Eer gy u in de muyl der prijkelen gaat steeken,
Waarom Cleonte V ootmoedelijk koomt smeken,
    Schoon 't voorneem lijt een krak.
De stroom Godinnen, en de vroolijke Dryaaden,
Die sullen Eliseen bepronken met Cieraaden,
En V Cleonte sal met Thym, en Roose-blaaden
    V Kransen, maar ay mijn!
Soo gy noch op de Golf van V gevaar wilt swerven,
Vaar wel, en keer haast weer het scheyden doet my sterven
Want wat het hert bemint dat kan het oog niet derven,
    Of 't moest van Mermer zijn.

♦♦♦

Ant-

Guard the entry, who through nose
And mouth breathe sheer hell
Lighting with sulphur the whole
Vault of starry heaven.
Megara, Tisiphone: Elise
You must face these furies
And unless you are the peer of Jason
Your heroic temper will not win.
Here is Scylla seizing and lifting her prey
Where Charybdis first ravens, then heaves
The sea into the sky. My new Proserpina!
Do not be tempted by that divine flower.
It is the lure cast by Pluto
To ravish you. Cléonte can't repel
The sardonic exercise of such force,
Her powers are too weak. Lady
Give up your plan before you throw
Yourself into the thorny bush.
You want anyway to lean over the abyss
Of your imperilment? Very well.
This parting kills me. What the heart
Loves the eye wants always to see
Or that organ must consist of marble.

◆ ◆ ◆

[69]

Op het onverwagte Leet, en Siek vinden van Eliseen.

'K Voel nog het vier in d'ooge randen
Ha! Eliseen van 't bittre leet
Waarop 'k onnosel kwam te stranden
Doe gy my deed' door schrift de weet
Te koomen om wat vreugt t'erlangen
Daar ik u vont met koorts bevangen.

'K sag door d'half ope siek-gordynen
Geslingert om 't bepylaart dak
De blyde Gitte-blicken schynen
Daar noch een vriendlyk vonkje stak
Die soete mont gelykse plagte
Begroete my, en minlyk lagte.

Maar ach! niet lang naar 't eerst omermen
De doot, die 't moort-tuyg had gewet
Had geen mêedogen met myn kermen,
Maar hield' de schicht op haar geset.
Ick stont als Niobé van krachten
Versteent, en smolt in droeve klachten.

Opt'laast door 't bang en jammer weenen
Het maagre spook kreeg mêedely
En schoot in plaats van Elisene
De pyl recht over t'hooft voor by

En

On Elise's unexpected taking sick and suffering*

My eyes sting like fire, red from harsh sadness,
Elise, after I passed a thoughtless judgement
When we had set a date to see each other –
Then I found you feverish, quarantined.
Peeking past the propped-open sick-
Curtain hung from the pillar-supported
Canopy, your jet-black glance pierced me,
Pricked, befriended me: your mouth teased,
Adorably laughed. But right after,
Death, who held his mortal weapon ready,
Ignored my plea, and aimed that lightning bolt.
I stood like Niobe stony, heaving sighs.
At last, the gaunt spook relented, melting,
And shot his dart not at Elise, but at

* Diana transformed Egeria, a nymph tearfully disconsolate at the death of her husband Numa, into a fountain. Like many of the poems involving Elise, this one pursues the protocols of love-elegy, inventing an episode in an ongoing affair. Elise's eyes are always characterized as black.

## [70]

En trof niet dan de wint en schimmen
Wyls' in de lucht scheen op te klimmen

Soo dat alree de bleeke kaaken
Berooft van bloos en leevens root
Beginnen weer op nieuw te blaaken
En stellen haar als buyten noot,
Waarom ik sal de Tempel-reyen
Oprechten en dank offers spreyen.
Jaa Eliseen myn tweede leeven
Ik waar als Orpheus neer gedaalt
En myn (waart gy me niet gegeeven)
Euridice weer om gehaalt:

'K waar als Egeria verdronken
In heet getraan, en tot een Bron,
(Myn waarde om u·doot) gesonken
Wyl my geen troost vertroosten kon,
Want sonder V vind ik verdrieten
Daar yder sou syn wensch genieten.

◆ ◆ ◆

Op de nieuwsgierigheyt van Juffer E. J. die midden door de Ruitery hene drong, en geen vrese had voor 't Paarde trappelen, en 't Schieten, daar sy gebeden wierd' niet te gaan.

'K Had nimmermeer gedagt dat gy
Soo boven Aart V Aart veraarde

Wijl

The space above her head, air and shadow,
Himself rising, ascending into sky.
Already pale cheeks bereft of bloom gleam
Red, reporting "She's out of danger now."
Therefore I will raise a temple after
The classical plan, to pour libations, plenty.
My other life, Elise, I verged on being Orpheus,
Going down to get you, lost Eurydice.
I was an Egeria sunk in streaming tears,
A deep well – yet overflowing. Your death
Moved me beyond any consolation.
Without you I detested anyone
Enjoying the fulfillment of a wish.

❖ ❖ ❖

On Miss E[lisabeth] J[oly]'s bold curiosity: despite being warned away, she thrust a passage through the midst of the cavalry and betrayed no fear of the trotting horses and the shooting\*

I had never thought I would say of you
Supernatural woman, to change your nature

---

\* Brongersma's poetry to Elise represents her in diverse situations, each of which illuminates a facet of her character. In France, her feminine virtue may suffer encroachment. In sickness, Elise displays her vulnerability, but also the resilience of her teasing nature. Here the same woman shows Achillean courage. Elsewhere Elise's intellect receives praise.

[71]

Wijl gy V aan der Dochtren zy
Als Thetis Soon: soo net verpaarde.
Maar 'k sie daar steekt een Helden moet
In 't Hert, en tragt als Amasone
Te grijpen Speer, of swaart, en doet
Daar door Natuir, en kragt vertoonen.
Want waar de Trommel Oproor slaat
Daar pronkt gy nooyt met gouwe draaden,
Of Mars sijn Vanen waayen laat
Soo Ciert gy u met Krijgs gewaden.
Schoon Cipris kroost u bidt, en smeekt
En soekt u van het spoor te leyden
Daar d'Oorlog moort, en bloetdorst queekt
In 't steeken van de velt Schalmeyen.
Gy draagt al eeven wel 't Helmet
En Veeder bos: gelijk de Mannen,
Gy bouwt de Flits boog aangeset
Om strijbre peesen in te spannen,
Iaa gy laat in V: sien Achil
Schoon hy niet waar als gy: in weesen:
Want tusschen Bey is geen verschilt
Alleen gy blijft: soo g'waar 't voor deesen.

◆ ◆ ◆

De klagende en verlangende ALCIONEE.

HElaas mijn Ceyx hoe kan ik langer leeven
Van U: daar gy U hertstogt hebt gedreven
In binnenst van mijn Ziel, ag ag! wat raat
    Alcyonee vergaat.

En

Among women you are Thetis's son,
Only he of his sex your proper peer.
Hero's courage flashes in your heart
Fit with Amazons to wield spear or sword
Infused with manifest Nature's might.
Where drums rattle you do not simper
In girlish golden dress: where the banners
Of Mars float on the breeze, you put on
The robes of his vocation. Already the children
Of Cypris appeal to you, to make you feel
Her touch, because war is murder and bloodthirst
Breeds in the tingling fifes of the muster.
You wear on your helm a plume like the men's.
You hold the bow bent to launch a fateful arrow.
Yes, you are the very image of Achilles
Yet he was ignorant compared to you
So there's really no parallel at all
And being incomparable, alone,
You prevail, unique woman! over him.

♦ ♦ ♦

The longing lamentation of Alcyone\*

Ceyx, how can I live any longer away
From you? You have kindled passion in
My inmost soul. Whatever sense Alcyone

\* Alcyone was a child of Neptune. In sailing to consult Apollo's oracle at Clarus in Ionia, her beloved Ceyx went to confer with the sun – hence the prominence (perhaps) of that luminary in Brongersma's poem. The daughter of Tiresias had founded this solar oracle, from which its patron god received the epithet "Clarius." A reader of Ovid (*Metamorphoses* 11.415–748) would know that Brongersma's Alcyone has not yet found Ceyx's corpse washed up on the shore. In due course, she will be with him transformed into that strong and beautiful bird the kingfisher. They will build a nest on the open sea, establishing the winter series of tranquil "halcyon" days. Mother Hyrie wept so much over the death of her son Cygnus (so Ovid reports in *Metamorphoses* 7.371) that she dissolved into a fountain. Cygnus, as his name suggests, suits with the book into which Brongersma's allusion obliquely enrolls him. Called "Swan," he assumed the shape of one. Prince Paris of Troy jilted the nymph Oenone, preferring Helen. The plaints of the bereft Alcyone resonate with those of Cléonte, expressing misgivings for a beloved making a journey by sea.

[72]

En smelt met Hyrie wijl gy sijt verdweenen
Naa my u Son een weynig heelt beschenen,
Daar nog den Oever rookt van mijn getraan
      En doet de weergalm slaan.
Gy gaat: en laat my op de strant verwringen
De handen, en het nare Scheyliet singen
Om met de Swaan een eynd' te maaken van
      Mijn Leeven, maar hoe kan.
Soo'n teedre borst alst mijne: dat verdragen
O neen: ik sal de Dodelijke plagen
Nu ik't bedenk, nog in mijn boesem voen
      Om u mijn pligt te doen.
Op hoop gy U sult haast weer herwaars spoeyen
Wijl'k laat het suyverst' bloet tot pekel vloeyen,
Want soo gy lang met suckelende straf
      My pijnt, ik daal in 't graf.
Hoe vaak sluyt ik mijn Oogen langs de baren
Als een Enôon: waar door gy sijt gevaaren,
U Psijche soekt, en sugt, nog menigmaal
      Om U: en het onthaal.
Daar gy op't laast door U vertrek ontruste
Mijn stil gemoet, en droeve Lippen kuste,
Daar daar ik met de Sonnelingen scheen
      Te plengent 't Barren steen,
Ik sal met Peneloop de Tijtweb weeven,
En op mijn Tong U naamen laten sweeven
Tot gy U naar beloft: weer tot my voegt
      En 't haakend' hert vernoegt.

◆ ◆ ◆

Aan

Had, she has lost it and melts with Hyrie:
By all appearances you have wholly vanished.
Your sun has shone on me in some measure
Yet my tears have misted our shore, and the echo
Of my lament persists. You have gone
And left me on the beach to wring my hands
And sing a wretched song of parting prepared
With the swan to end my life but could I, even?
How could I with such a soft breast as mine?
Then protract this vexed mortality instead
To render you my duty in the hope
You hurry back, while my rich blood converts
Itself continually to teary saltwater
Since your absence, like sickening punishment,
Pains me to the brink of the grave. How often
Like Oenone on her island, my eyes
Have quizzed the barren ocean. "Where are you?"
Your Psyche keeps on asking over and
Over, demanding our reunion. When
You left to consult the oracle my mind
Misgave; you kissed my miserable lips
Intending to tarry with the daystar while
Tears were mine. a Penelope to weave, unweave
The shroud, your name floating on my tongue
Till your promise is fulfilled and we join
And that coupling contents the heart.

♦ ♦ ♦

[73]

Aan Juffer KLARA BARTHOLS Die van voorneem waar my
te besoeken, doch belet door eenige voorvallen, wederom
genoot wert.

WYl my de Eer om V te sien mislukte
Van gister' doen Apol my deed' de weet,
En met een sachte stem in d'ooren drukte,
Stont ik om V t'ontsangen al gereet.
Maar stierd' een post verdrietig door't verblijven,
Verstont dat u een ander gaf belet:
Waarom ik ben genootsaakt dit te schrijven,
Dat ghy het woornemen noch hout vast geset.
Ik sal in't kleyn vertrek: met Baucis tonen,
Mijn hertendis: die voor u staat bereyt,
Schoon Goden in geen strooyen hutten wonen
Soo daalens wel om laag in nedrigheyt.
Wel dan u sal geen Berggedrogt doen schromen,
Vrees niet voor die: die u tot aller tijt
Vyt Konstgenootschap wil (soo ghy sult komen)
Omhelsen, en u misdaat schelden quijt.

◆ ◆ ◆

Op't seggen de Digt-konst uyt andre Boeken te soeken,
en te schrijven.

SOuw ik mijn Rijm: uyt andre digten soeken
Soo waar ik wel van doen al's wereldts Boeken,

O neen

To Madame Klara Barthols who really did intend to
visit but, impeded by various mishaps, receives from
me a second invitation*

I was deprived of the honour of seeing you
Yesterday. Apollo told me you were coming
Impressing the promise gently on my ears –
I was all ready to receive my welcome guest.
The post arriving brought disappointing news.
Someone else detained you. For which reason
I feel the need to write assuring you, you still
Must act according to our previous plan.
Venison awaits you on the dinner table
Of my little room – I, like Baucis,
Knowing even gods who hardly ever
Dwell in huts of straw condescend to call on
Humble lodgings. Don't fear that you will
Have to scramble to a mountaintop
To escape a flood. Relax. Contribute
Your usual sophistication, and so end
This prolix rebuke to a little peccadillo.

◆ ◆ ◆

On the commonplace that poetic power only comes
from reading and copying pre-existent books†

Draw my rhymes out of other books?
Where to stop? Consult them all?

---

* Brongersma writes another invitation poem. Ovid tells the story of Baucis and Philemon, a poor and aged mortal couple hospitable to sojourning gods. As a reward for their virtue, they escape to a Phrygian mountain sanctuary while an angry Jupiter floods and drowns the less generous remainder of humanity (*Metamorphoses* 8.631–724). It was from Barthols that Brongersma in an earlier poem borrowed Guarini's *The Faithful Shepherd*.

† Even in the eighteenth century, critics charged female poets, such as Charlotte Smith, with plagiarism when they merely practised the art of allusion. Brongersma's epigram insists on divine inspiration. But her God may like to display His wide reading.

[74]

O neen mijn vrient dat diende maar tot spot
Het geen ik heb dat is alleen van Godt.

♦ ♦ ♦

Op't Treurspel van Rodrik, Konink det Gotten, of de ondergank
derselve Regeringe in Spangien, Gerijmt door de hooch Geleerde
Heer Ludolf Smids, Medecijne Doctor binnen Groningen

Heeft Roderik de staf der Gottsche Heerschappyen
Als dwingeland geswaayt in d'ongetoomde Min,
Florinde heel vergramt heeft al de Rasernyen
Om haar geleden smaat daar door gesoogen in:
Mit's Vaders hulp, als ook Tancredos veynseryen
Het Zarazeensche Heyr deed' klaatren op den Troon
Van Spangiens trots. Iae liet door Mooren overstryen
Haar schender selfs, uyt spijt, en roven Hooft, en Kroon.
Dus valt het Rijk ter neer door stoute geyligheden,
Wijl dat de Wraak hoog is op Moortsugt uytgespant,
Wiens Treur Toneel Heer Smids ons koomt in Rijm ontleden
Waar door de Lauwer op sijn voorhooft wert geplant.
Hy toont Toledos Ramp, en Kaboos yslijk wreeken,
Dog met dees Nederlaag beswijkt mijn Swanne veer.
En geeft bekranste Tolk tot Lof dit eenig Teeken
(Dat's soo ik yets verdien) daar van aan V de Eer.

♦ ♦ ♦

Op het Wangedrocht, de Tweedracht, Of Oorlogh

Andromeda sal dan onschuldig sijn verslonden
Te reeten, en verscheurt door duysenden van wonden,

Neen

Friend, people would deride me.
What I do have, comes from God alone.

◆◆◆

On the tragedy of Rodrigo, king of the Visigoths, or the overthrow of that very tyrant in Spain, versified by the much-praised Mr Ludolph Smids, Doctor of Medicine at Groningen\*

Rodrigo king of Visigoths twisted
The sceptre of his rule to despotic passion
Without restraint. Florinda embittered summoned
Furies to avenge that misdeed as bad
As sly Tancred's – enjoying, however, the Count
Her father's help. A Saracen army seized
Proud Spain's throne. In rage she stirred the Moors
To vindicate her rape. They took crown and head
Alike. Thus heedless licence destroyed the nation.
Vengeance cannot be kept from dealing death.
Smids offers us this episode in rhyme, earning
Him the laurel that ennobles his capacious brow.
Toledo's sack he describes, Cadiz's abject wreck.
At these portents this Swan's quill stops quite still,
Mute witness a garland to peerless art
So that in the miracle I yet retain some part.

◆◆◆

On Trespass – Discord – War†

Will Andromeda the innocent be eaten
Fettered, torn by thousands of wounds?

\* Smids's play bore the title *Rodrigo, or Florinda Raped*. It relied on the precedent of Lope de Vega (1562–1635). Amanda C. Pipkin quotes from this drama in her *Rape in the Republic, 1609–1725: Formulating Dutch Identity*. The Smids line that Pipkin cites reappears in Brongersma: "Yes, she herself allowed the Moors to overtake her violator and steal his head and crown" (204). Brongersma's encomium salutes Florinda's spirit, but notes the consequences of her intransigence: the destruction of entire cities, half of whose suffering population shares Florinda's sex. Smids drew on legend, not fact. Supposedly, Count Julian – governor of Ceuta (a Moroccan seaport opposite Gibraltar) – sent his daughter Florinda to the Visigothic court. From the palace window, King Rodrigo then saw her swimming at Cava's baths and assaulted her. In *Toledo: The Story of an Old Spanish Capital*, Hannah Lynch dissents from the tale: "There is no proof whatever that Rodrigo was the wretched sensualist the historians delight to paint" (58–9). Landing at Gibraltar (etymologically, Tarik's Crag), a Muslim army under Tarik defeated Rodrigo's forces around 711. Tancred, ruler of Salerno, comes from Boccaccio's *Decameron*. His daughter Sigismonda, early widowed, falls in love with the low-born Guiscard. Disapproving of his daughter's choice, Tancred takes her suitor captive and strangles him. He cuts out Guiscard's heart. Then he dispatches this organ to Sigismonda. She kisses it; she drinks poison; and

[75]

Neen Perseus, neen grijp aan het Schilt, de Helm, het Swaart
    Waar mee gy 't gruwsaam dier te strijden eevenaart,
Brengt dapperheyt, en kracht wilt V manhaftig tonen,
Laat sien het Slangen hooft, het pronkbeelt der Gorgonen,
    Verbriefsel dog die mont die happig open staat
    Te swelgen met een slok: d'onnosele, schaf raat,
Span in de magten van u groote moedigheden
Op dat g'Andromeda ontbint, en stelt te vreden,
    Wiens Moeder was de wrok van al haar droeve smert,
    Door Trotsigheen? om wien zy dus mishandelt wert,
Gy hebt den Athlas selfs hoe vreeselijk verscheenen
Verandert in een Rots, jaa bonderden in steenen,
    Gy koont ik weet wanneer gy't slegs in u besluyt,
    Dit wangedrogt wel haast het leven bannen uyt.
V staalen Erm swaayt niet dan blijde zeege-pralen
Daar Eendragt laat het oog van vrintlijkheyt op stralen,
    Voert in ons lant dat staag in Liefde heeft gebloeyt
    De vreede stroom: op dat het weer eens overvloeyt.
De Maagt bynaa u tot een waare Bruyt geschonken,
Sal haar verlosser dan met minnelijker lonken
    Beschouwen als wel eer, vermits se siet dat zy
    Behouwt het Leven: en van alle sorg is vry.

◆ ◆ ◆

Aan Phillis.

GY segt ik ben u hert, wel aan ik sal't geloven,
U Hert leyt onder en u tonge Phylis boven,
Seer verre van malkaar soo dat ik niet en weet,
Of dese eenigheyt ware gront bekloet.

                                                      Gy

No, Perseus. No. Take up against that gruesome
Beast shield, helmet, blade and bring
To bear your courage. Show heroic
Force and that snaky head, the gorgon's glory.
Shatter the gape that would devour in
A gulp. Caution! Clamp the monster with
Bold drive. Unbind Andromeda. Restore
The peace her queenly mother's pride has wrecked –
Cassiopeia's daughter has grimly suffered.
You have changed Atlas the Titan himself –
A wonder and a terror – into a crag,
Into myriad stones. You can I know
Deprive this offender of its offensive life.
Triumph doesn't make you swing your iron arm
For modesty glows from your gaze,
Directs streaming joy back into our land
Where it flowed before, and constantly
Flourished in delight. The girl is almost
Your true bride, her loving looks will linger
On you – provided that you rescue her
Preserving her life, freeing her from fear.

◆ ◆ ◆

To Phillis*

You say I am your sweetheart. I want to be.
But your heart, Phillis, lives below – your tongue
Up above. They are so far from each

she dies on the bed where she and Guiscard used to consummate their passion. Sigismonda and Florinda are figures linked by a proud assertion of their right to dispose of their bodies as they please.

† Andromeda's mother, Cassiopeia, Ethiopian queen, boasted that she surpassed the Nereids in beauty. Vengeful Poseidon sent a sea monster to afflict the coasts. Only the sacrifice of the princess would suffice to efface the insult. Equipped with Hades's helmet, Athena's mirror, and Hermes's sandals, as well as the petrific head of Medusa, Perseus prevailed.

* Phillis is probably Elisabeth Joly.

[76]

Gy zijt gelijk de Bye, die by gebrek van Rosen
De Distelbloem tot haar vermaking heeft gekosen,
Dog dat is my genoeg, ik neem het seggen aan.
't Is Beter half gekleet, als moeder naakt te gaan.

♦ ♦ ♦

Aan Juffer S. wilmsonn, Die bloemen gesonden wierde op Pinxter-
avont: van Caritate, die bestrooyt waaren met Silver-sant.

Geen Flora stuyrt dees gloende Pinxter bloemen
Maar Karitaat om V daar door te roemen
Want soo veel kleurtjes als dit Tuytltje geeft,
Soo veel gevalligheyt u waarde heeft
Seyt zy: en 't deeg van Apricosen
Vertoont het root uws Purperrose blosen,
Dog soo sy waar gelijk Vulcaan een smit,
Sy smeede Venus selfs het dool sijns wit.
Maar nu gaat op 't Poëtse ambalt klinken,
V Deugden, die gelijk als sterren blinken.

♦ ♦ ♦

Aan mijn waarde Suster A. BRONGERSMA

DAar hoort ge dan tot lof mijn Swaantje singen
Van yder die haar gonst genooten zijn,
Daar siet ge haar op Grunoos Bron-nat springen,
Schoon Soylus spouwt sijn adderlijk fenijn,
Daar hoort g'in spijt van Eris, haar gesangen
Geset op trant van heylge hemel klangen:

Waar

Other I don't know if they operate
As one, or not. You seem like a bee
For want of roses choosing for refreshment
A thistle. Yet that's enough for me.
I trust your words. It's better to go half-clad
Than to go naked, entirely naked.

◆ ◆ ◆

To Miss S[usanna] Wilmson with flowers sent
on Easter Eve, over which Charity has sprinkled
silver glitter*

No Flora sends these shining Easter blossoms.
Charity herself, rather, confesses
(Even boasts) that rich in colour as this
Bouquet is, you – her love – are richer still
In grace. And the blush of apricots only
Emulates the heat of your pink cheek.
Were you like Vulcan a smith you'd forge
For Venus something so very bright.
But I write verse here, and I must rhyme.
Like shining stars (see!) your virtues climb.

◆ ◆ ◆

To my worthy sister A. Brongersma†

Listen. My Swan sings praise to any
Who showed her favour, ever. Look.
She frisks in Groningen's spring-fed waters.
Let Zoilus spit venom: her song persists.
Let Eris curse. Still the bird blesses heaven

* I translate Brongersma's "Karitas" – the chief Christian virtue – as "Charity."

† Only this poem mentions Brongersma's sister. Zoilus of Amphipolis became a byword for griping when he reproached Homer's grammar. Eris is the goddess of strife. Brongersma uses the language of immersion to describe her sister's religious faith. It is in keeping with the Swan's well-waters.

[77]

Waar naar gy meer als and're wijsen dorst:
Wijl dat U hert daar vast leyt aan geklonken
En Geest'lijk laast U Godt geminde borst,
Wiens drift U ziel in yver doet ontsonken,
Daar hoort ge 't al, uyt haar verschorde keel,
Doch sal terwijl ik U hier door verveel
Versoeken dat ge wilt mijn drift verschoonen
En 't Swaantje voor een tijt laat by U wonen.

♦ ♦ ♦

Aan de jonge en Minnelijke Flora, Juffer H.J.

'K Sie Zephyrus verbleekt, en droef verschijnen,
't Schijnt dat hy om dien jongen Flora truirdt,
En wasems sugt op sugt, in het verdwijnen
Om dat haar weder keer te lange duyrdt.
Hy wagt, en oogt geduyrig naar het zuyden,
Hy vraagt de Lente waar sijn Flora blijft,
Die eeuwig prijkt in bloemgewas, en Kruyden,
Schoon het Saisoen op winter-pluymen drijft.
De Faunen quijnen en de vlugtige Dryaden
Vermengen haar geklag by 't Nimfedom,
De Bos-goon weenen, met de Oreaden
En d'Bron-maagt stort daar duysent tranen om.
Dog Cloris die se vaak beschonk met Rosen,
(Waar mee haar blonde tuyt is opgehuldt)
Versugt dewijl s'haar had tot lust gekosen:
Daar nu haar boesem is met rouw vervuldt.

Wat

For which you, more than others, know the thirst
Since you have bound your heart to holiness
And obliged your loving breast to God
Immersing your soul in ardent desire.
So her hoarse throat takes up that theme of yours.
Yet please, sister, in the meantime tarry,
Suffer yourself to beautify my music.
Let the little Swan dwell a while with you.

♦ ♦ ♦

To the young and loveable Flora, Miss H. J[oly]

Zephyrus pales, and casts his eyes downward.
He would grieve his young Flora gone away,
With sigh after sigh following her recession
From which her return must be too tardy.
He sways and gazes southward asking Springtime
Where does his Flora delay and where linger? –
Who always wears a nosegay and robe of leaves
While the Winter whistles past on icy plumes
And Fauns repine and fugitive Dryads
Multiply complaint with sister Oreads
And the girl of the spring drips tears in the slush
And Cloris whom Flora loaded with roses often
Binding her blonde curls with that crop of delight
Sighs, bosom brim with cold woe? What whisper

Wat luyster bragt haar soet, en lieflijk, wesen,
Wat morgen-son, of blijden Dageraat
Scheen door haar glans ten vollen op geresen,
Wanneer s'haar flikring schoot op elks gelaat.
Keer Flora keer, wie kan die geuren derven?
En laat u Zephyrus daarom niet sterven.

◆ ◆ ◆

Herders Klagt.

WAar vliet gy wrede! seg: waar heen Astré
Ik ben geen Wolf, geen Leeuw, maar hoed het Vee
In 't Reder Bos, en op de Heuvlen mee
  Van Pelens Weyden.
Ik bid u schoonheyt aan in mijn gemoet
Gy vlugt gelijk een Duif voor d'Arent doet,
Mijn ziel wert door 't gesigt van u gevoet
  En doet my leyden
Van d'een ind' ander plaats, ag ag bedroeft
Ik ben geen Polifeem dat dit behoeft.
Weet dat gy my daardoor te seer bedroeft
  O wrange pijnen.
Siet wie ik ben: en toont dog medely
Soo gy volhardt ik woed in Raserny
Want in de hoop van deese minnery
  Moet ik verdwijnen.
Ik laat mijn Lammen, en mijn Hut alleen
Om u: O Hert: veel herder dan een steen
Veel dover als de Zee voor mijn geween
  En droevig kermen.

*Keer*

Would summon that sweet and loveable being,
What morning sun, blithe dawn uprising in
Shiny brilliance opening her glittering
Breast to all? Return, Flora, how could
Any subsist without your scent? For the lack
Of that perfume Zephyrus is panting, perishing.

◆ ◆ ◆

The shepherd's complaint*

Where are you running to, cruel woman!
Tell me where Astrée's going. I'm no wolf,
No lion. I watch the flock in the Shipowner's
Wood, from the hill of Pelen's meadow.
I plead with your beauty, you flee from me
Like a dove before an eagle, my pained soul
Falls at your feet just for a glimpse of you
Flitting from one place to another, my
Lady, stay! True Polyphemus may
Deserve such treatment, but not me. Aching
Bitter grief you cause me. Look at me,
Show sympathy, you keep resisting,
I rave and rant in frustration, lost
In hope of love returned leaving hut
And flock alone for you, O heart harder
Than stone, deafer than the sea to imploring.

* The influential Luis de Góngora y Argote (1561–1627) wrote on the topic of the cyclops Polyphemus, the Nereid Galatea, and the mortal Acis. He used the precedent of the thirteenth book of Ovid's *Metamorphoses* (750–897). Uncouth and risible Polyphemus crushed the object of Galatea's love beneath an immense boulder. Galatea then transformed her beloved into a river god. The doting monster Polyphemus sings to Galatea in the eleventh of Theocritus's *Idylls*.

[79]

Keer wederom ik ben geen Slang geen Beer
Geen Appulus: 'k dee ooyt of nimmer meer
Geen Nimfies eenig leet, of voer geen speer
      Wilt u ontfermen
Ik heers dit wout dat Tempe geensins wijkt,
Met Vee, en Veld gewas ben ik verrijkt,
Ik buyg niet voor die geen die my gelijkt
      Maar voor u Voeten.
Soo u mijn Herders staf te laag doet sien
Ik wissel dees mijn staat op u gebien
Wat gy begeert sal datelijk geschien
      Soo g'wilt versoeten
Mijn qualen, maar helaas. O wrede spreek
Verlaat g'om mijnent wil dees heylge streek
Daar ik in 't boomrijk dal de Liefde queek
      Door u Godinne.
Ick splijt de Bergen, 'k ruck de Rotsen af
'K werp s'op de daken neer, ik wroet mijn graf
Op dees gewyde Laan: voort loon, en straf
      Om uwe mine.
De wanhoop dult geen reen, ik moet vergaan
'K plet acis: neen, my selfs, ag!'tis gedaan
De kereker sal my in haar schoot ontvaan,
      Wiens Yfre banden
Nog naar mijn Doot mijn Lyk klagt sullen doen
En op de houwt mijt in het smeulen Woen
Om het geheugen met mijn ass te voen
      Door d'Offerhanden.

♦♦♦

Aan

Turn back. I'm no snake, no bear, no
Asinine Apuleius, will never lust for
Another charming nymph, don't threaten harm.
Take pity. Tempe never will fail, livestock
And crops enrich me, I bend the neck to no
Man but fall at your feet. Does my staff
Look too low for you? My condition depends
Only on you. Whatever you want instantly
I'll gratify, if you sweeten my torment yet,
Cruel mocker, do you desert this blessed
Tract of land and valley thickly treed
Where leaves quicken in adoration of you
Goddess? I cleave the rocky hills, I do,
Pile stones and roof them, hollow a grave
Along this holy laneway: reward, toll
Of your love. Illusion excludes reason.
I am crushing Acis, my rival suitor –
No – alas, my sweet self – it is over.
The wrestler has embraced me lustily
Whose iron desire will do my body grief
Even to death, and raise a tomb over
My head and pulped carcass, for his trophy.

◆ ◆ ◆

[80]

Aan de Hoogwaarde Juffer J.B.F.

Roemt Lesbos van haar Sappho, laat het wesen,
Ik roem op u, en 't brave Iufferdom
Dat Groningen telt in haar cirkel om,
Want wie de roem verdient, mag zijn gepresen.
Dog niemant wint voor niet de Pallemkroon,
Maar eygen Eer vereyst sijn eygen loon.
Laat Theben dan Korin ten wolken voeren,
Mijn Swaan draagt V op pluymen naa de Son,
En singt de Lofgerugten in haar Bron,
Wanneer se die door 't swemmen komt beroeren,
En 't sal altoos soo veel als het vermag,
V schooner naam woort brengen aan den dag.

❖❖❖

Op een brandende Lamp, die geweldich spartelde, zijnde Pallas, en Vulcaan. Oly, en vuyr.

Pallas spreekt.

Ik die d'Olijve-blaan tot Vrede heb geplant,
Sie my met al haar geur in eenen ligten brant,
Ah! help! Mijn kuysheyt wert van Mulciber geschonden
Ik smelt van spijt, O vier! wat geeft u hette wonden,
Wat baart u vlam al smert, verminkte laat me gaan,
Berookte siel helaas! hoort gy me niet Vulcaan?
Sult gy u Venus om een Pallas dan verlaten,
Ah! 'k sie wel daar 't al doof is kan geen smeeken baten.

Onts

To the highly esteemed Madame J.B. F.*

Lesbos boasts of Sappho, let it.
I boast of you and Groningen's gallant
Female circle, for the woman who merits
Glory deserves her praise. No one wins
The crown of Pallas for nothing. Talent demands
Deference. Thebes may raise Corinna to the skies.
My Swan carries you on her wings to the sun
And sings a panegyric from her well
While she makes waves, swimming,
And will do so, so long as she has the power
Spreading your lovely name like daylight.

◆ ◆ ◆

On a burning lamp that glittered splendidly,
comprising Pallas and Vulcan – Oil and Fire†

Here I planted the olive of peace
Fragrantly kindled in light but help
Me, Mulciber touches my modesty
And I melt with chagrin. Fire why do
You deliver such wounds, why O Flame
Bring forth such agony? Let me go
Injured as I am, burning up, alas.
Do you not hear me Vulcan? Do you
Desert your Venus for the sake of Pallas?
Oh, I perceive too clearly that it is
Not possible to flatter a deaf ear. Com-

* Here Brongersma's Swan is confident. Her confidence comes from her belief in the woman whom she praises. Corinna of Tanagra, compatriot of Pindar, boasted in the sixth century before our common era that she was in singing the pride of Thebes (centre of the Boeotian league). This ancient celebrity is outshone by the woman Brongersma extols: also by the poet herself. The *hunebed* at Borger, elsewhere, eclipses Amphion's Theban wall.

† Brongersma's conceit unites Athena with the flammable oil of her emblematic tree. Hephaestus is, perhaps, the smith of the lamp's metalwork: but more assuredly limited (by metonymy) to a smith's major tool – fire. Anna may be Dido's sister, witness of the Carthaginian queen's despair when, in book four of Vergil's *Aeneid*, Aeneas abandoned her. Dido builds a funerary pyre, in conformity with Brongersma's fiery theme (634–705).

[81]

Ontfermend' Anna koom help Pallas uyt de pijn
Gy die wel eer my soo geneegen plagt te zijn,
Dat gy mijn Schilt, mijn Helm, en Speer selfs hebt gedragen,
En door de wolken vloogt met mijn gevlerkte wagen
Tot V geminde heen, Ah! laat ge my in noot,
Daar u gewelden zijn soo wonderlijk, en groot,
Heeft een Godin op u gemoet dan geen vermogen,
Soo sult ge sien dat ik vergaau sal voor u oogen.

❖ ❖ ❖

De klagende Melinde, over de doot van Tirsis

'T Herdenken doet me vaak veel lugtjes loosen,
Wanneer ik my bevind' in eensaamheyt,
Aan dese klare bron omset met Rosen,
By wien nog het geheug geklonken leyt,
Hier is de plaats waar Tirsis menig werven
My heeft geleyt, hier is 't waar dat hy plagt,
(Soo ik hem deed' een dag mijn by zijn derven)
Aan haare waterval te doen sijn klagt.
Dit is het Beekje ah! dit zijn de Bomen
Waar op de namen van ons beyden staan,
Hier rollen nog de ruyschelende stromen
Soo dikwijls door gemengt met sijn getraan:
Om mijn bevreest gemoet te doen versetten,
Maar ah! my wierd door dreygen ingeprent
Een koelheyt dat sijn hert bekans verplette
En my beroofd' helaas van dat Talent,
De wreetheyt van 't geval had my verbonden
In wetten om te volgen vrinden raadt

En

Passionate Anna, come assist Pallas
In her pain. God who once went to such
Trouble on my behalf, fetching me
My shield – my helmet – my spear
And who flew through the clouds aboard
My winged chariot would you please, ah,
Relent in your strength that is so wonderful,
So great: a goddess has no power against
Your intent: you will see me extinguished
Right before your eyes.

♦ ♦ ♦

Melinda, lamenting the death of Thyrsis\*

Remembrance makes me sigh whenever
I find myself alone by the side of this well
Roses encircle, to which my mind remains
Chained. Here Thyrsis heaped his compliments
On me, often – here often teased me – here
We dared one day to lie beside each other
By the cascade, and he confessed his passion.
This the little stream, this the tree in which
We cut our names, these are the murmurous waters
In tears compelled through a narrow passage
Besieging my shyness: but my pride, hardened
By warnings, infused me with coldness his heart
Nearly melted: but it wasted that precious
Good. Chill cruelty's mischance bound me

\* The theme of a lover departing by sea – here transposed into the key of pastoral elegy – may echo Brongersma's poems to Elise leaving for France. The image of the well conforms the poem to the Swan's overall figurative repertoire.

[82]

En al? hoewel mijn trotse borst vol wonden
Verquijnde, toond' ik 't nog niet op 't gelaat,
O! hert geweldt O! alte strenge banden,
Wat herten leedt te missen dien men mindt,
En daar men sig soo vast gaat aan verpanden
Wijl dat het hert 't vernoegen daat in vindt,
Hoe dikwijls Tirsis dunkt me nog te hooren
U nagt gesang voor mijn geslooten Tent.
Of op u Fluytje 't geen mijn rust quam storen,
Waar ik me dan liet vinden ook ontrent.
Ah! wat al tranen, wat al angstig hikken,
Wat woorden van beklag in u verdriet
Deed' gy uyt bersten, als ge scheent te stikken,
In overmoedt wat hoord' Melinde niet
Wanneer het laast vaar wel schoot van u lippen;
Doen doen ik u sag hobblen op de Zee,
Gy gingt van hier (wat laat ik my ontslippen)
Maar voor een tijt, en droegt mijn hertje mee,
Dog dagre niet u nimmer weer te spreeken.
O! doodt o! wrede doodt schoon gy u magt
Toond aan mijn trouwe slaaf, en nog doet leeken
Mijn Ooge bron, gy hebt hem maar gebragt
Uyt sijn elend, daar 't mijn is uyt gesproten,
Dies ik ontbloodt van sulk een Puyk juweel
Waar van ik soo veel diensten heb genooten,
My in dit bos door sijn geheugen streel,
Vaak vraag ik aan de driffies van de Beeken
Of sy nog van ons'kuysen ommgang
Wel weten, dat se dan eens willen spreken;
Maar niemandt hoort mijn stem, O! alte lang

Te

To bow to the counsel of friends though my breast
Full of pride and wounds pines away, O
Harshness of force, O old and strong fetters,
What heartache to miss the one you love. Therefore
Lovers exchange imperishable pledges, the heart
Seeking sufficiency in promises. Often
I think I hear Thyrsis singing without a care
Before my shut tent or your flute warbles
To stir me from my rest. What sighs, what
Lovesick words you burst out with, seeming
To suffocate from excess of feeling, what did
Melinda not hear when your final farewell
Broke from your lips and I saw you distracted
By the edge of the sea, you left and I
Let you leave but my heart drew me after
For a time and I really never thought
I never again would speak with you. Cruel
Death your might is plain in the extinction
Of my faithful slave and my eyes' full well
Overflows because you have freed him from
Misery only to aggravate my own,
A glorious jewel I lay bare now that serves
Me loyally in many ways in this wood
Where his memory caresses me and I ask
The fluent stream whether it recalls
Our chaste intercourse, I urge speech
But nobody listens, Death, so

[83]

Te lang vertoeft gy Doot coom met u pesen
Doorschiet dit pijnend' hert soo hert gequeldt,
'K wil in't gewoel der aartschen niet meer wesen
Maar heb mijn ziel op waarder goedt gestelt,
Ik ben gereet in Charons boot te treeden
Schoon my dit wouten en 't Nimfedom koomt bien
De grootste vreugt, neen 'k ben niet eer te vreden
Voor ik in't Salig veld mijn wens mag sien.

❖❖❖

Voor M.A.L.H.E.J. Vertonen een Zephirus.

Hoe liefelijk Zephirus speelt gy door Bloem en bladen,
Hoe stil en vreedsaam ag! bewaayt gy het Foreest,
Gy krult de vloeden daar u kalmte doet versaaden
'T vernoegen van elk een: dat haare kwaal geneest.
'T schijnt yder draagt u gunst, selfs Tempe quijnt met smerte,
En is verblijdt wanneer s'u waasem wert gewaar.
Gy pijnt den Aquilon, en Borëas aan't herte
Dog niemant vlamt door min, met tederheyt tot haar,
Om u truyrt Peneus, en sijn Nimphen storten tranen
Als gy haar by sijn schuwt, de Lugt swelgt u Parfum,
Vrouw Flora trekt de sugt uyt u begeurde kranen
Pomona haakt veel meer naar u, als naar Vertum.
Ia wat maar Asemt kan u Lock-aas niet ontvlugten
Gy maakt het al verlieft, de Rotzen om u sugten.

❖❖❖

Op 't Jaar 72.

De Roos verdort de bladen Ruyken niet,
De Lelijen verwelken als men siet,

De

Thrust your dart through my hurt heart,
I cannot stand any longer the tumult
Of this earth but have proposed to my mind
Something worthier, to embark on
Charon's ferry cheerfully
With the blessing of all nymphdom.
Not until I tread Elysium's
Blissful grass will I feel peace.

❖ ❖ ❖

A Zephyr for you, my most beloved and honourable Elise*

How amiably Zephyrus you play among
The flowers, among the leaves, quietly,
How gently you sway the forest tops, riffle
The pools, for your tranquility requites
The wishes of all things, order or disorder,
To their desire. You bestow your favour
Universally; even Tempe suffers
Yearnings soothed by your reach, your touch.
You pain the northwinds Boreas and Aquilo
To the heart, though neither flames with love
Or tenderness. Peneus and his nymphs
Mourn you and spill their tears when you shy
Away from them, sky guzzles your scent
Mannerless. Madame Flora draws her sighs
From your sweet-smelling tap, Pomona
Wants you more, much more than Vertumnus,
Even to breathe is to succumb to your allure,
You make the most forlorn of things, the rocks,
Languish in sighs breathed out for you.

❖ ❖ ❖

On the disastrous year 1672†

The Rose wilts and its leaves lack perfume.
The Lily withers, as you can see.

* Brongersma regularly associates Elise (Elisabeth Joly) with breath. The poet variously evokes the congealed breath of winter, or the sighs of the friend left forlorn on the shore while the sails of the beloved fill with the wind and bear her away. Here the poet would present a personified Zephyr to her friend, infused with delicious scents. Boreas and Aquilo both customarily denote the north wind. But Brongersma decides to distinguish them in this piece – as though the Zephyr scrupulously sifted Greek from Roman motifs, the better to diversify the possible sources of longing. Tempe, a vale in Sicily, ought to be self-sufficient in legendary beauty. Zephyr detects and magnifies the defect even of this perfection. The laurel tree, Ovidian and Petrarchan token of poetic kudos, came into existence on the banks of the river Peneus when Daphne, relinquishing female form, evaded the lust of Apollo.

† Dutch history remembers 1672 as the *Rampjaar*, or *annus horribilis*. England (the Rose), France (the Lily), and the German bishoprics of Munster and Cologne (the Mitre weed), declared war on the Dutch Republic. In just weeks, Louis XIV's army, which crossed into the Netherlands at Cologne, managed to occupy Overijssel, Gelderland, and Utrecht. The beleaguered Dutch created a "waterline," flooding the path of hostile advance and impeding the invader.

[84]

De Mijter-tronk vergaat en Rot al deur,
Maar den Orange-Bloem behouwt haar geur.

♦ ♦ ♦

Silindor aan Cloris.

ALleen op't klinken van U Naam
Ontluykt de Roos haar bloos, en bladen
(Mijn Cloris) die met geur: beladen,
Sich maakt tot uwen dienst bequaam.

Alleen op't minst uws oogewenken,
Schiet Lely, en Convaly uyt,
Viole knopjes, Loof, en kruyt,
Waar mee U d'aarde koomt beschenken.

De Hiacynt, en Amarant,
Filet, en Krokus, en Narcissen
Niet voor U, uyt te botten missen,
Om weer te sterven in U hant.

Het groen Tapeet bereyt U Cronen,
En offert al het bloem Cieraat:
Dat als een Bruyt te prijcken staat,
Met bloosjes op haar blanke konen.

Daar siet ge dan U groote kragt,
Haa! Cloris, wijl ge koont gebieden,
Want wat ge wilt dat moet geschieden
Om dat het all: is in U macht.

Souw

Over there, the Mitre weed rots away.
But the Orange blossom keeps her sweet scent.

◆ ◆ ◆

Silindor to Cloris

At the sound of your name the rose
Blushes, and her spread petals diffuse
Their smell, expectant they wait – they long –
To serve you. Only for the sake
Of your gaze the lily unfolds
Beside her sister in the valley,
And the violet buds, and leaves,
Herbs, too: and earth unwraps her gifts.
Hyacinth, amaranth,
Crocus and narcissus –
For the ground from which they were
Plucked they do not pine but would
Die of gladness in your hands.
The green field prepares your garland,
Every flower would adorn your glory
As a bride will flaunt herself posing
With blushes darkening her red cheeks.
O Cloris, your splendour is patent.
Anything you ask for, dear,
Will be performed because, dear,
All pledges your sweet service.

[85]

Souw ik dan niet door het vermogen,
O lieve Son, vol Tintel licht
Beswijken voor dat schoon gesicht
Van U ontsloten Gitte oogen.

Ik sieg, en werp me aan U schoot,
Gebiet me Cloris, want mijn leven,
Heb ik in U gewelt gegeven,
Doch wacht daar voor, niet, als de doot.

♦ ♦ ♦

Op een Woekenaar.

Dat waekheer wint weest daar niet in verwondert:
Want hy neemt pant, en dan nog thien van 't hondert.

♦ ♦ ♦

Aan de Trouwe Loose Odace.

MEedogenlose soo mijn lijden u nog deert?
Toon dat mijn smert u dan in 't lijden u nog deert?
Of soo ik op u trouw in trouwheyt nog kan hoopen
Maak dat dit sidd'rent hert in geen gevaar mag lopen
Soo sal ik als de muir van Theben rijsen op,
En boven Tifon trots verheffen mijnen kop,
Ik sal door Cadmus speer het lant gedrogt vernielen
En Hydra met de Schigt van mijn gewelt ontzielen,
Die onse mijn vergift, verseker het is schandt
Een schat te roven, en te breken sulk een bandt
Die vast in vastigheyt door vrintschap is gebonden;
Dog daar men dat gedoogt: gedoogt men ook de sonden.

♦ ♦ ♦

Aan

Should I not then before your might,
Beloved sparkling sun, effer-
Vescent, fall silent struck
By the jet-black eyes* you open?
I look, throw myself on your breast,
Plead with you, Cloris, since
I deliver my life into your power
Expecting, dear, nothing but death.

❖ ❖ ❖

On a usurer†

The nightwatch turns a profit. No wonder.
He pawns stuff, rakes in his ten per cent.

❖ ❖ ❖

On faithless Odace‡

Remorseless, would you make my passion worse?
Doesn't my manifest hurt overmaster
You so I can trust you more and be true,
Yourself faithful in return? If you pledge
My shaking heart may rely on you I will
Rise like the walls of Thebes, lift my brow
Above the pride of Typhon and with a spear
Like Cadmus's subdue the blasted land
And deprive the Hydra of heads and life.
What poisoned our love poisons me. Scandal
To loot treasure like that, to snap a bond
Friendship knots so tight! Would any accept
That? Well, they do welcome sin, don't they?

❖ ❖ ❖

---

* Cloris's black eyes link her to the figure of Elisabeth Joly.

† This epigram seems to accuse the usurer of behaving like a watchman who first pilfers, then fences his booty through a pawnshop, raking off a cut of the profit as he does so. John Gay's *Beggar's Opera* (1728) portrays a racket somewhat like this. The guard grabs the very possessions he is supposed to defend.

‡ Zeus's son Amphion raised the legendary walls of Thebes merely by making music. His melody persuaded the blocks of the fortification to fall in place. Brongersma alludes to this feat in her praise of the *hunebed* at Borger. Zeus precipitated the hundred-headed storm-monster Typhon into Tartarus. Cadmus founded Thebes, first destroying the dragon that dwelt where there was water for his intended citadel. Hercules subdued the hydra of Lerna, successfully cauterizing a monster possessed of proliferating regenerative heads.

[86]

Aan Laurane.

EY laat dog nimmer toe dat boos en schriklijk quaadt
Dat onse vrintschap wert verandert in een haat:
Ik eys geen anders goedt wat kan dat willen baten
Elk, laat my 't mijn, ik sal hem gern' het sijne laten.

♦ ♦ ♦

Hercules aan Dianire.

Ah! Dianier vint gy in and'ren nu vermaaken
Die van Centaurus uw laat weereloos ontschaken
Daar gy hebt kragts genoeg sijn magt te teegen staan:
Dog die te veel vertrout wert ligtelijk verraân.

♦ ♦ ♦

Op het vertrek van de Hoog Ed. Geboren Heer Mijn Heer
CAREL van ROLY, Baron van Rolij, en de Wel-Gebooren Vrouw
Mevrouw ANNA ELISABETH CONDERS, van Helpen Baronnesse
van Rolij.

Soo siet men dan de Son in 't Oosten weer verrijsen
Voor Anna, naa hy had sijn omme trek gedaan

Door

To Laurane

Let sour, dour malice never twist
Our intimacy into loathing!

I can see no other means to prevent this
Than to own what is mine. It belongs to me.
Then gladly what is his I will resign – to him.

◆ ◆ ◆

Hercules to Dejanira*

Dejanira do you now divert yourself
With someone else? You let a centaur ravish
You resistless, though you had strength enough
To resist his strength. Know that those who trust
Too much are lightly betrayed, Dejanira.

◆ ◆ ◆

On the departure of the most noble Sir Carel van
Roly, Baron of Roly, and the well-born Lady Anna
Elisabeth Conders van Helpen, Baroness of Roly†

As you see in the east the sun rising again
For Anna, after he has made his journey

* Brongersma occupies the perspective of jealous Hercules. In book nine of Ovid's *Metamorphoses*, Dejanira shows no particular complicity when the centaur Nessus would forcibly possess her (9–210). Dejanira had married Hercules after his defeat of the river god Achelous. On subsequent travels, the couple encountered another river in flood – the Euenus. The centaur Nessus volunteered to carry Dejanira across, but tried midway to rape her. Hercules shot him with an arrow rendered poisonous by a tip treated with the hydra's blood. The dying centaur told Dejanira to collect gore from his wound. It would (he lied) prevent Hercules from ever betraying her. She should smear this matter onto Hercules's clothing. She did not know the centaur's blood was contaminated by the hydra's. After Hercules fell for Iole, Dejanira prepared him a shirt infused with Nessus's mixture. Hercules died, but on his funerary pyre was admitted to immortality on Olympus. He married Hebe, the goddess of youth.

† Charles de Roly married Anna Elisabeth Conders van Hulpen (daughter of Frederic and Jeanne Spinosa) in Groningen. He died in 1748. Helios loved the Oceanid Klytie, but when he abandoned her for Leukothoe, she turned into a sun-gazing heliotrope; her name means "famous one." What unites the figures of Klytie and Penelope is a mixture of patience and passion.

[87]

Door Thetis golve-plas dien grooten Oceaan:
Om wederom aan haar sijn liefde te bewijsen,
Dien Klitie die sig draayt naar 't stralen van sijn Oogen,
En al seen Peneloop Vlisses heeft verwagt:
Die nimmermeer 't geheug verloor uyt haar gedagt
Maar in 't verlangen bleef stantvastig in 't vermogen,
Dog wijl een regte Son nooyt stil kan staan, nog blijven
Soo siet men dan dat Ligt (: in trouwheyt geen gelijk:)
Vertrekken naar de kust van 't grote Lelij-rijk
En met Elisabeth op Vlerken derwaars Drijven.
Dus voerdt de Son sijn Maan op sijn gareelde wagen
Naar 't blinkende Rolij, waar hy dat deugde-Ligt
Stelt in 't Paleys dat hy voor lang heeft opgerigt
Om daar met Haar Sijn vreugt te eyndigen veel dagen.
Wel aan gy gaat dan heen: en laat Iupijn V Vader
(Haa! Conders waarde kroost) wiens Blixemmende handt
De wereldt is bekent in kragten van 't verstant,
Die niemandt meer als gy koomt sijne flik'ring nader.
Gaat dan in vreede voort den Hemel wil u Kronen
Aal-Oude lieve Twee, en Zegenen voortaan
Op dat ge in geluk moogt vroolijk heene gaan:
En door V rugtb're Naam by d'Hemellingen wonen.

◆ ◆ ◆

Aan de seer geleerde Heer ANDREAS Ten HAVE Bedienaar des Goddelijken woords Ter Pekel A.

DUs voeldt men sig gesticht door U gestichte reden,

O gro-

Through the great gulf of Thetis, the ocean,
To pledge to her his affection, he whose
Klytie bends and twirls to bask in the beams
Of his eyes – and as Penelope waited,
Who never dismissed Ulysses from her heart,
But kept her power by unceasing longing,
Yet since a fair-minded sun never stays put
So see now that light (peerlessly faithful)
Depart for the coast of the kingdom emblemed
By lilies and on wings go, with Elisabeth.
So the sun leads the moon on the wagon
His team pulls toward the glittering Roly
Where he has set up long since the light
Of virtue in the palace where they will bring
Many glad days to an end. You take your leave.
May Jove, whose lightning-wielding hand is known
To the world, foster your father, that man of intellect,
Dear worthy offspring of Conder: no one comes
Closer to that god's fieriness. Go in peace.
Heaven will crown you, reverend pair.
May blessings attend safe travels, with fair
Fortune. Dwell by reason of your glorious
Name near celestials, immortals.

♦ ♦ ♦

To the very learned Mr Andreas ten Have,
servant of Scripture at Pekela*

Wonderful enthusiast, your rapt speech

* With this poem, Brongersma inaugurates a series of verses in which she returns compliments to the men who supplied prefatory rhymes to *The Swan of the Well*. Andreas ten Have (1639–1691), son of Helena van Steen and the Latin master at Zwolle, Nicolaus ten Have, enrolled at the University of Groningen in 1663. He married Sophia Sigersma. The fire of 1674 destroyed the Reformed Church building in Pekela. Ten Have zealously interested himself in the construction of a replacement. He dedicated the completed building in 1684. The "morass" into which Pekela was plunged by the destruction of the church consisted in the encroachment that the Lutheran faith made in the neighbourhood in the aftermath of the disaster, as well as in the scandalous erection of a Maypole, a heathenish totem to which ten Have objected.

[88]

O! grooten Iveraar, wiens krachtige gebeden
Veel hebben opgewekt, en in'er ziel geplant
Het leven dat sich vont versturven in't verstant.
Gy klooft de baren van het Rode Meir der sonden,
En peylt de diepten van de grondelose gronden,
Om elk te leyden, en te wijsen op de baan,
Waar men naar't heylich land kan droogsvoets hene gaan.
Gy slaat het Bron-nat door U Tong uyt herde klippen,
En laast daar mee den dorst door 't roepen van u lippen,
Dat is de staf waar door gy grove Rotsen weekt,
En 't hert all waar 't van steen aan duysent stukken breekt.
Gy schenkt het Manna van den hemel afgevloten
Door 't heylich woord dat op ons neder wert gegoten
Met stromen, en gy doet door 't bidden Son, en Maan,
Mee aan den hemel van het herte stille staan,
Dat's in verwond'ring om het luystrend' oor te strelen,
Wanneer g'op Davids toon soo minnelijk gaat quelen
De Lofgesangen van het groot' en opper All,
Gy weydt op Gilead U Vee in't Lely dal:
O! brave herder, waar ge d'Aspis houwt bedolven,
En waar se zijn bevrijdt voor 't scheuren van de Wolven.
Door U wert het Moeras geset op vaster grondt,

*Daar*

Convinces the listener of the power of prayer
That stirs and in the soul re-sows the very
Life that had found itself dead, in the intellect.
You split the salt waste of sin's Red Sea,
And fathom the deeps of unfathomable abyss
Guiding each congregationer, directing
Them how to pass with dry feet to the holy
Land. Go slake your thirst at the font that gushes
From the shepherds' cliff, and satisfy
Your lips there for your tongue is the staff to waken
The gross rocks, splintering the stoniest heart
Into thousands of pieces. You send manna
From heaven floating down and the holy word
Pours streaming on us, for us, and at your
Bidding the sun and moon together in heaven
With the heart stand still so the ear in astonishment
May listen to you orating, like David, endearing
Music: praise of the great and sublime All.
You graze your herd in Gilead, in the valley,
Among the lilies – gallant shepherd slashing,
Routing vipers, and at the cleft repelling wolves.
By your will the morass becomes Terra Firma.

[89]

Daar't Pekelige A voor lang te los op stondt:
Maar nu haar Letter-heldt staat het op sterke benen,
Nu siet men door U Leer haar aan U leer vereenen,
Nu gy U kudde voert in vree Ten Haven in
Van Sions Tempel, die alree in het begin,
Gezegent bloeyt, en sluyt in haar gewyde muyren
Thienduysenden, doch wens het Eeuwen mach verduyren,
En dat dat nieuw gebouw in stigting wert gestigt,
En door U Godtspraak voort ten wolken op gerigt.

◆ ◆ ◆

Aan de Hoog-geleerde Heer, en puyk Poët LUDOLPH SMIDS
Medecijne Doctor, Op sijn Gallery der Vrouwen.

WIe sag ooyt Gallery soo schoon doormengelt
 Met soo veel konst, en groote deftigheyt?
Wat hofprieel waar ooyt soo net bestrengelt
 Als dese: die heer Smids hier heeft bereyt.
Elk Tafereel vertoont besonderheeden.
 Elk pronkbeeld wijst de dapp're daden aan
Der braafste Vrouwen, in wiens moed'ge schreden
 Nog d'eeretitels van'et wond'ren staan.

Diens lof wert door sijn dichtveer uitgeklonken,
 Die scheller luyt dan Maroos mond trompet,

*En*

Quaggy Pekela quaked too long but now
You, heroic literary man, set the town
Upright again on steady legs. You show how
Life and doctrine may be united. More, ten Have,
You renew Zion's Temple, its re-beginning
Blooms in blessing and in its consecrated shell
Tens of thousands sit. May it endure for ages!
The new church inaugurated for our use
Your inspired speech raises heaven-high.

♦ ♦ ♦

To the learned scholar and glorious poet Ludolph
Smids, Doctor of Medicine, on his *Gallery of Women
Extraordinary Either for their Virtues or their Vices**

What design, what order, what excellence
And artfulness, what courtly arbour ever
Was so neatly wound and twined as this,
The one my Smids has prepared, here.

Each depiction emphasizes the unique,
Each glorious image of glory informs us
Of the gallant actions of the bravest women
In following whose footsteps we perceive
Even their honourifics dazzle us.

Their praise rings in his verse again
Which blares clearer than the trumpet
Vergil set to his lips and Apollo

* Smids's *Gallerye der Vrouwen*
appeared in 1685. After Lescailje's,
Brongersma contributed this poem
to the series of verse tributes that
prefaced his volume. Brongersma's
picture of Zenobia may respond to
Smids's rendition of the same figure
in his *Gallerye*.

[90]

En die Apol met lauwren had beschonken,
    Eer hy wier an der dicht'ren rey geset.

Soo priekt hy dan en drijft op Fenixpennen
    De wolken door, en dooft het flonkerlicht,
Die aan sijn snelle vlucht licht is te kennen,
    En voor geen Sophocles, nog Naso swigt.

Wie sou niet wenschen by dees Amasonen
    Geplaatst te sijn in uwe Gallery
O Smids! wijl daar geheylgde Vrouwen wonen,
    Die eewig leven door u Poësy.

Wel offer dan gewijde Lauwerieren,
    Bepruyk dat hooft waar uit een springbron vloeyt
Van hemelvaarsen die sijn scheedel zieren
    Wijl op dien kruyn niet dan sulk puykloof groeyt.

Neen vlecht een krans van dobble loversblaren:
    Geen godtheyt ooyt met enkel pronksel praalt,
Het mindre is genoeg voor aartsche scharen:
    Want sulk een Son het maanlicht overhaalt.

◆ ◆ ◆

Aan de Hoog-geleerde Heer M.H.L.F.

WIe heeft de steyletrap met rasse schreden
Waar Grieken staag op roemt so nauw betreden

                                          Als

Honoured with the laurel before it ever
(At his grace) graced the brows of poets.

So plumed, he glides on phoenix wings
Through heights, and snuffs the flaring lights
Only glimpsed in the brilliance of his quick flight.
Even in the presence of Sophocles
Or of Ovid his voice does not falter.

Who would not want to join these Amazons,
Each niched in your "Gallery," great Smids!
Since there the blessed women dwell
Destined to live forever in your verse.

Then let us make our offering of laurels
To him whose mind flows like a pure well
From high on the slope of heaven, token
Of singular mental beauty, since
On his crown there does not grow
Such leafy proof of his glorious election.

Let us even weave a crown of double laurel.
No god parades with merely one distinction.
That lesser prize befits the herd of mortals
But our sunburst excels wan moonlight.

◆ ◆ ◆

To the most learned Mr M.H. L[uderus] F[lugger]*

Up the staircase with quick steps
Where Greeks climbed to attain Fame

---

* In 1677, Luderus Flugger became advocate of Groningen and the lands surrounding it. He may have died in 1694. Flugger was probably the father of the young artist Aleyda Flugger, elsewhere celebrated in Brongersma's verse.

[91]

Als hy die Flugger al seen Arent sweeft
En in sijn asch gelijck een Phaenix leeft,
Wie ist die 't Lof-boek van de Letter daken
In Themis school doet als een Aetna blaken?
En toont dat hy een Suil, en wonder is
Haars Capitools, en Raats geheymenis,
Ick seg't is Hij die swiert op sneege vlerken
En met een Flugger Vlugt door boort de swerken
Als wel de Son: mits sijn besleepen tong
D'Atheensche volkren steeds door 't Herte drong
Iaa schoon de Tuilbant flitst met stale peesen,
Diens kragt, soo is tot Gruno weer verreesen
Het Rijk Parnas: waar op Latonaas Soon
Met Flugger praalt, en voert de Lauwer Kroon.

♦ ♦ ♦

Aan den seer geleerden Heer en soet vloeyende Poët
SAMUEL MUNKERUS.

WAt dankbaarheyt sal u mijn Swaantje tonen!
Met wat gesang sal sy u deugt beloonen
Wijl het haar siet haa! dobblen Letter-Heldt

(Dog

Flugger has swept swifter than an eagle
And in his intensity like a phoenix lives.
How his book in praise of letters blazes
In the school of Themis, bright as Aetna.
What a pillar he is, what a wonder,
Intimate of its capitol, counsel.
I say it is he who soaring on sharp wings
And with ever faster flight – Flugger
Pierces the clouds as easily as clear sky
Like the sun: and his keen tongue
Pierces, too, the hearts of the Athenian
Folk. Even his head-dress gleams, bright as wit!
Such is the man's strength that Groningen
Is the country of Parnassus where
Latona's son communes with Flugger
Bringing the laurel crown.

♦ ♦ ♦

To the very learned scholar and sweetly fluent poet
Samuel Mun(c)kerus

What thanks my little Swan will sing to you,
With what melody your virtue reward,
Since she has seen (ha) that you, hero of literature
Twice over, in her and your own behalf,

## [92]

(Dog onverdient) te hoog ten Throon gesteldt
Voor u, die selfs het Y, en d'Yssel stromen
Den groten Rijn, laat tot u herwaarts komen
Op 't schel geluyt dat uw Rijm-schagt geeft,
Waar aan dat elk een groot behagen heeft.
V slag veer uyt een Arents wiek getogen
Verbaast benaa van wat gy koont beoogen,
Want gy verbeelt een tweden Mantuaan
Wijl men u door het wolken drift siet gaan,
Die soo in 't Grieks, als in 't Latijn geklonken
De werelt heeft daar gonstig mee beschonken,
Soo dat Korinn, nog Sappho u gelijkt
(Waar mee gy my onwaardig hebt verrijkt)
Maar toont veel eer dat Naso is u Vader
En dat Homeer, en Maro u sijn nader;
Waar om tot Lof mijn singens waarde swaan
V brave Naam sal door de swerken slaan.

◆ ◆ ◆

Aan de Hoog-geleerde en Soet vloeyende sinrijke Poët
Mijn Heer M. GARGON,
Toen sijn Ed. my eenige verssen op mijn Bronswaan gemaakt had gesonden.

Wijk Orfeus wijk: ontschroef de fedel snaren,
  V sangen Evenaren,

               Niet

Have placed her, however undeserving,
On the throne of literary fame.
You sat there already by reason of
The rivers your poetic quill has made
Bring their tribute to you – the IJ, IJssel,*
The Rhine itself in all its branches
Clearly sounding, offering pleasure
To everyone. You plunge on a wing
Strong as an eagle's astonished almost
By what you can perceive, for you
Embody the model of a second Mantuan
Roaming amid the clouds in Greek
And in Latin the world awarding
You favour so you equal
Corinna and Sappho (into whose
Presence you have ushered humble
Me): which deed shows your parentage
Is Ovid, Homer and Vergil are your
Comrades. Therefore my music-minded
Swan will trail your brave name through the sky.

◆ ◆ ◆

To the learned, mellifluous, intelligent poet, my dear
M[attheus] Gargon, after his honour had sent me
some verses on the topic of my *Swan of the Well*

Come Orpheus, tune up your fiddle strings,
Select an apt song for the occasion

* The IJssel is a branch of the Rhine
that flows through the provinces
Gelderland and Overijssel.

[93]

Niet by de klank van dees Gargonsche Luyt,
Die V in spele strijt komt dagen uyt.

Gy weet niet hoe die toverende streken
    Het mensen hert kan breken,
Daar gy maar Dieren lokt, 'k sie reets V kroon
Het hooft bepruycken van Apolloos soon.

Die lieflijk tokkert met gewiekte ving'ren
    En koomt het vlak besling'ren
Met hoeve nat geschept uyt Pegaas Bron
Nee 'k dool 't druypt uyt de Digiveer van Gargon.

Geen Hengst behoeft in 't slaan sich meer te moeyen
    Hier koomt een Rijm-stroom vloeyen,
Niet uyt een reep van Klip, of berg gevaart,
Maar uyt een Hersen-kloof: die wond'ren baart.

Die Haarlem Cranst, en uyt'er gront doet rijsen
    Een Delos, om te wijsen
De Loverbeemt, in wiens beschaduwt Dal
De drifties woen van sijnen hemel val.

Wat hant sal magtig zijn het Loof te plukken,
    En Telgen af te rukken,
Om hem te pronken die mijn Swaan verciert
Met geurig groen, als 't in'er Brontie swiert.
En op sijn pluymen doet door goude slagen
    Bekans ten wolken dragen,
Niet dan een dankbaarheyt: O Letterhelt,
Kan V omwinden, van mijn swak gewelt.

Maar soo my 't Negental wouw helpen vlegten
    Ik souw de Lauwren hegten

                                    Voort

In cadence differing from Gargon's own music

That you will match antiphonally now.
You have no concept how enchanting
The strokes of a fiddle bow may be
Since you attract an audience consisting
Of beasts, mostly, though I acknowledge
The garland on your head, son of Apollo.

With winged fingers the amiable plucks his strings
Flinging rustic water from Pegasus's spring –
No, it drips from Gargon's quill, no farmstead
Need feed this sound, a stream

Of poetry flowing not from cliff or mountain
But from a recess of mind birthing
Marvels that crown Haarlem: and a Delos
Rises from the ground to make plain
The rich meadowlands in whose shady hollow
Graze the little flocks of his sublime expression.

What hand can possess the strength to pluck
The leaf and pull the fruit to adorn
Him who lends lustre to my Swan
With fragrant green while she stirs her pool,
And his pinions with golden wingbeats bear
Her nearly to the limit of heaven.

Not Gratitude itself, hero of literature
Can settle on your brows compensation
Adequate to what my weak
Sensibility feels, and cannot say.

But if the ninefold sisterhood should
Assist me in my weaving I would twine

Voort op U Cruyn, gegroeyt in Dafnes gaardt,
Wijl ik's V acht, soo wel, als Febus waart.

◆ ◆ ◆

Aan den seer geleerde sinrijke Poët Mons. J.J. MONTER Toen sijn
E.E. my enige versen gesonden hadde.

SPeelsieke Apol wat tonen doet ge klingen
Nu sig het bos gevoelt op losse gront,
Het schijnt om hoog uyt sijn gewrigt te springen,
En 't berg gevaart te sijgen in de mont.

Hoe soet Basuynt gy van Medéaas kragten,
Van Jason, en den Frischen Adriaan,
Die gy bekleet met U vergulde vagten
Gewonnen door bekranste Letterblaan.

Hoe lokt gy het Dolfijn uyt Pontus stromen
Op 't strijken van de Feel tot U te komen
Om als Arion hem te temmen, maar

Te hoog stelr gy de dorre en schorre klanken
Van Titia: haar Roem der veeder ranken,
Die segt dat gy: zijt Drenth: een wonder raar.

◆ ◆ ◆

Aan de Sinrijcke Friesche Puik poët ADRIAAN TIJMENS.

SOet vloeyende poët met welk een toon van Reden

Sal

The laurel for your crown grown
In Daphne's bower, for you
I esteem as much as I do Phoebus.

◆ ◆ ◆

To the very learned and witty poet
Monsieur J[ohan] J[acob] Monter*

Apollo, lord of the contest, what sounds are those?
Now the trees shiver, the ground loosens up;
The roots jump out of their dirty sockets
While the hulking mount would slump down
Into the estuary. Your bassoon
Booms Medea's powers, and Jason, and
The chill Adriatic Sea, all topics that you drape
In the Golden Fleece you won through your laurel-
Earning feats of literature. Out of the Ocean
You summon the dolphin, bowing your viol
Like Arion ready to tame the sea beast but
You do esteem too highly the dry and throaty
Music of your Titia, you glory of higher
Ranges of attainment for, as Drenthe says,
"You really are a rare miracle, dear man."

◆ ◆ ◆

To the witty Frisian, that poetical splendour,
Adriaan Tijmens

Shall I begin to praise your incomparable pen –

---

* Johan Jacob Monter (biographical dates unknown) dwelt in Assen, a friend of Smids. The ancient lyric poet Arion lived on Lesbos. While travelling by ship, he became the object of a conspiracy by thieves to rob him. He pleaded with them to let him at least sing one last song before they cast him overboard to drown. He finished his piece; the thieves threw him into the sea. Dolphins, allured by his performance, however, carried the singer to safety. He awaited the arrival of the ship, and saw the men crucified who had wanted him to die. I preserve in my translation Brongersma's pun on Monter's name (mont or "mount").

[95]

Sal ik beginnen om u weergalose veer
Te schakelen aan haar behoorelijke Eer
En soete wonderen aanvaarden te ontleden,

Waar ik een Sappho, of had maar van Meles Swaan
Een slag pen, ag; wat sou ik wondre wond'ren schrijven,
Of op de vlugge vlerk der Mantuaan mogt drijven
Ik sprak o Adriaan u veel volmakter aan,

Maar nu de wijl mijn schagt te lag sweeft by de Aarde
En kan niet opwaars door de hooge wolken heen,
Versoek ik door een Reex van smekende gebeen

De slegre swieren van haar logge drift t'aanvaarden
Hoe wel 't wel billijk waar u gootse vaarse klang
Waar mee gy't luystrend' oor der Friessen soet komt strelen
En als een Sofokles u goude Lierslag deelen
Te stellen op de trant van Nasoos hemel-sang:

Maar

Or change the topic, to your honour, so great –
Or list in perfect order the welcome and
Delightful wonders of your sundry work
According to the laws of panegyric?
Were I Sappho, or had in my hand the quill
Of the Swan who swam in the Meles, Homer,
What marvels I would write and on the swift
Wings of the Mantuan I would speed, so much
More eloquently, Adriaan, I would speak:
But since my nib contends too close
To the earth's surface and cannot keep
Such altitude, I substitute this series
Of pleas, to render acceptable to you
The crude contraption of her slow flight.
Whatever her flaws she acknowledges
Your Gothic novel sound with which
You rinse clear the ears of listening Frisians
And share with them like Sophocles
The gold vibration of your lyre strings
Which admit you into the order of Ovid's
Heavenly song. But now your might

[96]

Maar nu de magt ontbreekt, sult gy niet meer begeren,
Voor my'k heb eer genoeg om u daar door te Eeren.

♦ ♦ ♦

Aan M.J.J.M.

Dewijl gy waardig agt te nuuren mijn gesangen
Die vind' ik my verpligt te senden u begeert
Sy werden u op die voor-waarde dan vereert
Dat gy se slegts al seen Dankoffer moet ontfangen
Voor u gesonden werk: soo deftig in waardy
Dat ik geen stof genoeg kan vinden u te prijsen
Maar weest te vreden in die kleyne Eerbewijsen
Gevloten uyt mijn schagt, en doffe Poëzy,
'Tis waar ik heb geeyft u gootse Fenix digten
Die my vernoegen, en bedank u waardigheyt
Ik maak u versen tot mijn grote nut bereyt:
Wijl sy my als een Toors op donkre paden ligten,
Dog wijl niet meer u breyn ontroeren door mijn pen
Maar onder groetenis belijden dat ik ben.
U Konstgenoot soo voor als naa
En gunstige T. Brongersma.

♦ ♦ ♦

Aan de sinrijke Rijmdigter, D' E. Heer M. GARGON.

MYn Heer ik moet u dit nog schrijven:
Mijn Swaantie, is al aan het drijven,

Het

Manifests itself: you really could
Desire nothing more, not from me.
But, to excuse myself, I perform my duty
In honouring you anyway, myself
Superfluous, for such completeness
Need rely on no one else's praise.

♦ ♦ ♦

To Monsieur J[ohan] J[acob] M[onter]

You nourish my songs and my duty and pleasure
Together compose this for you by way of thanks
For the work you sent, so eloquent I want the terms
But my pen still flows with toneless verse
To witness the chant of your phoenix, a Gothic\*
Subspecies of the ancient bird, and to declare
You lead me on dark ways like a torch.
But I don't want to distract your mind too long
With the maunderings of this pen so, dear
Colleague in art, your Titia Brongersma
Wishes you the best as she did always, before.

♦ ♦ ♦

To the intelligent poet the estimable
Monsieur Gargon†

Dear sir, I want to write to you again.
My little Swan is quite excited thrusting

\* Brongersma's use of the epithet "Gothic" throughout *The Swan of the Well* may simply denote a disposition to write in the vernacular. Her contemporaries are perhaps "Gothic" because they speak, compose, and live within a Northern European ambit. High culture has made a transition from the Mediterranean. Elsewhere, Brongersma makes even Pierre Ronsard drink from "Gothic" wells. The poet does not specify what works Monter sent her, but one of the complimentary verses of *The Swan of the Well*, describing its frontispiece, issues from Monter's hand.

† Mattheus Gargon, author of several complimentary poems for *The Swan of the Well*, was preacher and rector at Vlissigen after 1707. He published a book of pastoral poetry called *Walchersche Arkadia* in 1715. He also painted.

[97]

Het steekt sijn hooft ter Biesen uyt,
Maar dat het lang door schaamt' gescholen
Sich onder 't Lies-bos hield verholen,
En 't geeft alree een kleyn geluyt.
Maar of het durft de zee bepeylen,
Om 't groote Meirslot te bezeylen,
Dat weet ik niet, haar Golven gaan
Te hooch, en bars, te hol in 't woeden,
Doch soo het swemt naar and're vloeden
Soo koomt het eerst, U Oever aan.

♦ ♦ ♦

Aan mijn waarde Broeder CONRAAD BRONGERSMA.

'T Is V bekent voor lang, hoe dat mijn Swaan
Behagen had om in haar Bron te plassen,
Om haar misschien te baden, of te wassen,
Doch dorst' door vrees de stoutheyt nooyt bestaan
Maar nu gesterkt, soo heft se moet gegrepen;
En 't swiert alreets, en 't doppert op de vloet,
Waar het uyt vreugt wel duysent swieren doet,
Schoon Hydra soekt het beestje wech te slepen,
Doch 't wert bewaart van Febus gonstelingen,
Soo dat mijn Swaan daar heft soo licht geen noot,
De vree-Godes verbergt het in haar schoot,
Wanneer het gaat V Lofgesangen singen.
Leernes is dan (schoon Hy sijn swadder braakt)
Gemuylbant, en de Nijt leyt vast gebonden,

Dies

Her head up above the reeds but long
Schooled in modesty she is abashed
To be lifted into the company of Lesbos's
Heroine and she sings this – a small song.
If it is necessary to sound the sea's depths
And glide along on the open swell –
Well, I know nothing of that, the gulfs
So barren, fathomless, cresting and troughing
In their rage. Yet this Swan still swims
On other floods coming first, always,
To your bankside.

◆ ◆ ◆

To my worthy brother Conraad Brongersma*

You have known the longest the pleasure
My Swan has splashing in her well
Bathing (it looks) or washing: yet fear
Prevented her from avowing her
Perversity, of verse writing. Heartened now
She takes courage and whirls about
And paddles in the flood making dozens of circles
In her joy. Of course the hydra tries to snatch
The little creature: yet Phoebus favours her
And my Swan lives exempt from panic.
The goddess of love protects her in her lap
As she sings a song of thanks to you.
Lerna's monster is muzzled now, let it
Vomit up its poison. Envy is bound and tied.
With love my Swan sends these lines

\* Mute Swans really do turn in quick and graceful circles on the water. This buoyant rotation is part of a bonding ritual. Several birds may spin simultaneously, in close proximity to one another. Nothing is known of Brongersma's brother.

[98]

Dies wert mijn Swaan in vree V toe gesonden
Die V haar meedevrint, uyt vrintschap maakt.

♦ ♦ ♦

Op het uytnemende Tekenen, en Rekenen van Mons. P. JOLY.

WEg seg ik met de verf van u penceelen
Stocade, en Percel nu dat Philip,
U toont de konst van sijne Tafereelen
En overtreft u al tot op een stip.
Sijn tekenpen kan grooter roem berek'nen
Als Testaas schetsen doen daarom hou stil,
Hy sal haar Lof kroon naar het leven teek'nen,
Schoon hy het ook met Cijfers prenten wil.
Dies so gy schildert wilt hem mee vercieren,
En krans sijn hooft met groene Lauwerieren.

♦ ♦ ♦

Op het ongemeen schrijven van Mons. J. JOLY.

WYk Koster wijk verberg U schrift in 't donker,
Jacobus Letters zijn als Christalijn,
Sy geven meerder glans, en grooter flonker
Als wel de luyster van een puyk Robijn,

Sy

To you, who befriended her: that friendship
Inspired her to compose them for you.

♦ ♦ ♦

On Monsieur Philip Joly's outstanding paintings and
their mottoes*

Away say I with any lines
Celebrating your brushstroke, Stockade –
Away with you too, Porcellis, sail away –
For it's you, Philip, who surpass the skill of their pictures
Reducing them to a blot and a splatter.
Your pen can garner greater glory
Than Testa's drawings, so shut up.
Let Philip depict to the life the garland of glory
And recount, too, the same subject in letters.
Thus does he coordinate his talents
Each bestows the prize on the other
Crowning his head with green laurel.

♦ ♦ ♦

On the deluxe editions of Monsieur J[acobus] Joly†

Quiet, old man Coster. Hide your impressions
In a dark place: for Jacob's characters
Read as clear as crystal, shine more deeply

* Nicolaes de Helt Stockade painted Ovidian scenes such as the fallen Phaethon amid his mourners. He lived from 1614 to 1669. Joost van den Vondel, a dramatist whose writings are well known to Titia, wrote a poem about this artist. Pietro Testa appears elsewhere in Brongersma's praise of the precocious Aleyda Flugger.

† Laurens Janszoon Coster invented a printing press in Gutenberg's time: around 1440. He lived in Haarlem. The Cyprian goddess is Venus. Jacobus was related to Elisabeth Joly.

[99]

Sy staan geset op maat in goude spangen,
Als duyven opgekropt voor Cypris kar,
En in gareelen met Turkooys behangen,
Wiens glinster men siet flikkeren van vat,
Sal dan die handt die voortbrengt sulke swieren
En pen, niet zijn beslingert met Lauwrieren?

♦ ♦ ♦

Den Ontwapende Mars, Minerva Spreekt.

Wat hadt ge voor te Leunen op de Drempel
In het gewyde Choor van Iovis Tempel
Wat lonken gy ontharrenasden Heldt
Op Nisa, doen het offer waar gesteldt
Te raken voor het oog der Hemel-Scharen
Het wier ook op de Heylige altaaren,
Ah! Alte kuys bild Nisa haar gesigt
Neer slagtig, en wat want gy dat mijn Nigt
Soo redeloos ontsneeuwde haar geweeten
Dat sy om V haar pligten sou vergeten?
Neen Mavors haar behaagt geen ydel kaf
Van grootsheyt, al waar't Alexanders staf,
Schoon opgepronkt met V loftuyteryen,
Sy is mijn Priesteres hier helpt geen vryen:
Noch snorkery van Pol, of Roffiaan,
Vergeefs roept gy de Harpespeelders aan
Om Nisaas hart, of muyren te bewegen,
Slaa Trommel, en Trompet, en stapel op
De Brantkolk Etna sijn gehoornde kop,

Die

And with finer lustre than amethyst
Faceted elegantly, closed by gilt
Clasps like doves coupled to the Cyprian
Goddess's car in bridles lavish with
Glittering turquoise, gleaming from afar.
Shall the hand that holds the pen that inscribes
Such whirling flourishes not grasp the laurels, too?

◆ ◆ ◆

Minerva addresses Mars disarmed*

What were you thinking, lolling on the hill
Amid the blessed choir of Jove's temple?
What were you doing ogling
Nisa, hero divested of your armour
Sacrifice set to smoke at the altars
Under the gaze of the sky-dwelling
Host? Familiar picture of purity, Nisa,
Her face downcast – what had she, my niece,
To do with unreasonable you
Parrying her misgiving so that she
On your account might forget
Her obligation? No, Mars, she does not
Delight in the presumptuous
Appurtenances of greatness though it were
Alexander's sceptre or you, pompous
In a phalanx of sycophants.
My priestess does not go about flirting,
Not with Apollo's or a ruffian's bravado.
Go ahead, call on the harpist
To move walls for Nisa's sake –
Let the stones show sympathy,
Beat drum, blow trumpet, heap on
Smouldering Aetna! That molten
Summit, that mound of shattering

---

* Vergil's eighth eclogue includes a passing reference to "Nysa," a married countrywoman (18); Elizabethan drama adopts the name in courtly contexts. The Italian pastoral connects the figure of Mopsus with that of Nisa. Venus or Eros often assists in the stripping of Mars. In Renaissance painting, Minerva protects personified Peace and Plenty from Mars. She usually wears, like him, the panoply of a warrior. Minerva's jealous virginity would imply the celibacy of her servant Nisa. By suiting up, Mars will relinquish his amorous intention.

[100]

Die puynhoop, die se sal terstont verswelgen,
En V misschien met al de rest verdelgen
Dat vrees ik, dies grijp weer de Wapens aan,
Soo gy wilt in de gonst van Nisa staan.

◆ ◆ ◆

Antwoort aan Monsr. J.J.M.

Mijn vrient gy vraagt me naar het wedervaren
Van mijne Bronswaan, ah! die duykt in 't Lis,
Die vreest voor 't Ongediert, dat lichtlijk is
Geschoolen in het diepste van de Baren.

De moet ontsinkt'er wijl se is bedugt
Dat haar geluyt te schor valt in de Ooren
Van die gewoon zijn 't soet gesang te hooren
Van Nagtegaalen, in een Lente Lugt.

Dies gaatse op haar logge pennen strijken,
En laat de Bron, we leer haar toegewijdt,
Waar sy van laster meent te zijn bevrijdt,
En Momus klap, soo als haar dunkt, ontwijken.

Het is dan prijselijk, en best gedaan
Te swijgen, daar 't niet past te mogen spreken,
Doch d'Alderwijste valt wel in gebreken,
Daar hebt gy dan de meening van mijn Swaan.

◆ ◆ ◆

Eynde der Lofgedigten van de Vrouwen en Mannen.

De Gee-

Rock and the horror will devour
You, too, along with all the rest.
Put your armour back on, then,
If you would stand in chaste Nisa's
Good graces, again.

♦ ♦ ♦

Answer to Monsieur J[ohan] J[acob] M[onter]

Friend, you ask after my *Swan of the Well*
And her adventures. She dives amid
Irises nervous at grander expanses
Since she is lightly schooled only
In the deeps of the open sea.

Her courage flags because she thinks
Her sound hoarsely strikes the ear
Used to sweet song, nightingales',
On the balmy breeze of springtime.

So she flaps her sluggish pinions
To leave the well dedicated to her
Where she meant to escape vexation
And mordant Momus's scandal mongering.

Laudable therefore is it to keep pretty
Quiet since speech does not always avail
Yet the All-knowing will insist
Regardless, insist. There you have then
The opinion of my spring-haunting Swan.

♦ ♦ ♦

End of poems in praise of women and men.

De Geestelijke stoffen.

Op KARSTYT

NOoyt heeft de Maan een blijder nacht bescheenen
Als doen het Licht daar in geboren wiert
Waar door een damp van lijden is verdwenen
Want nu geen Doot met droeve wimpels swiert,
Maar als een Son ontlast van dicke wolken
Pronkt dese pragt vol van Genaden Glans
En bralt in't oog van sijn verkore volken,
Die eeuwig blinken aan sijn vreugdekrans.

♦♦♦

Op Goede Vrydag.

Maar heeft de Son ooyt droever dach beschenen,
Als doen het Licht van't stralen wierd berooft
Neen: maar het Leven selfs gink sig vereenen
Door't vast besluyt van't Eeuwig levend' Hooft.
In doots gevaar, verselt met Helse banden,
Waar't bloedig sweet het heylig heeft bemorst,
Waar't Iodenrot met onbesuysde handen,
Soo plomp, soo wreet, beknelden kaak, en borst.
O! vreeselijk gewelt, wat Donderslagen,
War baren van tempeest omringden Dien,

Diens

Religious Poetry\*

On Christmas Eve†

Never has the moon shone on a blither night
As though it were a light that naturally
Dispelled a fog of suffering for now
No Death waves banners but
Loosed, like a sun, from thick cloud
This beauty glimmers with the brilliance of mercy
And shines on the eyes of his chosen people
Who forever glow on his crown of happiness.

◆ ◆ ◆

On Good Friday‡

But has the sun ever shone on a day more dismal
As though the sky were robbed of every ray?
No. But the live resolve of that great rabbi
United with him all that breathes as he faced
His death, led in infernal chains, bloody
Sweat smearing him, nape and breast mauled
By Jewish rabble's hands. Violence,
Thunderbolts, tempestuous terrors surrounded

\* Samuel Mun(c)kerus's dedicatory "Sonnet" acknowledges Brongersma's Christian poems. He salutes them with a neoclassical reference to Polyhymnia. The list of "mixed genres" promised by Brongersma on the title page of her book omits mention of them.

† Brongersma's poem conflates moon and sun, as though these conventionally female and male luminaries, emblems of night and day, death and life, might unite to echo God's impregnation of a virgin. Light is the pervasive topic of the verse.

‡ Christian anti-Semitism unselfconsciously infuses this poem.

[102]

Dien seg ik die de lasten heeft gedragen
Van die hem weer verheerlijkt sullen sien.

♦♦♦

Op Paaschen.

Dog naa soo wrang en fel gepijnt te wesen
Is Hy, die heeft het slangen hooft geperst,
Seer Vorstelijk en Triomphant verresen,
Daar Hy ter rechterhant als Koning herst,
Om wiens vertoog veel duysent Gootse Eng'len
't Haleluya verbreyden door gesang,
En voorden Throon haar soete keelen meng'len
Ter Eer, en Lof, met Musicaal geklang.

♦♦♦

Op Pinxter.

Nog is hy naar 't vertrek ter sluyks gedrongen
In 't midden van sijn Tolken op de Zaal,
En blies met kracht op yders kruynen Tongen,
Waar door sijn Geest haar bracht een Hemeltaal,
Soo dat sy al vol Heylge wonders staken,
Niet denkende dat haar van d'Hemel voocht,
Dewijl sy voort met vreemde tonen spraken
Op sulken wijs, haar zielen had verhoocht.

♦♦♦

Toe-matje

Door al dit woen, en treflijk zeegevieren
Van Hem die 't Lam des Jammers is geweest

Sal

Him who, I say, carried the very burden
By which he will be restored to glory.

♦ ♦ ♦

On Easter

Though so bitter, so intense an agony
Was his who pierced the serpent's head
Sovereign, triumphant he departed
For he, a king, rules on God's right hand
And on his behalf, once he has spoken,
Thousands of Gothic angels hallelujah
And mingle their notes, their sweet throats
To his honour, before his throne resounding.

♦ ♦ ♦

On Pentecost*

Driven by fraud and force to take his leave
In the midst of his witnesses in the hall
He blazes out in power on each crested tongue
And the spirit breaks forth in heavenly speech
And manifold wonders awe them who do not know
Here is the king of heaven. So they speak
Strange, strange things their souls exalted.

♦ ♦ ♦

The Addition†

Consider the striking triumph of him who became
The Lamb of Misery meekly led to death.

\* Pentecost is the seventh Sunday after Easter when, according to the Acts of the Apostles, the Spirit possessed the disciples with flame and with foreign languages. It was on Pentecost in 1685 that Brongersma visited the *hunebed* at Borger; the gift of tongues perhaps allowed her to sing the praises of the long-forsaken goddess Natura.

† Here Christ resembles Hermes the psychopomp.

[103]

Sal Hy' die Geen die't wenst gewillig stieren,
Zijn Troostenstaf, Geleyder in den Geest.

❖ ❖ ❖

Troost-Borne.

COom al tot my Gy die V vint beladen,
Roept selfs de mont van't opperste vermooch,
Gy sult u in het Bat der volheyt baden,
En streelen in die vreucht het Geestlijk oogh.
Iaa salich zijn de arm versufte geesten,
Want selfs het Rijk bekranst haar met het goet
Sy smaken al de sauws der g'nade Feesten,
Dat dropelt uyt het dierbaar hemels soet.
O! waarde Troost, wat Heyl, wat Nardus vloeden
Bestroomen my nu ik daar aan gedenk,
Nu sal mijn ziel in't vrolijk Canaân woeden
De wijl het heylsaam sap dient tot geschenk.
Het lest den dorst van mijn versmachte Nieren,
En stilt de loop der grooten Iammerzee:
Ik neem het aan om my daar mee te Cieren,
Op dat de rust my schakelt aan de vree,
Want hier is nu verdoemenis noch smerte,
Noch hooploosheyt (wiens sickels maayen pijn)
Voor dien, die't zegelbaak plant in sijn herte,
Waar door zy al: aan't Lam geketent zijn.

❖ ❖ ❖

Op

He acquires His staff of solace, that great guide of souls.

♦ ♦ ♦

The well of consolation*

Come to me you who find your burdens heavy,
Mouth crying as loudly as it can.
Bathe in the pool of consummation,
Let your enlightened eye flash on the joy.
Yes, blessed are the poor in spirit whom
The kingdom crowns with good. They taste the gravy
Of the feast of mercy that sweet and adorable
Heaven serves. Solace – restoration –
Spikenard flows, and eases me even thinking
Of it. My soul will prophesy in happy Canaan
And the healing oil be a benefaction.
Relief comes to my reins, my lamentation
Is quieted, tranquillity attaches me
To love where there is not damnation
Or sorrow or despair whose scythe harvests
Human pain – none of those where love
Has impressed his seal on the heart, sign
By which they all are enrolled in the Lamb.

♦ ♦ ♦

*Brongersma here baptizes, so to speak, her favourite image. The well is a font.

## [104]

Overdenkinge op het Lijden Christi
En aanspraak tot de Pijnigers sijns Lichaams.

Met neer gebogen knien koom ik omhelsen
De plaats waar mijn gedagt my hene voert
Daar waar ik sie mijn Heylant knelsen
En daar het schendig rot te schimpig boert,
Met hem: wiens onschult is ontlast van sonden
En truyrt onnosel als een Offer-Lam:
Die door sijn Doot mijn doodelijke wonden
Geneest die my met regt, en reen toe quam,
Ik had gemaakt helaas die sware schulden
En op mijn ziel gelaan een rots van sorg:
Wiens Helsche last hy voor my koomt te dulden
En wert voor mijn Talent, een vaste Borg.
Omenschelijk gebroet, het Groot der Grooten
Helaas is door de prang van u gewelt:
Geschupt, gescheurt, geperst, gesteurt, gestooten,
En met een vuyst by naa ter neer gevelt,
Het vlickerend' gesigt als Duysent Sonnen
Is door 't venijn uws Adder spoog bevogt
En door u gesselriem het bloet geronnen
Langs het Geheyligt rif, en nog gy vlogt
Een kroon, en prickel krans van scherpe Doorens
Die gy verwoeden op 't gewyde Hooft
Met magt van Tiranny, en Beulsche toorens
Soo ver het volgen kon hebt ingedooft,
Noch waar het niet genoeg, gy most nog drucken
Op dat elk stickel punt meer smarten bragt,

Gy

Meditation on the suffering of Christ and on those
who tortured his body*

With knees bent devoutly I bow to embrace
The place to which meditation leads me
Where I watch my saviour afflicted by injustice,
Where the sinful mob abuses him vilely, him
Whose innocence has no stain and suffers
Purely as a lamb at the sacrifice
Healing my mortal wounds through his
Though I received mine rightly, deserving them.
I had incurred heavy guilt and on my soul
Set a stunning boulder whose Tartarean
Weight he bears for my sake and embeds
In a mighty fortress built to defend
My talent. Inhuman brood you
Have felled the best of the best, kicked, torn,
Crushed, dragged, and thumped him, with fist
Struck him to the ground. Your viperous
Spittle muddies his face radiant as a thousand
Suns, conniving you gashed
His holiness and his blood has gushed and
You have woven your lacerating
Crown: a garland of thorns for the blessed brow.
Frenzied, frenetic wielders of tyrannous
Power and the executioners' toolkit!
As far as you can you have extinguished
Him. Was it not enough but you had
To press deeper each pointed tip to reach
The root of every nerve? You would have your man

* Brongersma perhaps connects Sisyphus's stone to the burden of guilt her speaker feels, when she uses the epithet "Tartarean." The Gospels recount how two thieves were crucified with Christ, on his right hand and his left. One vilified the Messiah for his inability to save them all by divine fiat. The other repented, Christ promising him that they would see each other that very day in Paradise.

[105]

Gy deed het Offer onder 't Altaar bucken
Naa gy de Rietstaff gaaft in s'Koninckx magt
Iaa spotters 't waar een Prins, een Hemels Koning
Die Israels Scepter voert en Vorstlijk overswaayt
Hy ist diedt heydendom belooft de Kroning
Van sijn Genaden Seys, die vreugden maayt,
Maar ag verstokt Geslagt dorst gy aanranden
Dien Simson vol van kragt, en Godlijkheyt,
Dorst gy op't Griekse Tauw die Heylge handen
Vastnagelen van Hem V Mayesteyt?
Ag moest gij wreder nog sijn: zij doorboorden
Met Spietsen, most gy noch met Gal, en Eek,
Sijn Klamme Tong daar door te wreder moorden
En sijnen dorst doen laven uyt die Beek?
Siet daar den Hemelsvoocht met vrees bevangen
En uytgestrekten Erm roept ay: my dorst,
Siet sijn gestraamde Leen aan't Kruyse Hangen
Daar't Bloedich Sweet het Heylig heeft bemorst,
Besiet hoe Iammerlijk sijn Duyven Oogen
En Git gekrolde Hair: dat Dijstels draagt
In plaats van glans nu is met Rouw betogen
En noch niet eens van smart of pijnen klaagt,
Maar roept in tegen deel voor u te gader
(: Wanner men sag sijn Geest ten Mond uyt woen)
Vergeeft het haar, ik bid u Hemels Vader
Sy weeten niet wat sy aan my missdoen,
Dog dit wouw Hy om mijn misdaden lijden
Op dat ik door die smaat van sulk een doot
Met hem en 's Moorders Ziel my souw verblijden
In 't Paradijs: den regten Abrams schoot.

♦ ♦ ♦

De

Crouch at your altar clasping a sceptre of weeds
But, you scoffers, he really is prince, king
Of heaven who wields a true sceptre, Israel's,
In regal largesse imparting a promise to all
The Gentiles of his mercy, and the edge
With which he makes a harvest of endless
Happiness. Generation self-deprived
Do you dare banish this Sampson strong and
Pious and nail to the murderous Tau
His holy hands and majesty? Must you
Drive your spikes through his side, mock
His parching tongue with oak gall not
The refreshing stream? See heaven's regent
Arms outstretched, fear seizing even
Him crying "I am thirsty!" In a loincloth
He hangs from the cross bloody sweat staining
His holiness, his doves' eyes bruised, jet-black
Curls crusted with gore from the thistles'
Pricking. Sorrow sees his radiance. He does
Not complain but asks instead that you espouse
Him and he says "Heavenly Father forgive
Them. They know not what they do." All this
For my trespasses, the degradation
Of such a death but he – and that killer's soul,
Too – will today in Paradise rejoice,
In Abraham's bosom.

◆ ◆ ◆

[106]

De Lijbanonsche Herderin, spreekt.

DUs drijf ik't wollig Vee van mijn gedagten,
Langs Sions klavergront vol honigraadt:
Op dat mijn vagt haar vrolijk kan vernagten,
In't Cedrenbos van een verblijde staat.
Want in de geur van haar begroende bladen
Geniet ik vaak mijn ziel en herten lust,
Die mijn begeert ten vollen kan versaden,
Dewijl het staag het groot verlangen blust,
Jaa soo de Son te brandich door het loopen
My door de dorst doet snellen tot de vloet,
Soo laat ik my met Christalijne droopen,
Van het Jordaansche vogt, wiens hemelsoet,
Mijn vlauwe borst door Goddelijcke werken,
Als een vermoog, of Palestijna toont,
En soo met kragt' en moet my koomt versterken
Dies niet dan lieflijkheyt dit velt bewoont.
O! wonderbare plaats waar mijn beminde,
Mijn Herder, en mijn Leeuw, mijn Ariël,
My plag in schaduw van Cipres te vinden,
Waar ik nog naa de komst sijns wonder hel,
Siet dus bekranst met Roosjes van genade,
Vind ik mijn kruyn bestrengelt al den dag,
En voer een staf my strekkend' voor cieraden
Waar mee dat ik de Lamren hoeden mag.
Op het gebergt van Hermons vette weyden,
Daar Amana, en Semirs Nardus-plas;
My nooyt doet van het een of't ander scheyden,

Maar

The Lebanese shepherdess speaks*

So I drive the fleecy flock of my thoughts
Through Zion's clover, amid its honeycomb
Into cedars happily situated where my charges
May spend the night and where in the odour
Of verdant boughs my soul, my heart delight
Feeding desire to fullness for such constancy
Tempers my yearning, which is huge. Yes
When a sun too fiery aggravates my thirst
Into a flood of sorts when I ramble far
I cull crystal drops from Jordan's wave
The heavenly sweetness of which refreshes
My fainting breast with celestial effect
Or I glimpse Palestine so strength and courage
Come, combine to fortify me. Does not
Sibling bliss then dwell, too, in this field, mirific
Place where my beloved, the shepherd, my
Lion, my Ariel, can find me on the turf
In the shadow of the cypress crowned with balmy
Roses a garland of which I twist all day
Swaying my staff just for the grace of the gesture
Yet protecting the lambs? On the fat
Slopes of Hermon and rich Amana and Senir's
Streams fragrant as nard may neither of us

* Brongersma writes Christian pastoral. The bride of Solomonic song is represented in the manner of a figure from Ovid's *Heroides*. En Gedi is the largest oasis on the shores of the Dead Sea. It was at one time the asylum of King David. Brongersma's place-names are derived from the Song of Songs: Amana, Senir, Hermon. Her well now supports the image of a woman in love. Compare this piece with "Melinda, lamenting the death of Thyrsis." Like her contemporary John Milton, Brongersma draws from the repertoire of both Athens and Jerusalem with ease. Quite beside the impulse of Renaissance syncretism, the finesse with which this alternation can be performed arises from the uniformity of the Mediterranean setting common to Judaism and Christianity, to Hellenic and Roman culture.

[107]

Maar geeft het geen voor lang haar eygen was,
Noch pluk ik menig tros van Druive telgen,
Wanneer ik op het hoog van Engedie,
Het hongren mijner ziel mee poog te delgen,
En yder door het soet versadigt sie,
Ag! smakelijke spijs gy doet my haaken,
Om met mijn Lief, en uytgelesen Son,
Het Manna van sijn minlijkheyt te smaaken,
Op 't opperst van het Hemels Libanon,
Coom dan verlaat de scharp gedoornde dalen,
En kies het velt met Lelyen beplant,
Laat ik mijn heyl uyt U vertoning halen,
Op dat geen storm mijn Levenschip bestrant.
Ik wacht U dan, en schuyl in koele Lommer,
Terwijl dat gy U gangen hebt gewent
Tot hier, waar over ik myy steeds bekommer,
En soo in mijn lieve Schaapjes aasen,
Aan Giliad, van uytgekipte blaan
Een kroon bereyden daar veel danklof grasen
Van 't steyle toppigront der Sinay staan.
Welkoom dan, koom, ay! wilt niet lang vertoeven
Op dat ik door de hoop, mijn Levensbron
Niet al te seer mijn ziele mag bedroeven,
Koom koom ik wagt U aan dees Libanon.

◆ ◆ ◆

Op

Part one from the other though we each
Were single a long – very long – time. Yet
I pluck grapes in clusters on the heights of En Gedi
To still the hunger of my soul and the sweetness
Saturates me. Delicious spice you seize me,
To taste the manna of my dear sprawled
Sun's amiable self on the summit of
Divine Lebanon. Come forget the valleys
With their thorns and choose the field
With lilies thickly sown, restore me
By showing yourself: for then no storm
Can strand the vessel of my life.
In the refuge of the cool shade I wait
Until you turn your footsteps this way.
I think of you always, into my mind
I slip your very being, very deep. Meanwhile
I graze my sweet sheep on Gilead's
Nibbled grass and weave a garland
Of the ungrateful herbs of Sinai's
Barren summit. Come, do not tarry.
I am your living well of waters, waiting.

◆ ◆ ◆

[108]

Op de geoboorte onses Heeren JESUS CHRISTUS

Toon: Lorains Mars, of Tromp.

NOoyt heeft de Maan beschenen
Op aard soo'n blijde nacht
Als dees, waarin verdweenen
Is 't geen ons hielt ontmagt,
Want siet het licht dat praalt,
En is ter neer gedaalt
Uyt den Trone
Daar Godts Sone,
Ons bestraalt.

Hy heeft de duystre Wolken
Het lastigh rif ontgort,
Waar door de Hemels Tolken
Een gloir is ingestort,
Jaa al de Werelt jeugt,
En is daar in verheugt
Dat gebooren,

Is 't

On the birth of our Lord Jesus Christ

Air: "Lorraine's Mars," or "Tromp"*

Moonbeams never made earth glow
For a night more joyous than this
In which none of us disappears
And none forfeits vitality, either.
For look: this splendour of light
Glorifies, descending to us here below
From the throne where God's star
Irradiates us. The swag he pulls aside
Of obscuring cloud, heavenly
Witness alights, rejuvenates
The world gladdened that to bliss

* There exists no tune entitled "Lorraine's Mars," but one does bear the name "*De Franse Mars*" ("The French Mars"). Brongersma's point of reference may be a song in celebration of a victory of Admiral Tromp set to a pre-existing French melody in 1670. Cornelis Tromp participated in many sea battles. Two notable fights in which he partook were the Battle of the Downs in 1666 and Kijkduin, or the Battle of Texel, in 1673. The English were the foe.

[109]

Is't verkooren
Kint, tot vreugt.

De Son is opgeresen
Waarin de rust bestaat,
Wienst luysterrijke weesen
Beflikkert het gelaat
Van die (hem alle magt)
En Goddelijke kragt
Uyt den Hemel
Sijn gewemel
Heeft gebragt.

Wel dang gy wijste Bende,
En Herders die van ver
Den Koning, vol Elende
Saagt, door de Vreede-ster
Op't soobre Ledicant,
Met strooy, en hooy beplant,
U getuygen,
Doen my suygen
't Waar verstant.

❖ ❖ ❖

La bel-

Is born the chosen child.
The star has risen in which calm abides
And humble shepherds discussing
The king of peace peaceful
In a manger strewn with austere straw,
You witnesses nurse me
Until I too can understand, truly.

◆ ◆ ◆

[110]

La Belle ire.

SChoon de Son door heet geblaak
My te seer heeft over scheenen
Waar door is ter schuyl verdweenen
Mijn gedaant', soo is't vermaak
Dat ik heb veel lieflijk heeden
Die de Tenten deysen doet
Van de opgerechte Treeden:
Daar men Keder mee begroet,

Ben ik breyn ik heb geweyt
Aan't gebergt der Druyve bressen
Daar ik waar als waarderesse
En tot hoeden, staag bereyt
Maar helaas ik heb verlooren
En de Heuvels niet bewaart
Die my waaren uytgekooren,
Waar mijn hart door is beswaart,

Ach! ik socht hem die mijn Ziel
Als sijn eygen selfs beminde
Die ik elders dacht te vinde
Voor wiens macht ik neder kniel,
Doch ik vant hem daar hy ruste
By de Herders in het wouwt

Wiens

Air: "*À la belle Iris*"\*

Though the sun has shone on me too bright
So shelter evaporates and I am exposed
Yet I am delighted I have plenty
Of amenities to stretch their tent for me
On the upright pole for here
The cedar grows and greets us.

I used to graze in the passes
Of the vineyard hills
Where I was a watchwoman
Perpetually ready to protect.
But I alas am lost and do not
Defend the hills that I chose
For myself: and so my heart
Is heavy burdened.

I seek him whom my soul loves
As itself thinking to find him
Somewhere else, before whose strength
I kneel: there he is, I find him
Resting with shepherds in the woods.

\* Another Christian pastoral here takes a cue from the Song of Songs. "*La belle ire*" appears to be a title marred by a compositor's error; this melody may in fact be "*À la belle Iris*" – an air Brongersma uses elsewhere.

[111]

Wiens Kourale mont ik Kuste,
En my vast gebonden houwt.

Iaa soo haast hy herwaarts quam
Gaf mijn Nardus soete geuren
En de bundels Mirhe kleuren
Die mijn boesum willig nam
By de tross van volle Wijnen
Of gerukt tot Engedie
Die my doen van vreugt verdwijnen
Wijl ik my vervrolijkt sie.

♦ ♦ ♦

De Geestelijke Bruyt
Toon Courante La Raine.

ICk voel mijn ingewant
Door Goodelijke Stroomen
Ganslijk in genoomen,
En bevind mijn Hert in heete brant,
Om op het Choor van s'Hemels Throon
Mijn Ziels verlangende begeer te doôn
Op dat voor my mag sijn bekoomen
'T Lof der Englen Croon,

Maar wie ist die s'bereyt
Het is die d'Englen looven
Waar in ook Jehovae

Met

His coral lips I have kissed
And I have held him tight to me.

Yes he hurries forward, hands me
Aromatic nard, bright bundles of myrrh,
I take them gladly to my breast
By the cluster of ripe grapes
Collected at En Gedi. Bliss
Almost dematerializes
Me, joy penetrates me.

❖ ❖ ❖

The Spiritual Bride

Air: "*La nouvelle courante, à la reine*"\*

Godlike rays beam in my heart's depth
Possessing it entirely, and they find
A breast hotly burning to act my soul's
Strong desire in the choir at heaven's
Throne: to merit for myself the prize
Of an angelic crown. But how prepare?

The topic is seraphic praise on high
Where Jehovah, with El Shaddai, in eternity

---

\* "*La nouvelle courante, à la reine*" appeared in print at Rouen as early as 1649. From the Reformation onwards, Christians adopted the Masorete practice of referring to God as "Jehovah" (a version of the tetragrammaton). El Shaddai is conventionally translated as "God Almighty." The name of God known to Abraham, Jacob, and Isaac, it originates with a word meaning "Destroyer." Immanuel means "God with us," and the Gospels allege that this was the name prophesied to be borne by the Messiah. Elohim is a plural noun designating "Deities." Christian contexts treat it as singular.

[112]

Met Elschadday glanst in Eeuwigheyt
Het is dien Rots, d'Emmanuel
Die dieper oogt dan d'Afrgonts vlamme well.
Iaa Hemel, aarde gaat te booven
En beheerst de hell.

Het is het Groote ligt
Voor wien elck Knie moet buygen
En die drie-heens tuygen
In den Heemel sijn vermoogen stigt
De Geest, en 't vogte water 't bloet
Op aard' mijn Tong uyt Vreugde Jeugen doet
En soo den Honig coom te suygen
Van het smaaklijk Soet.

Ach mocht mijn sondig Oog
U Elohim beschouwen
En een Tempel Bouwen
Op de eenigheyt uws Liefde Boog,
Ick plant dan 't Zeegel, en het woort,
'T begin en 't eynde, op mijn herte voort
En smeeke aan U kragts vermoogen
Dat gy my verhoort.

Want U Medogenheyt
Reykt hooger dan den Heemel

                                                    Iaa

Glows. It is the Rock of Immanuel
That peers profoundly into the abyss's flame,
Hence heaven and earth both lord it over hellfire.

It is the great light before which every knee
Must bend, and all must gird up their loins.
The spirit in heaven its power establishes,

Water blossoms forth on earth and my tongue
Must rejoice rejuvenated, in felicity.
And so I suck the honeycomb's sweetness.

Ought my sinful eye even to look at you, Elohim,
And build a temple on the arch of your loving bow?
Then I set the seal, the Word, alpha and omega
On my heart and beseech you, Omnipotence,
Listen to me. Since your compassion
Extends higher than heaven, the strew

[113]

Jaa het Ster geweemel
Is uws wonderheden overspreyt,
Maakt doch Alwijse, Levensbron
Door U genade ik U Glinsterson
Mach heylig, heylig, heylig roemen
Eeuwich Helion.

♦ ♦ ♦

Toon: La Duchesse.

HOe vraagt gy waar mijn lief sich hout,
Of vinden laat?
Ik seg hy heeft gekoosen
Het hof der Roosen,
Daar hy treden gaat
Om 't Ceder van haar groene steel te rucken
En ook om Mirh, en bloemtjes of te plucken,
Hy weyt stagg in de daalen
Daar de hooning vloeyt,
Daar Nardus is te haalen,
En 't Saphyre groeyt,
Mijn lief is mijn, en ik ben sijn,
Geluckig is mijn Ziele
Ah! voor wiens glans ik kniele,
Door een vreugde pijn.

Weet gy dan nu waar dat mijn Son,
Sijn gangen went,

Of waar

Of stars overspread with your wonders,
Prepare me, All-Wise One, great well of life,
Glimmering sun, eternal Helios:
Show me your mercy that I may sing
"Holy, holy, holy."

◆ ◆ ◆

Air: *"La Duchesse"*\*

Why ask where my beloved hides
Or intends that he himself be found?
I say that he has chosen the court of roses
Where he goes stepping to collect
The boughs of the cedar, and to pluck
Myrrh and small flowers. Constantly
He wanders in the valleys where
The honey flows, where nard abounds
And sapphires gleam. My love
Is mine, and I his. My soul
Is blissful and before its radiance
I kneel, struck with happy agony.
Do you know where my sun took his path
Or what region his rays brighten?

---

\* *"La Duchesse"* was a *courante* popular in seventeenth-century Versailles. Joshua overthrew Tirzah, royal city of the Canaanites; it became in due course the capital of the northern kingdom of Israel. Aminabad was father to Elisabeth: possibly another oblique reference to Elisabeth Joly insinuates itself into this Christian pastoral. Shulamith is the female version of the male name "Solomon."

[114]

Of waar sijn stralen lichten,
Die mijn gewrichten
Zijn te wel bekent,
Ik moet sijn schoon gestelt u gaan afmalen
En u met eer en lof sijn roem verhalen:
Hy flickert als de Maane,
Of den daageraat,
Vervaarlijk als de Vaane
Van een Krijchs gewaadt,
Doet hy verbaasen al de kracht
Die tegen Tirsa strijden,
Maar hy doet weer verblijden
Mijn verlieft gedacht.

Soodanich een is hy die mijn,
Gemoet bewoont,
En die my soekt in't minnen
Te overwinnen,
Doch dewijl sijn schoont,
My hout beducht soo keer ik naa de beeken
Om sien de wijntros, of die dobblend leeken
En of de telgen groeyen
Van het teer Granaat,
Waar aan de vruchten bloeyen
Van mijn blijden staat,
Ik vind mijn ziel soo vast bevrijdt

Tot

Myself I am too well known but
Would shape for you his lovely form,
And expound for you, with praise
Equal to his honour, his glory.
He shines like the moon or sunrise,
Terrible as the banners of an army.
He strikes awe in all who, with him,
Fight to overthrow Tirzah
But he infatuates my thought again, again.
So unique is he who occupies my mind
Alluring me in love, overcoming me.
I am anxious, I return to the stream
To view the vineyard or the rushing brook
And inspect the green clusters
Of the fragile pomegranate tree
Where all the harvest of my happy state swells.

[115]

Tot Aminabats waagen,
Die my ter Throon sal dragen:
Van mijn Sulamijt.

◆ ◆ ◆

Courante La Reine Nouvelle.

Bruydegom.

GElijk een versse Roos
Zijt gy mijn ziels beminde,
In het wout te vinde
Daar ik u in't dal der scherpe doornen koos,
Staat op mijn lief mijn vreugde Choor
Koom dog tot my en geef mijn stem gehoor,
Soo sal de Libanonse Linde
Juichen u te voor.

Bruydt.

Ach Sonne van mijn hart,
Ik koom door u gebeden,
Vroolijk tot u reden,
En bevind my in u sterke min verwart,
Beschaauwt my onder u banier,
En breng u Hardus reuk waarande hier,
Op dat mijn ziel mach sijn te vreeden
Door u gonsts geswier.

Bruydegom.

Mijn schooner twijfel niet

Die

My soul is enlarged and at large in Aminabad's ways
Leading me in time to the throne of Shulamith.

❖ ❖ ❖

Air: *"La nouvelle courante, à la reine"*

Bridegroom

You are a fresh rose discovered in the forest,
Beloved of my soul. In a thorny valley
I selected you. Love, stand up, happy
Singer stand: approach: listen to my voice.
The Lebanese linden tree\* will rejoice before you.

Bride

Sun of my heart, I come when you ask
Striding up to you happy, safe
In your protection, conscripting
Myself beneath your banner, bringing
Aromatic nard so my soul may rest
In the pledge of your favour.

Bridegroom

Do not doubt my beauty. Spring

---

\* Brongersma appears to cite a linden tree in connection with Lebanon, though her usual reference, to the cedar of that country, is more in conformity with Scriptural precedent.

[116]

De Lent sal u behagen
Want de Winter vlagen
Zijn ten eynd gedroopt van u te lang verdriet
De regenplas is wech gegaan,
Gy sult nu zijn met Mirtheloof belaan,
De Wijntelg bloeyt de bergen dragen,
Siet dees volheyt aan.

Bruydt.

Wel aan ik ben gerust,
Gy hebt door u vermoogen
My dus seer bewoogen
Dat ik schep alleen in u mijn herten lust,
Ey laat mijn ziel met bloem gewas,
En koel mijn hart met fruyt en ratig gras,
Want ik ben krank van liefd 'om toogen
Stut mijn traane plas.

Bruydegom.

Koom dan mijn Suiv're Son
Geniet de hof Granaden,
Wily u lust versaden,
Smaak de wijn uyt mijn geheylgde Nectar bron
Ik heb hier tot u komst bereyt
Veel geurich kruyt met hoonichdauw bespreyt,
Wort vroolijk, gaat u tong beladen,
Met haar soeticheyt.

◆ ◆ ◆

De gee-

Will delight you, the pennants
Of winter droop that oppressed you
Too long. Rain has stopped at last,
Now myrtle leaves will deck you,
The vineyard blossom on the slopes
Fattening the clusters, a consummation.

Bride

I am placated. Your power moves me.
My desire takes ship in your heart,
My soul I give leave to flourish with flowers,
To cool itself with fruit and foliage,
For I am sick with love, and onto my table
Fall my wet tears.

Bridegroom

Come then my pure sunlight,
Accept this princely pomegranate.
If you wish to slake your thirst
Taste the wine from my consecrated
Nectar-well. I prepared it against
Your coming. Fragrant spices
Sprinkled with honeydew make
You merry, freight your tongue
With their virtue.

♦ ♦ ♦

[117]

De Geestelijke Bruyt spreekt:

Toon, Schoon Catrijn.

ACh waar zijt gy mijn beminde
Alderbeste Bruidegom?
Vliet niet als een bloode Hinde,
Maar siet eenmaal wederom.
Op dat ik V mach omermen,
Siet ik weet gy mijn bemint,
Wilt u over my ontfermen
Die V als haar selfs besint.

Of zijt ghy ter schuyl geweeken
Achter heg, of doren wijk,
Soo verwaardicht my te spreeken,
Want ik schier om V beswijk,
Ach mijn brakke traantjes hangen,
(Die al bruysend' stromen neer)
Over mijn besturve wangen
Koom mijn Liefste keer ay keer.

Immers hebt ghy my geropen
Flusjes doen ik lach en sliep,
Daar mijn oogen schenen open,
Als V stem te komen riep,
Maar belaas te lauw van herten

Toond

The Spiritual Bride Speaks

Air: *"Schoon Katrijn"**

Where are you, beloved, most
Beloved bridegroom? Do
Not fly like a timid stag,
Be present here again. I would
Embrace you. Pity me, beloved
Whom you know as your own self.
Do you forsake me behind
A hedge, behind a thornbush
So guarded your address, reserved?
My salty tears brim to stream
Hotly over my harrowed cheeks.
Come, my beloved, turn,
You have always called on me.
Now I laugh – now doze –
But in sleep my eyes stay wide
Open when your voice calls
On me to come, alas too
Lukewarm at heart, attuned

* *"Schoon Katrijn"* ("Pure Katrijn") is a seventeenth-century melody (attested by 1690); the song's plot focuses on a woman wooed by a man who has left another woman pregnant. She persuades her suitor to take up his responsibility. God is presumably a different kind of suitor. Like Alexander Pope's Eloisa, however, Brongersma appears strongly aware of how the figural repertoire of the church, relying on the experience of eros to communicate intensity of feeling, tends to mix or cross secular love with holy.

[118]

Toond'ik my tot V gestreel,
Koom genees mijn zielens smerte,
Want ghy zijt mijn hoochste Deel.

♦ ♦ ♦

Toon, Engelsche Gique.

WAt blinkende lichten,
Wat stik'rende schichten,
Wat glans?
Koomt tintelen boven de stal uyt een hemelse trans?
'K sie Engelen tieren,
Swieren,
Die komen uyt den Throon
Beneden,
Ontleden
De komst van Godts eenigste Soon.

Ook sie ik de scharen
Met vreugde vergaren,
Wiens galm
Vuldt velden, en bossen doot't schat'ren haar's vreugdigste psalm.
Zy queelen den Heere,
Eere
Sy Godt in't hoogste hoog,
En wenschen
De menschen
Behagen naar yders vermoog.

Daar sie ik de herders
By't Kintje, en verders

In't

As I am even to illusion,
The illusion of your touch.
Come, heal the pain of my heart
Since you are all my highest part.

◆ ◆ ◆

Air: "English jig"

What light shines or sconce flickers,
Irradiates the height of heaven
Over the stable? Angels I see swirling,
Twirling from the throne observing
The advent of God's singular son.
The host gathers in visible gladness
Whose echo fills fields and woods scattering
The joyous hymn. They warble, "Glory be
To God on highest, and let each man
Feel content to that man's measure."
Shepherds I see beside the little child

[119]

In't groot,
Wien dat heeft verwonnen de helle, jaa Duyvel en doodt.
De slang is vertreden
Heden
Alwaar de reyne Maagt,
Het Lam
Uyt de stamme
Van Jesse zaligheyt draagt.

Noch sie ik een wonder
Hoe dat hy is onder
Het vee,
Wien hemel en aarde verrijkt met een eeuwige vree,
Is dit voor een Koning
Woning,
Ah! al te slegt geval:
Besluyten,
Dees muyten
De prijs van he Goddelijk al?

O! Betlehem waardlich,
Ik nader U vaardich
En kniel
Voor Jesus wien dat ik aanbid uyt een nedrige ziel,
Laat doch al mijn sonden
G'bonden
Sijn aan U slegt gewaadt
Daar hooyen,
En strooyen,
U dienen voor 't eerste Cieraadt.

◆ ◆ ◆

Toon

Who defied Hell, Death, and the Devil,
Now nestled in shadow. The serpent is trodden
Underfoot today, today she who is chaste
And the Lamb from the branch of Jesse
Are delivered into salvation. A miracle I see,
He who abides with beasts rules heaven and earth
With eternal love. Is this the palace for a king?
O Fortune, is this the reward of godhead?
Bethlehem, grave, I approach you and kneel
Before Jesus whom my humble soul
Beseeches. Let my sins be joined with you
There in the wretched straw – your first home.

♦ ♦ ♦

[120]

Toon: Titer.

DUs belommert van de boomen,
Soek ik daagelijks mijn rust,
Daar het ruysen van de stroomen
Mijn begeerlijkheden sust,
Want hoe kriel de drifjes woeden
Van de Libanonse vloeden,
Soo ontfang ik buyten haar
Nooyt, dat aangenamer waar.

Mits dat ik hier plach te vinde,
Dien, wiens Schaduw ik bewoon,
En mijn ziele soo beminde,
Dat Hy achten al het schoon,
Waart te zijn aan my bekoomen,
Dies roept Hy, Gy hebt genomen
Door U oogen, dit mijn Hert,
Dat U opgeoffert wert.
Ach gelijk een hert door 't jagen
Snelt en spoeyt hem tot een Beek,
Soo verlang ik alle daagen,
Jaa wel duysent werven spreek
Van het schoon en Deftig weesen
Dat in Hem (mijn uyt-gelesen)

Staat

Air: "Titer"\*

Thus shaded by trees
Daily I look for repose
Where the murmur of the stream
Quiets desirousness
For though the waves may race
And rage along their banks
Never anywhere else
Would I be comfortable.
So long as persists
Adversity, so long
In his shadow will
I dwell, whom my soul
Loves, who attends me
As I revive and cries,
"Your eyes have made my heart
A sacrifice."

Like a deer by the hunt
Harried to the riverside
So I yearn every
Day, and thousands of things

---

\* "Titer" is Dutch for the Vergilian shepherd name "Tityrus"; Brongersma previously used "Tyter" in her "To the estimable and benevolent gentlewoman Miss Anna Marg[areta] Valcke." The poet mixes Hesiodic with Scriptural authority. "Philotée" is likely a Gallicized version of "Philotes," the Greek daemon of friendship, affection, and copulation. Cicero translates "Philotes" as *Gratia* or "Grace," a concept conformable, over the course of history, to Christian theology.

[121]

Staat geprent, haa! Helion
Als een soete morgen Son.

Coom dan Hoop van mijn gedachten
Laat U Herten Philotee
Door't verlangen niet versmachten
Maar breng haar de wijn tros mee
Daar de lieflijke straalen
Mijn Geheemelt koomt bepraalen
Coom ey koom mijn Helion
K'wagt U aan dees Libanon.

♦ ♦ ♦

Toon: Reveille vous.

Ik waar't in't sagte dons geweeken,
Wanneer mijn waarde Minnaar riep,
Die door sijn soet en lieflijk spreken
Mijn hert deed waken schoon ik sliep.
Maer siet de deur waar toegesloten,
Gegrundeld met een ijsre bant,
Doch vant het werk nochtans begoten
Door 't Nectar druypen van sijn handt.

Ik die mijn Lief en uytverkooren
Door sijn geklop wouw laten in,
Maar open doende waar verlooren,
Mijn Herder dien ik seer bemin.

Daar

Speak out of the beauty
And grace in him imprinted,
Helios of the early day.
Come then, hope of my
Reveries. Let your heart's
Philotée die not of longing.
Bring her grapes in clusters.
Charming radiance, celestial:
Come my Helios, come.
I summon you to Lebanon.

◆ ◆ ◆

Air: *"Reveillez-vous"*\*

I was from soft down awakened
Whenever my worthy lover called
Who speaking sweetly, amiably
Woke my heart though I still slept.
But see the door was firmly locked
Barred tight with an iron bolt.
Yet his fingers dripping nectar
Made that barrier all in vain.
My love could tell whose hand
Was knocking, and admit him here.
To stop him was a wish forlorn.
I serve my shepherd, all besotted.
Then afflicted I must complain

---

\* Henri Havard mentions the popularity in the Netherlands of a French tune called *"Reveillez-vous"* in his 1874 book *La Hollande pittoresque*. Perhaps its remote antecedent is the song *"Reveillez-vous, Picards!"* ("Wake up, Picards!") – composed around 1479.

[122]

Daar ving ik aan seer droef te klagen
Door het afwijken van mijn Son:
Ik gink rondom de wachters vragen,
Maar niemant mijn beminde kon.

Doch eer mijn hert van 't soeken ruste
Soo nam mijn lief tot my sijn gank,
Wiens Rooselippen ik doen kuste,
Vermits ik ben van liefde krank.

Ik bracht hem in dien eygen woning
Van die my eerstmaal heeft gebaart,
Daar hy als Prins en Hemels Koning
Tot mijn geluk noch wert bewaart.

♦ ♦ ♦

Eynde der Geestelijcke stoffen.

Aan

For my sun sank, my sun vanished.
I asked the watchmen all around
But none of them knew my beloved.
Yet before my heart from searching
Rested, my lover came walking in my way
Whose rosy lips I kissed and kissed
Because I was sick with love.
I brought him into his proper dwelling
In which I was born for the first time
For he, the prince and heaven's king,
To my great good luck preserved it.

♦ ♦ ♦

End of religious material.

## [123]

Aan de Welgeboren hoog Ed. Juff. CATHARINA ISABELLA
MARIA, Baronnesse van Heerema. Haar Ed. opdragende de
Gesangen, en de Vertalingen in 't besonder.

MYn Swaan heeft lang in het verlangen
Geweest, om u haar schorre sangen
Te off'ren, die se nu opdraagt,
En U om uwe gonsten vraagt,
Want seyt s'ik wil haar lof uytgalmen,
En overstrengelen met palmen,
Dien Terpsichoor die door geschal,
Besluyt in haar het Negen-tal,
Die als een tweede Canens gorgelt,
Dien Philomeel, die vrolijk orgeldt,
En hemelvallen dringt om hooch,
Die sy uyt Febus sangkruyk sooch,
Waarom de faam op vlugge pennen,
Haar doet de werelt over rennen,
Geen wonder dan dat U mijn Swaan
Biedt haar geringe stoffen aan.

◆ ◆ ◆

Op de

To the wellborn most noble Lady Catharina Isabella
Maria, Baroness van Heerema, in thanks I offer my
songs and translations*

My Swan has long in longing lived
To make an offering in her hoarse voice
Whose note she dedicates requesting
Forebearance from you, and grace:
For I, too, want to make echo, re-echo
The praise my Swan utters, and strew
Your way with palms. You for whom
Terpsichore dances, enlisting you among
The ninefold Muses – for whom Canens warbles
And a happy Philomela chants, while divinely
Inspired speech cascades down, begged
Of Phoebus and the urn at his well.
Therefore Fame swift in flight overruns
The world. No wonder that my Swan
Also makes her plea, humbly petitioning.

♦ ♦ ♦

* Brongersma also apostrophizes the Baroness van Heerema in the second poem of *The Swan of the Well*. The story of Canens and Picus is treated in a pair of poems that appear earlier in the book, suggesting the poet shared these works with the baroness. Brongersma thus imagines her Yeats-like circus animals performing for the baroness.

## [124]

Op de ongemene Lauwer-boom staande in 't Lusthof van de Ed:
Heer J.V.B. Die door de felle koude uytgevroren, en naderhant
afgekapt. Waarin als de Poëten seggen Dafne verandert is.

Die dus spreekt.

Toon: Machere liberté.

AY my! ik die de gloet van Febus min ontvloot,
Waar door mijn kruyn helaas! met Lauwer is omwonden,
Daar werd ik van Boreas geschonden,
Ay my! ik die de gloedt van Febus min ontvloot,
Staa in perijkel van de doodt,
Ah! help u Lief Apol, laat gy me soo vernielen
Van sulk een wrede, die in 't staal geklonken staat.
Helaas! helaas! 't is Mars die Dafne komt ontzielen
En wond' op wond' in haar verbroken spieren slaat.
Ay my: ik die de gloedt van Febus min ontvloodt
Waar door mijn kruyn helaas! met Lauwer is omwonden,
Daar werd ik van Borëas geschonden,
Ay my! ik die de gloedt van Febus min ontvloodt,
Staa in perijkel van de doodt.

◆ ◆ ◆

Op de

On the distinguished laurel tree that, standing in the
pleasure garden of the noble J.V. B., froze in a fierce
cold snap and suffered injury to its crown, whereby
(as poets say) Daphne was metamorphosed

Air: "*Ma chère liberté*"\*

I fled the heat of Phoebus's love that had
Torn from me my bough of laurel for
His badge of glory. Then Boreas defiled me
Cold as Phoebus, hot so I stood – and stand –
In mortal peril. If ever you loved me
Apollo do not abandon me to such assault,
Gouged and cut by steel, Mars's metal,
Militant striking to dispatch my soul,
Successive wounds dealing to my broken
Limbs. I fled the heat of Phoebus's love
That tore from me my bough of laurel. Then
Cold Boreas took me. I stood, I stand in peril.

❖ ❖ ❖

\* Proserpina sings the air "*Ma chère liberté que vous aviez d'attraits*" ("My dear liberty what charms you have") in the tragic opera bearing the heroine's name, composed by Quinault and Lully, and debuting in 1680. Brongersma alleges the presence or connivance of Mars, because arborists have employed edged weapons such as axes to remove shattered branches. The governing conceit contrasts the heat of the sun, Apollo, with the chill of the north wind.

[125]

Op de selfde Boom, wederom Uytloopende, die nieuwe Lootjes schiet.

Dafne spreekt.

Toon: Rochers vous este sourd.

IK voel me dan Apol door uwe min herboren,
Schoon d'ysre Mars my had ter aardt neergevelt,
Naar my den Aquilon bracht onder sijn gewelt
Waar om ik quijnden en mijn kragten had verloren

De locken die mijn Nek, en Schouderen beswieren
O! Mavors die hadt gy verwert, en uyt-gerukt,
Gy hadt de blad'ren van mijn lofkrans afgeplukt
Die sig verwiss'len in verweeuwigde lauwrieren,

Ik groen en bloos op nieuw, mijn leden sijn aan't groeyen,
Myn kruyn alree bepruykt (schoon g'op u tanden bijt)
Schiet males lootjes, u verwoeden bey tot spijt:
En sal soo lang ik leef ter eer van Febus bloeyen.

♦ ♦ ♦

Toon, Tranquille Coeur.

Cleonte aan Eliseen.

IK quijn gelijk de Tortel doet,
Die in een steen-reep sit bedolven,

Om

On the same tree renascent, producing new boughs

Air: *"Rochers vous êtes sourds"*

Though iron Mars nearly dragged my trunk
Earthward after Aquilo snapped my sinews
With the violence that withered me, that
Weakened me, Apollo, my love, you heal.
Locks that swirled on my shoulders, who
Dishonoured you by ripping you? Who tore
The leaves of the crown of praise from me
Promoted long ago to greatness's sign?
I grow green and bloom again like new,
My limbs proliferate, crown regenerates.
So your blades slashed me. Shoot tender twigs!
Rage is vain. I testify to Phoebus's honour
Which, at the same time, is my profuse blossoming.

◆ ◆ ◆

Cléonte to Elise

Air: *"Tranquilles coeurs"* *

Like a turtledove that moans and sits
On her dejected perch, a windmill's cable,

---

* The air that Brongersma supplies begins in this fashion: *"Tranquilles coeurs, préparez vous / À milles secrètes alarmes"* ("Calm hearts, prepare yourself for a thousand secret alarms"). So Venus sings in Lully's *Le triomphe de l'amour* of 1681. The melody was popular in Holland. This poem epitomizes Brongersma's method. She uses a technical term (*steen-reep*) in describing her turtledove's plausible perch, but modulates into description of a landscape discrepant from that in the vicinity of Groningen: rocky, mountainous, inhabited by the famous nymph Echo.

[126]

Om daar 't ontlasten 't droef gemoedt,
En sijne smerten uyt te golven
Door gesteen, en gekir, om dat het is ontbloodt.
Van sijne hert genoodt.

Soo truur ik om mijn Enigst' een,
Soo klaag ik in gekloofde rotsen,
En galm door herde klippen heen,
Die het bange geluyt doen bottsen
Aan de top van 't gebergt, in 't verwilderste wout,
Waar niemandt sig vertrouwt

Dan d'Echo, die door medely
Haar houdt in dat gehugt verholen,
Die dikwijls d'oorsaak vraagt aan my
Waar om dat ik dus sit geschoolen,
Ah! dan seg ik het is om het afsijn alleen,
Van u mijn Eliseen.

♦ ♦ ♦

Op het vertrek van ELISA naar Duytsland, dien geleyde wierde gedaan aan de Zuyder Zee waar het doen ter tijt geweldig Stormde, en Reegende,

Toon

Sobbing out of chagrin, ridding her breast
Of all that distresses her heart, I mourn
My dearest, voice echoing from the broken
Rock face to the height of wilder woods where
No climber dares to go. Then Echo who loves
That forsaken place and who shows pity asks,
"What is the reason you sit and cry there? – Tell."
Then I say: "It is your renunciation, Elise:
Your intolerable renunciation, Elise."

◆ ◆ ◆

On Elise's departure for Germany across the Zuider Zee, in heavy rain and wind\*

\* Brongersma's speaker imagines herself as the priestess Hero of Sestus who, adoring young Leander of Abydus, inspired him to swim across the Hellespont, a strait that – together with familial disapproval – divided the lovers from each other. She held a torch from a tower as a beacon, but he drowned anyway. Brongersma modifies the tendency of the tale. This Leander, now Elise, voluntarily departs into a storm, leaving Hero to pine. The "Gothic lands" are likely to be German-speaking parts of the Holy Roman Empire. The air from the tragic opera *Proserpine* reinforces the speaker's bereftness.

[127]

Toon, Machere liberté.

HElaas! de Hemel weendt, en stort veel dropen neer
De wint gevlerkt maakt dat de baren sijn aan 't woeden
Wijl mijn tranen leken in 'er vloeden
Helaas! den Heemel weent, en stort veel dropen neer
Om u vertrek Elisa ah! keer weer,

Siet gy niet schone Ziel hoe alles u is tegen;
Hoe Febus hem verschuylt en met een Wolk bedekt?
Schoon sijne Lauwren sijn aan uwe Kroon gereegen
Daar gy hem voor een Dafne steeds verstrekt,
Helaas: den Hemel weent en stort veel droopen neer
Om u vertrek Elisa ah! keer weer.

Maar neen het buld'ren en het bruysende gedruys
De golven, waar de Zee ontboeyt u mee gaat dreygen,
Daar men 't al siet naar u onluk neygen,
Maar neen, het buld'ren, en het bruysende gedruys
Schijnt u te sijn een lieflijk boom geruys,
Ah! siet gy Doris niet dien raserny ontvlugten

Die by haar Galathee in 't bolder klippen kruypt
Siet gy niet waarde (wijl haar nimfen om u sugten)
Hoe mijn geschrey de stranden over druypt,
Maar neen het buldren, en het bruysende gedruys
Schijnt u te sijn een lieflijk boom geruys.

Ik sal dan wijl g' op uytgspannen wieken drijft
Naar 't Godtse-rijk met smert u wederkomst verwagten
Daar, waar ik verquijnen sal in klagten,
Ik sal dan wijl g' op uytgespannen wieken drijft

My

Air: *"Ma chère liberté"*

Heaven weeps tumultuous tears, the wind's
Wingbeats stir the sea to fits while
My subtler tears slip into the stormy flood.
Heaven weeps tumultuous tears as you,
Elise, leave. Return. My pure soul, see how
Phoebus hides. Cloud occludes all except
The laurel on your brows, his persistent
Token which you wear as constantly
As Daphne herself. Heaven weeps, Elise,
Tumultuous tears. Return, please. But no.
You hear the booming and raving of the gulf,
Harassing seas harrying your vessel to
Disaster, as the rustling of leaves like Daphne's.
Doris flees the madness, Galatea
With her creeps into sea-grotto security.
Other nymphs conduct their quest for you.
You hear the booming and raving of the gulf
As soft as the rustle of leaves like Daphne's.
Full sails float you to the Gothic kingdom.
In music therefore my pain poses you
A warbled question: "When will you return?"

[128]

My troosten, soo ge maar in welstant blijft,
O! laast vaar wel, hoe hert, hoe hert, valt my dat scheyden
Geen Hero immer meer droeg groter Zielen leet
Als ik, helaas! helaas! mijn Hert sal u geleyden
Dat om u staat te volgen algereet,
Ik sal dan wijl g'op uytgespannen wicken drijft
My troosten, soo ge maar in welstant blijft.

◆ ◆ ◆

Toon, Rochers vous este sourd.

O! Aangename Bosch, en lust prieel der Goden:
Hoe Lieflijk overdekt U Lommer my altans,
Wanneer ik't blader loof hegt aan een Rose krans
Hoe vaak schijnt gy elk op u Boom-cieraad ten oden;

Om daar een Loflied van U waarde op te singen,
Want onder het gewulst: waar Philomeel van roemdt:
Daar vint men't Velt besaayd met weeldrig gebloemt
Waar langs een Suyvre-Beek haar golvig nat doet springen.

Waar't Flugge reetje speeld'en huppeld door de paden
Dat sig vermeydt in 't groen: en graast in 't lekkre kruyd,
Waar't Nagtegaaltie slaat haar Ziel roerend geluydt
Om't Luystrend Nimphedom door Sang strijd te versaden,

En

Farewell hits me hard, keep well my darling.
No Hero ever suffered worse. My heart
On wings will float if, darling, you keep well.

♦ ♦ ♦

Air: *"Rochers, vous êtes sourds"*

Pleasant woods, pleasure-bower of the gods,
How amiably you cover me over with shade
Every time when I, subduing twigs
To the end of proper praise, twine
A garland. Invite me, tree-civility.
Allow me only to describe your stateliness.
Under your tousled crowns, euphonious
Philomela dwells, and there widens out
A thick meadow light with flowers. A spring
Gurgles into a glassy creek. A quick
Fawn leaps on confluent paths, and green
Abundance hides it, freshening dainties feed it
While nightingales call their various audience:
Contesting birds conciliate nymphdom listening.

[129]

En waar het Jager-rot het Wilt fangt in de heggen
Door strikt met net gespan, waar 't schouwe Corhoen duykt
En 't anstig Haasje vliedt dat nimmer oog'leen luykt
Maar slaapend' houwt de wagt om hem geen laag te leggen.

Waar Pan sijn herders riet doet voor Sijringa klinken
Om haar verherde Hart te lokken tot sijn min
Waat sig Endimion voor sijne nagt Godin,
Gebogen houwt, en waar men Febus glans siet blinken

Om Dafnes Lauwren: die hy haar ter eer doet groenen,
O! Bosch bekoorlijk Bosch O! Schuylplaats mijns gemoet
Daar ik mijn Lamm'ren wey, O! Bosch hoe lief en soet
Spreydt guy u Lovren die malkand'ren minlijk soenen.

Wijl Zephirus komt om sijn Flora te begroeten:
Die van de Lent bepronkt haar goude hairen kruld,
Die 't gansche woud al om met Nardus geuren vuld,
O! Bosch geen bosch komt my (als gy) soo schoon ontmoeten.

✦✦✦

Op de Vermaaklijkheden van BORGER, in Drenthe.

Toon: Had ik een Koninks kroon op 't hooft.

Wijk Tempe, wijk, want gy zijt niet,
    Wijk Pindus u geboomt,

Is

The hateful hunter kills wild music's sources
Stringing nets in the gaps of the hedges where
Shy quail scuttle dodging, and the anxious
Eyes of the hare stay open as she dozes.
There Pan plays his reed for Syrinx – for her
For whom his reed is named – to soften
Her hardened heart until it admits his love.
In bed Endymion dreams his lunar goddess.
For Daphne Phoebus dazzles, laurel glows
In ardent light. Resort of the mind, forest,
You spread and turn your leaves to kiss one another
As Zephyr greets his Flora, the blonde whom Spring
Has curled and combed where earth smells good as nard.
No other forest lets me think as well as this.

◆ ◆ ◆

A poem on the amusements at Borger, in Drenthe

Air: "Had I a kingly crown upon my head"\*

Low Tempe yield, you are next to nothing:
Pindus withdraw your forest heights.

---

\* The melody "*Had ik een konings kroon op't hoofd*" ("Had I a kingly crown upon my head") is still popular with Dutch choirs. Borger, the village beside the great *hunebed* that Brongersma identifies as a temple to the goddess Natura, or Nature, here appears in entirely neoclassical guise. The poet subordinates indigenous motifs to pastoral commonplaces mellowly orchestrated. Brongersma displays familiarity with the personnel of Honoré d'Urfé's influential seventeenth-century fiction *L'Astrée*.

[130]

Is by dees Eyken als het Riet,
En 't Beekje dat der stroomt
Rilt sachter als den Liganon
Waar sich Astré verhouwt,
Die by haar trouwen Celadon
Daar rust in 't lomrich wouwt.

Geen Laetmus: schoon het van Diaan
Wel eer wierd' seer bemint,
Koomt by dees hooge heuv'len aan,
Want alles wat men vint
Is ongemeen, en aangenaam,
Jaa selfs de bruyne key
Is voor het wollich vee bequaam,
En dient haar tot een wey.

Geen Satyr hoe vol minne vier
Vermeyt sich hier ontrent,
Noch Veltgedrogten snufflen hier,
De Nimfjes sijn gewent
Te speelen by het lieve Vee,
In vreed'en soete rust,
Waar Coridon sijn Dorilee
Uyt reyne liefde kust.

Daar nimmer Leeuw, noch Tyger huylt,
Maar waar Endimion

In 't

Beside these reeds, beneath these oaks
Passes a gentler stream than the Lignon
Where Astrée rests in shade beside
Her faithful Celadon. No Latmos,
No matter how Diana loves it, rivals
The tall hill here where the visitor
Sees the uncommon and the agreeable.
Even hay-stems less than green please
The fleecy flock as it softly forages. Satyrs
Chase no one, and no swine snuffle.
The nymphs have gone to play with herds
Charming, happy, and sweetly tranquil.
Adoring Corydon kisses chaste Dorilée.
Does a tiger or a lion howl? No. Endymion

[131]

In't diepste van de Boschen schuylt
Voor 't straalen van de Son,
En't vluchtlich Reetje rennen siet,
Doch voor sijn schicht vervaart,
Dat over berg, en daalen vliet
Het geen sijn smerten baart.

En daar men veelderhande taal
Van pluymgedierten hoort,
En't singen van de Nachtegaal
'tgeen meenich hert bekoort,
Waar onder Damon lieflijk speelt
Als hy de schaapjes weyt,
En voor sijn lief een veltdeun queelt
Dat haar de ziel verleyt.

Wie souw niet wenschen staag te zijn
By dees' vermaaklijkheen,
Sach het den DonderGodt Jupijn
Hy daalde wel beneen,
Of soo het Hermes wier gewaar
Hy vloog ten hemel af,
En het sijn schoone Herte daar,
Soo men hem't Borger gaf.

♦ ♦ ♦

Op de

In the deepest covert of the woods retires
With misgiving for the arrow that over
Hill and valley fleets, infixing pain.
Feathered musicians whistle and mingle
But the nightingale, choosy, worshipping
Selectively, sings at length. Beneath
Its perch Damon pipes while grazing
His sheep, seducing his beloved's soul.
The minute you wish you have fulfillment.
The lord of thunder Jupiter
Would dwell down here below
Or Hermes did he only know
Would stoop from heaven and,
As a man of Borger, court a sweetheart.

❖ ❖ ❖

[132]

Op de Weder-komste van ELISA uyt de Pals en het onder wegen zijn,

Toon, Sombre Forest.

Rys op Rijs op, O Son van mijn gemoet,
Al lang-genoeg ter schuyl gekropen,
Schoon men V drenkt met lekker druyven bloed
In 't Palatijnsch gebergt, en let in 't ommelopen,
Ey dring V Paarden aan, vertoef niet, wijl gy weet
Hoe ik door groot verlangen
Als een Klitie staa gereet:
Om V mijn Ligt t' ontfangen
Die me laat vol herten leet.

Siet Gy niet hoe Auroor de weg bereyd
Die op haar Safferaane wagen
U vliegend Rosgespan de teugels leyd,
Om haar te rasser door de wolken heen te Iagen
Ik heb hier nog bewaard dat kost'lijk Hert-klenoot
Waar mee 'k V sal bepronken
Soo ge my waar haast weer bood
Een straaltje van V Lonken,
Want mijn lijden is te groot.

                                                                                        Ah!

To Elise en route from Palts-Tweebrugge*

Air: "*Sombres Foretz*"

Rise, rise sun of my mind
Too long sunk under horizon.
The tasty blood of grapes may toast you
In the Palatine tavern, but stop
Your delay now, tack your horses up,
Linger no longer knowing I stand
Like the Oceanid Klytie ready
To embrace you, my life, passion, heart.

See how Aurora lights the road
Who from her saffron wagon leads
Your flying pair by their bridles
To urge them faster amid the clouds.
I will lavish my heart on cherished you
So hurry back. Yield me a healing
Ray, from your flirtatious pupil.

* The Duchy of Pfalz-Zweibrücken was part of the Holy Roman Empire. The House of Wittelsbach ruled it. Elisabeth Joly must have visited this duchy. Born in Picardy, Thomas Gobert (ca 1600–1672) composed the air that Brongersma has in mind: "*Sombres foretz où régne le silence, / Je ne viens pas ici vous faire violence / Par triste recit de mon malheureux sort*" ("Gloomy forest where silence reigns I do not come here to do you violence by the sad recital of my unfortunate lot"). The forlorn nymph Klytie also appears in Brongersma's poem about Ceyx and Alcyone.

[133]

Ah! Coom, of ik beswijk, helaas! hoe kan
Ik V geflonker langer missen?
Of laat gy my geheel vernielen van
Het schriklijk Moort gedrogt der nare duysternissen,
Maar neen ik sie van 't hoog V goude wielen gaan
Die gy allenx doet dalen,
Ah! se schieten op my aan
Verberg niet meer V stralen,
Kom mijn Son, verligt V Maan.

◆ ◆ ◆

Op't Verjaren van de hoog E.G.V. M.V. H.M.B.V.S.

Toon: Ach mijn Credijt is doot.

NU dat den Oceaan
Met barre Noortsche Golven,
Koomt aan den Oever slaan
Van Kresus rijke kolven,
En laat het Zee-gesuys
Uyt Tritons hoor'nen schat'ren,
Wiens bulderend' geruys
Doorkrielt de souwte wat'ren.

Soo treedt Neptunus voor
Met sijn geschubde troepen,

Eu

To die now would hardly manifest
More devotion than my present pining
And wasting away. Abandon me?
Abuse and abase me? Let Death take me?
On high I spy your gilded wheels slowly
Turning, descending: glide toward me,
Hide no more those beams by which I, moon, glow.

❖ ❖ ❖

On the birthday celebration of the noble E.G.V. M.V. H.M.B.V.S.*

Air: "Ah, my faith is dead"

Now that the ocean's salt
Barrens and northward tides
Drive breakers against Croesus's
Coastlands and Triton's horn
Booms, shivering the sweet
Waters, Neptune progresses
With a scaly entourage

---

* The array of dedicatory initials is confounding. The pomp, the invocation of Thetis, the mention of a landgravate – all point to the celebration of local or visiting nobility.

[134]

En laat het schelpig Choor
Door't paarde bruyschen sloepen
Langs d'onbebaande strant,
Waar't galmen der Sirenen
Op Godenoffer-Brant
Haar vroolijk gaan vereenen.

Want maar de Monarchy,
En 't groote heyr der Baren
't Geweschte jaargety
Eendrachtich komt verklaren,
Van Haar wiens Adelfaan
Sich Forst'lijk gaat vertoonen:
Dien, sal men nu voortaan,
Als Friesche Thetis kroonen.

Op op dan Nimphedom
Van Pontus silte Ad'ren
Maak lieflijk Sang gemom,
Pluk groen bemoste blad'ren
Bestrengel klip, en Duyn:
Op dat gy moogt beswieren
Dien hooglansbergsche kruyn,
Om mee haar Feest te vieren.

❖❖❖

De ver-

In a sloop drawn by
Hippocamps by the edge
Of trackless sand where Sirens
Echo, meeting to make
Their happy sacrifice.
The lord of Ocean and
His dynasty proclaim
The day of her whose nobleness
Crowns her, glorious in song,
As the Frisian Thetis.
Up Nymphdom of Pontus's
Pulsing brine! Begin
Your masque, and pluck sea wrack,
String the bluffs and dunes
With the stuff and twine
The landgravate's garland.

◆ ◆ ◆

De vernoegde Herderin,

Toon: Carolus.

GElukkig die geen pracht en kent,
Noch daar sijn tochten ooyt toe sent,
Want het baart niet dan droeve qualen,
Veel beter is het naar het licht
Sijn oog te stieren dat den hemel sticht,
Als al de Koninklijke zalen.

Wat baat my Perel of Gesteent',
Als 't quijnend hert inwendig weent,
Ag 't geeft doch nimmer geen vernoegen,
Een kransje met der hant gestrikt
Van versse Rosen dat de ziel verquikt,
Sal tot mijn rust veel beter voegen.

Geen gulde Scepter, maar een staf
Van eenig Telg gesneden af,
Kan in mijn hant 't vermogen swaayen
Wanneer ik in het Veldt, of Dal,
Of langs de bergen 't Vee verweyden sal,
Waar nooyt geen vley gedrogt komt waayen.

Ik ben een Coningin van 't wouwt,
Mijn Hutje is van strooy gebouwt,
Omlommert van veel Else bomen,
Voor Lymonaad' of lekk're wijn
Kan my een rillend' beekje dienstig zijn;
Of 't vocht uyt klare waterstromen,

            Ik

The content shepherdess

Air: "Carolus"

Fortunate who no splendour knows,
It entails nothing but trouble. Let
The eye avoid the lustre of courtly halls
Preferring the light that issues out of heaven.
Pearl or gemstone only panics the heart
That the rose garland twined by hand delights.
Let me wield not a golden sceptre but a branch
Cut for a walking staff as I pass through
Meadow or valley grazing the herds where never
A woman is basely compelled to flatter.
Queen of the wood, under the ash trees I build
A thatch cabin and serve neither wine
Nor lemonade, but the fine liquor of the stream.

[136]

Ik kies een krans, voor goude kroon,
Een Herder voor een Princen Soon
Die onbekommert konen rapen
Haar voedsel uyt het grasich velt
Waar op ik houw mijn voorneem vast gestelt,
Vaar wel ik gaa, en hoed' mijn schapen.

♦ ♦ ♦

De verlangende TIRSIS

Toon, Tranquille Caeur.

VErgeefs beklim ik berg, en Duyn
En staar op t' woensdag der holle baaren,
Vergeefs betreed' ik strant; en puyn
Waar langs Elisa is gevaaren,
Ah! ik smoor in verdriet, soo se langer vertoeft
Dat my nog meer bedroeft.

Den Oever rookt van mijn getraan
De golven swellen door het sugten
En doet de stroom te rasser gaan
Wijl d' Eb haar vloeden koomt ontvlugten
Want de vrees van 't gevaar dat een gifts doot pijl is
Baart myn bekommernis.

Ah! mogt ik haast die schone mondt
Waar uyt bezielde woorden vloeyen
Genaken, opwiens malse gront
Het puyk van Vlees Robijnen groeyen,

Siet

Flowers round my temples better than gold.
The shepherd behaves more princely than a prince.
Rabbits nibble nourishment in the grassy field
Where my sheep, too, derive an equal banquet.

◆ ◆ ◆

Thyrsis full of longing

Air: *"Tranquilles coeurs"**

I may climb the hills and dunes and gaze
Out on the raving of the hollow seas,
I may pace the beach and scuff the shingle.
But Elise has sailed long since and if she tarried
So much the worse my sorrow would afflict me.
Tears mist my prospect of the shore, the gulf
Might swell with the heaving of my sighs.
The current rips faster, as the tide goes into ebb.
My fear for Elise's safety is the dart of death.
Her lovely mouth that forms her lovely words,
That place of tender eloquence ruby-tinted!

* The air that Brongersma supplies here (used elsewhere in *The Swan of the Well*) begins in this fashion: *"Tranquilles coeurs, préparez vous / À milles secrètes alarmes"* ("Calm hearts, prepare yourself for a thousand secret alarms"). Venus sings these words in Lully's *Le triomphe de l'amour* of 1681. Palinurus, helmsman of Aeneas's ship, fell into the sea – surviving that accident, only to be murdered on the coast by those who found him at the tideline. When Aeneas visited the underworld, he consulted with Palinurus's shade. The hero promised a monument to the helmsman's bones. The relevant promontory was named "Palinura," in honour of the murdered man. Brongersma's Thyrsis, stationed on a beach, perhaps feels himself close emotionally to Palinurus's dreary fate. Yet Elise has her share in it, also. Elise is like the lost pilot, for the speaker would gladly preserve his Palinurus safe from brute extinction in the surf. This poem belongs with the sizeable minority of pieces in *The Swan of the Well* that feature friends or lovers ruminating on the shore, often about a figure called Elise.

[137]

Siet ik schaaal gereet met de Ermen omhoog
En haal V met het Oog.

Koom dan ik wagt, ah! hoort ge't niet?
Of sijt ge doover van de Rotsen?
Heel door V weerkomst mijn verdriet
Laat m' aan geen klip van Wanhoop botsen
Maar drijf voort op't gevleugelde water Dolfijn
En set V koers op mijn.

Ik ben de Baak: daar V gemoedt
Door't onophoudelijk verlangen
In't weeder Lieven werdt gevoedt
Schoon my die harde ketens prangen
Doch ey kont door 't besluyt van V herts Palinuur
Versoeten al mijn suur.

◆ ◆ ◆

Toon, Sombre Forest.

Gy sijt dan tot getuygt O! naar geboomt'!
Van mijn onnoosele vermaken?
En gy O Beekje die langs keytjes stroomt;
Wanneer 'k slegs door 't gesigt Elisa mogt genaken,
Weest dan van nu voortaan't geheym van mijn verdriet
En deel met my de pijnen
Wijl de droefheyt voor me vliet
Ah! Ah! ik moet verdwijnen
Want Elisa is hier niet.

*Elisa*

It makes me raise my arms as though to signal,
The gesture over distance would seize your gaze.
"Can't you hear me?" I bawl. "Are you as deaf as rock?"
My woe flows back. I would fall from delusion's
Cliff top, unless you rode a wingèd dolphin's back
Plotting a course to me, over water.
Let me be the coastal beacon never dim
Inextinguishably kindling your kindly mind.
The bonds that chafe me only you can loose,
My heart's consolatory Palinurus.

◆ ◆ ◆

Air: *"Sombres Foretz"*\*

Witness, thick woods, my simple declaration
And you too, little stream flowing over rocks.
When I crave to bring my face to Elise's face
You hear, and alleviate that secret misery
While the tumult of my mind finds a covert
Among your branches, or gently flows away:
"How, Elise, could your heart, so hard, live on
Without love? Love wastes away out of love,

---

\* This poem features a sylvan complaint to Elise. The setting owes to Vergil's eclogues. Elise may be called "the lily of the east" because she travelled into a German-speaking land – the Duchy of Pfalz-Zweibrücken. But the lily also recalls the verses that deplore Elise's journey into France as well as the triumphal arch of *The Swan of the Well*'s program poem.

[138]

Elisa ah! hoe is V Hert, soo hert
Hoe koont ge sonder Leven Leeven?
Dog 't is vergeefs de min, om min gesert
Geen doode kan een rif doot is 't leven geven,
Maar gy die leeft door veel gun my het Leeftogt ree
Het hert is my ontstoolen
En ge voert het over zee
Gedenk, 't is V bevoolen
Breng het onverkreukt weer mee.

Dog ik sal schoon ge door de wolken streeft
U nimmer laaten, maar op wieken
De lugt door kerven, die me hoope geeft
Om V mijn Lelij-bloem in 't Oosten op te rieken,
Of dat ge meely hat? O lang gedooken Ligt
Om door de duysternissen
Voort te dringen, wijl ge stigt
De Dag dien ik moet missen
Al te lang uyt mijn gesigt.

♦ ♦ ♦

De onvernoegde Doris.

Toon: Suis je donc.

Oppervoogt ontsach der Goden
Die de Son, en maan gebiet,
Nu is my u hulp van noden,
'k Bid van 't hoog Olimpi siet,
Dwing Vulkaan dat hy gaat smeden
Weer u Blixems onder een,

Om

And no dead thing can raise to life a corpse.
Elise you have so much – give me some.
You took my heart with you abroad, and now
You must bring it unbroken back to me.
My lily of the east, if you flew I would
Follow you on wings through the cloudy sky.
My light long sunk rise again, and drive,
Bright as day, my turbid thoughts before you."

◆ ◆ ◆

The malcontent Doris

Air: "*Suis je donc né*"*

Leader of the gods whom sun and moon obey
Have Vulcan fashion lightning at his anvil
To free me, and to send me to the realms below.

\* Brongersma identifies her melody as "*Suis je donc*"; probably she means to indicate Claude Le Jeune's "*Suis-je donc né*," or "Was I born to live like this?" The composer lived from 1530 to 1600. The poem takes the form of a prayer to Jupiter.

[139]

Om my hier te doen ontleden!
En te voeren van beneen.

Hebt gy niet een drom doen sneuv'len
Doe der Reusen dwinglandy
Deden proppen top op heuv'len
Tegen al u heerschappy?
Hebt gy niet om 't dertel mallen
Uyt de wagen van de Son
In den Eridaan doen vallen,
Dien vermeet'len Phaëton.

Waarom dan een dit geweygert,
Wijl 't u aan geen macht ontbreekt,
Die u Majesteyt besteygert,
En u om een wel daat smeekt,
Want de wreetheyt van Clorinde
Doet my wenschen ach Jupijn!
Om een beter plaats te vinden,
Waar ik meer gerust mach zijn.

◆ ◆ ◆

Toon, Ah! qu'un fidel Amant.

HH! ah! waar vlugt ge voor
Mijn Arethuse?
Gy siet dat ik u volg in 't rennen op het spoor.
En langs mijn voeten heen een vloet van tranen brusen
'K ben geen Ascalafus, maar Alfeus geef gehoor,

Ach

Was it not your hand that chained the giants
When Pelion was piled on Ossa as a challenge?
Did you not spill the sunny car into Eridanus
Precipitating down the arrogant Phaethon?
Why would you hesitate to end my longing,
Kind as you are, in contrast to cruel Clorinde?
No power surpasses you. God, grant me peace.

♦ ♦ ♦

Air: "*Ah! Qu'un fidèle amant*"*

Where are you running off to, my Arethusa?
You can see I run right after you, on your traces,
And my tears hotly fall by my feet as I go.
Ascaphalus I am not. Give Alpheus a hearing.

* Brongersma gives no title to this verse. The air derives from Philippe Quinault and Jean-Baptiste Lully's opera *Le triomphe de l'amour*. The sea goddess Amphitrite, having long resisted the advances of Neptune, at last surrenders herself: the reverse of Arethusa's case. Amphitrite sings, "*Ah! Qu'un fidèle amant / Est redoubtable!*" ("Ah! How frightening a faithful lover is!"). Ascaphalus, son of Acheron or of Styx, informed Pluto that Proserpina had eaten pomegranate seeds, resulting in her detention in the underworld. Ovid declares that an enraged Proserpina changed this betrayer into an owl, by sprinkling him with water from the river Phlegethon (*Metamorphoses* 9.539–550). The riverine theme is apt. The speaker of Brongersma's poem – the stream Alpheus in Elis – chased a daughter of Oceanus, Arethusa (the addressee of the poem). To evade this unwelcome suitor, Arethusa petitioned Diana's help. The goddess compliantly changed her into a fountain. Brongersma's poem portrays a wooer who, despite his persistence, promises to refrain at last from mingling his waters with Arethusa's.

[140]

Ah! ah! waar vlugt ge voor
Mijn Arethuse
Gy loopt te ras de Bosschen door
Men hoort van ver U lokken rusen
Vertoef, vertoef, eer ik versmoor,
Ah! ah! waar vlugt ge voor
Myn Arethuse.

Schoon dat ge my nu siet
Tot Vogt verdruypen
Om U ontdankb're, die sig wisselt in een vliet,
Soo sal ik evenstaag U snelle loop naa kruypen
Ah! Arethus bedaar, O wrede hoort ge niet,
Schoon dat ge my nu siet
Tot vogt verdruypen.

Ik sal nogtans in mijn verdriet
Van U gesmolten Bron nat suypen,
Die gy uyt volle kruyken giet,
Schoon dat ge my nu siet
Tot vogt verdruypen.

◆ ◆ ◆

Silvander aan Hylas,

Toon: Tranquille Coeur.

WAar is nu al het lief vermaak,
Ah! Hylas! als een rook verdwenen,
Waar is Diaan, die deugde baak
Die my soo gunstich heeft bescheenen,

Sech

Where are you running off to, my Arethusa?
I can hear the wind rustle, is it in your long hair?
You run in the forest so fast my sweat
Will melt me away. I am dripping with wet
While ungratefully you transform into water.
I will constantly follow after your current's course.
Pitiless Arethusa come to your senses, listen.
In my distress I will never drink from your well
That pours out from a full jug though you see me
Myself flooded with the sweat of long pursuit.

♦ ♦ ♦

Silvander to Hylas*

Air: *"Tranquilles coeurs"*

Where now have they gone, those times that were
   so charming?
I can't grab Hylas back more than a wind-blown coil
   of smoke.
Diana, virtue's beacon, who (what goodness!) used to
   beam on us –

---

* Hylas is a male name. The poem imagines male friendship. Hercules and Hylas, fellow Argonauts, loved each other. But the desirous nymph of a well on the coast of Mysia abducted the handsome friend of the renowned hero.

[141]

Seg waar is toch dat licht dat soo heerelijk praalt,
En 't gantse ront bestraalt.

Ah! 't duykt voor my: ik sie niet meer
Het schitt'ren van die schoone oogen,
Wiens weerglans slaat een blixsem neer
Op mijne ziel, ay hebt medoogen,
Nu sy by u op't hoog van haar Latmus gaat treen,
Wijl ik hier dwaal alleen.

Hoe menichmaal gedenk ik aan
Dat soet, en minlijk ommetrekken
Wanneer we langs de Yper laan
Ons voor haar luyster moesten dekken,
Ah! het lommerig Bos groende op het gesicht
Van dat bekoorlijk licht.

De graasjes schooten weelich uyt,
De bloetjes pulyden uyt'er knoppen
Haar Asem overgoot het kruyt,
En baarde niet dan Nectar droppen,
Waar in gy u versuypt nu ik in't jammer-dal
Beween mijn ongeval.

                                                                       Doch

What happened to the lamp that she raised to light
   our friendship?
Her light dwindles. I can glimpse nowhere the glitter of
   those eyes
That always lanced mine like lightning. Have pity! She
Climbs with you perhaps on the heights of Latmos now,
While I linger here alone. That walk we always took
Along the Ee, that glittered! We used to flee the glare
Into the shade of trees, above which sky blue presided.
Succulent grass blades, budding flowerets,
The juicy luxury of wholesome nectars dripped
And we pleased ourselves here where single I patrol,
In the present tense, in the vale of my misfortune.

[142]

Doch wijl mijn lot hier in bestaat
Om sonder haar te moeten leven,
Soo bid'ik dat ge somtijts gaat
By mijn Godin' om troost te geven,
Want de hoop die de trouw van u aart my laast gaf,
Draag ik tot in het graf.

❖ ❖ ❖

Aan de slapende ELISE

Toon, Nimphes des Eaux.

STaak V geruys Ay wind beroer geen bladen,
En gy O Beekje schiet kabblend' V stroom
Wijl dat Elise door een Droom
Haar schijnt in vreugd' te baden.
Kleyn Filomeeltje swijg weer houwt V keel,
De wreetheyt slaapt met haar wien is mijn waarste Deel,
Laat s' in Rust haar Lust versaden
Slaap Oogjes slaap minlijk gesigt:
Voor wien de Son in 't stralen swigt.

Treed' soetjes ag! mijn Lammen wilt niet bletten
Steur niet de Nimph die doet quijnen mijn Hert
Ah! dat se tog niet wakker wert,
'K sal haar selfs niets beletten:
Schoon sy m'ontrust, O neen! en dat Iupijn
My schonk voor haar sijn Troon't souw dog al ijdel sijn,
Niets kan mijn Liefde versetten,

Slaap

My Fate declares, "You must live without him"
So I ask you to frequent that goddess, to offer her
Some solace. Diana at least may be happy though the hope
You gave me has grown very grave, and heavy over time.

♦ ♦ ♦

To the sleeping Elise

Air: "*Nymphes des eaux*"*

Shush all rustling. Wind, do not touch a leaf.
Little stream, suspend your current's murmur.
Elise in a dream bathes in fine felicity.
Stop, Philomela, your gorgeous warble.
Her cruelty sleeps in her who is my truest part.
Let her in repose satisfy desire.
Sleep bright eyes, sleep all you charming features.
Sun beaming down, orchestrate the silence.
Lightly step. My lambs, refrain from bleating.
I would myself prevent her from awaking.
The throne of Jove is worth less than this moment.

* "*Nymphes des eaux*" is a melody that may derive from Quinault and Lully's opera *Atys*. The hero of that tragic opera loves someone other than the goddess Cybele: the deity exacts her revenge.

[143]

Slaap Oogjes slap minlijk gesigt;
Voor wien de Son in 't straalen swigt.

✦ ✦ ✦

Voor L.E.C.

Toon, Un Berger charmant.

AH! waar vind ik troost
Nu mijn smert op 't groost,
Haar in het Hikken verpoost
Wijl 't hert veel bange sugtjes loost:
Waar door 't sig staag in vlammen roost,
Of sal dees grove Rots
Daar Menig scheeve Schots
Sig toont ter sijden
My in mijne Druk verblijden?
Neen O neen, dees Eensaamheyt
Selfs in een diepe rou bedolven leyt.
Want geen Tijger-dier
Nog geen Leeuw Brult hier
Of men hoort gans geen getier
Van Wolfgehuyl, of Slang geswier,
Nog nimmermeer de greetse gier
Die haar in 't nare wout
In mos Spelonken hout
En ijslijk Schaatert
Dat het door de Booschen klatert
Waar geen wint swalk ruijst ontrent
Nog son een flikker van sijn stralen sent.

Daar

Nothing can replace the slumber of my lover.
Sleep bright eyes, sleep all you charming features.
For you the sun orchestrates this silence.

◆ ◆ ◆

For L.E.C.

Air: *"Un berger charmant"* *

Where find solace now my pain is at its worst?
I sob and when I cease to sob I sigh.
My heart feels scorched by the flame it feeds.
Shall I complain to this enormous, craggy rock?
Its loneliness, too, looks overwhelmed in sadness.
No tiger, and no lion howls: no wolves
Rove, or serpents twist their spires menacing.
The avid vulture of cavernous heights
Neither croaks nor hisses. Wind is still.
The rays the sun sends down fall, tranquil.

\* Brongersma's frequent source for melodies, Jean-Baptiste Lully (1632–1687), composed *"Un berger charmant"* ("A beguiling shepherd").

[144]

Daar sal ik de Rust
Soeken, wijl't me lust
Hier door te werden gesust
Nu al mijn vreugt is uyt geblust
'T geen ik de Bergen maak bewust,
En ook dit graasig Dal,
Dat mijne Ween-plaats sal
Voor altijt weesen,
Wijl ik miss mijn Uytgeleesen
Om wien ik in Rouw verdwijn
En in dees woesteny alleen verschijn.

♦ ♦ ♦

Toon: Tranquille Caesar.

Dido spreekt.

Trouwlooste die op aarden leeft
O! Lafhert, durft ge noch verschijnen?
Sult gy die soo veel wonden geeft
Aan uwe ziel, niet gans verdwijnen?
Gaa Verrader ik sterf, schoon de doodt voor me vliet,
En eynd' dus mijn verdriet.

V Dido sal voor V gesicht
Meyneed'ge ijslijk koomen spooken,
Schuw schuw vry't klaare Hemels licht,
Geen Wierook sal ooyt voor V rooken
Maar Kartaag, O Tiran; en Barbaarse Troyaan,
Sal om V daadt vergaan.

                                        Vrees

I am calm, the requisites are met.
Let me tell the hills, all my fruit is ripened.
I descend, too, to the grassy valley.
I repeat, I want the one I chose. That's why
I wander in the wasteland here, alone.

◆ ◆ ◆

On the death of Dido, otherwise known as Elissa*

Air: *"Tranquille César"*

Desolating man, worst on earth,
Coward: Ought you still to languish in this life?
Wound after wound you deal to your own heart.
Ought not you to vanish of your own inflictions?
Go, traitor. I die. Already Death stands before me,
And proposes the term to my unhappiness.
Perjured Dido will give up the ghost, right before
Your eyes. Free air, light of dearest heaven!
No consecrated sacrifice smokes for you
But Carthage; tyrant, barbaric man of Troy,

* Jilted by Aeneas, Dido queen of Carthage killed herself. Her alternate name was Elissa. Brongersma may thus as a testament of love draw Vergil's heroine into the radiant allusive halo proceeding from the idea of her friend Elisabeth Joly (often "Elise"). What kind of "vengeance" can Dido have? She snubs Aeneas when he visits the underworld. But she also ensures the hatred of Carthage for Rome – a prophecy fulfilled in the three Punic wars that ended when Carthage was sown with salt by Scipio Aemilianus. In order to become a civic hero, Aeneas cauterizes his heart; through Mercury, Jupiter enforces this renunciation.

[145]

Vreest gy niet dat een nickerdrom,
V sal van lit, tot lit vernielen
De hel gaapt reets, en went sich om
Met al de ofgepijnde zielen,
Om te sien naar u vlucht, toef ontdankb're keer weer,
Of denkt ge aan my niet meer.

Soo denk dan aan V Trouw, en Eet,
Bedrieger (schaam u noch te liegen)
Die gy me duysent werven deedt,
Eer g'u Elisae kost bedriegen,
Doch 't Gewis is versengt, dat gebaart heeft mijn doodt
Die u ter Vierschaar noodt.

Daar gy O Roover! van mijn Eer,
Voer 't grootste Groot u sult beklagen,
V Trotsheyt quetst mijn hert geen weer,
Mijn sterven sal u eeuwig knagen,
En geloof waar gy zijt, dat de smaat, en mijn pijn
Noch sal gewrooken zijn.

❖❖❖

De Klaagende Melinde.

Toon: Tranquille Coeur.

DEes Populier, wiens wortel heeft
Wel duysent tranen in gesogen,
Sal: schoon se Amberdroopjes geeft,
Met mijn getruur noch zijn bewogen,
Want de gront, hoe verdort, sal door 't droevig geschrey,

                                            Bevoch-

Will be obliterated by your unkindness.
Don't you dread one suffering after another?
Hell gapes, and devils swarm, and souls are writhing:
Turn back to me, ungrateful. Tarry. Think of me.
Recall your vow, deceiver. You assisted me
Before you cheated Elissa of all her sweets.
My conscience burns, it brings my death.
And my death arraigns you for your grand injustice.
Pirate, robber of honour, in time to come
You will grieve worse than you can imagine.
My fate will gnaw at you forever. Trust
Whatever you do, I will have – just wait –
   my vengeance.

◆ ◆ ◆

Melinde's expostulation*

Air: *"Tranquilles coeurs"*

This poplar's root has drunk up many tears
And Phaethon's sisters – the same kind of tree –
Have wept out as many drops of amber.
Yet I will stir this poplar with my sorrow,
And the ground so parched now will be watered

---

* Elis is a territory west of Arcadia, in the Peloponnesus; the river Alpheus flows through it. It has an acoustical affinity with "Elise" and "Elisabeth." In an earlier poem, Alpheus the river god chases Arethusa without success. *Metamorphoses* 2.340–66 relates how Phaethon's sisters, viewing the wreck of the Sun's chariot and their brother's body, wept amber when they were transformed into poplar trees. *"Tranquilles coeurs"* ("Calm hearts") derives from Lully's *Le triomphe de l'amour* of 1681.

[146]

Bevochtigen haar Wey.

Geen Beekje, dat haar stroomtje schiet
Of 't sal van Tirsis min getuygen,
En van Melindaas ziels verdriet,
Die al haar leet komt in te zuygen,
Ah! het weer, hoe het Lot: door een wrev'lig besluyt
Sijn leven blusten uyt,

Wijl ik mijn klacht vaak heb gedaan
Aan haar, hoewel vergeefs gestreden,
En riep de mogentheden aan
Van 't bossig wout door mijn gebeden,
Maar helaas! 't is al doof, niemant hoort mijn geween
Hoe bitter dat ik steen.

'k Sal dan U doot, mijn Herder, die
(Sijn schaapjes by my placht te hoeden,
Hoe ver ik van my selver vlie)
Bejam'ren, en met suchtjes voeden,
't Quijnend' hert 't geen verlangt om in 't Elische velt
By u te zijn gestelt.

Waar ik u sal (schoon my de Nijt
Belet heeft om met u te paren)
Omhelsen, spijt dan die het spijt,
En u in mijn gedagt bewaren,
Ah! wat noot, heeft dan 't Aartsche gewelt ons ontvoegt.
Daar blijven wy vernoegt.

◆ ◆ ◆

Voor

With the steady rain of my afflicted outcry.
The stream of sadness is no little torrent.
It witnesses my love for Thyrsis, and my distress
At Fate's ignorance of the surly harm it does.
Forest powers I have called on you, as on him.
Deafness only requites my bitter weeping.
I would die, but you left your sheep in my charge:
A duty keeping me alive and sighing
Here in the fields of Elis longing to lie
Beside you. Although Envy holds me
Back let Spite itself be spited. I preserve
You, and hug you in my thoughts. Power
Cannot sunder us: on earth we remain
Contented, Necessity impotent against us.

◆ ◆ ◆

[147]

Voor Mejuffer A.D.B.

Toon: Air.

U Schoonheyt schoone Dorilee
Doet kille klippen blaken
Gy sengt de Alpen die alree
Versmelten, en doet haken
De noortschen Ysvorst naar u min
Daar Aquilon de stranden
Beherst, en geeft sig willig in
't Gewelt van uwe banden.

Soo Phaebus u maar eenmal sag
Hy souw sijn Dafne laten,
En Acis in de holen lag
By Galathee, haar haten,
Soo Polipheem u wierd' gewaar
Hy souw de Rotsen kloven,
En u op sijnen offer snaar
Met velt gesangen loven.
Selfs Psiche wijkt voor u, in kragt,
Gy doet de Liefd' verlieven,
Gy hebt de flitsboog in U magt
Om ider te doorgrieven,

Ja

For my Lady A[ngenis] D[e] B[asco]*

Air: "Air"

Your beauty, beautiful Dorilée,
Warms chill cliffs, melts
The caps of the Alps, seduces
The north's icy ruler
Aquilo who may have
Seized our coasts but
Yields in your homage
To your bondage. Phoebus
Beholding you
Would disdain Daphne, Acis
Desert Galatea, Polyphemus
Cleave rocks for an altar
At which to make
The sacrifice of an inept
Hymn. Psyche herself
Capitulates to you, every
Beloved is less loveable
Than you as you wield
The bow, fire the arrow
And no heart evades it

* Angenis de Basco is the beneficiary of two previous poems, both of which celebrate this woman's charm and musical ability.

[148]

Jaa Dorilee al wat sig roert
Moet in u boeyens quijnen,
Gy hebt mijn zieltje mee vervoert
Wijl'k gaa om u verdwijnen.

♦ ♦ ♦

A.G.K.

Toon, Schoon Catrijn.

'T Lomrig Wout bekranst het streekje
Daar de kuische Jagt Godin:
Dikwijls aan u soomrijs Beekje
Rusten en daar baden in
Daars' Endimion verwagten,
Wijl's het voor een Latmus nam,
En in 't strelen der gedagten
Haar daar vaak vermeyden quam,
Want Actëon schuwt dees weyen,
En geen Appulus verbaast
Daar nooyt bloode Nimfe reyen,
Nog geen Glaucus woedend' raast
Om het bloos van Scylaas kaken,
Schoon een Circe dat benijt
Nog geen Leet met wraak siet wraaken;
'T is daar in de Gulden tijt,

Want Pomoon schenkt Boomgewassen,

Flora

And, because everything endowed with motion
Must languish, enchanted, in your chains,
My soul, too, a prisoner of yours,
Will, like this poem itself,
The charming topic
Departed, disappear.

◆ ◆ ◆

To A.G.K.*

Air: *"Schoon Katrijn"*

Shady forest crowns the tract
Where often by your foamy stream
The hunt's chaste goddess rests
Or swims, where Endymion
Kept his watch mistaking the place
For Latmos, and contrived cover
To shun the Dawn's caresses.
Actaeon never visits: Apuleius
Never visited, to wonder: nymphs
Do not go naked, and no Glaucus
Raves about the blush in Scylla's
Cheek, though Circe envies it:
No passion need avenge itself.
Here it is still the Golden Age.
Pomona hands out bouquets,

* "Ephydridae" are technically shore-flies, but here Brongersma intends them to be nymph-like entities that live from and on the water. Circe jealously transformed Scylla into a six-headed monster incorporating whining dogs. Glaucus by eating transformative herbs eventually graduated to the form and status of a minor sea-*numen*. "Limnae" are ponds; Brongersma seems to name Diana, in her aspect as Lady of the Pools, by the honourific "Limnaea." The goddess oversaw the fertility and harvest of aquatic populations.

Flora ciert het velt Tapeet,
Limnea de water plassen:
Faunus d'ackers over kleet,
Selfs siet men d'Ephydriaden
Bortelen uyt haare Bron
Om haar in u te versaden
Wijl men nooyt veel schoonder von.

♦♦♦

Op de Heerlijkheyt van de THEE,

Toon, Entré d' isis.

SWijg schempers van de Thee,
Laat die Goden-Plant in vree,
Want gy sijt te ver gemist,
Ah! dat gy haar Deugden wist',
Seeker gy souwt beswijken in die twist,
Want haare kragt bestaat
Tot in den thienden graat:
Het suyvert bloedt, en 't dringt quaa dampen voort
En met een
Ongemeen
Voor de winden, daar men veel van klagen hoort.

Ook maakt het Long, en Maag
Driftig, en tot Spijsen graag:
'Tis voor duysendt qualen goedt
Voor die geen, die 't maat'lijk doet
Want selfs wijn is fenijn in overvloedt,
Ook vaagt het van 't gesigt

*Verd*

Flora weaves the meadow
Tapestry, Limnaea curates
Her pools, the hooves of Faunus
Clatter on the stony paths,
Ephydridae, even,
Burst from the springs
To satiate themselves in you
Than whom nothing lovelier can be found.

❖ ❖ ❖

On the excellence of tea*

Air: *"Entrée d'Isis"*

Silence, you who insult tea.
Leave the divine plant in peace.
You must not know its virtues,
Or you would stop the dispute.
It deserves praise's tenth degree.
It cleanses blood and drives vague
Fatigue away, and bloating too.
It quickens lungs and appetite, and
Palliates or cures a thousand disorders.
Even wine, a rival, in over-plus
Poisons, and muddies the complexion.

---

* "Fronteyn" is presumably an error for the last name of Nicolaes Fonteyn (1601–ca 1655); a druggist, he lived in Amsterdam, compiled an *Institutiones pharmaceuticae* (1633), and wrote plays including *Esther, or the Picture of Obedience* and *Casta, or the Mirror of Chastity*. Brongersma mentions theriac, an antidote to poison (*Triaac*). Edmund Waller (died 1687) wrote in English a birthday poem for Catherine of Braganza in praise of tea. As Charles II's queen, she popularized the custom of drinking this beverage.

[150]

Verduyst'ring, en 't verligt
De hersens, en het maakt een vrolijk hert,
Pijn in 't hooft
Wert gedooft
Door haar kragten, als 't op tijt geoevent wert.

De kost'le Orvitaan
Coomt niet by die Lof spruyt aan
Schoon Fronteyn die dapper roemt
En 't met schijn vernis verbloemt,
Wijl hy 't selfs 't puyk der arzenyen noemt
Weg weg Veneets' Triaac
By U is geen vermaak,
Maar Thee, dien Thee dat schoon, en Heylig kruyt
Is voor mijn
Medecijn
En ik suig daar Lekk're honigraten uyt

Dank heb, den Indiaan
En die geen, die dese blaan
(Schoon van duysenden gelaakt)
Heeft by ons bekent gemaakt,
Naar wiens geur menig braven kenner haakt
Schenk dan haar dierbaar nat
In 't Parsaleyne vat
En drink ter eer van dien gesonden Thee,
Vry en soop
Van een stoop,
Maar deel spotters, nooyt van dese Nectar mee.

♦♦♦

A.M.

Tea sharpens wit, cheers a merry
Heart, and drunk at the right time
Ends the headache. I am
Not the first to sing its powers.
Courageous Fonteyn preceded
Me in panegyric – that druggist-
Dramatist who pictured Esther
And Casta too. Away with
Venetian proxies, pleasureless.
Tea the lovely and the holy herb
Is antidotal as the honeycomb.
Thank the Indies and their people,
Thank the thousands who tried tea
Early, teaching us the use.
The odour alone delights the connoisseur.
Steep the worthy liquor in your pot
And toast tea, preserver of good health:
But pour none for the contrarians.

♦ ♦ ♦

[151]

A.M. C.H. E.L. op't laaste afscheyt,

Toon, Schoon Catrijn.

AH! Droog af uw natte wangen
Schijn bedroefde Eliseen,
Neen neen laat die perlen hangen
'T is het pronk van U geween,
'T sijn gesmolten Couralijnen
Die gy plengt op 't Lely blank
Op getrocken uyt de mijnen
Van uw zieltogt, tegen dank.

Dwing uw sugtjes dat se swijgen
Stuyr haar weder naar beneen,
Laat uw boesem door het hijgen
Niet versticken Eliseen
Ag! het is genoeg: mijn tranen
Uyt te storten, en een Beek
Door die pekeldrift te banen
Om uw, in dees jammer streek.
'Tis onnut om my te truyren
'K ben niet een gedagtjen waart
Schoon mijn Liefde, sal verduyren
'T sterkste steunsel van de aard

Jaa

To Elise, on our latest farewell*

Air: "*Schoon Katrijn*"

Dry your wet cheeks, afflicted Elise –
No. Let those pearls hang
Decorous, and decorating your sadness:
Your lily-pale skin runs with liquid
Crystal, raised from the depth
Of your sad soul: I thank you.
Suppress your sighs, let them not
Smother your gasping breast.
My tears jump out and course
In briny ardour making tracks
Testifying to sorrow.
No comfort, no consideration
Avail but my adoration
Will endure: the strongest
Prop on earth. Let the sun

---

* This poem offers the strongest evidence of a decisive break between Brongersma and Elisabeth Joly. Van Gemert may have had it in mind when she hypothesized an end to the *amitié* between these women. Joly continues to recur as an addressee even after this apparent sundering of the friends. *The Swan of the Well* insists on the perpetuation of kindness and affection, ending not with estrangement but birthday wishes.

[152]

Jaa de Son sal eer verduyst'ren,
En de Maan haar Horenligt
Door een onder gank ontluyst'ren
Eer ik voor de Trouste swigt.

Weest versekert 'k sal nooyt scheyden
Wijl ge segt, vergeet my niet,
Woorden die de Geest verleyden
En versagten veel verdriet,
'K laat me van geen vleyers strelen
'K ben gelijk een Rots van steen,
Nog van Orfeus min bequelen
'K blijf voor U geheel alleen.

♦♦♦

Voor J.A.J.D.L.

Toon, Had ik een Koninks Kroon op't Hooft.

Waarom (: O kuysche Nagt Godin
Die met U hooren ligt
Het boss bestraalt) haat gy de Min?
Die U dreygt met sijn schigt,
Neen neen gy raakter soo niet deur
U luyster is te groot
Die meenig brengt in swaar getreur
En met' er schigten dood.

Heeft

Darken and the moon's bright
Horns darken with it I will
Not keep quiet all my faith.
I really will not say goodbye
For you have said: "Never forget."
Let all lovers who have desponded
See that I am steadfast as a rock.
Let them drivel about old Orpheus.
You alone are why I will exist.

◆ ◆ ◆

For Miss A.J. D.L.*

Air: "Had I a kingly crown upon my head"

Why chaste goddess of the night
Lighting the woods with lucent horns
Do you despise all love?
He who threatens you with his shaft

* Diana saw Endymion naked as he slept on Latmos; although he already had a wife and children, she visited him nightly to enjoy his oneiric embraces. Diana's brother Apollo, in Brongersma's version of the myth, kills Endymion out of fraternal misgiving. Renaissance interpreters saw in the figure of Endymion the contrary urges of mortals and gods. Human beings wish for union with the contemplative divine; whereas deities crave frank erotic release. Brongersma may modify the story in which, invited to Olympus, Endymion fell for Juno – an infatuation that Jupiter punished by sending the errant visitor to the underworld with a lightning bolt. The melody "*Had ik een konings kroon op't hoofd*" ("Had I a kingly crown upon my head") is still current with Dutch singers; a songbook of 1745 called *Apollo's nieuwe-jaers-gift: Aen het bekoorlyke Hollandsche jufferschapp* (*Apollo's New Year's Gift to the Amiable Women of Holland*) includes it. Brongersma shows marked fondness for the pose of the supplicating lover.

[153]

Heeft Febus niet door raserny
U Lief, Endimion!
Door flitst, uyt woede Jalozy
Aan dese water Bron,
Welk Jammer Delos is bewust
Die sijne Tomb' bewaard
Waar in d'gewyde lijkass rust
'T geen U nog pijnen baard,

Siet Zephijrus: hoe die bemint
Sijn Flora, siet om hoog
Hoe Jovis sig bewogen vind
Door Junoos minlijk Oog,
En Ariadne, Bachus liefd'
Ah! hebt doch medely
Met een die gy het Hert door grieft
En hout in slaverny.

Verlaat O! siere heerscherin
U al te strenge wet,
Voer soeter ordeningen in
Als gy m'hebt voor geset,
Werp pijl, en koker van u af,
En gun my weder min,
Of anders daal ik in het graf,
Om u mijn Afgodin.

❖❖❖

Aan

Cannot prick you. You glitter
Too proudly for him who brings
Those less haughty into heavy mourning,
Slaying them with his arrow.
Didn't maddened Phoebus crazed with
Jealousy strike Endymion with a flash
Beside this spring? The affair is known
On Delos. There his tomb is guarded,
There his blessed body pains you, still.
See how Zephyr loves his Flora,
See how Juno's darling eye arouses
Jove, and Ariadne charms her Bacchus.
Have pity on a heart gripped hard
Persisting in its servitude. Permit
Shepherdess, your law to be relaxed.
Lift the sanction you impose on me.
Throw your quiver away and grant
Your favour or I, your idolater,
Will sink down into the grave.

♦ ♦ ♦

[154]

Aan de kusche Jaght-Godin DIANA Die met haar Nimphjes op de Drijlsche hertejagt gaat.

Toon: Sombre Forest.

Gy dreygt dan noch Diaan het Drijlsche wout,
En trekt met koker, boog, en pijlen
Ten strijde, waar sig meenig hert verhouwt
Die gy langst' effen spoor op 't schigtigst' naa komt ijlen
 Om daar het vlugtig Wild helaas! te zien geknelt,
 Schoon 't poogt u magt t'ontspringen,
 Maar vergeefs al 't groot geweld,
 Gy koomt de flitsen dringen
 In de boesems, die ge veld.

Is't niet genoeg dat gy Endimion
Getekend hebt, O! strenge wreede,
Is 't niet genoeg dat om u quijnd de Sonn,
Of zijt gy noch niet met die schooner vangst te vreden
 Verniel dan wat ge koont, koom koom door schiet dit hert
 Dat voor u leyd gebogen,
 En u opgeofferd werd,
Doorboor het met u oogen,
Ach! Verlos het van sijn smerd.

Soo sal ik dan Diaan voor u gesicht
Mijn leven storten, en u vragen

Hoe

To the chaste Diana goddess of the hunt who with
her nymphs roves after the deer near IJlst*

Air: *"Sombres Foretz"*

Now you menace the woods near IJlst, Diana,
And scout with your quiver, your bow and darts
Campaigning where the deer conceal their bowers
Along whose faint paths you hurry,
Harrying skittish beasts, hoping for ambush.

You make a forceful evasive leap
But the great attempt fails for
A bolt pierces you in the breast, and fells you.

Not enough that you fettered Endymion with sleep,
Not enough that the sun languishes for you,
Does not even that blazing conquest quiet you?
Ruin then whatever you want, come shoot
The acquiescent hart that bows before you
And release it from its pain.

I shall throw down my life and ask you, whose charm
Has lofted me often to heaven, why
You, chaste night-goddess, deserving lover, lack
Mercy. Please at least prepare me cypress now.

---

* Brongersma collates Diana the huntress with Cynthia the moon, a legitimate synthesis even if Diana forfeits her legendary celibacy in the process. IJlst ("Drylts" in West Frisian) is a town a few kilometres from Sneek.

[155]

Hoe gy (die my door u bekoorlijk licht,
Op wieken menichmaal ten Hemel heby gedragen)
    Soo ongenadich zijt, O! kuyse nacht Godes,
    Ik gaa gewillig sterven,
    Koom berey mijn Lijk Cypres,
    Nu ik de Liefd' moet derven,
    Van mijn waarde Minnares.

♦♦♦

Apollo spreekt

Toon: Marchere Liberte.

MYn Dafne doot, O! neen ik voel het hert nog slaan,
De schors beweegt sig in 't verroeren van 'et lippen,
Wat is 't dat ge uyt u mont laat glippen?
Mjin Dafne doot, O neen! ik voel het hert nog slaan,
Ze knikt, en siet me droevig aan,
Wie heeft u dus mijn Lief mishandelt voor mijn oogen,
Wat schenner heeft u leên en schoonheyt soo verplet,
De Lauw'ren zijn verbleekt, en van u kruyn getoogen
Die ik u had in 't Dal van Tempe op geset,
Mijn Dafne doot, O neen! ik voel het hert nog slaan
Ze knikt, en siet me droevich aan.

Ik sal schoon gy mijn min O Dafne hebt versmaat
U blad'ren dragen en doen nieuw ranken schieten

                                                    Wat

♦ ♦ ♦

Apollo speaks*

Air: "*Ma chère liberté*"

Daphne dead? No, I feel her heart still beats,
The agitation of her mouth still stirs the bark.
What are you murmuring with your lips?
Daphne dead? No, I feel her heart still beats.
She nods, she looks at me full of sorrow.
How could you abuse my love right before
My eyes – how violate the beauty you fostered,
Cropping away what I planted in Tempe?
Daphne dead? No, I feel her heart still beats.
She nods, she looks at me full of sorrow.
Daphne, you may have scorned my love, but
I will prune your leaves to let new branches grow.

* As elsewhere, the occasion of this poem appears to be damage sustained by a laurel tree in a storm. In the wake of this event, ignorant or enthusiastic arborists may have trimmed the tree excessively. Brongersma's Apollo regrets the overreaction, but predicts the laurel's regeneration. The poet is fascinated by the psychology of Apollo in relation to Daphne, and of Daphne in relation to Apollo. Laurel is the token of literary excellence. Yet for a female writer, especially, the origins of this traditional honour must remain fraught. In the first book of Ovid's *Metamorphoses*, Cupid imposes lust on Apollo; afflicted Apollo chases reluctant Daphne. She escapes him, transformed by her father, Peneus, into the shape of a laurel tree, but Apollo – with her consent – makes a perpetual trophy of her foliage (452–567).

[156]

Wat hebt gy m'al smerten doen genieten,
Ik sal schoon gy mijn min O Dafne hebt versmaat
U Lieven, daar gy my noch haat,
En wil het monster dat u kuysheyt dorst genaken
Vermors'len, en door flitzen met mijn schigt
'k Heb u vereeuwigt wijl mijn min noch is aan't blaken
Wast, groent, en bloeyt tot spijt voortaan in elx gesicht,
Ik sal schoon gy mijn min O Dafne hebt versmaat
U Lieven, daar ge my nog haat.

♦ ♦ ♦

T'Samen-Spraak,

Toon, La Princes.

Boerin.
Goen dey goen dey Laen Vrouw,
Hier bring ik yo hette aeyen
In twae hinnin uyte kouw,
'K hab se trije wijk in mest
Dir om togt mi wier it best
Dat ik brogt dit tiouke paer
Yise op mey ouws Lae en heer.

Land-Vrouw.
Trijntie wat is dit geseyt
Siet ik danck u gaat wat sitten
Wel hoe vaart u Man en Meyt,
Sijn u Kinders nog gesont
Wijf vien is dit mee u Hont

Mey-

You can recover from every pain I know it.
Daphne, you may have scorned my love, but
I will always love the one who hates me always
And I will cut to pieces any monster daring
To infringe your chasteness piercing him with
The lightning of my arrows. The blaze of my love
Is your immortality, from this time forward.
I will always love the one who hates me always.

♦ ♦ ♦

The Conversation\*

Air: "*La Princesse*"

The countrywoman:
Hey Lady! Good day! Good day to you!
Right here I have three eggs and a pair
Of chickens fattened three weeks
In the coop. Thought you ought
To have these plump birds,
You and your lord.

The lady:
Little Tryn, I'm sorry it's tough
Sometimes to get exactly
What you're saying.
But thanks – and take a seat.
How are you two doing, your man
And you? Your kids, they're
Healthy? Is that your dog,

\* The leaky churn may furnish a homely emblem of the linguistic difficulties which Brongersma's personnel experience. The farmwife speaks Frisian, whereas the lady speaks something closer to standard Dutch. "*La Princesse*" is probably "*La Princesse de l'Elide*," from Lully's 1664 *Les plaisirs de l'île enchantée* (*The Delights of the Enchanted Isle*). The tension between comic dialogue and sophisticated music anticipates the method of the Swedish poet and musician Carl Michael Bellman (1740–95), author of *Fredmans Epistlar*.

[157]

Meyden geeft hem dan wat Broodt,
En ik u ter Maaltijt noodt.

Boerin.
Vraeeg I Laeen Vrou ney mijn kij
Di beginne al to antien
In mijn man mey nogs wol brij
Maer mijn faam het pijn ijn't lief
Al har Laeen bin laem in stief
Yster soel si oof it hae
Dat ik togt ye bliuwter daee.

Land-Vrouw.
Neen ik vraag hoe dat het gaat
Met u Kinders Trijntie Iansen,
En u Huys gesontheyt staat,
Gy verstaat mijn taal niet regt,
Sijn dees eyers vers gelegt?
Seeker alsmer wel op let
Sijn dees Hoenders wonder Vet.

Boerin.
Ia ye habbe spijn sort spoon
In de aeyen swiet as moolke
Meytse Io de termin roon
Mae mijn hoes soeyt as ijen souw,
Deromis is it so Laeen vrouw
Dat ik yo nin meer bitins,
In nin tzies of boutir schins.

♦ ♦ ♦

Op

Dear? Girls, feed him some bread.
You, too: share some food with me.

The countrywoman:
Lady, asking after my cows?
They're about to calve. My man
Still has a huge appetite
For porridge, thank you. My maid,
Poor thing – she aches in every limb,
She toppled off a haystack
Yesterday, and almost
Died, right there and then.

The lady:
No, dear Tryn Jansen, I asked
About your kids, how
Their health is doing.
You don't follow everything
I'm saying. The eggs, they're new-laid?
The more I look at these hens
The plumper they appear.

The countrywoman:
Their fat will fleck your soup spoon!
And these eggs as sweet as milk
Will make your belly round.
But Lady, my churn is leaking
Like a sieve, so I can't give you
Any cheese, or butter.

◆ ◆ ◆

[158]

Op't gesicht van de Afbeeldinge van Eliseen, Cleonte aan Eliseen.

Toon: Air.

ALs ik mijn blacken opwaart slaa
Om u gestalt' te meten,
Soo dunkt my dat ik verder gaa,
En al u doen kan weten,
Want Eliseen ik sie u hals,
'k Sie ogg, en lipjes roeren
Soo 't schijnt, en 't hooft beveedert als
Een Mars: die krijch wil voeren.

Neen, neen gy zijt als een Diaan,
Wanneer se moe van 't jagen
Wil naar 't gebergt van Latmus gaan
Om daar naar haar behagen
Endimion te soeken, waar
Haar hert leyt in geklonken,
Of al seen Amasoon die haar
Ten strijde op doet pronken.
Soo schoon zijt gy haa! Eliseen
In mijn verliefde oogen,
Ik wissel voor u geen Heleen

Hoe

On a picture of Elisa: Cléonte to Elise*

Air: "Air"

When I turned my gaze upward to assess
Your form I thought I will go further
And assess everything about you, since, Elise,
I see your throat, your eye, and virtually
Touch your lips, and caress the head
Plumed like Mars relishing dear war.

No you really look more like Diana
When she would like to run hunting
On the mountain heights of Latmos
Seeking pretty Endymion, too,
To gratify her heart: or you resemble
An Amazon buckled up for battle.

Elise your beauty in my besotted eyes O
I would prefer you to Helen no matter

* In this poem, Brongersma performs an *ekphrasis* (she describes a picture) as well as a *blazon* – an enumeration of the beloved's beauties. Comparing Elise to Mars, Diana, and an Amazon, the poet rehearses roles into which she has already cast her friend, in previous verses. Sir Walter Ralegh marshals almost identical personnel to praise Elizabeth I, in a letter to Robert Cecil of July 1592: "I ... was wont to behold her riding like Alexander, hunting like Diana, walking like Venus, the gentle wind blowing in her fair hair about her pale cheeks, like a nymph; sometime sitting in the shade like a Goddess; sometime singing like an angel; sometime playing like Orpheus" (see Ralegh's *Selected Writings*, edited by Gerald Hammond [Manchester: Carcanet, 1984], 273).

[159]

Hoe krachtich van vermoogen,
Neen, neen gy zijt mijn herten lust,
De schuym Godes moet wijken,
U schets stelt het gedacht in rust,
Gy sult de prijs-kroon strijcken.

♦ ♦ ♦

De verlatene en stervende Acis.

Toon: Entré d'Isis.

O blanke Galathee
Wispeltuyr'ger dan de zee,
Koom beween mijn ongeval,
Sie waar Acis landen sal,
't Is genoech, nu dat ik werd' overall
Om uwe min belacht,
En van U selfs veracht,
Schoon gy wel eer mijn smerten hebt gesust.
  En in pijn,
   Waart te zijn
   Dat mijnn lust
Door u lipjes wierde menichmaal geblust.
Heugt U noch wel den dach
Dat ik in u ermen lach,
En die droeve morgen stont,
Doen ons Polifemus vont
In het hol, neer gekropen op de grondt

            Ach

Her glamour, the goddess conceived
Of ocean froth must acquiesce to you.
A simple sketch of you excites me
To the praise that, once I yield it, calms me.

◆ ◆ ◆

The forlorn and dying Acis*

Air: *"Entrée d'Isis"*

O gleaming Galatea more changeable
Than the sea! Come pity me, witness
I am everywhere mocked for my love
For you though you still will have
Compensated me if in the midst
Of my agony I remaining conscious
Of my desire's consummation
You press your lips to mine.
The day I laughed in your embrace! The dismal
Morning hour Polyphemus discovered us
In the grotto wound in each other's arms
On the ground! Acis (you said) Galatea will

* Uncouth Polyphemus, destined to be blinded by Odysseus, killed with a great stone his rival in love, Acis. Both the monster and the man loved Galatea. Accounts vary. Ovid reports that Acis, after his mortal death, became a river god mighty in stature, outstanding in beauty. The story of Acis appears in "The shepherd's complaint," earlier in this volume, when the distressed speaker prevaricates, alternately comparing himself to the monstrous Cyclops and the crushed lover.

[160]

      Ah! Acis seyde gy
      Staa Galathea by
Ik sterf, soo ik U noch eens missen moet,
      En met een
      Door gebeen,
      Wierd' begroet,
Wijl u oog uyt schoot, een soute trane vloet.

Is nu dien Polifeem
Voor u sulk een honichzeem
Die te vooren waar als Roet
En geschopt weird' met de voet,
Denk dan nu Galathea war ge doet,
      Schoon Acis wert verplet,
      En tot een roof geset,
Ik sweer dien Reus, dien Cyclops, dat ik hem
      Om die smaat
      Eeuwich haat,
      (Voor wiens stem
Yder schrikt) wel hast sal krijgen in de klem.

♦ ♦ ♦

A la chaste Diane, Mad. J. E. J. qui fait la chasse a drijlst avec ses Nimphes.

Voix, Vous Rochers De sert sauvage.

CHaste & froide Nimph Diane
Qui ne veu qu'on fait l'amour:

                                          Ny

Stand by you: and I said, I am
Dying, soon I have to leave
You, I am crushed and buried while
Your eyes stream and your sweet tears flow.

Now Polyphemus is your honey yet just
Yesterday you thought the monster trash, so
Clumsily made that feet rather than hands
Might have shaped his ugly body.
I may lie abandoned like something stolen then
Discarded, worthless, yet I swear
In that Cyclops's hearing because
Of the pain he has inflicted my hatred
Can never die, at least, and he too will
Suffer as one caught between great pincers.

◆ ◆ ◆

To the chaste Diana, Miss Elisabeth Joly who,
with her nymphs, goes hunting near IJlst in pursuit
of the deer*

Air: *"Vous rochers, désert sauvage"*

Cold and continent nymph, Diana,
Lady who spurns all flirtation,

---

* Brongersma wrote this poem in French. She promotes Diana from "nymph" to "goddess," an unorthodox procedure. IJlst ("Drylts" in West Frisian) is a town a few kilometres from Sneek.

[161]

Ny une chose un peu profane,
Mais qui aimera son tour.
Chaste & froide Nimph Diane
Qui ne veu qu'on fait l'amour.

Este vous a Drijlst deësse
Chez vos Nimphes dans ce bois?
Pour blesser les coeurs sans cesse
Par vos fleches, & quarquoy,
Este vous a Drijlst Deësse
Ches vos Nimphes dans ce bois.

Non, vous faille' a cette chose
C'est a Latmos j'avois peur,
Ou Endimion se repose
Qui possede votre Coeur,
Non vous faille a cette chose
C'est a Latmos j'avois peur.

Vos beaux jeux, & tous vos charmes
Son les fleches, & quarquoy,
On avec vous vous en arme
Mais helas! trop loin de moy,
Vos beaux jeux, & tous vos charmes
Son les fleches & quarquoy.

Brillé donc par l'air, & l'ondes

Vous

Never indulging the least indecorum,
Loving the circuit you make of the woods,
Cold and continent nymph Diana –

Are you the goddess of IJlst among your nymphs
In this plantation, piercing hearts
Without pause, your arrows flying
Out of your quiver, are you the goddess
Of IJlst among your nymphs in this forest?

Your inestimable eyes and all your charms
Are the arrows and the well-stocked quiver
Slung rattling round your sleek shoulder.
Too far from me you range in the forest
With inestimable eyes, with all your charms,
Your unerring arrows, your full quiver.

Shine therefore through the air, shine on the water!

[162]

Vous me trouverez ailleurs
Car ie suis encore au monde
Ou je verse pour vous mes pleurs,
Brillé donc par l'air & l'ondes
Vous me trouverez ailleurs.

❖ ❖ ❖

Tirsis a Elise.

Voix: Rochers vous este sourd.

QVe fertil que la douce, & la divine Flore
Me fait donner les lijs, & Roses de son front,
Que sert il que je voy les fleurs, & ses boutons
Si je ne voyez pas Elise que j'adore.

Elisemon object, Elise que j'honore
Vnique de mes soins, & mes chaste desirs,
Que sert un beaux printemp, que sert un doux zefijr
Si la plus belle fleur, que j'aime, n'est pas Esclore.
Ie sens deja l'odeur, je goute la merveille,
Ie perd dans un hijver (helas!) un vray Printemp,
Elise est loin d'icy qui cause mes tourments,
Ah! faut il que je perd la Rose nompareille.

❖ ❖ ❖

Sur

I find myself elsewhere run to earth
Where, in humility, I launch my faint plea.
I am elsewhere, if you choose to find me.

◆ ◆ ◆

Thyrsis to Elise*

Air: *"Rochers vous êtes sourds"*

Divine Flora as fecund as perfumed
Gives me the lily and the rose of her brow.
But what are buds and flowers worth, at all,
If I do not see Elise, whom I adore?

Elise, object of my zeal, the one I love
Uniquely among those my chaste desire
Cherishes, what does springtime signify
Or Zephyr's breath, if I do not praise
You first, consummate of flowers?
Almost inhaling her scent, almost tasting her wonder
I lose the spring around me in a winter for
Elise is far from me, the cause of this frost.
Let it not happen that I lose this peerless rose.

◆ ◆ ◆

\* Brongersma wrote this poem
in French.

## [163]

Sur un Bouquet des fleurs qu'a envoyez la jeune flore.
Mad. H. ISINGE a Philis, Mad: E.J.

Voix: lors que je pence a la peine.

VOy-la Philis les fleurs que Flore
A fait naistre il sons despeint
De la nature, & de sa gloire.
Elle se vons desja Esclore
     Mais pour mourir
Mais pour mourir sur vostre sein.

◆◆◆

Aminte a Philis.

Voix: J'ay beu pour chasser les Enneuit

Affreux Rochers soulagez moy.
Car Philis. Car Philis
La plus inhumaine,
Est changé & a rompu la chaine
Et tous les bandes de sa foy.

Si vous regardez mes soupirs
Cachez donc cachez donc
Tous mes maux, et Larmes
Dit a la perfide que ses charmes
Et cruautez me fon mourir.

◆◆◆

                                  Un

On a bouquet the young Flora bestowed
(Miss Heringa van Eysinga presented them to
Philis, namely, Miss Elisabeth Joly)*

Air: "Whenever I think of the pain"

Here, Philis, are flowers Flora sent,
Birthed and culled from nature,
Sharing in her glory.
She urges them to open,
Quickly, and blow, and die:
Die upon your bosom.

♦♦♦

Amintas to Philis†

Air: *"J'ai bu pour chasser l'ennui"*

Frightful rocks console me
For Philis – for Philis most
Inhuman woman has changed,
And snapped the chain, and broken
All the bonds there were, of trust.
If you respect my sighs
Hide all my woes,
Hide too my tears, and tell
The faithless woman her charms
And cruelty kill me.

♦♦♦

* The van Eysinga family belonged to the minor nobility of Friesland. Possibly Miss Heringa van Eysinga's father was born in 1653, in Werdum, just south of Leeuwarden; he became *monstercommisaris* or an inspector for Friesland at large, and died in 1690. Brongersma wrote this brief poem in French.

† It is a commonplace in, for example, Vergil's *Eclogues*, for a lover to complain to the rocks. Brongersma's melody may evoke a quatrain by François de Maucroix (1619–1708):

*J'ai bu pour calmer les ennuis*
*Que l'amour cause de mon âme;*
*Mais le vin n'éteint pas ma flamme:*
*J'aime, tout ivre que je suis,*

"I drink to dissipate the lassitude that love provokes in my soul. But wine does not dim my flame: drunk as I can be, still I love."

[164]

Un autre.

Voix: Aimons nous belle Silvie.

VOus Rochers, deserts sauvage,
Froides aux melez vos pleurs
Avec moy, car ce Boccage
Est touché de mon malheur:
Car ma Philis est volage
Qui me veu tirer son caeur.

Dite moy Philis ma belle
(Qui m'estois toujours charmant)
Pourquoy d'estre si cruelle
A un amoureux amant
Je vous aimeray fidelle,
Et je vis pour vous constent.

❖❖❖

T' Samen spraak

Toon, Belle iris.

de Boer

GOen joon boer faem goen loon
Heste toed' to haemir weysin?
Ia ik tins for schate reysin
Meye feynijn aek ijn 't roon
Ia ik gis dat sibirgs looskie
Di de knoote het bistioerd'

Tia

Another

Air: "*Aimons-nous, belle Silvie*"*

You rocks and savage deserts,
Cold waters mix your tears
With mine. My misfortune
Moves the forest. Philis
Is fickle and wants to root
Me right out of her heart.
Tell me Philis, lovely,
Perpetual charmer,
Why so cruel? I will love
You always, constantly.

◆ ◆ ◆

The Conversation†

Air: "*À la belle Iris*"

The farmer:

Evening, girl! Good evening!
Were you down at the tavern today?
Yes, I think you've been there often
Hanging out with all the boys.
I guess Sybrig's kid would knot a cloth
With you in mind, wouldn't he?

* Brongersma's model may be from Molière's *Mariage forcé* (1676): "*Aimons-nous, aimable Sylvie, / Unissons nos désirs et nos coeurs, / Nos soupirs, nos langueurs, nos ardeurs*" ("Let us love, loveable Sylvie. Let us unite our desires and our hearts, our sighs, our languishment, our ardours"). This lyric makes an appeal to "*la loi naturelle*" – "natural law."

† This poem is in Frisian dialect. The author of "*À la belle Iris*" may be A.L. LeBrun, called by one paradoxical authority "*un versificateur oublié.*" This LeBrun flourished around 1709. If Brongersma's model is LeBrun's poem, then her bucolic adaptation is ironic. His courtly lyrics run:

*Je pleure, je languis, je me plains,
   je souspire,
Je n'ai pas un moment de repos nuit
   et jour.
Je souffre, belle Iris, et je crois que
   l'amour
N'a jamais fait souffrir un plus cruel
   martyre,*

"I weep, I languish, I complain, I sigh, I have not one moment of rest by night or day. I suffer, lovely Iris, and I believe cruel love never committed a more grievous martyrdom."

[165]

Tiala wol in mot aeek booskie
Oors lis ik op hotse sioerd'.

de Meyt

Ny ik wyt dogs nioornie fin
'K gis I miene Martzins Iantjen
Altijd lis i so to rantjen
Sioeg ik tioeg wol opp'erin
Hab i oors naeet nies to snappien
Haed de toet din nammirs to,
Altijd had i bett to gappien
In ik sis it is noet so.

Boer

Ey het biste maal in tyoe
Soeste der om hinne rinne
'K Laeeu de fammin baesig binne
As min praet sin Ionge lijoe,
Der ye nagts in deys om tinse
'K Laeeudu ingiste der oon
Woe ouws Ian dy 't yld'oors schinse
Du betrouwst him dijn pirsoon.

Meyt

Imme Ian sio ugt fiers to Haeg
Hi kin't lieppe aay naet sijna
Of hi mot die schoeg op byne
Ny 'k most aeftir ime waeg
Sok ijen feynt als ijmme Soentje
Wijt ik nioor ijn ous Laen,
Rin riuw hinne mey Ion Kroontje
Ik nim Tiale byer Haen.

♦ ♦ ♦

Hotse-

He needs a wife, or should I
Place a bet on Hotse Sioerd?

The girl:

No. I know nothing about all that.
I guess you mean Martijn's little Jan.
Well, here you lie ranting all day.
Do I really look bad in any way?
You make up stuff when there's no gossip,
So just shut up. You're always
Wanting to gawp at something –
In this case there's nothing.

The farmer:

You're a bad girl and stupid, too,
To go running off to that place.
Girls get hot when a man mentions
The boys they think of night and day.
You're obviously flustered.
If Jan proposed you'd say yes.

The girl:

Your Jan keeps his nose in the air.
He couldn't find a lapwing's egg
Unless he stooped to do up his laces.
To get him I'd have to go
To *your* house. Your precious son
Is the biggest fool around here.
So get out of here with your
Dear Jan Kroontje. I'll take
Tialle's hand instead.

◆ ◆ ◆

[166]

Hotse mans Vryery,

Toon, Lom'rig woudt.

WIer om wotte mi naeet habbe
Sis mijn soucker swiete laeem,
Of is Lolkmoers harre Tiabbe
Tho dijn Liaeef de moeest biquaam.

Wotte habbe sil ik stere
Sis ho biste nou so tioe,
Of mot ik eerst vryen lere
Fin ous Boermans jonge lioe.

Sioegste wol di tiouke knote
Sil ik di mijn gouden Iaen
Ister yoen yoeg Sibbils Bote
Mi dit woendre rinkel raen

Dog du dit dijn liaeeve Swobbel
Sey er, in ik ron rieuw fort
Maar di liltie rabbel wobbel
Die mi yn mijn dwaan tho kort,

Omye sey: wol motte booskie
Hotse tiene din tho wirk
Oors bitiugt di Taeetse looskie
Of ous Ian mieg, of Piers Drik.

Nim mi dogs mijn Swiete Fambke,
Siker wier ik bin so ing
Dat der om ous Beppe Ianke
Mey mi kibt dat bose ding.

Wor-

Hotse's courtship*

Air: "*Sombres foretz*"

Why not have me little
Lamb, so sugar-sweet?
Or is Tjebbe of Lolkmoer
The boy you really like?

You want me to die?
You're so hard and mean.
Want the farmer's children
To teach me how to woo?

Look at the knotted cloth
I'm giving you, my golden girl.
Yesterday Sibbel's Bote
Showed me this amazing ring.

"For cute little Swob,"
Said he. I ran off right away:
But the ugly little jerk
Cut me short.

Uncle said, "You have to marry,
Hotse: get to it, or Teatse's
Kid, or Jan, or Piers Dirk
Will steal the one you love."

Then take me, honey.
I'm so worried Granny
Yanke the malicious
Thing will nag me so much.

* Hotse and Bote are male names, Swob and Bauke female. Brongersma writes the whole poem in Frisian dialect. One folk custom of the region is to present an intended with a knotted cloth. Brongersma probably never married. She represents marriage here as a fate imposed on men as much as on women – and none too delicately proffered.

[167]

Wottit dwaan du schette lisse
Moorns oon agt, of nioe gen oer,
'K silit yten, lit dy sisse
For di sette op it sioer.

Wotte nogs naeet, 'k woe wol gale
Hestit birt so slagger ijn
Sis reys Iaa, allijk as Tiale
Tiebbis Breyd; di male Trijn.

Lit oes aek as oore minschin
Swobbeltie, ey you min pat
Dir's nin graeeter lok tho winschin
Wes so goed ik bid di dat.

Wotte naeet, du meystit litte
'K vraeeg nin meer, koens baauk wol wol,
Ey het minst du hone tijette
Wey, mey di du tirrel hol.

♦ ♦ ♦

Op een Swaantje T.H.S.

MYn Swaanelijn
Wilt met V Treeders roeyen
En door de baaren spoeyen
Op dat gy by my moogt sijn
V sagte pluymen die vermaaken mijn
De golvies die soo vaardig her waarts schieten
Die sullen V voort dringen met haar dertle vloet

En

Say yes and you'll sleep in
Till eight, till nine
And I'll set the meal
On the hearth, I promise.

If you say no I'll scream.
If you're listening, take my hand.
Just say "Yes" like Tjalle
Tjebbe's bride, crazy Tryn.

Dear little Swob, let's be
Like other people. Kiss me.
It'd complete my happiness.
Just do as I say, be good.

You won't? You don't need to.
I give up. Anyway, Koen's Bauke
Wants me. So there, you stuck-up
Bitch. Get out of here.

◆ ◆ ◆

On the Little Swan T.H.S.

Air: "Air"

Little Swan, would you with your web-feet paddle
Through the deep salt sea, to be with me?
Your soft plumage how pleasant to the touch
But the currents rush and push so rapidly

[168]

En op het spoedigst' door de waater vlieten
Doen sullen, aan de strant van mijn gemoet.

Schoon dat gy sijt
Vrouw Cipris opgedraagen
En haar Ivore Waagen
om te voeren: toe gewijdt,
Soo sult gy sijn mijn Lust tot aller tijdt,
Of Jovis schuymt, en meent V te vervaaren
Neen neen mijn Swaanelijn gy hebt soo ligt geen noet
Ik sal V voor die Blixem bulb bewaaren
En Bergen V als Leda in mijn schoot.

Daar sal ik dan
V Matte Leetjes decken
En 't lieve bekkie lecken
Iaa betoonen wat ik kan
Ge moedigt V mijn Swaantje en koomt an
V witte feders sijn 't die my doen branden
Gelijk den Phaenix door de hitte van de Son
Ik stier mijn sugtjes tot een offer-hande
En duyk reets in de poel van Acheron.

Maar soo gy wilt
Mijn beede gift ontfangen
En my het groot verlangen
Door V komste een maal stilt

Doch

Their hectic insolence might hurl you
Too hard, onto the beach of my desire.
You know, the Cyprian lady makes birds
Of your beauty draw along her shining
Chariot: so you are yoked to my love
For all time. Does Jupiter intend to foam
And frighten? I will cover you from his bolt
And hide you, like Leda, in my lap.
There I will embrace your modest woe
And kiss your delightful beak, yes,
Show my affection any way I can.
Courage my Swan, approach. Those bright
Feathers set me on fire like a phoenix's
Kindled by the rays of the sun. Let me
Send my sighs as a sacrifice diving
Even into the eddies of Acheron.

I dread the coldness of your bosom
Yet court your coming to end my longing,

[169]

(: Dog vrees V boesem al te ijsig kilt:)
Soo sal ik V als in een wolk alkoven
'Ten Heemel voeren op de kamer van vulcaan
Daar sullen V de Gooden t' samen looven
En neemen V daar voor haar Venus aan.

♦ ♦ ♦

Toon: Courante simple.

HOe lang verkoren Adamant
Heeft sig't geval seer nijdig tegen kant
En my belet om niet te moogen zijn
By u mijn Alderwaarste Engelijn.

Het schijnt dat water, vuyr, en lucht,
Jaa gans de aarde met Firandus sucht
Wijl het Climaat daar Janus over herst
Te wrang de ijs schigt in veel boesems perst

Niet dat ik daar voor heb geschuwt
Of schoon Borëas hagelbergen spuwt
Neen: maar ik heb my selfs te veel verschoont
En u mijn ijver daar in met betoont.

Doch nu de son wat hooger gaat
En met de Ram springt in de Lente graat
Nu sal ik botten met gebloemt en kruyt
En schieten weer aan u mijn diensten uyt.

♦ ♦ ♦

Toon,

I will cleave the clouds to lead you
To Vulcan's chamber where gods in chorus
Must praise you, taking you for Venus.

◆ ◆ ◆

Air: *"Courante simple"*\*

Dear diamond, deserving angel, Fortune
Has how long opposed itself in envy
And hindered me from being with you?
Water and fire alike feel desire, yes:
The whole earth with Firandus feels desire.
The month named for Janus presses
Icy shafts into every bosom though
I would not desist for that reason.
Let the north wind belch heaping hail.
Passion mine, I only am to blame
For not pursuing you the harder.
Yet now daylight lengthens, the Ram springs,
And with flowers and with leaves I bud
And burst to pledge fealty to you, again.

◆ ◆ ◆

\* A *"courante"* was a dance popular in the seventeenth century; the "simple" variant is the most basic form that the dance could take. Firandus loves Leonora in the prose chronicle *De wonderlijke vryagien en rampzaalige, doch bly-eyndige, Trouw-gevallen van deze tijt* (1668). Brongersma appears to adopt the persona of this male lover.

[170]

Toon: La Mignonne.

SChoon de Griexske Phoebus dondert
Van sijn breyn gedaakte school,
En den Atlas sich verwondert
Acht nochtans het Capitool
Waar Atheenen mee gaat pronken,
Niet soo veel als Philis lonken,

Jaa schoon dat het wert beklaatert
Van de aldoorsiende Goon,
En van Janus uyt geschaatert
Soo vermach Latona soon
Niet op mijn verwonnen spieren,
Maar tracht Phylis op te cieren.

Phylis die ik uyt wil terten
Tegen al de grootste pracht,
Sy gebiet geen mensen herten
Maar den hemel houwt ontmacht,
Phylis is vol waardigheeden,
Dies wert Phylis aangebeden

Phyilis schoonste van de Werelt
Gy zijt meerder dan Diaan,
'k Houw u als de Son beperelt,
En roep staag u machten

Phy-

Air: "*La Mignonne*"*

Let Phoebus boast his sophisticated school.
Let Atlas gawp at the acropolis where
Athens struts, and Athens preens. Phyllis
Allures me more. Let Providence see
To everything, let Janus rule
The year. Set your bow aside, Apollo.
Labour to adorn adorable Phyllis.

Phyllis, that is, whom I extol
More than the greatest glory possible.
Human hearts? She makes heaven swoon.
Her Excellency I propitiate
Like a goddess, purest in the world.
Adorable, more adorable than Diana,
Pearl of pearls the sun is dim beside you.

---

* "*La Mignonne*" means "The Adorable Woman." Pierre de Ronsard wrote an ode beginning in this way: "*Mignonne, allons voir si la rose / Qui, ce matin, avoit disclose*" ("Adorable, let's go look at the rose that has this very morning, bloomed"). Brongersma's stanzaic pattern does appear to substantiate Ronsard's sixteenth-century precedent.

Phylis gy zijt Grunoos luyster,
En u licht maakt alles Duyster,

♦ ♦ ♦

Toon: Povre Gruselle.

HElaas waat baat het Phylis dat ik kom u ween,
Seg eens de reen,
Waarem gy my dus tert,
Ach al te herden hert
Woont in u sachte borst hebt doch medoogen,
Siet ghy niet schoone de tranen mijns oogen
Die van mijn pijn
Getuygen konnen zijn.

Het Beekje Phylis dat gy siet in dese Wey
        Is door 't geschrey
Gesprooten: mits ik staag
Hier aan haar boorden klaag
Hoe dat gy noch u ermen Tyter mertelt
Waar van het brakke vocht dat niet meer dertelt
Maar sich weer houwt,
En nu met Tyter rouwt.

De Else boomen die gy daar van verre siet
        Zijn vol verdriet
Iaa Kruyt, en Graasjes staan
Beswangert met getraan,
De Rotsen slaan de galm van al het suchten
Bossen, en Bergen zijn sonder genuchten
Om dat het niet
Haar Herder by u siet.

Geluk-

Groningen would go dark without you.
Your bright powers I petition, charmer.

♦ ♦ ♦

Air: *"Pauvre Gruselle"**

Phyllis what could you want? I weep.
Say at least the reason, hard heart.
In your soft bosom compassion
Must remain. Don't you see the tears
In my eyes, witnessing my misery?

The meadow stream my tears feed.
I wander its banks in constant grief.
If you sought out Tyter's arms
The brackish flow would stop
But it has to grieve with Tyter now.

The ash-trees there writhe with woe
With the herbs and the little grasses
Heavily laden with a burden of tears.
The rocks echo sighs, the woods and hills
Hear no consolation for they do not now
See their shepherd by your side, fortunate

* The melody *"Pauvre Gruselle"* ("Poor Gruselle") is often attested after 1655. The title recollects the heroine from Boccaccio's *Decameron*, who famously endures a husband's deliberate infliction of a series of inordinate ordeals.

[172]

Gelukkig is het wouwt waar dat mijn Phylis vvoont
    En als bekroont
Door Telges gaat en pronkt,
En menich hert ontfonkt,
Gelukkig seg ik is het schauw der bladen
Waar Sy haar staag in de koelte komt baden
En met Diaan
Daar schouwt veel soetheyt aan.

Ik sal dan wijl gy lacht en met de Nimfjes speelt,
    En kluchjes deelt,
Mijn graf bereyden daar
De Eliseesche schaar
Haar klachten storten met het nederklimmen
In het gepekelt nat van al de schimmen
Daar u mijn smert
Sal knagen doen het hert.

♦ ♦ ♦

Eyndigen de Gesangen

Af-beel-

The forest where my Phyllis crowned with boughs
Parades her charms, wounding hearts.
Happy the leaves that flourish
Where she goes to bathe in the cool
Her nakedness sweeter than Diana's.

Since you laugh performing skits
With the droll nymphs playful and petite
I'll prepare my tomb there: the whole
Elysian host will break out in lamentation
At my descent, briny-wet, amid the shades
Since my pain will gnaw away, at your heart.

◆ ◆ ◆

Here the songs end

[173]

Af-beeldingen.

Aan de Geestrijke, en in Deugt uyt Muntende Juffer, ELISABETH
JOLY, Haar E. opdragende, De afbeeldingen in't besonder.

GEdoog, wijl 't Swaantje vaardig staat
Dat met sijn witte wieken slaat
Om door de Lugt te dringen:
Dat het voor u mag singen,
Den Eeren trant op Schildery
Van u, en anderens waardy:
Op dat het op die wijsen
U doe ten Hemel rijsen,
Want u Alwaarde waardigheyt
Verdient veel meerder aardigheyt
Als't Beestje uyt kan geeven:
Schoon 't werdt door moet gedreven.
Neem dan in Dank haar schor geluydt
Wijl't sig in uwe gonst besluyt.

◆ ◆ ◆

Op de

Ekphrastic poems

A special dedication of my ekphrastic work to the
brilliant and virtuous Elisabeth Joly*

Patience, dear one. The little Swan would beat
White wings and sing aloft a panegyric
Of your painterly gift and everything else
Worthy of your exaltation to the skies,
All-worthy woman deserving of much
Greater delights than this petty creature
Could express – though she tries her courageous
Best. Tolerate the hoarse uproar then
Since it would only with fervour favour you.

♦ ♦ ♦

* Brongersma avows Elisabeth Joly's
graphic talent here.

[174]

Op de Af-beelding van J. van VONDEL.

SIet vry dit heerlijk beeld verwondert aan:
Dees voert het puyk der Nederduytse Digten
Dit is de Fenix daar de Grieksche Swaan
In 't vliegen naar de wolken voor moet swigten
Dit's Febus soon die om d'onsterflijk heyt
De Lauwer Croon te dragen is bereyt.

♦ ♦ ♦

Op de Afbeeldinge van de Coninginne DIDO haar met een Swaardt Dodende.

KArtaagschen Elisae moet gy dan
Dus sneuv'len om te trouwe daden?
O! Dido wraak u selfs niet van
D'ondankbre gast die u versmade,
Maar ... ah! gy toondt dan door dit swaardt
Dat Eerverlies de Doodt is waardt.

♦ ♦ ♦

Op de Afbeeldinge van de Keyser NERO, hangende in een duystere kamer.

Het oog beelt uyt de togten der gemoeden
Besie't gelaat hoe fel, en straf het sy:

Men

On a portrait of Joost van Vondel*

Take a look at the picture. Magnificent.
It shows the glory of Netherdutch verse.
Phoenix, the Hellenic swan's late avatar,
Through the clouds he flies on wings of courage,
Scion of Phoebus reaching to attain laurel,
The warrant of his immortality.

♦♦♦

On a picture of Dido killing herself with a sword†

Elissa, queen of Carthage, must you really
Die, in order to prove your loyalty?
An ingrate guest defiled you: do not
Harm your body, Dido. Yet you, your sword
Still show us how honour lost may choose
A decent death.

♦♦♦

On a portrait of Nero hanging in a dim chamber‡

Squint, and see that eye evincing violence:
The unambiguous sponsor of state terror!

---

* Born in Cologne, Joost van den Vondel lived from 1587 to 1679; his family moved to Amsterdam. His early drama *Palamedes* (1625) resulted in state persecution. Critics call his *Lucifer* (1654) the best of his plays. He matured slowly, only beginning to reach his literary peak at the age of sixty. Brongersma calls Vondel "the Hellenic swan's late avatar" probably because he translated a Greek tragedy (Sophocles's *Electra*), and modelled other pieces on Greek precedent. Brongersma alludes to Vondel's nickname *Rijnzwaan*, Swan of the Rhine.

† Assisted by her sister Anna, Queen Dido of Carthage resolved on suicide. Her perfidious beloved Aeneas had defected from her side, under orders from Mercury to hold for the Italian peninsula and so fulfil his destiny of founding Rome. Brongersma is aware of the similarity of Dido's alternate name, Elissa, to Elisabeth Joly's. The poet salutes the impulse to self-preservation but – since the epic will not allow for the prevalence of that impulse – she reverts to the ethos of female honour, elsewhere embodied in the resolution of Hippo to die rather than to submit to rape.

‡ Notorious for his misrule, Nero tried repeatedly to murder his mother, Agrippina, using such expedients as a booby-trapped boat. Finally he commissioned assassins to break into her bedroom: she was slain.

Men leest uyd' op slag daar de tirany,
Die Romen heeft gesmaakt door sinen woede
Daar d'asch sijns Moeders dekt door wraak 't gesigt,
Wijl hy hem schaamt, en schuw is voor het ligt.

♦♦♦

Op de Af-beeldinge van den Eer-waarden, Wel-geleerden Heer
Mijn Heer NICOLAUS BLANCARDUS, Professor tot Franeker.

WAnneer men staard op het besaad, en deftig wesen
Van Blanckaard: treflijk door Pencelen afgemaeld
Soo schijnt het dat men uyt sijn Ogeligt kan lesen
Hoe hy de Griekse Homeer, in weetkund' overhaalt,
En hoe sijn Taal-lit nog veel vloeyender sou spreeken,
(Soo het niet waar gehegt aan 't effene Paneel)
Als een Plutarch, die door 't vertoog kon Rotsen breeken
Die sig in hem vertoond, op't konstig Tafereel,
Schooon wit besneeuwd', dog dat is het Trofeen der wijsen,
Geen Loverkransen, nog gekromden Passem Tak
Ciert ooyt een schedel meer, de kennis is aan 't grijsen
En lijt nooyt door de tijdt, de alderminste krak:
Maar d'Wijsheyt als gesterkt kan veel gewelt verdragen
'k Sie Blancard' dan bevrijd voor 't slaande blixemvier

                                        Gehar-

Tyranny drives us mad. His mother's
Ashes darken his face. Even his picture
Suspended in darkness shuns our exposing light.

♦ ♦ ♦

On a portrait of the honourable and learned Nicolaus
Blancardus, professor at Franeker*

The very gaze of this decent, appealing person
Rendered accurately by the artist's strokes –
The light in those eyes alone, we imagine –
Tells us he can translate Homer and discourse
So well he might break the picture-plane's
Restraints, and improve on Plutarch's talent:
Plutarch, the man to offer this scholar's "parallel
Life." That hair of his, white as snow, rewards
Wisdom better than laurel or the palm frond
Bent; it distinguishes the head of a true
Intellect. Philosophy resists time's
Attrition. Lightning's fire only liberates

* Nicolaus Blancard contributes prominently to the commendatory verses with which *The Swan of the Well* begins. Plutarch, a Greek writer born at Chaeronia, lived from around 46 to 120 CE. Brongersma mentions his most famous work, *Parallel Lives,* which pairs for illumination the life of a notable Greek (such as Demosthenes) with that of a notable Roman (such as Cicero).

[176]

Geharnast tegen't gift, en felle donder-slagen
Wij hy omwonden is met dobble Lauwerier.

♦♦♦

Op de Af-beeldinge van de Deugt, en Geestrijke Juffer Mejuffer
CORNELIA BLANCAARD.

WAt siet men daar de Schets van U Cornelia,
Dat kan men zijn: wat hand heeft u soo net gedreven,
Wat Konstpenceel, wat verw boetst soo het weesen naa
En doet u op het doek als oogenschijnlijk leven.
Hier staat Natuyr verset, en ijder die u kend,
Of vind' ik my ook door dien Schildery bedrogen?
Neen, 'k weet et immers, schoon gy wel getroffen bent,
Dat gy het zijt, door 't ligt en 't flonk'ren van u ogen.
Wat hert souw niet wijl gy u hert schenkt aan de konst
Veroverdt werden, en u beeld voor Pallas roemen,
En offren dienst op dienst aan u begeerde gonst
Wijl men U waarlijk moet een Thiende Musa noemen.

Doch soo u Aftrek elk verbaast, van die u siet,
Seg Blancaards kroost wat doet u eygen selfs dan niet?

♦♦♦

Op de

Blancardus, proof against all poison: for
My verses hereby confect him protective laurel
As the painter's loving skill did, before I came.

♦♦♦

On a portrait of Miss Cornelia Blancardus, a woman
as virtuous as intelligent*

Cornelia, what paintbrush can have caught your
Elegance? You seem a living being, there,
And canvas breathes like you, so like nature
No one could not recognize you. Am I
Bewitched? No, I know what lures me,
It is the brightness of, the gleam in your gaze.
To the execution of this art
You gave yourself wholeheartedly.
Your picture is an Athena's and we offer
Sacrifice after sacrifice seeking favour,
Acknowledging you our new, tenth Muse.
If to turn my back on this lovely
Picture pains me, young and darling Blancard,
What effect must you have, seen, scanned in the flesh?

♦♦♦

\* Cornelia Blancard may be
Nicolaus's daughter.

[177]

Op de Af-beeldinge van de seer Geleerden heer, mijn heer
JOH. MENSINGA, Professor tot Groningen.

SOo siet men dan haar braven Letterheld
Door't konstpenceel u beeltenis afmalen,
Soo siet men op het Tafereel gesteldt
Het wesen dat de Son gelijk in't stralen,
Die door d'invloeying werkt op het verstant,
En stort een stroom van kennis neer van boven,
Waardoor de kragt der wijsheyt werdt geplant
Op't logge breyn van die u moeten loven.
Gy zijt een ware Bron der wetenschap,
De zedekonst, en u oprechten handel
Verheften U om hoog op d'Eeretrap
Die gy verdient docr d'eerlijken wandel,
U moet men dan, O rechten Majaas soon:
De Lauwer-tak toevoeren die voor desen
Den Mantuaan versstrekte tot een kroon
Die uyt de gront van Andes quam geresen,
De wijl dat gy een Ligt voor Gruno zijt,

War

On a portrait of the very learned Johannes Mensinga,
professor at Groningen*

Gallant literary hero, the paintbrush
Catches the being who burns like the sun
Kindling the understanding, sending
Rays of wisdom from the heights to warm,
Enlighten the muzzy minds of those who would
Affirm you. Moral philosophy, fair
Dealing lead you up the stairs to honour
You deserve for your conversation
And kind bearing, good son of Maja.
Vergil himself, the man of Mantua, weaves
Laurel from his hometown Andes since
You illuminate Groningen, sweep

* Brongersma, fond of synonymy, refers to Vergil in multiple ways (Maro is the last of these). Eloquent, interpretative Hermes is the son of Maja. Johannes Mensinga contributes commendatory verses to *The Swan of the Well*.

Waar in gy drijft op sneege Arents pennen,
Daar gy U doet (in't aansien van de Nijt)
Seer loflijk voor den tweeden Maro kennen.

♦ ♦ ♦

Op de Af-beeldinge van de Deugd en Konstrijke Juffer, MeJuffer
ELISABETH JOLY.

DAar siet ge dan het Beeld van dien Elisabeth
Wiens Deugd: geschakeld aan de schrandre Wetenschappen
Haar hooft bekranst, wijl men haar Lofnaam uyt trompet,
En triompherend voor Minnerva heen doet stappen.
Daar siet g'het wesen van dien Geestigen Joly
Dat Pronkbeeld, voor wiens geest de braafste geest moet Wijken,
Daar vind g' het leven in de doode Schildery:
Dat geen Pigmalion kan nader doen gelijken,
Maar schoon d'Afbeelding van dien tweeden Dafne toont
Door haar ge-eerde kruyn omvlogten met Lauwrieren,
Dat sy gesegent by d'onstervelingen woont,
Soo sal ik haar nog met een vaarse trant beswieren
Te meer om dat se werd, door Phaebus heyl'ge min
Vergood, en meest geliefdt van sijne Priesterin.

♦ ♦ ♦

Op de Af-beeldinge van de Deugtrijke Juffer MeJ. ANNA MA.
BLANCAARD.

DUs siet men toegelijk in eene Schildery
D'ontfermend' Anna, en een treurende Mary,

Geen

On an eagle's rapid pinions past
Envy's grimace as our second Maro.

♦ ♦ ♦

On a painting of Elisabeth Joly, a woman as virtuous as artistic*

There is our Elisabeth. Virtue and knowledge,
Twined, crown her head. People praise her
Above Minerva. Effervescent being,
Mind revered by potent minds, you shine
In the deadness of mere paint, though no
Pygmalion could beat the original, live.
Yet even this image of a second Daphne,
Beguiling in her crown of laurel leaves,
Adored by mortals, makes me here adorn
Her freshly, in this way, endearing her
Further to the sacred love of her Phoebus
No less than to his deeply smitten priestess.

♦ ♦ ♦

On a portrait of Miss Anna Maria Blancard, a woman rich in virtue†

Combined in one in this picture see the pitying
Anne and the mourning Mary, Anne grieving

---

* Brongersma performs yet another *ekphrasis* on her friend. On this occasion, Joly's mental power receives the poet's emphasis. Brongersma intriguingly explores a neglected dimension of Daphne's story. The transformed nymph herself has won the laurel: after all, she is the essence of that triumph. The poet imagines officiating as Apollo's priestess – a role in which Samuel Mun(c)kerus places her, too, in his complimentary verses.

† The addressee is likely another young relative of Nicolaus Blancard. Da Vinci's representation of St Anne and the Virgin Mary is possibly the most famous; it is unlikely that Brongersma knew of it. Brongersma emphasizes the civilizing power of Miss Blancard's eloquence, paradoxically conveyed by her mute portrait.

[179]

Geen treurende die treurd om dat Maria weende
Neen! maar om dat'er naam sig met die naam vereende
Want haar bevallig oog schiet andre stralen uyt,
En wijst hoe dat haar geest een groter geest besluyt
Wijl gy geoffend met haar sagte tong kan weken
Het alderruwst gemoed door't soet en minlijk spreken.
Doch schoon de Beeltenis die doot is 't leven toont
Van haar die van de Deugd met Eerloof werd bekroont,
Soo sal nochtans mijn schagt, die sig in't git gaat betten.
Haar lof beschrijven, en haar gaven nyt trompetten.

♦ ♦ ♦

Op de Af-beeldinge van de hoog Ed. Geb. V.M.V.
TITIA RUFFELART A.B.V.M.

WAnneer ik sie U schildery, en wesen
O! hert vrindin, soo denk ik hoe voor desen
De vrintschap bloeyden als een Cederboom
Die nu verloopt gelijk een waterstroom.
Hoewel aan mijne kant stantvast sal blijven
Schoon dat gy neffens my niet koont beklijven,

U goet

For the sobbing Mary. No. I say that
Only because the sitter possesses both these names.
From her charming eye shoots a light of another
Kind expressing the spirit and gentle tongue
That can tame raw violence with its clear speech.
True the painting is dumb and dead yet in it
Is a hint of the life of her whom goodness crowns
And my black ink inscribes her worth, resounds
Her gifts and manifold capacity.

♦ ♦ ♦

On a portrait of the most noble and high-born lady
Titia Ruffelart*

When I see this painting, darling of my heart,
I recall the friendship that flourished like a cedar
Tree. It courses away now like a torrent.
For my part I stand fast and abide for you
Although I know you cannot cleave to me.

\* Properly the name is "Ruffelaert."
Minor nobility, this family was
notable in Groningen.

[180]

U goetheyt staag getoont vergeet ik niet,
Maar sal (hoewel gy my niet by U siet)
Altoos soo lang mijn aders sullen rukken
U in het hert, en mijn geheugen drukken,
Ik sal tot blijk al spuwt de Nijt haar gal
U Eer en Roem Trompetten over al,
Want gy verdient veel meer als ik kan uyten
Doch sal u in de Rang der wijsen sluyten
Wijl nimmermeer de deugt, in kennis slijt
Maar sulk een kost lijkheyt duyrt voor altijt,
Dies laat dan toe dat sonder my te roemen
'k U voor als naa, noch mijn Vrindin mag noemen.

♦ ♦ ♦

Op de Af-beeldinge van de hoog Ed.Geb. V.M.V.
THEODORA LOUISA STERNZEE, A.V.M.

Daar braldt de Ster in Zee, daar flikkeren de ligten,
Die deugde Sonnen, op een aangeverft Panneel,
Daar siet men hoe de konst verbeelt op 't Tafereel
Louisaas waarde, die voor niemant hoeft te swigten
Want selfs de goetheyt schijnt haar tot de oogen uyt,
Wijl sy die nimmer voor haar gonstelingen sluyt.

Daar kan men soo veel nut uyt haar gedaante lessen
Gelijk het inder daat in 't rechte leven is,

              Daar

The picture constantly declares your goodness.
As long as my heart keeps beating you will
Make your impression on my thoughts.
Let Envy spill its bile, I shall trumpet
Your fame, your glory since you merit more
Than I can phrase but let me say you will
Be inscribed in the rank of the wise for such
A precious thing as virtue never passes.
Permit me, dear woman, only to remain
What I was before and would still be, your friend.

◆◆◆

On a portrait of the most nobly born
Theodora Louisa Sternzee, A.V.M.*

On a painted panel see the star of the sea,
The sun of virtue glowing. Art on canvas
Can image Louise's goodness beaming from her eyes.
This woman never excludes them from the sight
Of promise, or of neediness. She looks as she lives.

* Brongersma puns on Sternzee's name: "star" and "sea."

[181]

Daar siet men door de verf haar ware Beeltenis,
Die als een morgen Son komt uyt de Zee geresen
Om elk te toonen dat haar Hemels klaarheyt straalt,
Waar mee sy Eer, en Gonst van al de werelt haalt.

Want waar Godtsdienstigheyt verselt gaat met de reden,
Daar steltse selfs de Nijt in tegen wilt te vreden.

♦ ♦ ♦

Op de Af-beeldinge van de hoog Ed. Juffer MeeJuffer
HOUWKJEN van GLINSTRA

MEn speurt dan uyt de Schets, en 't ster uws oogen
Haa Glinstra dat gy zijt een Glinster Ster,
Wiens zede flickering men siet van ver
Die gy hebt uyt u Moeders borst gesoogen.
De Deugd blinkt Sonne klaar uyt al u wesen,
De Leersugt schiet, (O pronk van 't Friesche landt)
Haar stralen voort, en toont op het verstandt
De grootheyt van U kragt, van elk gepresen,
Het is vergeefs geweest u staal te slijpen,
Wijl 't van natuyr een heldre luyster geeft,
Gy zijt dan 't licht dat door haar lichten leeft,
Wat hoeft men dan 't onnodich te begrijpren?
Dog 't spreekwoort seyt tot voorbeelt van de wijsen
Dat d'Oeffening noot saakelijk is nut,
Wijl het de geest dient tot een vaste stut,
Soo moet ik voor natuyr Geleertheyt prijsen.

Het

Pigment depicts her truth and true likeness
Rising like the sun from a morning gulf
Lucidly blazing and winning honour, the world's
Goodwill. Where service of God goes united
With eloquence, there Envy against its will
Is made glad and kind, blithe and festive.

❖ ❖ ❖

On a portrait of the most noble
Miss Howkjen van Glinstra\*

This sketch and the light of your heavenly eye,
Glinstra, prove you to be a glistering star
Whose moral radiance sparkles far and wide.
You sucked that virtue from your mother's breast.
The sunny glow irradiates your whole person:
Your love of learning, Frisian splendour, shines
And everyone acknowledges your mental power.
Steel such as yours is not to be evaded
Since by nature it glitters brilliantly.
You are then the light by which such light lives.
Do we ourselves really need to seize it?
The principle suffices: study is a good.
It serves the mind as a fulcrum and a basis.
Let me praise education more than nature.

\* Brongersma puns on Glinstra's name, a quibble that I attempt to convey with the sound-alike epithet "glistering."

[182]

Het geen U waarlijk koomt op't schoonst' bekronen,
En waar door dat gy wert by 't Jufferdom
Geëert, gelieft, in uwe stadt al om,
Want elk wil geerne by soo'n puyk licht wonen.

◆ ◆ ◆

Op de Af-beeldinge van de hoog Ed. Juffer MeJuffer
LOUISA van GLINSTRA.

'K sie dan U Beeld in Schildery,
O! soete Glinstra, die voor desen
My placht tot een vermaak te wesen,
Maar nu is al de vreucht voorby.
Nu vind ik dat Louisje niet,
Dat elk soo minlijk weet te streelen,
Dat yder van haar gaaf wil delen,
En men altijt soo vrolijk siet,
Dat lieve kint van deugt, en aart
Dat waardich is een kroon te dragen
Van Perelen in Gout geslagen,
Dat van de hemel werdt bewaart

Tot troost en heyl van dien: die't sorglijk hoeden:
Die't eygen zijn, en met haar Liefde voeden,

             Dien

You win the crown in purity of endeavour,
All the city's women revere you, prodigy,
And linger freely near you, luminary.

♦♦♦

On a portrait of the very noble
Miss Louisa van Glinstra

While I gaze on your image in paint, sweet Glinstra,
What afflicts me – your absence – becomes a pleasure.
But when I wake from the trance, petite Louise
In whom everyone finds perfection bright and dear,
I discover anew that you are not here for me.
You wear in the eyes of all the pearl- and gold-
Adorned crown of virtue guarded by heaven.
You are heaven's solace, and integrity.
You belong to it and it protects you
Who are fed by its love, and by mine.

[183]

Dien seg ik die ik wens (tot spijt der Nijt)
Een zegen, en altoos, een gulden tjit.

♦ ♦ ♦

Op de Af-beeldinge van de geest-rijcke Juffer
MARGARETA G. de DAVID.

Hoe meer men staart op 't wesen van Margreet
Hoe meer men sich moet om haar geest verwond'ren,
Wyl sy als Kato welt te spreeken weet,
En op de trant van Sappho uyt komt dond'ren
Haar Helden sang, daar d'Yssel-Swaan van singt
Die haar op syne schagt voert naa de tronen
Waar Febus Lier op maatse tonen klingt,
En doet haar by het konst'bre Neegen wonen,
Dies Sy haar daar als opgeslooten vindt,
En voor de Thiende siet ten Hemel dragen,
't Is dan vergeefs men haar met Lauwren bindt
Dewijl Sy die daar plukt naa haar behagen.

♦ ♦ ♦

Op het uytgehouwen Beelt van de Friesche Puik, dichter
ADRIAAN TYMENS, gedaan door F. staande in sijn E. Kamer op
een Pylaar, hebbende geen Crans om 't hooft.

SONNET.

SOo pronkt het Beelt in blanke Mermersteen
Van Adriaan: naar 't leven uytgehouwen,

En

I bless you: I wish you with heaven a golden
Life, in spite of loveless, scheming Envy.

♦ ♦ ♦

On a portrait of the ingenious
Miss Margareta G. de David

We all want to look at Margaret's person,
Still more we are astonished by her mind
Since she speaks with Cato's fluency and
Adopting Sappho's mode like lightning
Blazes in heroic song. So the Swan
Of the IJssel* sings of her who upon strong wings
Bears her to the throne where Phoebus's
Lyre keeps good measure inviting Margaret
To join the artful Nine entranced by her.
Their Tenth, she is a heaven in herself. Vain
Gesture here to bind her brows around with laurel,
Elsewhere she plucks the stuff to her heart's delight.

♦ ♦ ♦

On F.'s bust of the glory of Frisia, the poet Adriaan
Tymens, standing in the gallery of worthies on a
plinth without a garland on his head†

Sonnet

Adriaan shines in marble sculpted to the life,
Face distinctive, his irrefutably, a look

---

\* "The Swan of the IJssel" is probably Katharina Lescailje.

† The Leeuwarden littérateur Adriaan Tymens published his *Meditations on the Birth of Our Saviour Jesus Christ* in 1680. His verse appeared in *Frisia Nobilis, of Lyk- en graf-sampt mengeldigten* (*Noble Frisia, or Various Elegies and Eulogies*). The sculptor Lysippus of Peloponnesian Sicyon flourished around 325 BCE. He was famed especially for his skill in rendering hair, and for specific statues of Alexander and Socrates. Tymens is the author of commendatory verses at the beginning of *The Swan of the Well*. The identity of the artist F. is unknown.

[184]

En streeft met het geischt door wolken heen
Als of hy wilde daar de konstklip bouwen

Om sijne Schets te richten op'er stangen,
Dat ingewijd op een Colomne blinkt.
O! groot verstant, hoe veel doet gy ontfangen
Een hemel val, wanneer u Lier uytklinkt

De Heldendaân, en tokkert op de snaren
Een Veldtliet, of het lof der Letterscharen
Daar mee ge bralt, en door de hoef vliet plast.

Maar had Lisip de Beytel aan geklonken
U hooft waar met een Lauwer krans beschonken,
Die U soo wel als Alexander past.

◆ ◆ ◆

Op de Af-beeldinge van den Franschen P. RONSARD
Prince der Poëten, met devis.

Laurier Immortelle.

SIe daar de Gootschen Lely-bron
Uyt wiens doorvloende Ad'ren,
Den grontstroom van den Helicon
Sig koomt door hem vergad'ren,
Daar is het hooft vol hemels vier,
Daar 's Ronsard' wiens Gesangen

Sijn

Resolute as one who would establish his image
On Parnassus, on a column set up
Gleaming sanctified: an initiate.
O mind inspired, your lyre sounds,
Pastoral song is plucked from your strings
Or praise of makers, whom you exalt
Rushing and sparkling like the horse's well.
But had Lysippus managed the chisel
He would have granted your head the laurel.
It suits you as well as it did Alexander.

◆ ◆ ◆

On a portrait of Pierre Ronsard, Prince of Poets,
with his device: "Immortal laurel"*

There is the Gothic spring
Where lilies flourish.
It feeds the Heliconian stream. Head
Full of heaven's fire he drank here,

* Pierre de Ronsard (1524–1585) was a member of La Pléiade. The reason why Brongersma chooses to call Ronsard's well of inspiration "Gothic" is unclear. The epithet may identify the great poet's willingness to compose in a vernacular language.

[185]

Sijn kruyn met eeuw'ge Lauwerier
Onsterffelijk behangen.

◆ ◆ ◆

Op de Af-beeldinge van een Gans vluchtende voor de
Lauwerboom, Met Devis
L'impureté suit la vertu.

'K Sie met vermaak de wulpsche vogel vluchten
Voor't geurig Groen van Dafnes Lauwerblaan
Doch kent hoar waarde niet dan door geruchten,
Dies poogt d'onsuyverheyt, de Deugt t'ontgaan.

◆ ◆ ◆

Op't gesigt van een vliege, vliegende om een brandende Fackel:
Met Devis
Temerite' dangereuse.

HEt Vliegje schept vermaak in't Fackellicht,
Het swiert soo't lijkt voorby die goude stralen:
Maar 't weet niet dat het brant 't gaat naa't gesicht
In't vliegen, in die schone flammen dalen,
Elendig dier: wijk eer g'u vleugels sengt
Want: reukeloosheyt veel in p'rijkel brengt.

◆ ◆ ◆

Op de Af-beeldinge van een Hert luysterende naar't gespeel van
een Feel, Met devis.
Dangereux d'ecouter les flateurs.

DVs lokt de soete galm het Hert te nad'ren
En't schijnt te luystren naar het spel der Feel.

Diens

Ronsard, brow shadowed with laurel
Unfading, enduring, like his song.

♦ ♦ ♦

On the picture of a goose flying away from a laurel
tree, with the motto: "Impurity flees virtue"

See with amusement the defamatory bird flap
Away from Daphne's green and scented laurel leaf.
Don't assess her worth by gabbling rumour, then.
Gossiping vice gracelessly flees fragrant virtue.

♦ ♦ ♦

On the likeness of a fly orbiting a burning torch, with
the motto: "Dangerous temerity"

The bright torch amuses the fly
Contracting circles to intermit the rays
Unconscious how flammable its form
Descending to the central heat.
Wretch, before you scorch go.
Recklessness kindles calamity.

♦ ♦ ♦

On the picture of a heart inclined to the playing of a
fiddle, with the motto: "Perilous to listen to flatterers"

The heart leans closer to the sweet solicitation
Of strings, and trustful joy swells its arteries,

[186]

Diens vreugt kruypt door't gehoor langs sijne ad'ren
Wijl het sig laat verleyden door't gestreel,
Het is perijkel't oor naa vleyery te hangen,
Want't is het rechte Net: om yder in te vangen.

♦♦♦

Op de Af-beeldinge van een die wel gestevelt is, gaande door een weg vol dorens, met devis
Faut estre bien chaussé, pour marcher entre les Espines.

DEes Reysiger schijnt onbevreest
Te treeden door de scharpe stickels
Wijl hy geschoeyt op deugdens leest
Vermorst door het getrap de prickels,
Dat is, wie ongequetst wil gaan
Door't steek'lich bos der Lasteraren,
Die moet al wel sijn aangedaan,
Om sig voor't onheyl te bewaren.

♦♦♦

Op een Geschilderde Bloem: die verslenst haar blaatjes laat vallen, Met devis,
Ainsi se passe la beaute.

DEse bloem weI eer vol geuren
Die'er blaatjes vallen laat,
En verlenst te truyren staat,
Om't verlies van verf en kleuren,

Wijst

Seduction engrosses the organ beat after beat:
The ear that depends on praise is such a heart
As each and every one of us bears in our breast
Spilling lifeblood to the glib and dangerous.

♦ ♦ ♦

On the picture of a walker whose thick clothing
resists thorns, with the motto: "Get proper gear
together, before you face brambles and nettles"

This pilgrim marches ahead amid the prickles
Proof against any spiny vines, branches.
Would you advance without blood and bruising
Through masses of stinging and tearing plants?
Prepare your defence against godless growths.

♦ ♦ ♦

On the picture of a flower bloomed out and dropping
its petals, with the motto: "Even so beauty passes"

This flower lately brim with scent
Casts its petals, droops dimming
Lustre, pigment, displaying not

Wijst ons met haar voorbeelt aan
Hoe de schoonheyt moet vergaan.

♦ ♦ ♦

Op de Af-beeldinge van Polixena Die geoffert wert op het graf van Achilles door Pyrrhus.

ACh Pyrrhus ach! ik schrik, O wree barbaar
Hoe durft gy in die blanke boesem steeken?
Kan u dit bloedt, bloet dorst'ge offeraar
Van vaders doodt: en bloetvergieten wreeken?
Ik sie ghy schreyt en antwoort door geween,
Ag! siet haar schoone borst, haar mont, en oogen
Het schijnt sy Triomfeert, haa Polixeen
Wat Lauwerkroon sal't lof bereyken moogen
Van dees u daadt, nu is Achil gerust
Nu 't overschot van Troyen leyt verslagen
Op 't graf van hem: wiens wraaklust is geblust,
En aan de saam geeft stof dit voor te dragen.

♦ ♦ ♦

Op de Afbeeldinge van een Sater die een Nimf vervolgt die in 't rennen van vrese omsiet wiens Minnaar haar volgt, om 'er uyt sijn klaauwen te redden.

Die spreekt.

STaa Sater staa, of houw u wat ter zy?
Siet gy niet hoe de Nimf u vreest in 't rennen

Staa

Beauty: beauty's evanescence.

◆ ◆ ◆

On a picture of Polyxena by Pyrrhus sacrificed on Achilles's grave*

Cruel defiler Pyrrhus could you knife
That shining breast? Does bloodshed solve
Your father's slaying? I see you cry, howl by way
Of answer. Breasts, and mouth, and eyes,
Only look at them, so pure she triumphs.
What laurel wreath could commemorate
Your feat, Polyxena? Achilles lies at rest.
You master Troy's remains on his grave whose
Desire for havoc is extinguished, transformed
Into the matter with which fame may play.

◆ ◆ ◆

On a picture of a satyr chasing a nymph who in panic reverts her gaze at the pursuer, eager to escape his clutches†

Her defender speaks:

Stop, satyr. Stop. You want to paw her?
Her fear is evident by her flight.

* Pyrrhus is the son of Achilles, Polyxena daughter of Hecuba and Priam. Achilles had desired Polyxena. Willingly or unwillingly, the Trojan woman was sacrificed on Achilles's grave: one account has the ghost of that warrior appear to the Greeks, demanding this monstrous offering. Brongersma appears to imply that Polyxena's death ends the war, and makes it susceptible of artistic renditions. Homer's *Odyssey* advances such susceptibility as the saving grace of war. William Blake abhorred the Greek and Roman classics for just this reason, claiming that (extenuating bloodshed as matter for epics and tragedies) they persistently devastated Europe with war.

† Brongersma has imagined a Sri Lankan satyr. Admiral Joris van Spilbergen arrived in Sri Lanka in 1602. Cinnamon was already known in the Mediterranean habitat of satyrs when the Greeks first imagined them. The Carthaginian deity Moloch demanded victims immolated in fire.

[188]

Staa Bockx voet 't schijnt ge loopt u selfs voor by
Men kan u nauw van spoken onder kennen,
U Trony brant gelijk een Aetnaas gloet
Neen 't Boscornoelij doet u dus vermommen:
Of is door Febus wrok het weeldrig bloet
Van Marsias, u in 't gesigt geklommen
Dat's wel geraan, O snoeper daar gy sijt
Gy meent te sijn in u kaneel waranden
En in 't Ceylonsche bos, waar gy verslijt
U dertle tijt in 't snuff'len, op'er stranden,
Neen neen dit's Canna niet staa snoo Moluk
'T is mijn Lerinde die ik sal beschermen,
Blijf agter, of ik u te morsel druk
Geen Nimf past in u klauw, maar in mijn Ermen.

❖ ❖ ❖

Op de Afbeeldinge van de Verloste ANDROMEDA door
perseus! die haar de geboeyde Handen ontbint, geschildert
door STOCADE.

HOe vlamt het oog van Perseus op sijn Bruyt
Hoe Liefijck strookt hy haar geboeyde handen
En schiet een vier vol stralen op haar uyt
Wijl hy s'ontkeetent: van de Ysre banden.

Andromeda verbleekt, en bloost van vrese

Belonkt

You belong among your brother ghouls,
Face burning sullen as Aetna's fires,
Congested monster of the wood. Marsyas's
Plethoric purple mounts in you – Phoebus Apollo
Skinned that bloody beast. To gluttony
All's food. Go range in Ceylon's cinnamon,
Rummaging, nosing on the jungle shore:
This nymph is not spice. Desist, malicious Moloch.
I would tutor – would protect the woman.
Listen: I'll tear you into bits unless
My arms, and not your claws, receive her youth.

◆ ◆ ◆

On Stockade's painting of Andromeda, whose tightly
shackled hands Perseus loosens\*

Perseus's eye burns bright as he unchains
His bride: Andromeda glows unmanacled
Then pales, then flushes: fearful, yet enchanted.

\* The painter Nicolaes de Helt Stockade (1614–1669) often treated topics from Ovid. Andromeda's mother Cassiopeia boasted that her beauty surpassed that of the Nereids. Aggrieved Neptune sent a sea monster to ravage the coasts of her kingdom, Ethiopia. The oracle at Ammon advised that the naked Andromeda be exposed to the monster's rage. The hero Perseus intervened, wielding Medusa's head in his defence. Brongersma mentions Stockade in connection, elsewhere, with the art of her personal acquaintance Philip Joly.

[189]

Belonkt nog van ter zy haar Bruydegom
Sy siet voor haar Triomfen op gereesen
En om die vregut verblijden 't Hemeldom

De Lant plaag drijft op 't bloedig pekelnat
En stort sijn gift en leeven in de golven
Daar d'Erm van Dana'as kroost die zeeg om vat
En hout hem daar door 't moedig staal gedolven.

'K sie Cassioop, en Cefeus d'handen klappen
Van vreugde, schoon een Ammon 't vonnis velt
En Perseus met Andromeda heen stappen
Verwinnaars van het Monster, en 't geweldt.

◆ ◆ ◆

Van een Rose-tak, waar op een Bye sit, suygende Honig uyt eene
van die Rosies, met Devis.
Ie vit de la douceur.

HEt nerig Bytje suygt van Rose-bladen
Sijn voetsel, en het trekt daar Honig uyt,
Om door dat ratig vogt sig te versaden:
En 't schijnt of het hem in dat Bloemtje sluyt,
Om beter van de grond het sap te halen.
Het geen my leerd te denken aan het soet
Van d'Hemel Roos, geplant in Sions dalen,
En dat ik selfs het Bytie wesen moet,
Want tot die geur werd ik door pligt gedreven:
En roep met hem, die soetheyd doet my leven.

◆ ◆ ◆

Op de

She could have ascended then in triumph
Enjoying a share of heaven's happiness.
Her nation's terror heaves in brine and vomits
Poison with its life. The arm of Danaë's
Son has won the victory, gallant steel
Split the whalish monster's skull. I see
Cassiopeia, Cepheus clapping despite
The oracle at Ammon's counsel, while Perseus
Revels with Andromeda, ugly
Violence vanquished very beautifully.

♦ ♦ ♦

On a spray of roses, from one of which a bee sucks
honey, with the device "I live on sweetness"\*

The petite and energetic bee sucks in the midst
    of petals
Her nourishment, and bears the nectar out to please
Her wise monarch. It looks like she is quite shut
In the blossom, all the better to get at
The sap collected in the bottom. Heaven's
Rose, sown in Zion, tempts me to imitate that bee.
I would root in aroma doing her duty, and summon
The one who, all sweetness, honeys my life.

♦ ♦ ♦

\* The commonplace of the bee is flexible. Sometimes the insect stands for industriousness, sometimes for the citizen of an ideal commonwealth, sometimes for luxurious or inconstant eros. Here sensuality is emphasized, but chastened (or diverted) into the sphere of holy devotion – Brongersma's familiar rose of Sharon.

## [190]

Op de Af-beeldinge van Juffer Anna Maria Schuirmans, hangende in 't voor huys van J[uffers] J.K.

SIet hoe het konstig werk van dese schets verbeelt
Het pronksel van Euroop: uyt Pallas breyn geboren
En doet een ider door 't gesigt benaa bekoren
Niet om haar schoonheyt, maar om dat sy heeft geteelt
Een Reex van wondren, wijls' door ongemene gaven
Ver boven 't Vrouwe sex naar waan heeft ingestelt
'T geheym der wet, waar in sy onvermoeyt gink slaven,
Dog schoon se overtrof soo meenig Letter Helt:
Is door 't afleydent spoor van 't regte pat geweeken,
'T schijnt dat hoe sterk een suyl sig toent, wel ligt kan breeken.

♦♦♦

Op de Af-beeldinge van Cefalus, en Procris daar zy hem de schigt, met de hont Lelapa vereert, die nooyt misten.

HOe Procris gy schenkt aan Cefaal
Soo 't schijnt u Lelapa van herten,
En ook de goutschigt wiens metaal
't Venijn uyt braakt om u te smarten,
'K sie Aura schuylt daar achter 't bos
Daar gy u dootnet hebt gespannen,
Zy maakt u Jagthonts banden los,
En poogt u uyt haar oog te bannen.

O blint

On the picture of Miss Anna Maria van Schuirman
hanging in Miss J[oanna] K[athius]'s vestibule*

Look at how the artful work of this sketch images
The glory of Europe, from Pallas's mind
    brought forth.
No sooner does a viewer see her face than
    she's beloved
Not by reason of her beauty, but because she
    has partaken
Of a realm of wonders assisted by gifts uncommon
Raising her above her sex to surpass many heroes
Of literature, instilling in her the secret
    of governance
In whose behalf she labours incessantly.
She illustrates for all that no matter
How strong a soul it can shatter easily.

◆ ◆ ◆

On a picture of Cephalus and Procris, with the dog
Lelapa unerringly sure of his prey†

Procris, sincere of heart you gave your beloved,
Cephalus, both Lelapa and the dart whose gold
Dipped in venom will poison and pain you.
Sexy Aurora skulks in the woods it is true.
Trustless you still connive in your demise.
The goddess frees from the leash your hunting dog
To send you, woman, from her sight forever.

---

* In the last two lines of this poem, Brongersma alludes to van Schuirman's choice to become a member of the religious commune of Jean De Labadie. This decision cost van Schuirman her reputation. She died in the commune; its founder predeceased her entry into the organization. It was located not far from Leeuwarden, in Wieuwert.

† Cephalus the hunter, beloved of Procris, attracted the goddess Aurora's lust. Though the divinity flirted with Cephalus, he remained faithful. Suspecting him regardless, Procris hid in the forest, to spy on him as he hunted. He mistook her commotion in the underbrush for an animal's, and transfixed Procris with an arrow she herself had furnished him. Brongersma's pitiless poem alludes to this sad mistake. The hunting dog Lelapa had detected Procris who, expiring, was often, in the seventeenth century, portrayed with the deadly dart piercing one visible breast. Odysseus is a descendant of the house of Cephalus (see *Metamorphoses* 7.694–862).

[191]

O blint Geval hoe licht raakt gy
Door eygen stricken in de ly.

♦ ♦ ♦

Op de Af-beeldinge van mijn Eerwaarde versturvende
Vater en Moeder, hangende in mijn Kamer.

HIer sie ik twee die my de werelt deden kennen
Haar oogen stralen nog vol troost op mijn gesigt
En schijnen wijlse my soo waarde panden bennen
Te willen seggen iets van grooter reen gewigt
Daar 't spraak-lit dat wel eer met tedre minlijkheden
My streelde, is beklemt, hoewel de lippen gaan
Soo 't schijnt, en my helaas! voel in het Hert gesneden
Als ik met aandagt Schouw mijn lieve Ouders aan,

Dog wijl de Doot te vroeg m'Haar by sijn quam ontschaken
Soo troost ik my! dat my haar Schetsen nog vermaken.

♦ ♦ ♦

Op de Af-beeldinge van Hoop, Geloof, en Liefde, klimmende op
een Piramide met devis,
Ainsi on monte au Ciel.

DVs treet de hoop op d'eerste Trans
Wijl het geloof de tweede nadert,
Daar Liefde wint de Olijf krans,

En

Fortune, almost frivolous, wreaks revenge.
You set the net, the snares: into them
You stumble. The forest whispers. Dawn returns.

◆ ◆ ◆

On the sketch of my late honourable father and
mother, hanging in my room

Here I see two who had the means to grant me all
The world. Their eyes retain the power to beam
Solace into mine. And they look as though
They want with dignity to tell me something
Serious and significant. But since that speech
On the verge of streaming tenderly to my ears
Remains constricted and withheld on lips
Shaped to impart a message, cut to the heart
I can only gaze. If death untimely
Ravished them, contemplation of their picture
Restores me: though not my parents, or my loss.

◆ ◆ ◆

On the emblem of Hope, Faith, and Charity
ascending the side of a pyramid with the motto,
"Even so, one climbs to heaven"\*

Onto the first tier clambers Hope,
Faith balances on the second.
Charity wins the olive crown,

\* The motto is originally in French.
Brongersma uses two different
words to designate the same thing,
namely Charity or Love: the translation imitates her variation.

[192]

En op de Opper-top vergadert
Het Lott voor't moeyelijk gewelt
Tot blijtschap van de Heyl'ge schimmen,
En't Troost-woort uyt te roepen stelt
Alsoo moet men ten Hemel klimmen.

Daar Liefde trekt geloof en hoop
En bint haar drie in eene knoop.

♦ ♦ ♦

Toon: La Cardinal.

SIbrig sis wier rinste sey
Bring ous de ky vinne ickers mey
Maar lit de kaeelin rinne: maer lit,
Driuw de aeede Ruyn
Ynne kaemp by de tuyn
Inne rieren ijnne finne.

Sioeg reys ijnne Jarre slaeet
Of daar de tourle leyt of naeet?

Du moste fiouwir meltie: du moste:
De oore sex of agt
Nim ik din wol to wagt,
Of sist laeer oon ouws Jeltie.

Rop dat Dirk in swetse man
De bry poot bringt in drinkins kan

In

Straddling the apex has exchanged
Worldly trouble for heaven's bliss,
While encouraging, while consoling:
"Climb after." Love, and Faith, and Hope
So bind their triune-ness, into one knot.

◆ ◆ ◆

Air: "*La Cardinale*"\*

Sibrig, say, where are you running?
Bring us the cows from the fields
But let the calves – let them run.
Drive the old gelding
Into the paddock by the garden,
The heifers can head into the fenny patch.

See if the milking stool was left
Lying by the dunghill drain.
You have to milk four cows: do it.
I'll take care of the other
Six or eight – or get Jentje
To do that, you tell her.

Call Dirk, the bigmouth, to bring
A bowl and a drinking can.

---

\* This poem is entirely in Frisian dialect. The song "*La Cardinale*" was current in the Netherlands as early as 1658. The placement of this poem among the *ekphrases* implies that Brongersma describes (or pretends to describe) an actual painting.

[193]

In reuwe din twae weynnin: in reuwe.
Fird ijmme hette fort
Die tied valt oors to kort:
Mi engit joed for reynin.

Harck reys joo eer ik't for ijt
Dat swetse di den menne lit
Du kinste best di herne: du kinste:
Finne schoere door
Du witstit for ijen oor
Maar gied for al ous tierne.

Flye jouwir ijnne hoek
Du wistit wol eij spoed di kloek
Ik mot it ijt in kootse: ik mot it:
Rep ijm hette tel
Ouws boete komt meij snel
Nu mot ik't flaaks eerst plootse.

◆ ◆ ◆

Eynde der Af-beeldingen.

Aan

Harness two waggons – two,
Do you hear? Go: time's wasting.
The sky looks like rain, I'm worried.

Before I forget – remember:
You're driving, Dirk may talk big
But he doesn't know the dairy.
You recognize the barn door.
Make sure you pour off
The liquid from the churn.

Set out oats in the corner,
You know where I mean. Hurry.
I have to cook a meal – I have to.
Speed it up. Here comes Bote with Snel
And now I have to pluck some flax.

◆ ◆ ◆

End of ekphrastic poems.

[194]

Verjaar-Dichten.

Aan de snege Juffer JOHANNA KATHIUS.
Haar offerende de Verjaar Gesangen, in't besonder.

DAar drijft mijn Swaantje in den bron
In't aansien van de gulde Son
En dobbert op de baren
Om naar U toe te varen,
En om te vragen of het mach
Wel quelen als het eertijts plach
Dat's van verjaar Gersangen?
Wan't hadde groot verlangen
Aan U te offren wil, en gonst
Hoewel 't niet singt op maat, of konst
Maar 't wil alleen doen blijken
Sijn drift al souw't beswijken.
Doch wijl het sig nu horen laat
En U verdienst op tonen slaat,
O! wijse maagt, wiens gaven
De werelt overdriven
Soo smeekt het, en het wenst dat gy
Vernoegt zijt met sijn harmony.

◆ ◆ ◆

Aan

Birthday poems [Brongersma's own generic allocation]*

To the witty Miss Johanna Cathius, offering her especially these birthday poems†

Over the waves my Swan is drifting, beneath
The gleaming zenith. In the current she dabbles,
Swimming your way to ask you may she
Muster, as before, a song for your birthday,
Not promising perfect metre, diction, pitch
But her passion finding what form it can
Tuning herself to you audibly now,
Learned lady whose gifts embrace the world,
She asks you, please, take her intention
As that harmonious achievement: a gift for you.

♦ ♦ ♦

* Collections of birthday poems were not uncommon. When Katharina Lescailje's collected verse was published, for example, her editors chose to cluster all of her birthday poems together.

† An Andreas Cathius living at (or near) Groningen had seven children with a Jetske van Bouricius. This woman died in 1687. Miss Johanna Cathius is undoubtedly a relative, and possibly a daughter of the same Andreas Cathius.

[195]

Aan Juffer Mee-Juffer SYBILLE BOTHENIUS.
Op haar E. Verjaren.

ICk werd genoopt haa Kroost van Themis Soon
Met vrolijkheyt u jaardag op te singen,
Dog bring geen Rose Telg nog Mirthe kroon
Om uwe blonde Lok te doen omringen.

Maar velgt een Letterkrans: daar mijne schagt
(Die kruypend' met de Tamarind langs d'aarde)
In ijverlust, wil door haar kleyne magt
Het Wierookgeur doen rooken voor u waarde.

Neem dan dees plicht als gulde gunsten aan,
Denk dat u Delos heeft met heyl'ge bladen
Bepruykt, en op dees Feesttijt aangedaan
Waar in u't Iufferdom pronkt met cieraden.

Maar waar ik Sappho 'k souw naar hooger wil
V schand're kruyn met goude veder slagen
Beswieren, en O Groninger Sybil
D'Orakels, van u wijse Lippen vragen.
Daar staag een Hemelval koomt druypen af,
En't rijp verstant dat volle Nectar-stroomen
Doet vloeyen, dat bereyt u kroon, en staf
Om als door het geluk, tot staat te koomen.

Het

To Miss Sybille Bothenius, to mark her birthday*

I am obliged, ha! child of Themis's son
With gladness to sing your birthday song,
Yet bring with me no roses and no myrtle
To grace, superfluously, your sweet blonde hair.
I weave instead a wreath of words since my pen
Creeping like the tamarind on the ground
Will try what strength it has in your behalf.
Set rivals aside: receive my offering: imagine
Delos has distinguished you with holy leaves
On a day when womankind adores you
Universally. Were I Sappho, I would
Lift your glittering crown still higher with
Golden flourishes of the quill, O Sybil
From whose prophetic lips I beg an answer.
From that mouth sublime speech always wells.
Ripest comprehension flows like nectar
Preparing your crown, your sceptre's sway.

* Aeschylus says the son of Themis was Prometheus. That tormented titan may embody the power of intellect for Brongersma: his name means "forethought." Sybille Bothenius was born in 1661, in Scheemda. Her father was Henricus Bothenius, her mother Ettien Aylkens. The latter died around 1669. Sybille's siblings included Aylcko, Casparus, and Regina Elisabeth. Scheemda lies just east of Groningen. The tamarind tree – which attains a moderate height, and is by no means a variety of low ground-cover – is said to produce fruit at once the most acidic and the sweetest of any plant. Dutch trade with Asia may have introduced Brongersma to the tamarind or its products. Possibly, she even saw a botanical specimen that gave her a misleading idea of the tree's habit of growth and stature. One of the three Parcae or Fates, Atropos was represented as inflexible, bearing the scissors with which she cut the thread of life.

[196]

Het geen ik wens: verschoon mijn moedigheyt
Begaafde Maagt; leef lang in veel gelukken
Tot Atrops u van hier naar 't rustperk leyt
Daar u de Nijt nooyt sal aan 't herte drukken.

❖ ❖ ❖

Verjaar-groet Aan de Hoog-geëerde, Deugtrijke Juffer,
Meejuffer. BARBERA SYGERS.

'K Heb bloem nog Mirthe-groen, nog telgen van Lauwerieren
Om u (waar my de bandt van Eerbied toe verbind)
Te kranssen, maar dewijl sig mijne Sang-nimf vindt
Verbonden om u op u Iaarfeest op te cieren:

Soo bid ik dat gy wilt (wijl 'k anders niet kan schenken
Als mijn geringen dienst geschakelt aan de gonst)
Aanvaarden dese Gift, die u sal doen gedenken
Dat het meer pligt verbeelt als schijn van eenich konst,

Mijn lome Digtveer kan niet op de wolken drijven
Gelijk de pluymen van den braven Mantuaan,
Se moet beneden by de logge Geesten blijven,
En wijken voor de vlucht van Meles blanke Swaan.
V rijp verstant sal licht dees kleynigheyt verschoonen,
En sloffen noch op Niet: doch 'k ben daar meet tevreên
Wijl dat u Geest u meer als mijn Gedicht kan kroonen
Want waar de kennis woont daar rust een schat van reen.

              Kwens

I wish for it. Excuse my boldness gifted
Lady, live long in felicity till
Atropos makes your restful bed for you,
Envy able never to crush your heart.

♦ ♦ ♦

Birthday greetings to the most noble, honourable,
and virtuous Miss Barbera Sygers*

I have brought no blossom, myrtle, laurel
To bind around your head a flattering garland
Yet my muse is bound to adorn the occasion,
Your birthday, by asking that you take this
Evidence of love's devotion as
Your gift, in lieu of what my little art
Fails to convey. This dawdling quill travails
Near the ground, below the gallant Mantuan's
Flexing pinions. It bumbles below among
Muzzy minds, and humbles itself before
The epic flight of Meles's brilliant swan.
Your loving gaze excuses this minor trifle
Objecting to nothing: for your spirit, I know,

---

\* Homer was supposedly born beside the Ionian river Meles, and was figured as a swan – like Horace and like Brongersma. In Brongersma, even Sophocles features, once, as a swan. Some say that Homer wrote in a grotto on the banks of the Meles. Croesus of Lydia held the reputation of being the wealthiest man of his time. Defeated by Cyrus of Persia in 548 BCE, he was spared at the very moment of punitive immolation and even cherished by his conqueror, whom he outlived. Brongersma writes elsewhere that Zenobia had riches beyond those of Croesus.

[197]

'K Wens dan dat dese dach van u gewenst Verjaren
V toevoer sulk een schat die Kresus schat verdooft,
En die een Heyl'ge rust mag in u rusten baren
Wanneer men d'Eere kroon sal stellen op u hooft.

Ik sluyt: en sal in plaats van Somerloof, en bloemen
V offeren mijn Hert: dat u van herten mint,
En send voor dropen Goudt, een blijk van schralen Inkt,
Dog sal soo lang ik leef van uwe Deugden roemen.

◆ ◆ ◆

Op het Verjaren van de Deugdenrijke, en geestige
Juffer ELISABETH JOLY.

Men sond wel eer Minerva Offerbloemen,
En hield' een vierdag om haar naam te roemen
T'Athenen in den Tempel daar die pracht
    Door Maagden wiert volbracht,
Sy strengden, en beslingden de pijlaren
Met Lovergroen, en op de Lof-altaren
Daar sag men niet dan kost'lijk land cieraat
    Gewrogt op Sang, en maat,
Souw dan Elisabeth een Pallas wijken
Neen, Sy kan door haar konst de Lauwren strijken,
Waarom dan niet met kranssen op het hooft
    Haar Jaardag ook gelooft?

Haar gaven noden my met Herse te tonen,
't Borduyrde Veldtapeet op Somer-tronen

*Waar*

More than my verse is able to crown you:
Wisdom where it dwells supplies all defects.
For your hoard of knowledge would daze
Lydian Croesus with his simple gold.
You are philosophic before a needless
Effort to honour eminence with a wreath.
Therefore I resolve not to offer summer's
Bounty, but a heart that loves you to its depths –
Not molten gold, but the homely promise
To praise lifelong your very many virtues.

♦ ♦ ♦

On the birthday of that most richly virtuous and
ingenious young woman Miss Elisabeth Joly*

Once upon a time people gathered flowers
In honour of Minerva, and a festal day
Glorified her name. In Athens in a temple
Women performed the rite, they strung, garlanded
The columns with green leaves and on the altar
Of their Lady's veneration a song
In stately measure attended elegant
Local votary offerings. Well, Elisabeth
Ought not to acquiesce before Pallas.
Her art has earned her the laurel. Let me crown
Your equal powers, on your proper day.
The festive rug laid on summer seats where

---

\* Brongersma may associate
Elisabeth Joly's August birthday
with the period in the middle of
that month (13 or 14 August) during
which antique Athens celebrated
the Panathenaea in honour of
its patron goddess, known to the
Romans as Minerva. A statue of
Athena was disrobed and washed by
women, then dressed in a fresh robe
woven by the hands of women.

[198]

Waar haar de tijdt in d'ingank van August
    Met saal'ge lippen kust.

JOLY, u aardigheyt, u deugt, en zeden
Verlokken Roedrig als gy door u reden
't Vertoog bereykt in driederhande Taal,
    Dog soo ik meer verhaal

Van 't geen u treft, mijn pen souw d'adem geven
Die van de doodt ontfangt het tweede leven,
Maar weest vernoegt dat u mijn Liersnaar bindt
    Die sig verpligtig vindt.

◆ ◆ ◆

Op het verjaren, van de seer geachte, en Deugtrijke
Juffer HENDERIKA TYMANS.

'K Heb dan geen Rosetak, nog Palmekroon bereyt,
Maar bind u met de strik van mijn genegenheyt,
En sing het Loflied van u Deugdt op Hemeltonen,
Ik queel u goeden aart die u veel meer sal kronen
Als menich perelkrans schoon door gewrocht met gout,
Het Lof te melden is my door u gunst vertrout,
Want niemant u verstant, en wesen af kan meten,
Soo naa als ik van die u soete wond'ren weten,
Doch heb voor lang gewilt u met een Vaarseirant
Van mijne Poëzy (O puykbeeld van het landt)
Te cieren, en ter eer u Iaarfeest op te singen,
Met wensing dat u nooyt den Aspis aan komt dringen
Van 't Helse wangedrecht de Niit dat Ziel Serpent,

                                                Maar

Early August kisses the special woman
With happy mouth invites me, too, to linger,
Ponder how best to get across her talents.
Joly, delectable soul, conversant with
Three tongues, seducer of glib Hermes by your
Very virtue, could my pen touch the limits
Of the topic "Elisabeth," it would bestow
Breath escaping death to grant a second
Life. It can and would affirm only this:
You stretch and tune my lyre's strings and they
Are fated to proclaim your service, always.

♦ ♦ ♦

On the birthday of the honourable and virtuous
Miss Henderika Tijmens*

I do not have ready a branch of roses
Or a crown of palm fronds but I twine
The band of my fond affection around you
And intone your panegyric, virtuous lady,
And warble the good nature that adorns you
Better than a gold tiara dropping pearls.
Your favour licenses my praise of you
For no one knows your intellect and essence
So intimately as I, my sweet marvel.
How long I have wanted to house you in
The building of my verses, you pattern
For the countryside, to sing, to wish
Happy birthday and may no viper strike you.
From your mind be it driven, Envy I mean,
That serpent of soul. Instead, observe your triumph.

* Henderika Tymens is probably
a relative, possibly a daughter, of
Adriaan Tymens, who contributed
commendatory verses to *The Swan
of the Well*.

Maar dat gy zegeviert, en't Heel-all maakt bekent
Wie dat gy zijt, en hoe de Grootheen van u gaven
Door Famaas Loftrompet de werelt over draven,
En dat gy in geluk, en vree u soetsten tijdt
Vernoegder als voorheen ter salicheyt verslijt
Op dat gy 't Opper-all, en't Heylichdom hier boven
Voor het genooten godet daar voor moogt eeuwich loven.

◆ ◆ ◆

Op't Verjaaren van Mee-Juffer. ESTER PERSON.

DEwijl de dach van U Verjaren
Verschenen is, soo breng ik voort
Mijn gunst, en koom nu openbaren
De rechte tijt van U Geboort.
Met wensing van Geluk: en zegen,
En dat u nooyt de Aartsche wrang
Tot herten leet mach stromen tegen
Maar daar voor alle heyl ontvang.
Den hemel gun veel vreugde dagen
Aan U: met die: wie met u is
Een steunsel om te onderschragen,
En dat hier naar 't geheymenis
U voert door d'Engle rey hier boven!
Om eeuwich Elion te loven.

◆ ◆ ◆

Geboor-

Potent as heal-all, the grandeur of your talents
Conquers the world at the blast of Fame's trumpet.
Relish of good times and contentment improving
On your prior life may you taste and savour
While you praise, unendingly, the One
Who abides above, for the delight that is all yours.

♦ ♦ ♦

For the birthday of Miss Ester Person

The day of your birth circling round again
Tells me: Multiply wishes, magnify
The hour Ester came to be on the world's coast.
Be happy, never taste bitterness,
Be hale, your days merry, your heart staunch.
You and yours are a rock here on earth.
May divine mystery, when the hour arrives,
Spirit you sublimely to praise Zion, forever.

♦ ♦ ♦

[200]

Geboorte-kroon Ter Eeren van de Hoog-geleerde Heer en Puyk-digter LUDOLF SMIDS. Medecijnen Doct. binnen Groningen.

SONNET.

DVs plagt men Cesars hooft met Lauwerblaan te pronken
Wanneer de zeegekar hem bracht op 't Capitool:
Gelijk O Smids de schaar u kranst van Phaebus school
Met Dafnes kruinloof uyt Castalius spelonken.

Wijl Gy als stichter van het nieuw herstelt Parnas
Soo heylsaam op die Rots het Dichterdom doet groeyen
Dat zy als stroomen uyt de Watersprongen vloeyen,
Op wiens tweespitse Top nooyt soo veel speelstrijt was.

Hoe klinken daar ay! hoor: die deftige Gesangen,
Wat Eng'le tongen slaan die boven mensche klangen
Soo ziel verruckend' op een volle Fluit accoort.

Iaa 'tis om dat dees Dach van u gewenst Verjaaren
Die Gorgeltoon doet aan besnaarde Lieren paaren
Die uyt Trompetten het geluk: op u Geboort'.

♦ ♦ ♦

Eynde der verjaar Gedichten.

Aan

A birthday crown in honour of the learned scholar
and glorious poet Ludolph Smids, Doctor of Medicine
at Groningen*

Sonnet

Ancient custom encircled Caesar's temples
With laurel when the triumphal car swept him
To the Capitol. Dear Smids, the students of Apollo's
School wreath you just the same with Daphne's branch
Castalia's cavern watered. You have founded
New Parnassus, on the slope establishing
Soundly a kingdom where artists draw
Their eloquence from the wellspring
Below the double peak where never before
Such rivalry ever sharpened wits.
The artful songs transcend mortal
Musicality; tongues angelic shake
The soul tuned to the source, munificence.
Let organs vibrate your anniversary,
Strummed lyres likewise. Trumpets
Blare a flourish for your birth – and birthright.

♦ ♦ ♦

End of birthday poems.

* Ludolph Smids was born on 13 June 1649. The original rules for the celebration of a triumph stipulated that the victorious general would have conquered on land or at sea, with a minimum of five thousand enemy deaths bringing to conclusion the pertinent conflict. A procession began at the Campus Martius, and ended at the temple of the Capitoline Jupiter. The triumphator did not wear, but carried laurel in his uplifted right hand. This arboreal token was deposited at the temple. A slave, however, sustained a golden crown above the triumphator's head while the procession advanced. For the poet, Smids's "triumph" is the willingness to teach, to be a mentor and an example.

[201]

Aan de geestige Juffer MeeJuff. CORNELIA BLANCARDUS. Haar
E. opdragende de Lijk-gesangen, En Raatsels in't besonder.

Het is dan eens gelukt te horen
Het Swaantje dat uyt blijtschap singt
En vrolijk op de baren springt,
Wijl dat het moedich komt te voren.
't Waar lang gedoken onder 't lies
Daar 't klevend' mos sijn hooft bewies
Waar onder 't scheen van druk te smoren,
Het swiert op pluymen spoedich heen
Tot u, en wil de Lijkgesangen
Opdragen, en Geraatselklangen,
Het komt gemoedicht tot u treen:
O! schandre Maacht: om u t'ontdekken
Hoe 't nu sijn kromme hals mach rekken,
Die eerst als ingekrompen scheen.

En 't sal wie 't spijt het lof uytgalmen
Van die, verdienen d'Eere-palmen.

♦ ♦ ♦

Lijk

Dedication to the intellectual Miss Cornelia
Blancardus of my elegies and riddles*

What was that? The noise? The Swan, now loud
With pleasure, breasts the waves she makes
And patters brim with spirit, lifting
A throat algae- and duckweed-flecked,
Long immersed. She beats away on pinions
To praise elegies, ingenious riddles,
Alighting to stalk, all gallantry,
Toward you, clever woman, her neck,
Once bowed, for you standing straight.
Envy cannot silence her resounding
Praise of those she knows merit the palm.

◆ ◆ ◆

* The addressee of this poem also received ekphrastic treatment from Brongersma, in "On a portrait of Miss Cornelia Blancardus, a woman as virtuous as intelligent."

[202]

Lijk-Gesangen.

LYK-KLAGT Op het haastigh Overlijden van de Hoog Edele
Personen: voor de eerste de Deugtminnende Heer mijn Heer
OENE van GLINSTRA, Ende daar naa de uytmuntende, wijse, en
Eerwaardige Vrouw Mevrouw ELEONORA BOURITIUS, Anders
GLINSTRA, Soon en Moeder.

Wat Hecuba, bejammert Polydoor,
Wat Moeder siet m'om Faëton besterven,
Om Memnon weer, verbleken een Auroor,
Ag! Ag! kan ook Eleonora derven

Haar Oene! haar Kroost haar jongen Benjamijn,
Haar Stam'pijlaar daar soo veel heldedaden,
Van Deugt uytblonken al seen puyk Robijn
Gestreeken op de Keur van pracht-cieraden.

Dien Thetis ach! besweek op't kouwe Graf
Van haar Achill, en golfde met'er tranen

Eer

Elegies.

An elegy on the untimely deaths of two noble
persons, namely the virtuous, loving Mr Oene
van Glinstra and the insightful, honourable
Eleonora Bouritius (otherwise Glinstra) –
a son and his mother*

Hecuba's woe over Polydorus, Aurora's
Over Phaethon or over Memnon: can
Eleanor's lack for anything they felt?
Her Oene! Her child, a youthful Benjamin,
Was to her as a staff incised with heroic
Deeds. His virtues gleamed like glorious rubies
One after another, loading a rich string.

And she a Thetis to succumb on the grave,
Her son Achilles's – so cold. She sobs; her soul

* Oene Frederik van Glinstra, born in 1656, died in 1682. His mother, the poet Eelkje Hectorsdr van Bouricius, died in April of the same year, in Leeuwarden. Her other sons were Hector and Vincentius; the former name perhaps motivates Brongersma's resort to Iliadic allusion. Hecuba, queen of Troy, was mother to both Polydorus and Hector. First Polydorus, then Hector, died in the contest for that city. Aurora, goddess of dawn, was mother to both Phaethon and Memnon. Both the latter perished (like Hecuba's Polydorus and Hector) on the field before Ilium. Vincentius, born in 1650, had died long since – in 1665. Genesis relates that Benjamin was the youngest son of Jacob. He remained the favourite sibling of Joseph, too young to have assisted the treachery that the latter's brothers had perpetrated. Brongersma dedicates poems elsewhere to other van Glinstras; as in the present piece, she puns on the family name, associating it with ideas of glimmering and shining.

[203]

(Eer haar de ziel glee van de lippen af)
Gelijk een stroom, om soo de wech te banen.

Maar ag! siet daar een Hector staat omgort
Met Rouw, en went om 't sneven van sijn broeder,
En op het Lijk een zee van tranen stort,
Om 't storven weer op nieu sijns waarde Moeder.

Wiens luyster sal de lichten van de Maan
Bereyken, en de glinsterende sterren,
Het vlik'ren door haar Glinster doen vergaan,
En ook de Lof straal in haar praal verwerren.

Wat hert souw niet, al waar 't van Mermersteen
Versmelten, om haar beyder overlijden,
En om soo'n zede Son, die elk bescheen
Niet truyren, schoon haar zielen sig verblijden

In 't Lusthof van de saal'ge Eng'len schaar,
Waar Elohim de heyl'ge Lauwerkronen
Sal stellen op haar kruin, en quelen daar
Het hemel-liet geset op Davids Toonen.

O! Glinstra eenig Erf, van dese Suylen
Sluyt toe de kranen van u Ooge Bron
Haar staat: is voor u staten niet te ruylen,
Sy wonen in 't Paleys van Helion.

♦ ♦ ♦

UYT-

Streams on a breath from her lips, to guide him.

Ach: there survives a Hector in his panoply of woe,
Pouring seas of tears on the corpse of his brother.
His mother will die twice – once with each son's death.

But Glinstra's lustre glisters past the moon
Far as stars. Their flickering, weaker than her light,
Dims at the splendor of her streaming merit.
A marble heart would cave at the double death:
Good son, imaginative mother – for both whom
We need not mourn. Their souls in bliss, in the pleasure
Palace of the angels, take at the hands
Of the Elohim their crowns of holy laurel
And loudly sing at the foot of David's throne.
O Hector, last Glinstra of this sad estate,
Dry your eyes. For things will not change.
You remain; they live in luxurious Helicon.

♦ ♦ ♦

[204]

UYT VAART Van de Hoog Ed: Gebooren Vrouw Meevrouw
HELENA MARIA Baronnesse van Zchwart-senborg, en
Hoog-lants-bergen, met 3 van haar Ed. Kinderen. Gemalinne
van den Hoog Edelen Gestrengen Heer T.V. AILVA.
Grietman op Rinsema-geest.

DUs draayt de spil op d'ass van haar veranderingen:
Moet dan mijn Treurheldin: naau van de Rouw ontlast
Al weer het klagliet van Heleenaas Lijk vier singen
Ag ag! barbaarsche Doot gy hebt my overrast,
'K dagt niet de Trant op soo een droevewijs te setten
'K dagt niet gy sulk een Telg op 't kragtigst, sout verpletten.

Waar't niet genoeg dat gy de Lootjes seysden af
Moest yust de Tronk soo vast nog op haar Edle stangen
Met eenen slag ter neer verhuysen in het Graf
En van de hout mijt haar de Tombe mee omvangen?
O Lant-plaag ag het schijnt geen offer stilt u wraak
Gy neemt in't vellen, van de braafsten u vermaak,

Die schone bloem: die Roem, van't Trotse Hoog-lants Bergen

Maria

For the funeral of the most noble Mrs Helena Maria,
Baroness of Schwarzenberg and Hohenlandsberg
with her three noble children, she the consort of the
most noble and dignified T.V. Ailva, judge-mayor
of Rinsumageest*

The thread of fleshly fate at last is severed.
Courage, muse of grief. Lamentation
Summons you to offer song for Helena's
Funeral. Sing all four: the mother, three
Children who predeceased her. But ach, Death
You truly overwhelm me. Theme so sad!
I did not expect to bend boughs this dark and sober
Into a wreath – hard trial of my power.
You stole the acorns. Did you have to knock
The whole oak over, every stately bough
Subdued by gravity, level with the grave?
Plague, no sacrifice requites your appetite
For malice. Must you cull, amused, the best,
The gallant – bright, blossoming Baroness,

* Brongersma mourns for Baroness
Helena Maria thoe Schwarzenberg
en Hohenlandsberg, who died
in 1682. Her dynasty began with
Hildebrand von Seinsheim around
1230. The Frisian branch of the
family was established in the sixteenth century.

[205]

Maria 't kostle schat van onwaardeerbre prijs?
Die nooyt aan ymant quam met hooghmoet d'ogen tergen
Maar d'arme onnooselheyt dee voen met reden spijs.
En laaf de weeuw, en wees: gelijk een milde voetster
S'waar de verdruckeling een steun, een troost, een hoetster,

Helaas dat puik Juweel is ons te haast ontrukt
En in het nederdal der stoffen op geslooten,
Die Hemel Roos is met haar knoppies af geplukt
En waar aant stamhout tot de wortel om gestooten
Soo niet de spruiten van haar eerst begroende Lent,
Op d'Erf-tak van haar Beelt, en Naam was ingeënt.

Waar op nu bralt haar glans geset in eygen wesen
Daar d'Zchwerzenbergsche pronk beperelt in de Rang
Koomt uyt d'aal onde asch als Phaenixen gereesen
En hout de voortogt van der duitsche helden gang,
Die die nu sijn berooft van 't waarste deel der aarde
Van haar Vrouw Moeder die nooyt 't Liefde voor haar spaarde.

Om wien dat jder truyrt en met haar kroost versmelt
In klagten, en om wien een stenen hert moet sugten?
Ag ag! is sulk een suil soo plots ter neer gevelt
Wat swakheyt sal die slag van 't groot gewelt ontvlugten
Geen Zee van tranen hout de Dootsche schigten in,
Die maaken al een eynd' daar 't schijnt maar een begin.

Wat

Mary most precious treasure, priceless?
She never bullied with a hard look but fed
Simple innocence with kind words
And walked the way and showed the way to go,
Like the gentle wet nurse of her people.
As a rock, and a solace, and a guiding star
She shone, she soothed, and she protected.
The glorious gem is torn from us too soon
Sunk in the abject valley of surcease.
The holy rose, its thick buds are plucked.
The tree of dynasty displays its torn-up roots.
No early, hazy spring can grow and leaf on
The branch that bore her likeness and her name.
Her radiance remains there, bright still and burning
Where ancestral glory, pearl of her rank,
Leaps up like a phoenix to vindicate
The clan of German heroes bereaved now of
An honest piece of nature, much-adored mother
Who never stinted on love, for whom and for
Whose offspring the world is melting in regret
Making the hardest, intractable
Heart quiver, sigh-shaken. So great a prop
Subverted, who can evade the force of death?
A sea of tears cannot snuff the unkind lightning.
Her prime turned out to be her peroration.

[206]

Wat helpt dan 't naar gekrijt ey Ailva staak het wenen
U waarde Gemalin, u Troost, u Morgen Son
Is neer gedaalt, zy heeft u Orisont beschenen,
Zy rust nu van haar loop: en slorpt de Nectar Bron
In 't Saalige Eden hof daar Hemel Aders vloeyen,
Die haar bekroonde Ziel met Nardus dau besproeyen.

Daar waar de Heylgerey der groote wonder schaar
De zeegesang verheft voor d'Opper Godt der Goden
Daar waar zy queelt op maat met Jesse Harpenaar:
En komen Duysenden met Englen keelen noden
Om voor Elschaddys Troon, en sijne Mayesteyt:
Te Looven Elohïm: in alle Eeuwigheyt.

♦♦♦

Graf-Dicht Op het overlijden van de hoog Edele Geb
Juffer MARIA ELISABETH Van MARCKELSBACH,
mijn waarde Vrindinne.

'K heb om het sterven van Mary
Helaas mijn oogen root gekreten:
Diens yd'le gaaf geen medely
Heeft koonen voen in haar Geweten.

Het koude Lijk heeft geen gehoor
Het blijft als Rotsen onbewogen,

En

Ailva, stop your weeping. That daystar is dead:
Sunk deep. She kindled your horizon, now rests
And drinks from nectareous wells in Eden.
Sweet veins of heaven deliver nard
To anoint her crowned and consecrated brows.
The blessed chorus, wingèd wonders, sings
Of triumph before the lofty God of gods
Where she warbles in measure meetly to Jesse's
Harp and throats in thousands hymn majestic
El-Shaddai at his throne for all eternity.

◆ ◆ ◆

Elegy on the death of the most noble Miss Maria
Elisabeth van Marckelsbach, my worthy friend*

I have wept my eyes red over the death of Mary
Whose integrity, whose nobleness
No grief, no expression of pity
Can affect any longer, to her knowledge.
Her cold body lacks capacity to listen.

* Aurora is mother of Phaethon. Ovid recounts how Phaethon's sisters wept tears of amber for their sibling – aetiology of that petrified resin. The rationale for associating van Marckelsbach with the ambitious charioteer is unclear, unless perhaps Brongersma studied *Metamorphoses* with her.

[207]

En of ik d'hemeldak doorboor
Of in den afgront waar getogen.

Niet helpter aan't verstijfde Rif,
Jaa schoon ik stremd' tot herde stenen
En slingde my gelijk het klif
Rontom de droeve Graf-baar henen.

Of als de Dochters van de Son
In Amberdropen waar gestollen,
Of in een bitt're waterbron,
Of hooge klippen opgeswollen.

Het is vergeefs, en al om niet,
Auroor heeft door haar bracke regen,
Haar zielkroost, die sy sneuv'len siet,
Nooyt naar haar wens weerom gekregen.

Dies gaa ik met dien Morgen-roos
Verbleeken, en des avonds deelen
Mijn Tranen dauw op kruyt, en bloos,
En eeuwig 't Lof haar's Deugden quelen.

◆ ◆ ◆

Lijk'

It remains as unmoved as rock though I wail
To crack the top of heaven or shatter
The abyss. She stays stiff and stony and I
Resolve into rock around her dismal bier.
Just as the daughters of the Sun distilled hard
Amber droplets, or as bitter water leaks
From a sterile cliff's parched face, it is
For nothing: just as Aurora shed salt rain
For her offspring whom she saw dying
Never again to be embraced, so I pass
Like morning's pink, and pass like dusk
Tears dewing flowers, chanting her virtue
Imperishable, which eternises my praise.

◆ ◆ ◆

## [208]

LYCK-TRANEN, Gestort over de Doodt van de Eer-bare
Deugdenrijke Juffrouw MARIA A TINGE, Huisvrouw van de
hoog-geleerde heer LUDOLF SMIDS, Medecijnen Doctor
binnen Groningen.

Ter Aarde bestelt den 8. Iul. 1672.

Mijn schagt leg af het kleed bepruijkt met pronkcieraden
Hang aan de wimpels van de droeve Lijk-gewaden
Wilt u in plaats van inkt met pekeldauw versaden
    Nu gy gedompelt siet

Maria 't waarste pant van Smids in donk're Mijnen
Wiens Deugde Son voor hem soo lieflijk plag te schijnen,
Maar die nu vrolijk queelt in 't Choor der Cherubijnen
    Een heylich Hemelliedt.

Wel aan dan waarde Heer sluyt toe de Tranesluysen,
En laat niet meer die stroom van d'oogeranden bruysen
Wiens doffe dampen doen vermaak, en moet verhuysen
    O! Phaenix, die Parnas
Hier als een vaste zuyl haar last koomt ondersteunen,
En op wiens schouders gy het groot Gebou laat leunen
Diens dapp're Veederslag den Helicon doet dreunen
    'k Vraag dan komt dit te pas?

                                        O neen

Funeral tears spilled over the death of the
honourable and virtuous Mrs Maria Tinge, wife
of the most learned Mr Ludolph Smids, Doctor of
Medicine at Groningen, laid to rest in Earth on
8 July 1682*

Pen, do not depict cloth dyed with glamorous motifs.
Hang banners rather of sad and sober make.
Dip yourself not in ink but in deep tears.
In dark times Maria was a surety
With amiable virtue shining like the sun,
A light to her husband – with cherubim now
Warbling a paradisal psalm so, decent man,
Close the sluices of your tears snugly,
Let the stream be checked at the brink of your lids
Even if to weep gives a commonplace pleasure.
Parnassus, dear phoenix, must assist
Like a sturdy pillar to support the burden,
Bearing the weight of a huge estate. Helicon
May rumble with the power of your quill

* Maria Tinge married Ludolph Smids (1649–1720) in February 1674. After her death, Smids married Anna de Groot. This second marriage occurred in 1684. Note that funerary urns emerge as a shared topic between Smids and Brongersma, when she investigates the *hunebed*.

[209]

O! neen de Bootbus hoort naa geen geween nog klagen
Gy moet Belauwert hooft: de nootlots wrange plagen
hoe swaar die zijn, voor licht, in ut gemoet verdragen.
   Hoewel het heeft sijn reên

Dat gy u helft betruyrt, die gy hadt uytgekoren
Met wien gy al de lust, en vreugde hebt verlooren
Doch dit, is Haar, en u, van d'opper Godt beschoren
   Daarom stelt u te vreên.

❖❖❖

LYK-KLAGT Over de Dood van de Deugtrijke Juffer, en Nicht
MARGARETA GRATEMA, Overleden binnen Groningen den 1686.

WAarom O! straffe Dood hebt gy u schigt gedreven
In 't hert van Margareet, en haar berooft van's leven,
Waarom u moortgeweer juyst op haar aan gestelt
Die gy gelijk een bloem ter neder hebt gevelt,
Wat kan 't u baten ah! vernielder aller Mensen
Gaa flits die boesems door die naar u pijlen wensen,
En die als afgeleeft het stervelingschap haat,
By veel komt gy te vroeg by vele weer te laat,
Doch gy zijt doof, en blindt van aanbegin geboren
Geen Tranen, noch gekerm koont gy noch sien noch horen,
O! Wreed'aart moest ge dan die Perel in het graf

            Bedel-

But the urn can hear neither weeping nor complaint.
Destiny's affliction however heavy
Has its reasons, wearer of earned laurels.
Mourn her who helped you, whom you adored,
With whom you have forfeited desire and
Contentment. Great God supports you, and her.
It is right therefore that you express your love.

♦ ♦ ♦

Lamentation over the death of my niece, the virtuous
Miss Margareta Gratema, who died in Groningen,
in 1686*

Why plunge a shaft into Margaret's heart
Driving the life right out of her? Assassin
Why did you pick her from among so many?
You slashed her like a flower from a stem.
What plea would make you lay aside your gun?
You kill everyone. So go spear bosoms
That crave your thrust: the wretched, the starving.
You come too early, you come too late, deaf
To moaning, blind to tears. Did you have to
Roll my pearl into the grave, quell her blush

---

\* Brongersma wrote a birthday poem for Margareta Gratema who must have died abruptly close to the time of *The Swan of the Well*'s publication.

[210]

Bedelven, en haar bloos, en luyster stropen af.
Moest gy dien maacht soo vast en sterk noch op haar benen
Vermorselen tot niet, en stooten voor de scheenen,
Om haar te domp'len in ons Aller moeder schoot,
Doch sal weer leven naar dees tijdelijke doodt
Wanneer de Troostbasuyn sal werden aangeslagen,
Want in den Hemel hoort men jammeren noch klagen
Maar blijde tonen slaan in volle vrolijkheyt,
Die haar voor't aartsche leet op't salighst is bereyt.

En daar sy't Heylich Liedt gesteldt om Godt te loven
Sal singen met de schaar der Engelen hier boven.

♦ ♦ ♦

LYK-KROON Gevlochten: op het haastigh, doch Godtsalich overlijden van de Hoog-waarde, en in Deugt uytblinckende JUFFROUW MARIA Van AMAMA. Gemalinne van de E. Heer JOHANNES JONGHBLOEDT.

Mijn Heer

Gedoog dat mijn Treur-Sangeres
Het Lijk, en dootbaar mag bestrengen
Met raaye rancken van Cypres
En haar geklag in d'uwe mengen

Wijl

And lustre? Did you have to trip her and send her
Headlong into our universal mother's lap?
I hear the bassoon of solace sounding, she lives
Again after transitory death.
Heaven hears neither grievance nor sorrow,
Blitheness alone resonates in bliss.
To the degree she suffered, she now is joyous.
Before her God she sings. Angels join her.

♦ ♦ ♦

An elegiac wreath woven for the premature though
blessed death of the most worthy and virtuous
Mrs Maria van Amama, spouse of the noble
Mr Johannes Jonghbloedt*

Please accept, my lord, the sprigs of stubborn,
Woven cypress the muse of sorrow braids

* Johannes Jongbloedt and
Maria van Amama had married on
22 March 1684.

[211]

Wijl dat de bits' en greetsche doot
U heeft van 't Liefste deel ontbloot.

Maria ah! met recht Mary
Die Deugde-baak, die schoone en waarde,
Dat pronk-beelt van u hert, en zy,
Wert nu geoffert aan de aarde
Die al wat eens ontlevent is
Bewaart in haar gevangenis.

Geen Scepter-swaayer hoe gekroont
Kan sulk een hert gewelt ontwringen,
Noch Herderdom wert ooyt verschoont
't Sijn altesaamen stervelingen,
En 't Schat waarom gy bloedich weent
Is U maar voor een tijdt geleent.

Zy gaat naar 't hooge Heldenschap,
Waar d'Engle schaar haar komt ontmoeten
Wijl gy noch aan de werelt trap.
In 't nietich puynstof legt te wroeten
En haar ijs koud, en dorren ass:
Bevochtigt met een traane plas.

Die Kronedraagter van U Ziel,
Die purpre Roos soo nieuws ontlooken,
Die in de Trouw haar trouwlijk hiel,

Die

Round the body and the bier, her lament
Mixed with yours, for bitter, avid Death
Has stripped you of your dearest part.
Virtue's beacon, pure, worthy, glorious
Idol of your widowed heart, Maria
Descends underground into Earth
Who keeps imprisoned all things inanimate.
No sceptre-wielder can disarm such power
Save the holy pastors whom God instructs,
Though even they are, at last, only mortals.
The treasure for whom you are weeping blood
Was loaned to you a brief – the briefest time.
She soars to join the lofty band of heroes,
The host of angels flies to greet their conscript.
Yet here on Earth you heavily tread you must
Blend the quick lime and use it on her flesh
Ice cold, barren, wet with coursing tears.
Your soul was set as a chaplet on her head.
She was fresh as a rose, and she believed.

[212]

Die Son: helaas! te vroeg gedooken,
Doch schoon sy is ter neer gedaalt
Zy d'hemel-kimmen weer bestraalt.

Souwt gy dan die'er heylich mint
Haar dat genot onttrekken konnen
Wijl zy daar al't gewenste vint,
En haar de Zalicheyt misgonnen?
O neen: 'k weet beeter, want u Hert
Heeft nooyt op weederwil gespert,

Wat helpt het of gy Bronnen weent
En door gekerm een Rots doet beeven?
Haar Rif is Hert, en als versteent
Ze kan u vraag geen antwoort geeven,
Daarom ai! maatig dan u druk
En stel u Troost in haar gelnk.

Zy die de Loop-baan heeft vol endt
Hoeft voor geen doot-schigt meer te gruwen
Zy smaakt het soet van haar Talent
En gaat haar Heyl: aan vreugde huwen,
Daar waar men Lof-Basuynen klingt
En 't Driemaal heylig Eeuwig singt.

Ik sluyt dan wyl mijn Sangerin
Met my Ontlost haar peekel kranen

Om

The sun plunges all too soon in darkness,
Yet, buried, she flashes across our horizon.
Ought jealousy now to afflict you since she
Whom you have loved devoutly prefers to
Earthly passion the bliss she finds? No – your
Heart understands, is soft and yielding.
Yet like a spring you weep, and shake the rocks
With grief. Her body stiffens flintily supplying
No answer to any question that you ask.
Impose measure. Believe in her felicity.
She has run her full career and does not
Shudder. Let untimely Death thrust away.
She elsewhere tastes the sweetness of her talent.
She prepares to wed her saviour where bassoons
Sound praises. A choir extols the trinity
Eternal. I see, therefore, as my muse
Decants her urns of brine (my friend, my country's

Om 't sterven van mijn Lants Vrindin
Die 'k mee bedolf in brakke tranen,
Dog 't is vergeefs 't besluyt getert:
Wijl 't nimmer meer verandert wert.

◆ ◆ ◆

LYK KLAGT Over de Doot van Mijn HEER J. de BRUYN,
Predicant binnen Doccum.

WEen nu en stort een beek van bracke dropen
Gy Sions kudde die op Doccum berg
U Zielens spijs by Bruyno plag te kopen
Waar door de geur van 't bladerrijke merg
Soo heerlijk scheen ten Hemel op getoogen
Dat selfs het All, door sijn Geheylgde schaar
Geen wegen heeft gebaant of kon door oogen
Het regte wit, O wondre Iveraar,
Die niet alleen de herderlijke pligten
Door 't hoeden van het sorg vuldig hieldt
Maar als een Son: de Aarde quam verligten
Van wiens vermoog nog al de werelt krielt,
Ag 't moedeloose volk vol klaag ellende
Is nu de Nek tot aan de gront gedrukt
Het roept, en krijt, O sondigbaare bende
Nu is de kroon ons van het hooft geruckt,

Friend being dead), how useless brackish
Woe presides, useless protests and blames
The end that can never again be mended.

♦ ♦ ♦

Eulogy over the body of J. de Bruyn, preacher at Dokkum*

Weep now, pour out a river of salty drops.
Zion's flock, you who on Dokkum's hill
Sought aliment for your hungry souls:
The leafy exhalation and odour of sap
So freshly lift toward heaven that God
Almighty has never tasted or seen this degree
Of candour, or of righteousness. O
Exemplary in your pastoral mission keeping
Watch on your charges attentively
As the sun warms, rising, and superintends
The globe fecundated, cherished, ach how
People go unnerved, Grief and Misery
Bow their necks, deplorable sin they see
Tear their crown from their heads for prostrate

* Dokkum was probably Brongersma's birthplace. In 716, the Wessex missionary Boniface, later sainted, travelled to Frisia, on a mission to convert the heathen. Locals martyred the saint near Dokkum in 756. The sixteenth-century visitor Cornelius Kempius records that the relics of the holy man at Dokkum included skull fragments, an ivory crook, a gold chalice, a chasuble, a cope, and a gospel in Boniface's own transcription. Protestants plundered the abbey at Dokkum in 1572; it was abolished a decade later; the relics vanished. Fulda may have spirited some of them in 1580 to the Cathedral of Fulda. By the end of the sixteenth century, the skull fragments, the cope, and the chasuble had made their way back to Dokkum. Brongersma's theme of sources and springs naturally prompts mention of Boniface and his well, still famous in her hometown.

[214]

Nu leyt dien Roem met Duysent waardigheden
(: Die op dit hoog veel planten heeft gestigt:)
In een Gedolven Mijn, wiens Engelreden
Nog naa sijn Doot vertoonen 't heldre ligt
Daar van getuygt de Priesterlijke drempel
Die 't ganse steunsel, en de lasten draagt
Van het gebouw der Godt gewyde Tempel
Die als een Suil van hem wier d'onder schraagt,
Of schoon de top van haar verheven Daken
Door groote storm te wreet wierd' aan geranst
Soo stelden hy een stut voor 't siddrig kraken
En flux waar het met Iver-sugt beschanst,
O gadeloose Beelt, al waar den hoeder
Hoe hebt gy opgewacht in kouw, en wint
V schapjes nu ontbloot, van heer, en voeder,
Doch meer van d'Oppervoogt, als hier bemint,
Want daar hy in het dal van Aartse volken
Als een Profeetsche slaaf staag heeft geslooft,
Daar rust hy by een Reex van Hemel tolken
En draagt de krans van Glory op het hooft,
Daar hy omringt van soo veel saal'ge Eng'len
't Haleluja verbreyt op Gootse trant,
En voor Elschaddays Throon, haar galmen meng'len
Daar riest sijn heyl in 't eeuwich Vaderlandt.
Weld an benauwde Vacht en droeve Lam'ren
Schoon Bonifaci Bron haar Golven bint

Door

Lies your splendor, your merits attending it,
A thousand (see: they foster shoots like themselves).
The crypt awaits: yet your seraphic words
Flutter splendidly, imparting good light
Whose counterpart, the sacrosanct threshold,
Bears great weight, and like a pillar, centres
And shoulders its enormous load. Let a
Brutal storm tear away at the lofty roof.
The prop, immune, would rebut the assault,
The very agitation strengthening the spire
Ambitious to endure: paragon
Nonpareil! Protector you kept guard
In the cold, in the wind, warden of sheep
Bereft now of their lord and food alike, for
Heaven's regent loves you even more
Than we did when you, our prophet, drudged
In our vale, interpreting for us the kingdom, up above.
You rest there, wear a crown of glory, angels
Numberless, delicious, crowd you
Singing hallelujah in the Gothic style
Where before El-Shaddai's throne echoes
Unite. Your salvation finds its fatherland.
But austere rites and grieving lambs! Such is
The lamentation, the bitter, intimate
Complaint drains the well of Boniface

Door't naar geluyt en't bitterlijke jam'ren
Gelooft da thy daar soeter stromen vindt,
Mits uyt dien Beek niet dan genaden vloeyen
Voor hem, en dien het ramp draagt met gedult,
Daar sal tot troost een nieuwe Ceder bloeyen,
Maar dit verlies is onser misdaadt schult.

◆ ◆ ◆

Op het Godtsalig overlijden van den Hoog Edele Gebooren Heer, mijn Heer ONNO TAMMINGA, In sijn leven heer van Luydema, en Dynasta, in Ulquert, &c.

DAa leyt dien Suyl dien steunpost van het lant.
Daar leyt de Deugt, en Wijsheyt t'saam geklonken,
Gesneuvelt en bedolven in het Sant
Die op de Throon der Raden placht te pronken.
Dien Vader, en beschutter van de staat
Die onverkreukt de Vree-banier deed' swaayen,
En 't Recht dat regt op vaste beenen gaat
Noyt door 't gewelt der Twistdraak liet verdrayen,
Maar die altoos door een gedweêgen aart,
D'onnoosle heeft rechthertigheyt geschonken
En Weeuw, en Wees, voor ondergank bewaart
Helaas! is nu ten gravewaart gesonken.
Doch schoon de Tomb bedekt het koude Lijk
Van Tamminga, diens onberisplijk leven

Hem

To its bottom. You, however, drink
Waters sweeter. Mercy flows for all
Who suffer defeat with patience. Solace will
Flourish as a cedar, in spite of all iniquity.

◆ ◆ ◆

On the blessed death of the most high-born
Onno Tamminga, in life Lord of Luydema and
Dynasta in Ulquert, etc.*

The pillar and mainstay of the land, in whom
Virtue and Wisdom coincide and chime, lies
Slain and buried in the sand, adorner, once,
By his attendance, of the throne of counsel.
That father and defender of the state
Unbowed bore, waved our standard, and Justice
So often hampered on hobbled legs he
Never left to the vile distortions of
The destructive serpent's instinctive cruelty.
He dispensed his righteousness to innocence,
He kept the widow and the orphan from
Going under, but has sunk now, himself,
Low as the grave: alas. Yet though the tomb
Shuts away Tamminga's frigid body

\* Possibly Brongersma's Onno Tamminga died in October 1674. This man, promoted captain in 1667, fell in the successful siege of Grave, in North Brabant. Henri de la Tour d'Auvergne, vicomte de Turenne, had seized Grave on 14 July 1672; the Dutch retook the city on 16 October. Ambiguities in Brongersma's poem imply that it may commemorate the reinterment of Tamminga's remains, in a tomb already occupied by his spouse. The date of Tamminga's death is otherwise rather early for Brongersma to undertake an elegy for him. The record does testify to a surprising number of men bearing that name – many of them apparently descendants of the first of the line.

[216]

Hem door de Dood voert in het Eng'len Rijk
Soo koomt hy noch de Heylberg op te striven
Daar hy sijn Helft dat kostele Juweel
Elisabeth, hem in't gesicht ontdragen
Gaat vinden, daar hy wint sijn Erref-deel,
En nimmer reên sal hebben om te klagen,
Wat hert souw niet al waar 't van herde steen
Door Rouw verweeken om dit droevig sterven
Daar zy veel meerder dan dit aarts beneên
In't hooge Heyligdom sullen beërven.
Nochtans waar dat soo'n vasten pijlaar breekt
Waarop de hooftstof rust en staat te brallen
Daar is't geen wonder dat elkx ooge leekt
Want een gebouw moet sonder grontvest vallen,
Wel aan dan ween, en stort een tranen vloet
Besproey de Zerk wiens swaarte hout beslooten
· Twee die maar een geweest zijn in't gemoet
Doch in dees enge Mijn het grootst vergrooten
Daar zy gepaart (schoon haar de greetse Dood)
Gerukt heeft uyt des werdelds ijsre banden,
Noch sullen zijn malkanders zijd'genoot
Wijl 't graf bewaart dees Hoog-gebooren panden,
't Is dan genoech doch wense eer ik sluyt
Dat gy U Rouw Doorlugt'ge Adellooten
Wilt matigen, Sy treden vooren uyt,
En wachten U by Saalge Huysgenooten
Om weer op nieuw haar naagellaten kroost
Te sien bepruykt met Goodse Lauwerkronen
Daar gy tot haar en uwer zielen troost
Sult Eeuwich by malkander blijven wonen.

♦ ♦ ♦

LYK-

That life to which none could take exception
Lifts his soul past death into the kingdom
Of angels, and he mounts the strenuous holy
Zion's slope. The jewel from him long stolen,
Elizabeth, assists her man. To see
Face to face he longs, and he would win
His share of his estate, never having reason
To grieve again. What heart though coldest stone
Would not waken deathly sorrow at his
Passing, even when he far more than
On earth below in heaven's height inherits.
Did such a column ever break on which
Weighed such a splendid superstructure?
No wonder every eye is oozing sadness.
A building without its basis must collapse.
Weep then floods of tears. They splash and run
On a monument whose black wood encloses
Two who had a single mind between them.
In this crypt the greatest grow still greater
For made a couple after former parting
They burst the iron shackles of this world
Remaining spouses here too for the grave
Conserves their noble promise. Therefore woeful
Nobles, illustrious, woeful nobles
Suspend your lament, resign yourself and
Keep your vigil with your blessed families.
You will see afresh your relatives
Graced with God's laurels and to their
And your own consolation will abide
Dwelling by one another eternally.

◆ ◆ ◆

## [217]

LYCK KROON Gestrengelt Over het afsterven van den Hoog
Geleerden heer THEODORUS ALMA UCHTMAN, Griekx en
Latijns puyck Poët binnen Groningen.

GY hebt dan strenge Doodt op uwe Wagen
    Heer Uchtman wech gedragen,
Wiens Ris, in't Graf, ter neder is geleyt
Terwijl sijn ziel vliegt naar d'onsterflijkeheyt.

Dorst gy die Bye (die soo veel Hoonichraten
    De werelt heeft gelaten)
Vernielen, en waar uyt een Zeembron vloot
Die langs den Gangus in den Tages schoot.

Daar, Hy uyt soo veel keur van geurge blaren
    Het Heyl-sap gink vergaren
Waar mee hy't blakens hert, hoe krank het was
Gelijk een Peon van'er quaal genas.

Die dreef, door swerken been op dunne wieken
    In het beroemde Grieken,
Daar Hy de Riem: aan Amaranthis schonk
Waar op het Beelt van sijn Christina blonk

                                                              Met

A wreath placed in memory of the most learned
Mr Theodorus Alma Uchtman, Greek and Latin poet
resident in Groningen*

So, dull Death, have you dragged off Uchtman in your hearse,
His mortal remains impounded in your grave
While his soul wings away invincible, immortal?
Would you crush the bee that fashioned honeycombs
Dripping thickly as Ganges's wells, as those of Tagus?
See the choice he makes of fragrant petals, of balms
To heal the heart however wasted blossoming
Stout as peonies. His thoughtful humming soothes.
He soars in circles on slender wings, joining Greeks.
Undying amaranth rewards his talent, and at its centre
Blazes the picture of Christina, with her retinue of roses.

* The protector of the Latin school at Groningen was one Uchtmannus who, in 1663, brought out *Carminum Virgilianorum Supplementa* (*A Supplement to the Works of Vergil*). His wife was probably the Christina mentioned here; it is characteristic of Brongersma to remember and to emphasize spouses.

[218]

Met Rosen, om gepruykt, diens Bloemvergaring
     Hy brachte in Bewaring
Van sijn doorbreynt gewelf, en in wiens mont
Men het Orakel der Latijnen vont.

Daar Hy het Ionglingschap, door deede spijsen
     Soo veel als d'oude Grijsen,
Hy leest dan (schoon u Zickel hem ontzielt)
In 't Salig veldt daar het van schimmen krielt.

Alwaar Hy door een snelle drift gedreven
     Gaat door de wolken sweven,
Soo siet men Alma dan ten Hemel gaan,
En door sijn Doot, herleven met de Swaan.

Men hoeft geen tranen op sijn Lijk te plengen
     Maear wilt een Lof telg brengen
Voor Hem geplukt uyt Napels LauwerMijn,
Wijl Hy voor Gruno moet een Maro sijn.

♦ ♦ ♦

Graf-schrift,

Hier leyt in 't Graf gevelt
Alma dien Letter-helt,
Die door sijn puyk Gesangen
Den hemel deed' verlangen:
Waar hy die nestens Son, en Maan,
Onsterflijk sal te blinken staan.

♦ ♦ ♦

Eynde der Truyr-gesangen

                                                    Aan

He collects and he curates in safety all the flowers
In his spiritual museum, his mouth professes
Oracles in behalf of Latium. His youth he nourished
There, and in Hellas, and your sickle missed him.
In thronged Elysium he thrives befriended.

♦ ♦ ♦

Epitaph*

Here lies fallen in the grave
Alma, hero of letters who
Lofted by the glory of his songs
Touched the sky in which he will
With sun and moon glitter on
Immortally in his station.

♦ ♦ ♦

End of Elegies

* This epitaph is evidently meant for the same Uchtmannus as in the elegy above.

[219]

Aan de Hoog-Geëerde Juffer Meejuffer SUSANNA WILMSONN, haar Ed: opdragende de Bruylofs Gedigten, met de Omgeefsels, in't besonder.

IK offer dan dees rijmeloose Sangen
Aan u die my daar toe soo vast verbindt
Door d'Eer die ik heb van u deugt ontfangen
Dat sig mijn hert daar in begraven vindt.
Daar siet ge dan mijn Swaan voor windt af drijven,
En swabbren op het nat van Grunoos Bron
Daar het sijn dienst aanbiet, en wenst te blijven
In het geheugen van haar Willemsonn.
Het Beestje swiert op kronkelende baren
Om metter haast u Oever te betreen,
Het komt met vlijt op't roey-tuyg aangevaren,
En streeft voor by den Helsen giftbeek heen,
Waar het een Bruylofts-Liedt komt op te singen
Voor d'Nimfe-schaar uyt lust en vrolijkheyt,
Waar het sijn tonen doet door wolken dringen
Daar't heeft alree sijn wieken uyt gespreyt
Om met Eerbied de wonderen te quelen
Van dien: die't Swaantje gaan haar gonsten delen.

♦ ♦ ♦

BRVY-

Dedication to the very honourable Miss Susanna
Wilmson of my epithalamia and riddles in particular*

I offer then this immethodical song
To you, dear, who are so intimate by virtue
Of that virtue you have graven in my heart.
Look and see my Swan fly before the wind,
Paddle in the gush of Groningen's splashing spring
Where she offers her service and wishes to remain
Loyal to her ideal – to her friend, Wilmson.
Riffling the surface, making eddies and a wake,
She hurries to reach and clamber up your bankside
Plying webfeet briskly as rowers at the oar
Passing fast the tributary stream to sing a song
With the choir of nymphs ardent and elated
In tones to pierce the clouds, the theme your wedding,
Where she spreads her wings as wide as possible
To warble with the chorus musing upon marriage –
Your marriage: for which she would supplicate all favour.

◆ ◆ ◆

* Brongersma treats Susanna Wilmson in two earlier poems in *The Swan of the Well*. One epigram flatters her as a consummate blossom, while thanking her for the gift of some flowers. The other, addressing her with the Vergilian-bucolic pseudonym "Amaryllis," praises her agility in climbing Parnassus. This friend possesses the literary capability to act as an editor.

[220]

Bruylofts-gesangen. Ter Bruyloft Van de E. seer geaghte HEER Mijn HEER. JACOBUS GROOTHUYS als BRUYDEGOM. En den Hoog begaafde en Deugden rijke JUFFER Mee JUFFER, SUSANNA van WILMSONN als BRUYT.

WIe helpt me nu een Throon van Bloemen vlegten
Of een festoon van 't alder geurigst' Cruyt,
Om in de Bruylofft zaal die op te regten
Tot pronksel van de Bruydegom, en Bruyt.

Wijl Wilmsonn heeft, door smekende gebeden
Haar Hert, (: dat ijsig kout te vooren Scheen:)
Door Groothuys Tover-taal, doen overreden
Waar mee al 't leet ten eene maal verdween.

Nu Dafne heeft haar Lauweren geschonken
Aan febus, die niet meer van pijnen klaagt
En hem begloort met kuyse Ooge lonken
Wanneer hy haar om weder Liefde vraagt.

Gy

A song for the marriage of the noble and most
honourable Mr Jacobus Groothuys and the talented
as virtuous Miss Susanna Wilmson*

How would I furnish the wedding chamber best?
I might wreathe their chair in flowers, or festoon
The sweetest-smelling plants in swags on high
To reward with ornament the groom and bride.
For Wilmson's heart, once icy and unmoved,
Melted at Groothuys's eloquent enchantment.
Her numbness and his pain both vanished in a flash.
Daphne has tendered her laurel to her Phoebus
And she complains no longer of her loss.
Her look, though modest, allures and admires
When he inquires, "Do you feel the noble passion?"

* Brongersma appears untroubled here that the union of Venus with Mars was adulterous in nature. This sensuous epithalamium marks the marriage of Jacob Groothuys, an infantry lieutenant, with Susanna Wilmson; regimental records attest that the ceremony happened on 12 January 1684.

[221]

Gy nimfies die beroemt in aardigheden
U hout altoos ten voordeel op geciert
Coom wilt met my de feest vloer over treden
Waar men de Sitplaats van de Bruyt beswiert.

Schoon d'aard' die nu beschorst leyt, en bevrosen:
(Dat puyk Beelt, vol van Deugt en, held're glans)
Niet kan beschenken met een Reex van Rosen
Soo strik haar dan van Maagdepalm, een Crans:

Pluk Mirthe Blaan, bepruyk haar bruyne Lokken
Hegt op'er-kruyn, het Lieflijk winter groen
Schoon Boreas u dreygt met kille vlokken
Wilt daarom evenwel u pligt voldoen.

En aan den longe Mars, sijn Venus schenken,
Wanneer hy eyst dat uytgelesen pant
Die hem doet in haar zede stroomen drenken
Wijl hy, tot haar, in Reyne liefde Brant.

Die hem de Borst doet als een Etna blaken
Als hy een Kussie van haar Rosemont
Af lept, en wenst wel duysent te ontschaken
Soo maar dat willen, in haar wil, bestont.

Ick sal terwijl haar wensen Heyl, en Zegen
Met vreede op gevult, en dat voortaan
Een Nectar vloet haat beyde over Reegen,
En dat haar Echte Bant nooyt werd' ontdaan.

❖❖❖

BRUY-

Slender nymphs famous for good nature
Who, lovely, lucky, make your woods the same,
Come tread with me the festive, hymeneal floor,
Winding our way around the bride's own seat.
Though the earth is in suspense, all frozen,
And roses nicely ranged cannot be got,
Decorate the lady with a virgin's palmy
Crown: pluck myrtle adorning her brown curls
With a garland of winter greens. Boreas
Spangles you with chilly snowflakes, too,
And consummates duly his duty to you.
His Venus yields herself to her tall Mars
Whenever he eyes this exquisite pledge of his
To drink licitly of her natural goodness
Who would have him slake himself at her source:
For he burns for her, and parches in pure desire.
Her high breast blazes like glowing Aetna as
He gets a red kiss from her red lips.
Thousands he would take, many thousands
Provided she concurred in every one of them.
Health, prosperity, I wish the couple
Brim with joy: and may their nectar flow
Bathing them always, and their bond last long.

♦ ♦ ♦

[222]

BRUYLOFTS-LIEDT Uytgeschatert ter Eeren van den hoogh Eedele en Eerenfesten Heer mijn Heer GYSBERT MATHIAS KRIEX En de Hoogh-Eedele gebooren, en Zedenrijke Juffer Me-juffer, MARGARETA D' MEPSCHE Vereenicht in de houwelijken staat den 23. Sept. 1684.

Toon: Ma chere Liberte.

WAt dach glans schijnt soo klaar in mijn verdooft Gesigt?
Wat ugtent roos ontluykt soo schoon in't vroege krieken?
  't Is een lust de Perelbloem te rieken.
Wat Dag-glans schijnt soo klaar in mijn verdooft gesigt?
  Ag! t'is Margreta die dus ligt.
't Is Cyprus die haar heeft in't Parlemoer geklonken,
Waar Pafos Heerscherin haar blonde scheedel kroont.
Het is De Mepsche die door 't stralen van'er lonken
  Dien braven Kriex een gouden Son vertoont.
Wat dagh glans schijnt soo klaar in mijn verdooft gesight?
  Ah! 't is Margreta de dus light.

Wel

A merry song for the wedding of the most noble
and admirable Sir Gysbert Mathias Kriex and the
high-born, astute, and virtuous Miss Margareta
D'Mepsche, joined in matrimony on the twenty-third
of September 1684*


Air: "*Ma chère liberté*"

The light of day blushes on my dumbstruck face.
What frank true rose unfolds at crack of dawn?
I would inhale that pearl of flowers' perfume.
The light of day blushes on my dumbstruck face.
Ach, it is Margaret who glows so clear.
The Cyprian goddess (she of her pearly shell),
The Paphian lady, crowns her bright blondeness:
D'Mepsche shines, to light up gallant Kriex.
The light of day blushes on my dumbstruck face.
Ach, it is Margaret who glows so clear.

* Note that Brongersma puns in her Dutch. The family name "Kriex" sounds like *krieken*. That word means "dawn," or "matutinal splendour." The governing conceit of the epithalamium is that Margareta especially suits Kriex, because she resembles Aurora, the Dawn: her blonde radiance anticipates her destined husband's own name. I have attempted faintly to honour Brongersma's pun with the phrase "crack of dawn." Margaretha de Mepsche (1668–1736) married Gijsbert Mattheus Criex. The husband died in 1685; their son bore his identical name. The de Mepsches are a noble dynasty or *jonkergeslecht*, attested as far back as the thirteenth century in the vicinity of Groningen. The wedding ceremony actually occurred on 6 September 1684.

[223]

Wel aan dan Nimphe-Rey bekrans dit blijde paar,
Wijl 't Goden-dom bepronckt haar brede Dans-zaletten,
En de faam dees Feest komt uyt trompetten,
 Wel aan dan Nimphe-Rey bekrans dit blijde paar,
Vleght Mirth en Tijm-loof door malkaar,
Singh vry ten boesem uyt met hooge Hemel klancken,
 Slaa lieflijk u geluyt tot door de dunne lught,
En wens haar Twee, dat sy (dien Aadelijke Ranken)
 Staagh sijn in vree, en nooyt in droef gesugt,
Wel aan dan Mimphe Rey bekrans dit blijde paar,
 Vleght Mirth, en Tijm-loof door malkaar.

En ik (dewijl dat ghy u Bruylofft-dagen Eert,)
Sal schoon mijn Dicht-veer heeft, u mee door plight bekroonen,
 Doch versoek mijn vryheyt te verschoonen,
En ik: (dewijl dat gy u Bruylofts-dagen Eert)
Gun u het geen u Ziel begeert.
 Maar eer mijn schagt beswijkt, en Eerse u geleyden
 Waar Hymen heeft bereydt het Echtlijk Ledicant
Soo wens ik nog voor 't laast de Heyl-rust voor u beyden
 En dat ge staag in kuysche Liefde brant.
En ik (dewijl dat gy u Bruylofts dagen Eert:)
 Gun u het geen u Ziel begeert.

◆ ◆ ◆

Eynde der Bruylofts-Gedichten.

Verta-

Then, nymph chorus, garland the happy pair.
The entire pantheon flatters them, attending.
Trumpets blare the glamour of the dance hall.
Then, nymph chorus, garland the happy pair.
Weave the myrtle with aromatic thyme.
Sing while day wanes with all your lungs the joy.
Wish they may in their nobility never
Heave a troubled sigh as they dwell content.
Weave the myrtle with aromatic thyme.
Even I, since you celebrate your wedding day,
Dip my quill to adorn you as duty directs
Extenuating my licence with the excuse
I would grant you your souls' twined desire.

♦ ♦ ♦

End of Epithalamia

[224]

Vetalingen: Uyt de France Enigmes.

Toon: Doux habitans des ces bois.

SOete woning van het veldt,
Daar't geluyt der wederklangen
Op U tonen zijn gestelt,
Wijl ge antwoort op mijn sangen,
Rotsen, pluym-gediert' wat raat?
Ah! wy spreeken ons verlangen,
't Geen mijn Philis niet verstaat.

◆◆◆

Een ander

Toon: L'aimable Florae.

DE schoone Flora treedt weer in
't Gespeel, de wintjes, en de Min
Verkondigen het soet van d'aangename tijden,
De Lente herst in dit saisoen:
Maar ah! wat sal u Tirsis doen
Philis? die gy nooyt wilt verblijden.

◆◆◆

EEN ANDER

Toon: Rossignol que pretende vous.

SEg, wat versoekt gy Nachtegaal
Door u betoverende Taal,

Wat

Translations of French *Énigmes**

Air: "*Doux habitants de ces bois*"†

Sweet meadowland, a home
Where echoes await all sound –
Rocks, feathery flocks, would you
Requite my song with a sensible
Answer consonant to my call?
We confess, like you, our yearning:
Which Philis does not grasp at all.

♦ ♦ ♦

Air: "*L'aimable Flore est de retour*"‡

Bright Flora treads her measures,
Little breezes and Love together
Usher the advent of the sweet and
Comfortable season. Spring has
Sway but Philis what will Thyrsis do
Whom you deprive of bliss?

♦ ♦ ♦

Air: "*Rossignol, que prétendez-vous*"**

Tell me nightingale with your enchanting speech
What do you lack that you could desire

---

* Brongersma adapts these lyrics, sometimes with extreme latitude, into Dutch. They do not conform to the protocol of "enigmas" in any recognizable way – though Brongersma does omit the identity of their creators, a puzzle in itself.

† The air, credited to La Tour, appeared in the periodical *Le nouveau Mercure galant* (February 1678); its title means "Sweet inhabitants of these woods."

‡ One Mlle Sicard wrote this air. It appeared in *Le nouveau Mercure galant* (January 1678). Its title means "Loveable Flora has come back."

** François Martin wrote this air. It appeared in *Le nouveau Mercure galant* (April 1678). Its title means "Nightingale, what are you feigning?"

[225]

Wat koont ghy doch voor u begeren, en doen vragen,
Soo gy in liefde vlammen blaakt,
Gy hebt geen reden om te klagen,
En 't is voor my onnut, ik heb nooyt min gesmaakt.

♦ ♦ ♦

EEN ANDER

Toon: Agreable Ruisseaux.

Aanminnige water val, en gy bekruynt geboomt'
Houw op van my te noôn op u bekoorlijkheden,
Elisa is hier niet, schoon gy O beekje stroomt,
Hoe lang, ah! seg het my is het nu wel geleden
Dat ik ging dwalen in u Lommerige groen?
Dog 't waar om mijn getraan, en sugten te bedecken,
Helaas, soo haar gesigt u kon tot min verwecken,
Wat souwt gy my dan wel veel diensten doen.

♦ ♦ ♦

EEN ANDER

Toon: Amour Cruel Amour.

LAat my in rust O! Min, weg wreede ik scheld V quijt
Ontstel niet meer het soet van mijn gewenste dagen
'k Wil om geen Silvia meer klagen.
Laat my in rust O! min, weg wreede ik scheld u quijt,
'k Sal al de quelling, en verdrieten van my jagen,
Te minnen: zijn versotte plagen,
't Is my alleens, 'k heb lang genoeg gevrijt
Laat my in rust O! min, weg wreede ik scheld u quijt.

♦ ♦ ♦

Een

Igniting you with amorous fire?
You have no reason to complain whereas I
Live in vain. I have never tasted love.

♦ ♦ ♦

Air: "*Agréable ruisseaux et vous sombres forêts*"\*

Charming waterfall, trees with lofty tops
Exquisite though you are I renounce
Your invitation. The current races purely
But Elisa is gone, now tell me
How long ago did I first settle down
To camp in your green shade? It was
Only to hide my sighs, my tears.
Awaken me then to remembrance
Of her look. That service do me, at least.

♦ ♦ ♦

Air: "*Amour, cruel Amour! laisse finir mes larmes*"†

Leave me in peace, Love. Cruel! Quit my side and stop
Embittering the sweetness of my desirous days.
Then I would not moan after Silvia, or her like.
Leave me in peace, Love. Cruel! Quit my side
    and stop.
I will chase away all oppression's pleasing torments
For I am alone with lust and thoughts of touching.
Leave me in peace, Love. Cruel! Quit my side
    and stop.

♦ ♦ ♦

\* Jean Lafontaine wrote this air. It appeared in *Le nouveau Mercure galant* (July 1678). Its title means "You sweet streams and sombre forests." Brongersma introduces her favourite character, Elise, into Lafontaine's lyrics.

† After 1640, Sébastien le Camus, the author of this piece of music ("Love, cruel love, give me a chance to stop crying"), composed songs for Louis XIII.

Een ander

Toon: Le Soleil sur nos.

DE Son in dit gewest te lang haar woning hiel,
Verdroogde al't gebloemt' en bragt tot as dees streken,
Deed' quijnen kruyt, en gras, verdorde Bron, en Beken
Maar tegen wil van die mijn Ziel
Ontsteken heeft, en Somer-ligten,
De winter woont in't hert van die mijn vlam doet stigten.

♦ ♦ ♦

Een ander

Toon: Que vostre sort est doux.

GElukkig is u lot, O! Roosje vers ontsloten
Een minnend' hert meest naa u geur, en schoonheyt dorst
Gy wast by Flora, en schiet loten:
Maar sterft weer om op Philis borst.

♦ ♦ ♦

Een ander

Toon: Le printemp m'offre.

DE Lente offert my vergeefs haar wout cieraat,
'k Sie nimmer weer het schoon dat in dees bossen staat
Want Tirsis my helaas! soo vaak heeft doen verhaal
In U belommering van sijn te lang gevry
Maar ah! d'ontrouwe weet niet meer van pijn, of quaal,
Soo is der dan geen Lent', nog liefde, meer voor my.

♦ ♦ ♦

Een

Air: "*Le soleil sur nos champs trop longtemps arrêté*"\*

The sun in this province too long his sojourn keeps.
He desiccates the blossoms and makes a carcass
Of the country. Stream bed dries, and weed withers,
The grass shrivels, and my heart kindles
Against the will of her who has inflamed
That organ, my summer blaze: but winter
Lives intact, tyrannizes in her breast.

◆ ◆ ◆

Air: "*Que votre sort est doux*"†

Fortunate your lot
Little rose newly
Blown: A loving heart
Feeds on your odour,
Drinks your beauty. You
Grow alongside Flora
And bend from the stem that's cut,
Dying a second time
Settled on Philis's breast.

◆ ◆ ◆

Air: "*Le printemps m'offre en vain ses innocents plaisirs*"‡

For nothing Spring shines in woodland glory.
I will never see again the beauty who tenants the
    forest
Where Thyrsis used to tell under your shades
Extended stories of his lovemaking.
But ah! the infidel knows no pain or torment,
So neither spring is – nor affection – for me.

◆ ◆ ◆

\* This air appeared in *Le nouveau Mercure galant* (July 1678). Its title means "The sun on our fields too long tarrying."

† Brongersma quotes the second line of a chorus from Marc-Antoine Charpentier's *Actéon* (1684). A chorus of nymphs sings, beginning with the verse "*Charmante fontaine.*" The title means "How sweet is your lot."

‡ M. Marcelle composed this piece ("Spring offers me in vain its innocent delights") dating from 1679.

[227]

Een ander

Toon: Anfin de nos Bergere.

DE Velden digt besaayt, en overvloerdt
Met duysendt geurige, en schoone bloemen,
Daar 't quelend' Pluygedierte van gaat roemen,
En't Herderdom op nieuw met haar gesang beroert,
Maar de Natuyr vergeefs te lachend' wil me streelen:
Vertoont al het vermaak waar door sy my verblijt,
Mijn Philis maakt 't is Ernst, of speelen,
Mijn Winter, of mijn Lente tijdt.

✦✦✦

Toon: Pour quoy venir troubler.

WAarom O! min ontstelt gy dog mijn rustig leven,
Ik ben voor U, en voor u pijlen onvervaart,
En tegen u gewelt bewaart,
'k Heb al mijn smerten weg gedreven,
Dog 'k waar betovert, dat mijn lijden heeft gebaart,
Waarom O! min onstelt gy dog mijn rustig leven,
Ik ben voor u, en voor u pijlen onvervaart.

✦✦✦

Toon: Lors que je pence a la peine.

ALs ik gedenke aan de pijnen
Die ik lijde nacht, en dach,
Soo souw'k u haten Rosalijne,
Maar om dat quaat te doen schijnen
Helaas! mijn hert
Helaas! mijn hert sulks niet vermach.

✦✦✦

Toon,

Air: "*Ainsi la jeune bergère / Et son berger chaque jour*"\*

Meadows densely sown and carpeted
With flowery thousands pure and fragrant,
Feathered creatures whistling total praise,
Shepherds for their part piping music –
Nature herself would tickle me to laughter,
Displaying a lap of pleasures and delights.
But Philis alone determines whether
All is grave, or all is play,
June or November.

◆ ◆ ◆

Air: "*Pourquoi venir troubler le repos de ma vie*"

Why, Love, derange my peaceful life?
I do not fear you or your shafts.
Defending against your violence
I have purged all my discomfort
Yet I was ravished by what
My pain brought forth.

◆ ◆ ◆

Air: "*Lorsque je pense à la peine*"†

When I think of the ache
I suffer day and night.
Dear Rosaline,
I would hate you.
But a feeling so evil
Alas, my heart –
Alas, my heart can't feel it
Dear Rosaline.

◆ ◆ ◆

\* This air dates from 1672. Its title means "So every day the young shepherdess and young shepherd."

† This air's title means "When I think of the ache."

THE SWAN OF THE WELL ◆ 503

Toon, Ombre de mon amant.

O! Schaduw van mijn lief, beklagelijke lommer.
Helaas! wat wilt ge dog, ik sterf,
Toeft, vliet niet wijl 'k om u bekommer
O! doodelijk verblijf nu ik u by zijn derf,
't Is op de soom van dese stromen
Dat ik u lauwe bloedt sag woen in mijn getraan.
Niet kan mijn vlugt'ge ziel in dese rouw betomen,
'k Swijg dan, en sie mijn onluk aan,
O! schaduw van mijn lief, beklagelijke lommer,
Helaas! wat wilt ge doch, ik sterf.

◆ ◆ ◆

Toon, que sert a mon amour.

WAt baat mijn Liefde nu de Lente wert herboren,
Wat helpt, dat nu het wout brengt bloem, en kruyt te vooren
Nu sy me mijd, en vliedt, 'k sie meer die doen beklag
Maar Iris is te wreet in 't pijnen,
Soo vaak als ik Haar vind doet sy me deerlijk quijnen,
Daar 's dan voor my nooyt somerdag.

◆ ◆ ◆

Toon, Ah! que l'hijver.

O! strenge Winter vol verdriet
Sal ons u woede langer plagen?
Koom Flora, koom, wie kan 't verdragen,
Gy hebt nu alles in 't gebiedt,
Breng mee die schoone, die veragt mijn droevich klagen,
Vergeet gelag, nog speeltjes niet,

O stren-

Air: "*Ombre de mon amant, ombre toujours plaintive*"\*

Shade of my beloved, mournful spectre,
What more do you want? I die, I wait,
I do not fly for I am flustered by you,
Fatally tarry for your sake
Lacking you, lamenting you
Here on the stream bank cursing
Your unimpassioned blood. Nothing
Can still my soul's wavering misery
Though my misfortune silences me.
Shade of my beloved, mournful spectre,
What more do you want? I die, I wait.

❖ ❖ ❖

Air: "*Que sert à mon amour que le printemps renaisse*"†

Ah! what does my love ask, now the spring returns?
Herbs emerge, the trees blossom, neither assists.
She avoids me, she flees, others too
Lament Iris excessively cruel
Who treats me bestially
Making winter of my balmy days.

❖ ❖ ❖

Air: "*Ah! que l'hiver est ennuyeux*"‡

Winter severe, oppressive,
How long will you rage?
Come Flora, come: I cannot bear it.
You know the country yields to you.
Bring me the pure despiser of my pleas.

\* Michel Lambert (1610–1696) is responsible for this Baroque aria. Its title means "Shade of my beloved, shade always doleful."

† *Le nouveau Mercure galant* published this air. Its title means "What fate for my love, now the spring returns?"

‡ Le Redde and Noël collaborated on this 1679 piece.

[229]

O! strenge winter vol verdriet,
't Gebloemte verbergt sig wijl het nog geen knopjes schiet,
Maar met u wederkomst sal alle vreugt opdagen.

♦♦♦

Toon, Lors que j'estois aimé.

WAnneer ik waar gelieft van d'Herderin Dorinde
Door u O! Moesel, wiens geluyt sy meer beminde
Als al mijn vleyery, wat smaakten ik al soet,
Maar nu se is, Helaas! verandert van gemoet
Nu koont gy my niet meer in al mijn Lijden
(Schoon ik m'aan u beklaag) verligten, nog verblijden.

♦♦♦

Toon, Ah! que je suis d'inquietude.

AH! dat ik voel d'onrustigheden,
Een een beweging die me nimmer waar bekent
O! soet en stil vermaak, waar zijt gy nu gebleven
Ik soek vergeefs, ('k weet niet wat reden)
De eensaamheyt, hoe komt het dat ik ween, en dut,
En 't hooft met handen onderstut,
En poog de bitterheyt door groot gewelt te breken,
Maar al om niet, 'k ben nooyt vernoegt in wat ik doe,
O! wrede min 'k staa u om my te straffen toe
'k Heb u versmaat, dies zijt gy schuldig u te wreken.

♦♦♦

Toon, je ne vien plus.

NEen, neen ik koom niet meer in 't woudt
Om u O! Nagtegaal (die sig hier staag verhout)

Om

Don't forget our laughter, our little games.
Winter severe, oppressive,
Not a bud grows plump, petals hide.
Flora will fatten buds, peel flowers.

◆ ◆ ◆

Air: "*Lorsque j'étais aimé par la jeune Lisette*"\*

So long as Dorinde the shepherdess loved me,
She loved you, too, dear bagpipe
Whose strains she loved more even
Than my praise. Alas! Her mind is changed.
And as for you, though I make my complaint,
You cannot lighten it, or gladden me.

◆ ◆ ◆

Air: "*Ah! que je sens d'inquiétude*"†

Ah, restlessness imparts a feeling to me
Never before known. O tranquil pleasures,
Where are you now abiding? I look in vain.
Why is it like this? Why? Why do I cry,
Rest my head on my hands, burst
With a bitter violence? No good, never
Enough. Cruel love, do you punish me?
Have I scorned you? You are guilty – you.

◆ ◆ ◆

Air: "*Je ne viens plus dans ces deserts / Inviter les oiseaux à faire des concerts*"‡

No, I visit no more the woods,
O nightingale, your retreat,

---

\* *Le nouveau Mercure galant* published this air in 1678. Its title means "When I was loved by the young Lisette." Gouët scored this piece for three voices.

† Antoinette du Ligier de la Garde, called Mme Deshoulières, wrote the lyrics to "Ah! how uneasy I feel," which were set to music by La Tour.

‡ The author is Sébastien de Brossard (1655–1730); the piece appeared in *Le nouveau Mercure galant* (August 1678). Its title means "I no longer go into the wilderness to solicit music from the birds."

Om Sang-strijdt uyt te noden,
Ik soek de stilheyt, en ben al 't gewoel ontvloden
Ag! ag! soo gy maar wist de quelling die ik ly
Bekruint geboom' ik weet u eensaamheden,
Die lieten willig toe: om 't geen ik heb geleden
Dat gy het ziel verdriet bedekten slegs van my.

♦ ♦ ♦

Toon, Vous de mandez.

GY vraagt waarom ik schuw u Son gelijke ogen
Ey! laat dog het verwond'ren staan,
Gy hebt veel schoonheyt, en mijn hert te haast bewogen
Verseng-de sig wel ligt daar aan.

♦ ♦ ♦

Toon, O! mort funeste mort.

O! Doot, koom eyndig dog dit mijn beweenlijk leven,
Mijn mede Minnares wert boven my verheven,
Wat sal ik lijden, soo ik niet van droef heyt sterf.
Haar groote vreugt baart my een onverdraaglijk streven,
De Nacht hoe schriklijk, voor bederf
Sal my nu min vervaartheyt geven,
O! Doot, koom eyndig dog dit mijn beweenlijk leven,
     Helaas! ik wens u menig werf,
Gy schijnt te vrees'lijk voor die, door geluk gedreven
Vervroolijkt zijn, maar wat is 't erf
Van een als ik? ah! niet dan een elendig streven
O! doot koom eyndig dog dit mijn beweenlijk leven

♦ ♦ ♦

Toon, Trancquille Coeur.

VReedsamig hert bereyt u dan
Tot veelderhande moeylijkheden

Gy

To compete with you in song.
No, quiet is what I want to strip
My cares, relieve unrest. Broad-crowned
Forest, if only you knew the torment
I have undergone, you would, I know,
Pity me, you solitudes: and discretely
Shelter the agitation of my soul.

♦ ♦ ♦

Air: "*Vous demandez des vers et si j'en crois vos yeux*"\*

You ask why I shy from your sun-like gaze.
Oh, let the perplexity remain.
Your beauty is so great, my heart so moved
Will just as likely burn itself there
As derive a portion of your cherished light.

♦ ♦ ♦

Air: "*O mort! O funeste mort / Terminez mon triste sort*"†

Death, come end my tearful life.
My mistress is exalted over me.
How can I bear the sorrow? Her
Felicity so great afflicts
Me, empty night depletes me.
Must love mean only feeling fear?
Death, come end my tearful life.
Lady, go enjoy your wooers.
Ignore the timid and oppressed
By fortune. Revel. But what
Fate awaits one like me?
Must love mean only feeling fear?
Death, come end my tearful life.

♦ ♦ ♦

Air: "*Tranquille coeur*"

Prepare, O careless heart,
For crowding troubles

\* *Le nouveau Mercure galant* printed this air in October 1679. Its title means "You ask for poetry, and if I trust your eyes."

† This air derives from *Amadis*, first performed in January 1684 at Versailles. In act three of this opera by Jean-Baptiste Lully, a captive sings these lines. Its title means "O death, O gloomy death, put a period to my sad lot."

Gy legt u soete rust in ban,
Dan gy mint meer Mins Toverreden,
Maar d'onrust van de Liefd' brengt meer aanloksels mee
      Als d'aldersoeste vree.

♦ ♦ ♦

Toon, Voy la Philis les fleurs que Flore.

SIe daar Philis het puyk der bloemen
Waar naar u hert verlangend' dorst
Die Flora schenkt, om u te roemen,
En haar natuyraas pronk gaat noemen
      Doch om de Doodt
De doodt te smaken op u borst.

♦ ♦ ♦

Toon, Nimphes des Eaux.

GY Nimfjes van het bos, en watervloeden
Bral nu met al u beminnelijkheyt,
Vermaak, maak ook u macht bereydt
Laat het al met ons woeden
Om te verbreyden d'eere van mijn soon,
Wijl hy een heerscher is van Mensen, en van Goôn,
En dwingt al de gemoeden.
De Liefde verwint al wat leeft,
Mits elk sich in sijn boeyens geeft.

♦ ♦ ♦

                              Toon

Now you love Love's witching
Discourse: and restless passion
Brings along temptation
Worse than placid peace.

◆ ◆ ◆

Air: *"Voilà, Philis, les fleurs que Flore"* \*

See there, Philis, glory of flowers,
How Flora gives a gift to you
To make you famous, plucking Nature's
Raving splendour, an end in mind:
To die and wilt upon your breast.

◆ ◆ ◆

Air: *"Nymphes des eaux"* †

Slender nymphs of woods and water
Boast your charms, adorable.
Amuse yourselves, prepare your powers
To diffuse the honour of my son
Ruler of men and gods, compeller
Of all minds who triumphs over
Everything that lives so long
As his fetters fit them tight.

◆ ◆ ◆

---

\* The title of this air means "Behold, Philis, the flowers that Flora."

† *"Nymphes des eaux"* is a melody that may derive from Quinault and Lully's opera *Atys*. The hero of that tragic opera – called "the King's opera," because Louis XIV enjoyed it so much – loves someone other than the goddess Cybele: she punishes him for that mistake.

[232]

Toon, Ah! qu'un fidel amant.

AH! dat een Minnaar is
Soo seer te vresen
'k Had wel gemeent t'ontgaan die herts verbintenis.
Doch ik geloofd' niet aan d'onmijdelijke pesen,
Waarom verplicht my dat ik mijn Eed vermis,
  Ah! dat een Minnaar is
    Soo seer te vresen,
Wel wat bemin ik soo onwis,
  Ik smaakt' een rust soo soet in wesen,
Gy drijft van my 't geheymenis,
  Ah! dat een Minnaar is
    Soo seer te vresen.

◆ ◆ ◆

Toon, Dans ce forest venez suivre nos pas.

COom hijr in 't Bos om tevolgen mijn schreen
Gy die het vuyr van de Min wilt ontvluchten,
't Is te vergeefs onse Ziel te doen suchten,
Sulk een beleyt verwint nooyt de reen,
Spijt selfs de Liefd' men veragt doch sijn krachten,
Ons fierheyt geeft sich niet in gedrang,
  Spijt dan sijn prang
    Wy lijden geen dwang,
Schoon dat dit Gootje hoe vreeslijk en stouwt
Sich doet vorschijnen, sal moeten verdragen
Dat sijn vermogen, ons is een mishagen
Wijl dat het hert sig onverbonden houwt,
Spijt selfs de Liefd' men veracht. bis.

◆ ◆ ◆

Eynde der Vertalingen.

Air: "*Ah! Qu'un fidèle amant / Est redoubtable!*"\*

That a faithful suitor should fill with fear!
I had meant to keep my heart un-entangled.
I did not believe in the inevitable.
Why oblige me to break my oath?
What do I adore so vaguely, sampling secret
Tingling sweetness that you probe, provoke?
That a faithful suitor should fill with fear!

◆ ◆ ◆

Air: "*Dans ces forêts venez suivre nos pas*"†

Come into the woods, pursue my steps
You who flee Love's fire: follow.
It is in vain to chase, cajole our souls
For we listen only to our reason.
Let Love wield all passion's arsenal
Our pride defies his might, his splendour.
Even if in the insolence of his awe
The little god should expose his power
Our mind will bear it, our hearts
Free from his bondage, and aloof. (Repeat)

Even if in the insolence of his awe
The little god should expose his power
Our mind will bear it, our hearts
Free from his bondage, and aloof.

◆ ◆ ◆

End of Translations

\* The Nereid Amphitrite, Poseidon's spouse, is the singer; Brongersma's translation is quite faithful. The song derives from *Le triomphe de l'amour* (1681).

† Diana sings in the midst of her nymphs, who dance – in this song from *Le triomphe de l'amour* (1681).

Omgeefsels.

EEN ROOSJE.

HEt Godenbloemtje praaldt
En prijkt in volle geuren,
Maar als Vrouw Cypris daaldt
Soo schiet se hemel kleuren,
Haar montje blaast Fiolen,
En sachte Roose blaan,
Doch heeft my jets bevoolen
In 't noemen van u naam.

Dat ik van u Robijn
Souw suygen 't Ambrosijn.

♦ ♦ ♦

EEN KRANSJE.

GEvlochten van veel Rosen,
En groene Mirthe-blaan
Die Venus heeft gekoosen,
Als Sy ter Feest sal gaan,
Sy gaat van al de bloemen
Haar Koninginne noemen,
Om 't Roosje gaf de zeeg
Dat sy den Appel kreegh,
Want om dat wel gevallen,
Streek Sy de prijs van allen.

♦ ♦ ♦

Op de

Poems to Accompany Gifts

A little rose

God's small bloom flaunts
Spilling scent while lady
Venus comes heavenly
Coloured, mouth persuasive
As the music of violins.
Tender petals I am happy
To speak your name suckling
Nectar from your ruby.

♦ ♦ ♦

A little garland*

Woven of plural blossoms
And green myrtle leaves
Venus herself picked
For the cider fest
The rose is chosen Queen,
Wins the contest rightly
Taking the prize, the apple:
O beloved victory.

♦ ♦ ♦

\* Venus was sometimes represented
with an apple in hand.

[234]

Op de Wraak.

DE wraak wert by een swartgebekte Raaf geleken
Die voor sijn roof, of prooy, den Scorpioen vernielt
Maar 't giftig Dier komt met sijn hoorne staart te steken,
Daar by de Raaf vol smert door sijn Venijn ontzielt,
So gaat het die door wraak de Doot steek meent te geven
Geniet de wraak tot straf en eyndigt soo het leven.

♦♦♦

Narcis.

DIe in de Beek
Sijn schoon gestalt' sag schijnen,
Het gene hem geleek
Dagt hem, in het verdwijnen,
Dies lieft hy selfs sijn beeldt,
Wat wonder uyt sijn weesen
Wierd' voort een Bloem geteeldt
Wiens naam hier staat te Leesen. Srasunsis.

♦♦♦

Sijn Liefste by een Roos te vergelijken, of Serviteur.

MYn Liefste is soo soet
Als enckel Gal en Roet,
Hy ruyckt gelijk als Roosen
Die in de Winter bloosen
En sijn gestalt is schoon
't Gelijkt geen Spaanse Boon,
Ook draagt hy aan de beenen
De Kuyten voor de Scheenen,
En ik bemin hem soo:
Als Meeuwes Hont de Vloo.

♦♦♦

Eynde van de Omgeefsels.

Plicht

On revenge

Before the black-beaked raven killed its prey,
The scorpion, the latter's armoured stinging tail
Pricked the raptor – who died in pain of poison.
The death blow you would deliver to your foe
May annihilate you both, in reciprocal destruction.

♦ ♦ ♦

Narcissus*

In the stream he saw his pure form
Look at him like him he thought
Vanishing into it out of love
Under the water. What wonder
That his being returns, flowers
Enamouring us with
The plant our title names.

♦ ♦ ♦

The beloved likened to a rose

My beloved tastes as good as ash and bile.
He reeks as sweet as roses withered by the frost.
His form is shapely as twisting string bean vines.
His calves bulge meatier than his skinny thighs.
I love him just the way a stray dotes on fleas.

♦ ♦ ♦

End of Poems to Accompany Gifts

\* Brongersma adds an obscure attribution, "Srasunsis." Possibly she models her piece after a precedent supplied by the epigrammatist Strasensis.

[235]

**BY-VALLEN**

Plicht-offer
Aan de E.J. de WOLFF, Puyk Tekenaar, en Schilder binnen
Groningen, die mijn Bron-Swaan, of Tijtel-Prent getekent heeft.

SOo siet men dan het Swaantje op de Golff
Van 't Brontje dert'len en aanminnig spelen,
Waar het sijn Gorgel slaat, dat van een Wolff
Begonstigt wert, die 't aangenaam komt strelen,
Maar 't is geen Wolff als and're wolven sijn,
Die sonder medely het al vernielen,
Neen 't is een Mens alleen in Wolve schijn,
Die doode Beelden kan door konst bezielen,
Dies leeft het al door sijne Teken-veer:
Waar van getuyge sijn dees Nimfe reyen
Die op de water soom haar setten neer
Om in de schaduw sig wat te vermeyen,
Waar 't Roots gevaart een Spring-aar vloeyen doet
(Door sijne Schagt:) die schijnt om hoog te springen,
Waar in men sig O Wolff verwondren moet:
En U ter Eer een Vrolijk Lof liet Singen,
Want geen Apelles komt by U in 't Schildren aan;
Dat toont ge door U Geest op 't wesen van mijn Swaan.

◆◆◆

Aan

Acknowledgments

To E.J. de Wolff, engraver and painter extraordinaire
of Groningen, who depicted my *Swan of the Well* for
the frontispiece of this book

There's the little Swan on the waves of her intimate well
Appealingly splashing and playing and proclaiming
A Wolff helped her loping opportunely along.
But this Wolff was unlike others of its kind
Who destroy wantonly, without compassion.
He's a man in the likeness of a Wolff who makes
Dead pictures come alive. Let's take a look –
A cluster of nymphs lazes by the side of the water
Diverting themselves in the shade of a rock.
Out of a cleft flows down a source – a source
Of wonder, my dear Wolff, for no Apelles
Rises up to you, your degree of talent. Your
Spirit proves this by the soul you impart to my Swan.

◆ ◆ ◆

[236]

Aan J. Purmerënt, en H. Vlaak, die mijn Bron-Swaan door de
Druk-konst hebben aan den Dach gebracht.

DVs moet Penceel, en Pen voor d'Eed'le Drukkonst swichten,
En Koster prijken by een Vlaak, en Purmerënt
Wijl hy de Letter snee heeft in het hout geprent
Daar't Sparen noch pronkt met die eerst geboorne lichten.

De werelt bromt, en sweeft op die doorgraven vlerken
En groeyt, en bloeyt, en roemt op sulk een schoone vont,
De Wijsheyt draagt het lof der Drukkonst in de mondt,
En prijst de Oeffening van die besaamde werken.

Geen Koningdom noch magt der vrye Republijken
Kan sonder haar bestaan, Sy plant op't blanke witt
De Heyl'ge wetten door het vast aanklevend' gitt,
En koomt het Heelal met die Lettergaaf verrijken.

't Is dan geen wonder dat men van die konst gaat roemen
En op die kennis stoft, terwijl het in der daadt
Het grootste wonder is, van wat sich vinden laat,
Dies men het waarlijk met dien Tojtel mach benoemen.

'k Sal dan tot dankbaarheyt voort't roemenswaarde Drukken
Van't Swaantje u ter Eer beschenken voor die Konst.
(Haa brave Helden) door de gisien van mijn gonst,
En voor u elk tot Lof, een Lauwer Tak afrukken.

♦ ♦ ♦

Dank-

To J. Purmerënt and H. Vlaak whose skilful printing has
ushered my *Swan of the Well* into the light of day*

Now to the art of printing, brush and quill surrender:
And Koster acquiesces to a Vlaak and a Purmerënt
Since he printed with clumsy blocks of wood and
The Sparen glittered then with the first light of dawn.
But now the world hums and sweeps on engraved wings
Widespread as that glorious invention, the metal plate.
Wisdom's soaring words praise the printing press,
Panegyrize the launch of works complete.
No kingdom, no republic can stand without
Printers who impress on shining pages
The holy law with jet indelible ink
Publishing for us a legible salvation.
Therefore do not wonder at our thanks
And our amazed desire to spread our thanks,
The greatest wonder ever discovered merits
Truly the honourific "most miraculous."
Grateful for my splendid publication I
And my little Swan esteem you for your art.
Gallant heroes in token of my favour
Wear on your brows the laurel I have wreathed.

❖ ❖ ❖

* Koster was a contemporary of Gutenberg, and contrived around 1440 a printing press much like that of the renowned resident of Mainz. Brongersma prefers the latest technology, metal plates, over woodblocks. The Sparen is a waterbody in Groningen.

[237]

Dank Offer aan de E. JOANNIS FEDENSMA Schilder, voor sijn
gesonden vers, op mijn BRONSWAAN,

GY Schildert dan O dobb'len Febus Soon
Soo wel met inkt', als met gemalen verven,
En steekt Apel, en Naso naa de kroon
Met wien ge door U Geest sult nimmer sterven,

Gy maaldt me door U pen soo deftig af
(Hoe wel het niet gelijk:) dat ik moet prijsen
De driften die voor lang Natuir U gaf:
Waar door U Sonn soo vroeg komt aan het rijsen.

Pictura lagt om dat se heeft gebaardt
Een Soon die haar gelijkt in eygen weesen,
Waar aan men kan de Moederlijke aart,
En uyt het oog, een Jongen Zeuxis leesen.

Hoe Net hebt gy Elisa ... af gebeelt
Die ik soo wel in mijn gedagt kan kennen,
(Schoon't leeven daar heel kennelijk in speelt)
Als gy koont schild'ren door Penceel, en Pennen.

Ik dank U dan Haa braven Iongeling
Voor uwe verse Trandt, en konst met eenen,
Weet dat ik nooyt een waarder Schets ontfing,
By welkens glans ik ben als uyt geschenen.

♦ ♦ ♦

Raat-

Thanks to the noble Joannis Fedensma, painter, for the verses he sent me on the topic of my *Swan of the Well*\*

You paint as well with words as pigments,
O son of Phoebus, and wear the crowns
Now of Apelles, now of Ovid.
By them ennobled, and by your spirit
You cannot die. Your pen makes me
More chic than I confess I am
But I will praise the aptitude
Nature gave you from the start.
Hence your talent dawned so early,
*Pictura* divinely laughing
To bear a child so like her essence
With the eye of a youthful Zeuxis.
You portray Elisa closely.
In phrases you incarnate her –
Or on your canvas she gleams bright.
Thank you, young and gifted man,
Artful, natural – what a likeness.
It outshines me who never will
See, let alone receive, a better.

♦ ♦ ♦

\* Joannis Fedensma may have painted the picture of Elisabeth Joly of which Brongersma gives *ekphrases*. Alexander the Great favoured Apelles, a celebrated painter. Augustus brought his depiction of Venus Anadyomene (Venus wringing the seawater from her hair) to the temple of Julius Caesar in Rome. Commissioned to represent Alexander's mistress Campaspe, Apelles fell in love with his subject; Alexander permitted him to marry her. Zeuxis of Heraclea refused to sell any of his own paintings, since he thought them priceless. They included a Jupiter among the clouds, a Penelope, a Helen, and the image of an ideal woman, whose composite features he derived from five virgins of Crotona.

[238]

Raatsels.

SOmers souw men my wel hangen
Winters ben ik elkx verlangen
Schoon ik kout ben van natuyr
'K draag nog tans het hert vol vuyr,
'K weet geen Manne Lief'te winnen,
't Sijn meest Vrouwen die my minnen.

◆ ◆ ◆

Een ander

'K Ben ongestadig als de winden
Waar mee dat ik my gaa verbinden:
Want als Boree op Vlerken drijft
En my tot herde Schorsen stijft
Soo ben ik als Christale Klijppen:
En draag mijn Dochter op mijn Lippen,
Maar als Apol my weer ontlast
En met sijn Lauwe wasem wast
Dan werd ik sagt, en weer herboren:
Van die ik baarde, en gaat verloren.

◆ ◆ ◆

FINIS.

Riddle*

In the summer I am hung up.
In the winter longing reaches for me.
Although cold by nature I bear
A heart of fire that wins some men:
Yet it is women, mostly, love me.

◆ ◆ ◆

Riddle†

I vary like the winds to which
I can attach at will and when
Boreas planes on frigid wings
He stiffens me in brittle shards
So I lengthen into pendent crystal
Bearing my daughter on my lips.
Apollo bathes me in his balmy
Breath that softens me, loosens
Me up again, reborn
In the very act of vanishing.

◆ ◆ ◆

\* The answer to the riddle is probably "bed-warmer." In the seventeenth century, bed-warmers featured a handle of wood or metal, with a perforated metal lid and pan into which coals were loaded.

† The answer to the riddle is probably "water." Brongersma's Swan swims in water; like the landscape of Friesland, her book flows – sometimes hardens – with water as it passes through all its states. Brongersma closes with water, and with the watery promise of a return.

# INDEX OF FIRST LINES (ENGLISH)

Adriaan shines in marble sculpted to the life, 415
Ah, restlessness imparts a feeling to me, 507
Ah! what does my love ask, now the spring returns?, 505
Alphesibé budding now and blooming, 173
Amaryllis, do not tempt or dare me, 151
Ancient custom encircled Caesar's temples, 449
Apollo, lord of the contest, what sounds are those?, 237
Arachne has lost a nest. For Boreas, 153
Arachne has woven a visual hymn to you, 91
As you see in the east the sun rising again, 221
At the sound of your name the rose, 217
Away say I with any lines, 245
A woman vowed to Apollo, young, 33
As gorgeously burns your glorious sun, 75

Before the black-billed raven killed its prey, 517
Boast, Achaea, Stymphalia's proud wood, 105
Boast, Rome, Vergil's epic trumpet's blare, 13
Bright Flora treads her measures, 497
But has the sun ever shone on a day more dismal, 251

Can you pluck grapes from thistles, figs, 157
Ceyx, how can I live any longer away, 191
Charming waterfall, trees with lofty tops, 499
Cold and continent nymph, Diana, 369

Combined in one in this picture see the pitying, 405
Come into the woods, pursue my steps, 513
Come Orpheus, tune up your fiddle-strings, 233
Come to me you who find your burdens heavy, 255
Consider the striking triumph of him who became, 253
Consummate model for all the righteous, 141
Cornelia, what paintbrush can have caught your, 401
Cruel defiler Pyrrhus could you knife, 423
Cyrus, was it not enough to lay waste the east, 85

Daphne dead? No I feel her heart still beats, 359
Darling swan, don't you leave my swan alone, 111
Dear diamond, deserving angel, Fortune, 387
Dear sir, I want to write to you again, 241
Death, come end my tearful life, 509
Dejanira do you now divert yourself, 221
Desolating man, worst on earth, 337
Dewed with pearl-like drops, your base supports, 47
Divine Flora as fecund as perfumed, 373
Dorimée, you're sighing, aren't you?, 173
Draw my rhymes out of other books?, 195
Driven by fraud and force to take his leave, 253
Dry your cheeks, afflicted Elise, 351

Elisa, queen of Carthage, must you really, 397
Euphemia, may your quick wits and obvious, 107
Evening girl! Good evening!, 377

Faithless Elise, can you really leave?, 181
Forgive me for magnifying your name, 85
For nothing Spring shines in woodland glory, 501
Fortunate who no splendour knows, 319
Fortunate your lot, 501
Friend, you ask after my *Swan of the Well*, 249
Frightful rocks console me, 375

Gallant literary hero, the paintbrush, 403
Garden-haunting Pomona, Frisian sister, 49
Godlike rays beam in my heart's depth, 271
God's small bloom flaunts, 515
Grand Duke Aquilo mellows, unlocks your source, 59
Gratitude to you, glory of Sharon's flowers, 143

Heaven weeps tumultuous tears, the wind's, 303
Hecuba's woe over Polydorus, Aurora's, 453
Here I planted the olive of peace, 209
Here I see two who had the means to grant me all, 431
Here is the charming image deriving from, 167
Here lies fallen in the grave, 485
Here, Philis, are flowers Flora sent, 375
How amiably Zephyrus you play among, 215
How can you do it? You pass with your, 165
How would I furnish the wedding chamber best?, 489

I am obliged, ha! child of Themis's son, 439
I could not possibly express your worth, 83
I do not have ready a branch of roses, 445
I fled the heat of Phoebus's love that had, 297
I have brought no blossom, myrtle, laurel, 441
I have wept my eyes red over the death of Mary, 461
I hear the old cock of Mars cackle, 127
I know well you never take delight, 153
I may climb the hills and dunes and gaze, 321
In the stream he saw his pure form, 517
In the summer I am hung up, 525
I offer then this immethodical song, 487
I rested on a bosom before I was buried, 65
I saw Daifilo with slavish submission by the cool, 121
I see the goddess of flowers bend and blush, 101
I send *The Faithful Shepherd*. It's, 119
I stand like one to stone turned staring, 61
I vary like the wind to which, 525
I was from soft down awakened, 291
I want to boast about you, Cathius, 97
I was deprived of the honour of seeing you, 195
I would like, a lot, to invite you, 99

Lady! Good day to you! Good day!, 361
Leader of the gods whom sun and moon obey, 325
Leave me in peace, Love. Cruel! Quit my side and stop, 499
Lesbos boasts of Sappho, let it, 209
Let French esprit, Spanish solemnity, 79
Let Phoebus boast his sophisticated school, 389
Let sour, dour malice never twist, 221
Let Titia be your name when you are Apollo's priestess, 23
Like a turtledove that moans and sits, 299
Little swan, would you with your web-feet paddle, 383
Little well deriving from the hoof-stamp, 27
Look at how the artful work of this sketch images, 429
Low Tempe yield, you are next to nothing, 307

Meadows densely sown and carpeted, 503
Minerva snatches your golden yarn, your weaving-, 89
Moonbeams never made earth glow, 265

Must I compose verse? No exemption?, 19
Must I remain so far from you, 145
My beloved tastes as good as ash and bile, 517
My dipped pen abstained a while, from staining paper, 43
My eyes sting like fire, red from harsh sadness, 187
My swan has long in longing lived, 295

Naïve lady, beset by pricking hazards, 295
Never has the moon shone on a blither night, 251
No, I visit no more the woods, 507
No wonder other people regard you as, 125
Now it doesn't snow as light as the petals, 117
Now that the ocean's salt, 315
Now the woman of the well breathes free, 139
Now to the art of printing, brush and quill surrender, 521
Now you menace the woods near Ijlst, Diana, 357

Off with you Dido. Off with you, too, 135
O gleaming Galatea more changeable, 367
On a painted panel see the star of the sea, 409
Once I'd seen *The Swan of the Well*, my spirit, 17
Once upon a time people gathered flowers, 443
Onto the first tier clambers Hope, 431
Over the waves my Swan is drifting, beneath, 437

Parnassus herself gives voice glittering, 179
Pallas hatched, Apollo nursed you, 169
Patience, dear one. The little Swan would beat, 395
Pausing at the midpoint, Costius, 133
Pen, do not depict cloth dyed with glamorous motifs, 465
Perseus's eye burns bright as he unchains, 425
Phantasmagoric god, flee, 25
Philomela, give up grieving old, 53

Phyllis what could you want? I weep, 391
Picus, oh, has vanished: Circe has changed him, 113
Pleasant woods, pleasure-bower of the gods, 305
Please accept, my lord, the sprigs of stubborn, 469
Pleasure garden of Assen, glorious valley, 103
Procris, sincere of heart you gave your beloved, 429

Quiet down, Hermes. Rhetoric, be silent, 95
Quiet, old man Koster. Hide your impressions, 529

Remembrance makes me sigh whenever, 211
Remorseless, would you make my passion worse?, 219
Rise, rise sun of my mind, 313
Rodrigo king of Visigoths twisted, 197

Sacred rose, goddess of flowers, 109
See Anna revel in festoons of petals, and, 147
See there, Philis, glory of flowers, 511
See with amusement the defamatory bird flap, 419
See Zenobia the queen like Achilles come again, 55
Shade of my beloved, mournful spectre, 505
Shady forest crowns the tract, 345
Shall I begin to praise your incomparable pen, 237
Should I dare where so many eagles glide, 145
Shush, all rustling. Wind, do not touch a leaf, 333
Sibrig, say, where are you running?, 433
Silence, leaden listless age! Listen, 25
Silence, you who insult tea, 347
Slender nymphs of woods and water, 511
So, dull Death, have you dragged off Uchtman in your hearse, 483
So I drive the fleecy flock of my thoughts, 261

So long as Dorinde the shepherdess loved me, 507
Squint, and see that eye evincing violence, 397
Stand aside, Cyprian goddess: in dance, 91
Stop, people! Stop vying to get at this resource, 39
Stop, satyr. Stop. You want to paw her?, 423
Supernatural woman, to change your nature!, 189
Sweet meadowland, a home, 497
Sweet noise delights my ears, 177

Take a look at the picture. Magnificent, 397
Tell me nightingale with your enchanting speech, 497
That a faithful suitor should fill with fear!, 513
The bright torch amuses the fly, 419
The day of your birth circling round again, 447
The field is bright with festoons of flowers, 163
The heart leans closer to the sweet solicitation, 419
The light of day blushes on my dumbstruck face, 493
The nightwatch turns a profit. No wonder, 219
The petite and energetic bee sucks in the midst of petals, 427
The pillar and mainstay of the land, in whom, 479
There is our Elisabeth. Virtue and knowledge, 405
There is the Gothic spring, 417
There's the little Swan on the waves of her intimate well, 519
The Rose wilts and its leaves lack perfume, 215
The sight of fireworks tinting summer skies, 69
The sun in this province too long his sojourn keeps, 501
The thread of fleshly fate at last is severed, 457
*The Swan of the Well* wears a bridle finely, 21

The very gaze of this decent, appealing person, 399
Thick elm woods grown tall on every path, 149
This flower lately brim with scent, 421
This pilgrim marches ahead amid the prickles, 421
This poplar's root has drunk up many tears, 339
This sketch and the light of your heavenly eye, 411
Though iron Mars nearly dragged my trunk, 299
Though so bitter, so intense an agony, 253
Though the sun has shone on me too bright, 269
Thus shaded by trees, 289

Unfasten the blindfold from Pomona's eyes, 101
Up the staircase with quick steps, 229

We all want to look at Margaret's person, 415
We praise perennial monuments of ancient, 15
Weep now, pour out a river of salty drops, 475
Welcome longed-for Prince, welcome Wilhelm, 75
Well, Susanna, what does gratitude send you now?, 53
What can I hear in this mundane place?, 49
What design, what order, what excellence, 227
What do you advise now the river stops, 57
What does it mean, your tongue split in two, 115
What envious steel has cut such a gash in you?, 171
What is that Owl doing, respectable familiar of Minerva, 51
What kind of love can conciliate spite?, 111
What light shines or sconce flickers, 285
What streams so sweetly to my listening ears?, 155

What thanks my little Swan will sing to you, 231
What the trumpet of Vergil, the lyre of Horace, 13
What was that, the noise? The Swan, now loud, 451
What were you doing, lolling on the hill, 247
When I on earth am no more, 165
When I see this painting, darling of my heart, 407
When I turned my gaze upward to assess, 365
Where are you, beloved, most, 283
Where are you running off to, my Arethusa?, 327
Where are you running to, cruel woman!, 205
Where can I find stuff equal to your quality, 175
Where find solace now my pain is at its worst?, 335
Where now have they gone, those times that were so charming?, 329
While I gaze on your image in paint, sweet Glinstra, 413
Who dares, famous heroine of song, 29
Who would doubt your education in art, 93
Why plunge a shaft into Margaret's heart, 467
Winter, severe, oppressive, 505
Witness, thick woods, my simple declaration, 323
Wonderful enthusiast, your rapt speech, 223
When I think of the ache, 503
Why ask where my beloved hides, 275
Why chaste goddess of the night, 353
Why did my niece forget to decorate me?, 123
Why doesn't Apollo preside with his nine, 37
Why do you forsake the ramparts of Groningen, 159
Why hide your light in the depths of the sea?, 97
Why, Love, derange my peaceful life?, 503
Why not have me little, 381
With knees bent devoutly I bow to embrace, 257
Woman, who will trumpet your deed? Say what, 87
Wonderful enthusiast, your rapt speech, 223
Worry does the mind no good. What can, 171
Woven of plural blossoms, 515

You are a fresh rose discovered in the forest, 279
You ask why I shy from your sun-like gaze, 509
You comprise, Auricula, an entire, 137
You consider it alarming, unrestful, 67
You filthy cauldron of magic, have you, 113
You have known the longest the pleasure, 243
You have woven and tied together a headpiece, 95
You missed the moment to rend sweet, briny, 51
You nourish my songs and my duty and pleasure, 241
You rocks and savage deserts, 377
Your art, Lady, placing these horns on my head, 133
Your beauty, beautiful Dorilée, 343
You say I am a thief and steal your rest, 169
You paint as well with words as pigments, 523
Your poems show so much intellect, dear woman, 41
Your virtue and personality oblige, 157

Zephyrus pales, and casts his eyes downward, 203

# INDEX OF FIRST LINES (DUTCH)

Aanminnige water val, en gy bekruynt geboomt', 498
ACh Pyrrhus ach! Ik schrik, O wree barbaar, 422
ACh waar zijt gy mijn beminde, 282
Affreux Rochers soulagez moy, 374
Ag! Moet ik dan soo ver van V gescheyden blijven, 144
Ah! Ah! waar vlugt ge voor, 328
AH! dat een Minnaar is, 512
AH! dat ik voel d'onrustigheden, 506
Ah! Dianier vint gy in and'ren nu vermaaken, 220
AH! Droog af uw natte wangen, 350
AH! waar vind ik troost, 334
Alleen op't klinken vam U Naam, 216
Als ik gedenke aan de pijnen, 502
Als ik mijn blicken opwaart slaa, 364
Als ik niet meer op aard' sal sijn, 164
Als ik u Bronswaan sag ging my mijn Geest ontspringen, 16
Althesibée uyt jlio gesprooten, 172
Andromeda sal dan onschuldig sijn verslonden, 196
Arachne heeft het Lof van V geweven, 90
Aragne is verhuyst en haar Tapeet gebrooken, 152
Assen Lusthof, Pronck Valeye, 102
AY my! ik die de gloat van Febus min ontvloot, 296

CHaste & froide Nimph Diane, 368
COom al tot my Gy die V vint beladen, 254
COom hijr in't Bos om tevolgen mijn schreen, 512

Daar braldt de Ster in Zee, daar flikkeren de ligten, 408
DAar drijft mijn Swaantje in de bron, 436
DAar hoort ge dan tot lof mijn Swaantje singen, 200
Daar is het aardig beeldt, 166
Daar koomt mijn Swaantje aan gevaren, 160
Daar leyt dien Suyl dien steunpost van het lant, 478
Daar siet ge dan het Beeld van dien Elisabeth, 404
Dat waekheer wint west daar niet in verwondert, 218
DE Lente offert my vergeefs haar wout cieraat, 500
De Roos verdort de bladen Ruyken niet, 214
De schoone Flora treedt weer in, 496
De Son in dit gewest te lang haar woning hiel, 500
DE Velden digt besaayt, en overvloerdt, 502
De wijl gy Costius reets op de middel trap, 132
De wijl gy niet en koomt om my de nek te breken, 50
De wijl gy waardig agt te nuuren mijn gesangen, 240
De wraak wert by een swartgebekte Raaf geleken, 516
DEes Populier, wiens wortel heeft, 338
DEse bloem wel eer vol geuren, 420
DEwijl de dach van U Verjaren, 446
Die in de Beek, 516
Doe dan Pomoon het masker van de Oogen, 100

Dog naa soo wrang en fel gepijnt te wesen, 252
Door al dit woen, en treflijk zeegevieren, 252
Dus belommert van de boomen, 288
DUs draayt de spil op d'ass van haar veranderingen, 112
Dus drijf ik't wollig Vee van mijn dedagten, 260
Dus praalt Parnas met ongemeene luyster, 178
Dus siet men toegelijk in eene Schildery, 404
Dus voeldt men sig gesticht door U gestichte reden, 222
DVs lokt de soete galm het Hert te nad'ren, 418
DVs moet Penceel, en Pen voor d'Eed'le Drukkonst, 520
DVs plagt men Cesars hooft met Lauwerblaan te pronken, 448
DVs treet de hoop op d'eerste Trans, 78

Een Maagd, Apollo toegewijd, 32
Euphemia V aart, V geest, en Goet gerugt, 106
Ey! Amaril 'k versoek my niet te weyg'ren, 150
Ey laat dog nimmer toe dat boos en schriklijk quaadt, 220
Ey Swaantje laat mijn Swaan niet sonder Swaantje roeyen, 110

GE vlochten van veel Rosen, 514
Gedoog dat mijn Treur-Sangeres, 468
Gedoog O! puyk heeld van de geestelijke scharen, 140
GEdoog, wijl 't Swaantje vaardig slaat, 394
Geen Flora stuyrt dees gloende Pinxter bloemen, 200
Geen wonder dat men V als opgesloten siet, 124
GElijk een versse Roos, 278
Gelukkig die geen pracht en kent, 318
GElukkig is u lot, O! Roosje vers ontsloten, 500
Gewyde Roos, Godinne aller Bloemen, 108

Goen dey goen dey Laen Vrouw, 360
Goen joon boer saem goen Ioon, 376
Gy doet my door U Const met Cippus schromen, 132
Gy dreygt dan noch Diaan het Drijlsche wout, 356
Gy gaat dan Eliseen Brittansche Leelien plukken, 182
Gy hebt dan snoode tover-boel, 112
Gy hebt dan strenge Doodt op uwe Wagen, 482
Gy Nimfjes van het bos, en watervloede, 510
GY Schildert dan O dobb'len Febus Soon, 522
Gy segt ik ben u hert, wel aan ik sal't geloven, 198
Gy segt ik bin een dief, en steel u rust, 168
Gy sijt dan tot getuyg O! naar geboomt'!, 322
Gy sijt dan als het schijnt verstoort, en ongerust, 66
Gy zijt gewis de konst school door getreden, 92
Gy vraagt me of men op Parnas wel droog kan sitten, 128
Gy vraagt waar om ik schuw u Son gelijke ogen, 508
Gy weeft, en knoopt van zy, en nette-garen, 94

Heeft Roderik de staf der Gottsche Heerschappyen, 196
HElaas! de Hemel weendt, en stort veel dropen neer, 302
Helaas is Picus dan niet meer te vinden, 112
Helaas mijn Ceyx hoe kan ik langer leeven, 190
Helaas wat baat het Phylis dat ik om u ween, 390
Het Godenbloemtje praaldt, 514
Het is dan eens gelukt groot-Vorst van Aguilon, 58
Het is dan eens gelukt te horen, 534
Het nerig Bytje suygt van Rose-bladen, 426
Het oog beelt uyt de togten der gemoeden, 396

Het schijnt dat gy Minerv' haar goude draân, 88
Het sneewt nu niet als winter-rosen, 116
Het Vliegje schept vermaak in 't Fackellicht, 418
Hier leyt in 't Graf gevelt, 484
Hier send' ik de Trouwe-herder, 118
HIer sie ik twee die my de werelt deden kennen, 430
Hoe heerlijk bralt dien Puik-Son in het westen, 74
Hoe koont gy met u Swane vlerken, 164
Hoe lang verkoren Adamant, 386
Hoe lieflijk Zephirus spelt gy door Bloem en bladen, 214
Hoe meer men staart op 't wesen van Margreet, 414
Hoe Procris gy schenkt aan Cefaal, 428
Hoe staat die trunk bedauwd met pereldroppen, 46
Hoe sugt ge Dorimeen om dat u Tirsis laat, 172
Hoe vlamt het oog van Perseus op sijn Bruyt, 424
Hoe vraagt gy waar mijn lief sich hout, 274

Ick voel mijn ingewant, 270
Ick weet weld dat ghy nimmer naamt behagen, 152
Ick werd genoopt haa Kroost van Themis Soon, 438
Ik die d'Olijve-blaan tot Vrede heb geplant, 208
Ik hor de oube haan van Mavors kraayen, 126
Ik offer dan dees rijmloose Sangen, 486
IK quijn gelijk de Tortel doet, 298
Ik sie de bloem-Godes ter schuyl gekropen, 100
IK voel me dan Apol door uwe min herboren, 298
Ik waar in 't sagte dons geweeken, 290

'K Artaagsche Elisae moet gy dan, 396
'K Ben ongestadig als de winden, 524
'K Dank U puyk van Sarons bloemen, 142

'K had lang mijn Schacht gedoopt om 't blank papier, 42
'K Had nimmermeer gedagt dat gy, 188
'K Heb bloem nog Mirthe-groen, nog telgen van Lauwrieren, 440
'K Heb dan geen Rosetak, nog Palmekroon bereyt, 444
'K heb lang gewenst haa! Cathius te pronken, 96
'K heb om het sterven van Mary, 460
'K sag Daifilo het koele Bron-nat langen, 120
'K sie dan U Beeld in Schildery, 412
'K sie met vermaak de wulpsche vogel vluchten, 418
'K Sie Zephyrus verbleekt, end roof verschijnen, 202
'K souw wel wensen V te noden, 98
'K staa, verbaast dees Steen Mijt aan te schouwen, 60
'K Voel nog het vier in d'ooge randen, 186

LAat my in rust O! Min, weg wreede ik scheld V quijt, 498
Laat vry de snege Frank, en 't deftig Spangien pralen, 78
Laudamus veterum monumenta perennia Vatum, 14

Maar heeft de Son ooyt droever dach beschenen, 250
Medogenlose soo mijn lijden u nog deert?, 218
Men noemt U Titia, als Febus Priesterinnen, 22
Men plukt nooyt druyven van een Distel boom, 158
Men sond wel eer Minerva Offerbloemen, 442
Men speurt dan uyt de Schets, en 't ster uws oogen, 410
Met neer gebogen knien koom ik omhelfen, 256
Mijn schagt leg af het kleed beprujikt met pronk cieraden, 464
Mijn vrient gy vraagt me naar het wedervaren, 248

Moet ik dan dichten? En hoort gy na geen' verschoonen, 18
MYn Dafne doot, O! neen ik voel het hert nog slaan, 358
Myn Heer ik moet u dit nog schrijven, 240
MYn Liefste is soo soet, 516
Myn Sangh-Nimph wil dat ik (wijl yder sigh vermaakt, 68
MYn Swaan heeft lang in het verlangen, 294
MYn Swaanelijn, 382

NEen, neen ik koom niet meer in't woudt, 506
Nog is hy naar't vertrek ter sluyks gedrongen, 252
NOoyt heeft de Maan beschenen, 264
NOoyt heeft de Maan een blijder nacht bescheenen, 250
NU dat den Oceaan, 314
Nu kan de Bron-Maagt eens haar asem weder haalen, 138

O! Aangename Bosch, en lust prieel der Goden, 304
O Blanke Galathee, 366
O Bloeyrijk Hof Iuweel Aurikula, 136
O Brontje! dat wel eer zyn oorspronk heeft genomen, 26
O! Doot, koom eyndig dog dit mijn beweenlijk leven, 508
O Friesene Hof-pomoon, en suster van de Musen, 48
O Philomeel, beween niet meer u ongeluck, 52
O! Schaduw van mijn lief, beklagelijke lommer, 504
O! Strenge Winter vol verdriet, 506
O Weeld'rig Yper wouwt begrandigt in V paden, 148
Oppervoogt ontsach der Goden, 324

Pallas heeft U uyt-gebroedt, 168

Quod tuba Virgilii, lyra Flacci, altusque cothurnus, 12
QVe fertil que la douce, et la divine Flore, 372

Roemt dan Achaia nog op 't Trotse bos Stymfaal!, 104
Roemt Lesbos van haar Sappho, laat het wesen, 208
Roemt, Romen, op't gedreun van Marôs Helden-Sangen, 12
RYs op Rijs op, O Son van mijn gemoet, 312

SChoon de Griexse Phoebus dondert, 388
SChoon de Son door heet geblaak, 268
SEg, wat versoekt gy Nachtegaal, 496
SIbrig sis wier rinste sey, 432
Sie daar den Gootschen Lely-bron, 416
SIe daar Philis het puyk der bloemen, 510
Sie daar Zenobia de Koningin, 54
Siet hoe het konstig werk van dese schets verbeelt, 428
Siet nu hoe Anna bralt in Bloem-festoenen, 146
SIet vry dit heerlijk beeld verwondert aan, 396
Soet vloeyende poet met welk een toon van Reden, 236
SOete woning van het veldt, 496
SOmers souw men my wel hangen, 524
SOo pronkt het Beeld in blanke Mermersteen, 414
Soo siet men dan de Son in 't Oosten weer verrijsen, 220
SOo siet men dan haa braven Letterheld, 402
SOo siet men dan het Swaantje op de Golff, 518
So staat u Bron-Swaan dan in het gareel geslagen, 20
Souw ik daar soo veel Adelaren groeyen, 144
Souw ik mijn Rijm uyt andre digten soeken, 194
SPeelsieke Apol wat tonen doet ge klingen, 236
Staa Cypria! U sool begint te kraken, 90
Staa Sater staa, of houw u wat ter zy?, 422
Staak V geruys Ay wind beroer geen bladen, 332
Staakt ijverschaar, staakt desen strijd, 38
Swijg Hermes, en Rethorica houw stil, 94
SWijg schempers vam de Thee, 346

'T Herdenken doet me vaak veel sugtjes loosen, 210
'T Lomrig Wout bekranst het streckje, 344
'TIs V bekent voor lang, hoe dat mijn Swaan, 242
Trouwlooste die op aarden leeft, 336

U deugt en aart, doet my aan U verbinden, 156
U Schoonheyt schooner Dorilee, 342
Uyt uwe groote Gees ten wonderbare wercken, 40

Verdigte God heên vliedt, vliedt negen zang-godinnen, 24
Vergeef me dat ik V naa waarde niet kan roemen, 82
Vergeefs beklim ik berg, en Duyn, 320
Vergeefsche sorg baart onrust in de geest, 170
Verlaat gy my Troulose Eliseen, 180
Verwaardig my dat ik V Eer-naam roem, 84
Vous Rochers, deserts sauvage, 376
Voy-la Philis les fleurs que Flore, 374
VReedsamig hert bereyt u dan, 508

Waar is nu al het lief vermaak, 328
Waar vind' ik stof genoech en eer bewijsen, 174
Waar vliet gy wrede! seg: waar heen Astrè, 204
Waarom mijn Nicht vergeetge my te binden, 122
Waarom (O kysche Nagt Godin, 352
Waarom O! min ontstelt gy dog mijn rustig leven, 502
Waarom O! strafe Dood hebt gu u schigt gedreven, 466
Waarom verlaat ge soo de sterke wallen, 158
Waarom verse huylt U Sonne-schijn, 96
Waarom zit hier Apoll, en't Negental, 36
Waar't Cyrus niet genoeg dat gy gans Orienten, 84
Waneer men staard op het besaad, en deftig wesen, 398
WAnneer ik sie U schildery, en wesen, 406

WAnneer ik waar gelieft van d'Herderin Dorinde, 506
Was raat Iolij nu't Water leyt beschorst, 537
Wat baat mijn Liefde nu de Lente wert herboren, 504
Wat blinkende lichten, 284
Wat Bloem festoenen staan op't blanke Veldt, 162
Wat dach glans schijnt soo klaar in mijn verdooft Gesigt?, 492
Wat dankbaarheyt sal u mijn Swaantje tonen!, 230
Wat doet den Uyl, de Eer-staf van Minerve, 50
Wat hadt ge voor te Leunen op de Drempel, 246
Wat Hecuba bejammert Polydoor, 452
Wat lief en soet geluydt slaat in mijn Ooren?, 176
Wat liefde draagt gy tot de Nijt, 110
Wat siet men daar de Schets van U Cornelia, 400
Wat sinnig staal geeft sulk een sneed, 170
Wat wild it wesen van V twee gespleten tong, 114
Ween nu en stort een beek van bracke dropen, 474
Weg Dido, weg Lucretia, 134
Weg seg ik met de verf van u penceelen, 244
Wel hoe Susann: wat stuyrd u Karitate?, 52
Welkoom gewenste Prins welkoom Wilhelm Georg, 74
Wie durft, vermaarde Sang-Heldin, 28
Wie heeft de steyletrap met rasse schreden, 228
WIe helpt me nu een Throon van Bloemen vlegte, 488
Wie hoor ik daar soo Hemels onder 't spelen, 48
Wie sag ooyt Gallery soo schoon doormengelt, 226
Wie sal O! Griekse maagt, V daadt trompetten?, 86
Wie streeldt soo soet mijn luysterende Ooren?, 154
WIer om wotte mi naeet habbe, 380

Wijk Orfeus wijk: ontschroef de fedel snaren, 232
Wijk Tempe, wijk, want gy zijt niet, 360
WYk Koster wijk verberg U schrift in't donker, 244

WYl my de Eer om V te sien mislukte, 194

Zwijgt grijse logen-eeuw, verdigtzel heeft nu uyt, 24